EUROPE'S BA...
AD 200–...

The Medieval World

Series editor: Julia Smith, The University of Glasgow

EUROPE'S BARBARIANS, AD 200–600

EDWARD JAMES

PEARSON
Longman

Harlow, England • London • New York • Boston • San Francisco • Toronto
Sydney • Tokyo • Singapore • Hong Kong • Seoul • Taipei • New Delhi
Cape Town • Madrid • Mexico City • Amsterdam • Munich • Paris • Milan

PEARSON EDUCATION LIMITED

Edinburgh Gate
Harlow CM20 2JE
United Kingdom
Tel: +44 (0) 1279 623623
Fax: +44 (0) 1279 431059
Website: www.pearsoned.co.uk

———

First edition published in Great Britain in 2009

© Pearson Education Limited 2009

The right of Edward James to be identified as author
of this work has been asserted by him in accordance
with the Copyright, Designs and Patents Act 1988.

ISBN: 978-0-582-77296-0

British Library Cataloguing in Publication Data
A CIP catalogue record for this book can be obtained from the British Library

Library of Congress Cataloging in Publication Data
James, Edward, 1947–
Europe's barbarians, AD 200–600 / Edward James. — 1st ed.
p. cm.
Includes bibliographical references and index.
ISBN 978-0-582-77296-0 (pbk.)
1. Rome—History—Germanic Invasions, 3rd–6th centuries.   2. Germanic peoples—
Rome—History.   3. Germanic peoples—Europe—History.   4. Roman provinces—History.
5. Europe—History—To 476.   6. Europe—History—476–1492.   7. Rome—Civilization—
Foreign influences.   8. Europe—Ethnic relations.   9. Rome—Ethnic relations.   I. Title.
DG312.J365 2009
937′.004—dc22

2009002079

A CIP catalog record for this book can be obtained from the Library of Congress

10   9   8   7   6   5   4   3   2
13   12   11   10

Set by 35 in 10.5/13pt Galliard
Printed in Malaysia (CTP-VP)

The Publisher's policy is to use paper manufactured from sustainable forests.

CONTENTS

SERIES EDITOR'S PREFACE

Why did the Western Roman Empire end? How and why did medieval Europe begin? These perennially important questions lie at the heart of some of the most vibrant historical scholarship currently being conducted. While some historians have breathed new life into the paradigm of 'decline and fall', others argue for a complex process of 'transformation' whether gradual or abrupt, peaceful or violent. What no one disputes is that barbarians from outside the boundaries of the Roman Empire played a part. But what part? Who were they anyway? How many were there? What were they like? In this book, Edward James guides the reader through these debates with a sure interpretive touch and an authoritative grasp of all the evidence.

He tells this story with a difference. Its central characters are never the Romans but always the barbarians. His theme is what the barbarians contributed to European history, and his geographical scope extends from Ireland and Scandinavia to the Mediterranean and the Danube basin. On this broad canvas, he takes account of a large number of different peoples, not only those who remain household names such as the Goths, Franks, Saxons or Picts, but also such half-forgotten groups as the Heruls, or Sarmatians – and he even mentions the Ohtgaga and Noxgaga, whose names only occurs once in the historical record.

James explains how new kingdoms emerged on Roman soil, taking their identity from barbarian armies and their leaders. His account balances narrative (Chapters 2–4) with analytic overviews (Chapters 5–12) of issues central to current debates: the changing character of late Roman provincial societies; the nature of early medieval ethnic identities; the multiple interactions of Romans and barbarians besides warfare; the problem of how many people may have migrated, and how far. The nature of barbarian kingship and governance, and the role of religion in political change and cultural identity also receive full attention. He closes by demonstrating that the barbarians' contribution to Europe's political mythologies remains potent.

A key feature of this book – as of Edward James's earlier work – is his skill in juxtaposing archaeological evidence with the historical record. By balancing material culture with the written word, he brings nuance and fair-mindedness to key controversies. He is also alive to the importance of complementary disciplines such as the history of language and of place-names, and introduces readers to the newest research methods, notably genetic anthropology.

All those interested in the early Middle Ages will find James an enlightening and often witty guide to the rich and fascinating story of Europe's barbarians.

Julia M.H. Smith

PUBLISHER'S ACKNOWLEDGEMENTS

We are grateful to the following for permission to reproduce copyright material:

Maps
Map 1 adapted from *The Decline of the Ancient World*, Longman (Jones, A.H.M. 1966) 100–101; Map 2 after *Tacitus: Germania*, by permission of Oxford University Press (Rives, J.R. 1999) xii–xiii; Map 3 from *Borders, Barriers and Ethnogenesis: Frontiers in Late Antiquity and the Middle Ages*, Brepols (Curta, F. 2005) 156; Map 5 after *The Making of the Slavs*, Cambridge University Press (Curta, F. 2001) 198; Map 7 from *Ethnische Interpretationen in der fruhgeschichtlichen Archaologie: Geschichte, Grundlagen und Alternativen*, Walter de Gruyter (Brather, S. 2004) 266; Map 9 after *Die Franken, Wegbereiter Europas*, 2nd ed., 2 vols., Mainz: Reiss–Engelhorn Museen Mannheim (Wieczorek, A., Perin, P., Von Welck, K. and Menghin, W. 1997) 98; Map 10 from *Les Invasions Barbares*, Presses Universitaires de France (Riche, P. 1968); Map 11 from *Die Franken, Wegbereiter Europas*, 2nd ed., 2 vols., Mainz: Reiss–Engelhorn Museen Mannheim (Wieczorek, A., Perin, P., Von Welck, K. and Menghin, W. 1997) 94; Map 12 after *The Blackwell Encyclopedia of Anglo-Saxon England*, Blackwell (Lapidge, M., Blair, J., Keynes, S. and Scragg, D. 1999) 456, reproduced with permission of Blackwell Publishing Ltd.

Figures
Figure 1 from *Topographies of Power in the Early Middle Ages*, Brill (De Jong, M. and Theuws, F. 2001) 477, From "Asgard reconstructed. Gudme, a 'central place' in the North"; Figure 2 from *Gudmehallerne: Kongeligt byggeri fra jernalderen*, National Museum of Denmark (Sorensen, P. 1994).

Picture Credits
The publisher would like to thank the following for their kind permission to reproduce their photographs:

Plate 1, p14 Diptych depicting Stilicho (*c.* 365–408), Serena and Eucharius (ivory) by Italian School, (5th century) Basilica di San Giovanni Battista,

Monza, Italy / The Bridgeman Art Library Nationality / copyright status: Italian / out of copyright; Plate 2, p37 Uppsala University Library; Plate 3, p79 Bibliothèque nationale de France; Plate 4, p84 by grant of the Ministero per I Beni e le Attività Culturali – Soprintendenza Speciale per i Beni Archeologici di Roma; Plate 5, p93 Reiss-Engelhorn-Museen Mannheim, photo: Jean Christen; Plate 6, p115 from *I Goti by Palazzo Reale di Milano*, Electa; Plate 7, p142 Fotosearch: AGE Fotostock; Plate 8, p151 Kulturhistorisk Museum/Photographer: Eirik Irgens Johnsen; Plate 9, p194 Rheinisches Landesmuseum Trier; Plate 11, p243 © The Trustees of The British Museum.

All other images © Pearson Education.

Every effort has been made to trace the copyright holders and we apologise in advance for any unintentional omissions. We would be pleased to insert the appropriate acknowledgement in any subsequent edition of this publication.

AUTHOR'S ACKNOWLEDGEMENTS

For six months during 1973, I looked at the archaeological remains of barbarians in every museum I could find in the former territory of the fifth-century Visigothic kingdom of Toulouse. At weekends and when museums were closed, my first wife and I sat in the local campsite and translated Lucien Musset's *Les Invasions: Les Vagues germaniques.*[1] Columba, a graduate in modern languages, agonized over every nuance, while I was more inclined to cut through the verbiage in order to tell Musset's historical story. We had numerous arguments, and it was a longer process than either of us had anticipated. I said at the time that it would have probably been easier to write a book on the barbarians myself. Now, some 35 years later, I have done; and I was wrong.

The field of barbarian studies has expanded enormously since Musset's book, and contributions are being made constantly in numerous European languages. Some of these I can read; but most I can't; and, since I wanted to finish this book within a year or three of the deadline, much of this scholarship I have simply not consulted. This book is very reliant on work in English, as a glance at the bibliography will show. Certainly, some of the most profound changes in our understanding of this period in the decades since Musset wrote his book have come from Anglophone scholars (which, it may be said, includes many colleagues from Scandinavia, the Netherlands and elsewhere in the EU). But I am guiltily conscious that there is much of value that I have not looked at, although the book would have been delayed for years had I read every relevant but tortuous paragraph of *Wissenschaftsdeutsch.*[2] However, I have gleaned a great deal from the treasure house of the 35 volumes of the *Reallexicon der germanische Altertumskunde*, which is not always acknowledged fully in my notes. I hope that my Anglophone bias will at least enable Anglophone readers who want to follow up my sources, both primary and secondary, to do so more easily.

I have many people to thank. I did much of the work and writing in the Alexander Library (New Brunswick, NJ), the British Library, the Cambridge University Library, the Firestone Library (Princeton, NJ) and the James Joyce Library at University College Dublin, and I am most grateful to all the librarians for providing such excellent facilities. I began this project while I was a Senior Research Fellow at Rutgers, twice teaching a course there on 'The barbarian invasions', and I would like to thank my colleagues in History there for their support, particularly Karl Morrison and James Masschaele. My colleagues in the UCD School of History and Archives currently have helped to create a very congenial working environment. Guy Halsall graciously allowed me to read his book on *Barbarian Migrations* in draft: his book came out as I was putting the finishing touches to mine.[3] And finally, and most particularly, I would like to thank those friends who read through all or part of this book before publication and offered many valuable comments (not all of which I have followed): Hilary Carey, Hugh Elton, Julie Hofmann, Antony Keen, Ann Marie Long and Farah Mendlesohn, and, course, the patient General Editor of this series, Julia Smith. Farah's help, of course, went way beyond the reading of the text: her constant support and encouragement has made the production of this book possible – and she did it while managing to write and publish two books herself.

ABBREVIATIONS

CIL	*Corpus Inscriptionum Latinarum*, ed. T. Mommsen *et al.*, 17 vols (Berlin, 1863–1986)
MGH	*Monumenta Germaniae Historica*
[*MGH*] *SSRM*	*Scriptores Rerum Merowingicarum*
PG	*Patrologia Graeca*, ed. J.P. Migne, 161 vols (Paris, 1857–66)
PL	*Patrologia Latina*, ed. J.P. Migne, 221 vols (Paris, 1844–65)
PLRE 1, 2, 3	*The Prosopography of the later Roman Empire*, ed. A.H.M. Jones, J.R. Martindale, A.H.M. Jones, J.R. Martindale and J. Morris, 3 vols (Cambridge: Cambridge University Press, 1971, 1980, 1992)
RGA	*Reallexicon der germanischen Altertumskunde*, 2nd edition, ed. Heinrich Beck *et al.* (Berlin: De Gruyter, 1973–2007)
TTH	Translated Texts for Historians (Liverpool University Press, 1985–)

When I refer to primary sources in the notes, wherever possible I give the reference followed by the name of a translator and a page reference to a translation; the full publication information will be found in the bibliography of primary sources.

chapter one

WHO ARE THE BARBARIANS?

'B arbarian' is a key word in European history, Arno Borst suggested; it has helped define Europe itself, and European civilization.[1] This book is about the various peoples, labelled 'barbarians' by Greeks and Romans, who transformed Europe between the third and the seventh centuries AD, in the period during which, traditionally, the Ancient World became the Middle Ages. Those whose interests are focused primarily on the culture of the Mediterranean world have, over the last 35 years or so, called this period Late Antiquity; those more interested in the world of northern Europe often call it the Migration Period. Most historians who have looked at the barbarians have focused their attention on their migrations or (in a different interpretation) on their invasions of the Roman Empire. This book will attempt instead to focus on the barbarians themselves, trying to see them not as faceless hordes who brought down a great civilization, but as individuals and groups who had civilizations and achievements of their own.

Barbarians and Barbarism

Attempting to gain some understanding of people generally viewed through the hostile lenses of both the Roman sources and our own prejudices is an exercise in deduction and imagination. It is a frustrating exercise, since there are many questions to which answers may never be found and many heated academic debates which defy reconciliation and conclusion. One major stumbling block is that our written sources come almost exclusively from Greek and Roman writers. The first barbarian to tell us about barbarians is Jordanes, a Goth, writing in the middle of the sixth century; but his *History of the Goths* may be largely derived from a lost history written by the Roman scholar Cassiodorus, and, even if it was not, it was written by a 'barbarian' who had lived his whole life, within the Empire had acquired a classical education and had a purely

Greco-Roman view of the world. The earliest surviving text in a barbarian language is the Gothic Bible, translated from Greek in the mid-fourth century by Ulfila, the descendent of Roman citizens captured in a Gothic raid, and written in a script which he devised to capture Gothic phonology. But otherwise, by the time barbarians learned to write in the Latin alphabet, they had, like Jordanes, been thoroughly Romanized and Christianized, and initially they wrote in Latin. One of the greatest works of Latin literature in the early Middle Ages was Bede's *Ecclesiastical History of the English People*, written by an Anglo-Saxon barbarian who could write Latin better than most Romans, who drew a discreet veil over the pre-Christian and hence uncivilized past of his own people, and who believed that the greatest event in his people's history was conversion by missionaries sent from Rome.

The English were, nevertheless, among the first barbarians in the post-Roman world to write in their own vernacular; the other pioneers were the Irish, through whose writings (it has been claimed) we can learn something of the world of the barbarians before 'contamination' with Roman ways. Some other barbarian peoples leave us no written records until much later; the Scandinavians not until the tenth century, and the Slavs not until the eleventh. Many others – the Huns and the Picts, for instance – disappeared from history without leaving any written records at all.

The history of the barbarians therefore, in the sense of the history of events and of individuals, has very largely to be written from the outside. And that is at the root of our main historical problem: how far can we trust sources written by people with deep-rooted prejudices against barbarians?

The question of sources has to stay uppermost in our minds throughout this book. As far as possible, I shall not be consigning the authors and words of our written sources to the decent obscurity of endnotes: it is important to know what our sources are, what they say and what they leave out and whether it is possible to get beyond them. It is rather too common in general books of this kind – or even in much more specialized monographs – to find bald statements of fact which, when one looks at the footnote or endnote with a trained eye, turn out to be nothing resembling fact at all. There is little point in repeating tabloid-style statements from our Greco-Roman sources without noting, as visibly as possible, that often such statements are no more than opinion or rumour.

Archaeology offers us a way of approaching the barbarians without the intermediary of a written source. Archaeologists have hugely increased our data-store over the last century and more. But, as has often been remarked, although the spade does not lie, neither does it speak. To make sense, the spade needs the archaeologist as an interpreter, and archaeologists, like historians, frequently offer interpretations which reflect theories and ideologies of the age in which they live. The most notorious example is the work done by Nazi archaeologists on the barbarian period, to support Nazi theories of race and culture. But other examples are numerous in the archaeology of the barbarians, and are far more numerous there, I suspect, than in the closely related fields of classical archaeology or later medieval archaeology.[2] This is in part, I believe, because the barbarians are still with us.

Barbarism haunts us: and by 'us' I mean 'many readers in the western European world and its former colonies'. We fear that we (kin to the perpetrators of Dresden, Auschwitz, Hiroshima, My Lai, Haditha and so on) may be barbarians ourselves, under the skin. At the same time we fear that our civilization is threatened by our own barbarians – fascists, communists, liberals, EU bureaucrats, fundamentalists, immigrants or any other imagined enemy.

The agonies of identification may be more acute for western Europeans than for anyone else. The English, for instance, or those with any sense of their own origins, note that they are apparently descended from Germanic-speaking barbarians, and indeed from a group who seem to have been much more successful than other barbarians in destroying the Roman civilization they found. In Britain, Latin disappeared; in other European countries once part of the Roman Empire the dominant languages, like French and Castilian, are still derived directly from Latin. In France and Spain, the historical myth used to be that the barbarians had imposed themselves as a military aristocracy, and that therefore the ruling classes of later centuries were descended from Franks or Goths. The French Revolution was thus portrayed by some as the attempts of Gallo-Romans to rid themselves of their Frankish masters.[3] The history of the barbarians, over much of Europe, is inseparable from the myths that created, and were created by, the nationalism that is still with us.

None of us (least of all myself) is entirely free from our own historical context, which not only helps us determine the questions we ask of the past, but also the answers that we give. I should be honest, therefore, about my own prejudices and ideological stand. I am English, although my surname (common in Wales) suggests that I have Welsh ancestors, descendants, that is, of the Romano-Britons who managed to preserve their independence from barbarian rule for centuries longer than anyone else. By the time of my retirement I shall have spent well over a third of my professional life in Dublin, capital of a country which was much less touched by the Roman world than most European countries. Perhaps this may give me a slant on the barbarian world which is a little different from those of other historians (though I am mindful that three of the greatest historians of this period – J.B. Bury, E.A. Thompson and Peter Brown – all came from or spent significant periods in Dublin and its surroundings).

I have problems with two approaches to the period. First, I cannot quite understand those historians who regard 'the fall of the Western Roman Empire' and its replacement by various barbarian kingdoms as a disaster. People who do are often the same people who regarded the fall of a similarly bloated, corrupt and exploitative regime in 1991 with enthusiastic (and uncritical) joy. I am not on the whole on the side of empires, whoever is running them. In that sense, therefore, my view of the barbarians could be said to be a post-imperialist or a post-colonialist one. Second, however, I find a problem with those historians who imply that the 'fall of the Western Roman Empire' was not really important, and who thereby imply that the barbarians were really not *that* barbarian. The barbarian invasions were just a blip in the development of late antique culture, they say; the emperors may have disappeared from the West, but when one looks at the Roman economy, Roman social structure and the new Roman religion (Christianity) what one finds is continuity. Tell that, one is tempted to say, to a Romano-Briton fleeing to Brittany to get away from the Angles and Saxons, or to the inhabitant of a Roman town near the Rhine or Danube frontier, whose world was similarly overturned or destroyed by barbarian incursions that the Roman emperors were powerless to halt. Tell that to almost anyone living in the former western Europe around the year 600, who, wherever they were, found themselves living in markedly less comfort than their ancestors had done two or three centuries earlier.[4]

A few years ago Guy Halsall suggested that most people who studied this period were either Movers or Shakers. Movers think that many of the changes that came to the late Roman world were the result of the movement of barbarians into the Empire; Shakers think that the Roman world was already riven with tension and change, and that the arrival of a few small groups of barbarian warriors was a symptom rather than a cause of these changes. Halsall suggested that a third group – who think that nothing very much happened at all – is really an extreme wing of the Shakers. Like Halsall – though not openly admitting, as he does, to be a curmudgeonly cove[5] – I am not a fully paid-up member of either the Movers or the Shakers. The trouble is (as the reader of this book will discover, possibly with some alarm) that the story of the ever-changing relationship between Romans and barbarians is an enormously complex and uncertain one, and that the history of each region of the Roman Empire, and of each barbarian group who came into contact with those regions, is unique and different. The complexity is enhanced by the problems we have with our sources (see below, p. 15); neither our written sources nor our archaeological ones speak with transparency, clarity or trustworthiness about *anything*.

In this book I am going to deal with the barbarians who lived in what is now regarded as Europe. I am going to ignore the barbarians of North Africa, notably the people who are still called by a word deriving from *barbari* (the Berbers), and the barbarians beyond the south-eastern Roman frontier, the Arabs, who would (around the time that this book ends) have more of an impact upon the Roman world than any other non-Roman people. And within Europe, some barbarian peoples are much better known to us (or sometimes, to be honest, to me) than others. In the West, the Irish, at least from the sixth century onwards, have supplied us with a wealth of material (even though they are frequently left out of any discussion of the barbarians). At the eastern end of the Continent, the various Slavic-speaking peoples have left us with nothing save archaeology, and much of that has been published in languages which I cannot read: for those two reasons the history of the Slavic peoples is not covered in nearly the depth that I would have liked, nor with anything resembling authority. What I shall do is remind readers that – despite what they might conclude from some books on the barbarians – by no means all Europe's barbarians were Germanic-speaking. There were three other groups of barbarians in this period who, like Germanic-speakers, spoke languages belonging to the Indo-European group of languages: that is, Celtic-speaking peoples, Slavic-speaking peoples and those peoples speaking Baltic languages like Latvian and Lithuanian. But there were also peoples whose languages were quite unrelated to Indo-European, like the groups of Turkic-speakers who arrived in Europe from Central Asia during this period (notably the Huns, the Avars and the Bulgars), and some of those who lived by the Baltic, like the Finns and the Estonians, who spoke varieties of Finno-Ugrian (although their linguistic cousins, the Magyars, did not arrive in Europe until after the period covered in this book).[6]

It needs to be emphasized that the barbarians I shall be writing about have nothing in common with each other except that the Greeks and Romans labelled them 'barbarians'. That word – *barbaros* (plural *barbaroi*) in Greek and *barbarus* (plural *barbari*) in Latin – had two meanings by the period which concerns us. Primarily it meant non-Roman, someone who came from outside the Roman Empire; but secondarily it meant 'barbarous', that is, someone who was not civilized. There may have been people who identified themselves in certain circumstances as 'barbarian', but for the most part it was a word applied to others, pejoratively, by Romans.

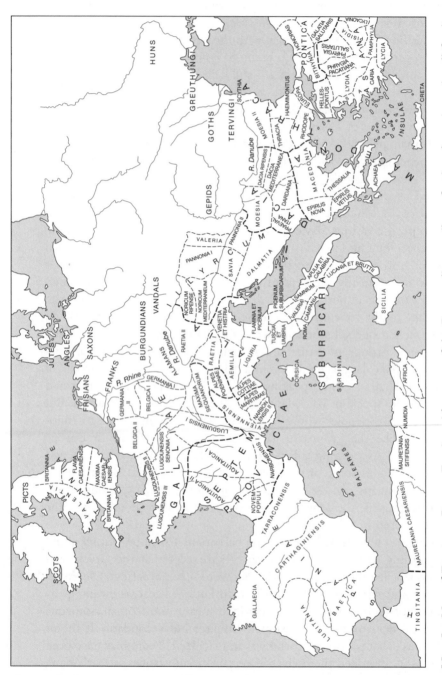

Map 1 Map of European Roman Empire with names of the Roman dioceses (large font) and provinces (small font) and the approximate location of various barbarian peoples. The provinces are those named by the *Notitia Dignitatum* in 400; the barbarians are as positioned before Goths moved into the Empire in 376. (Modified from A.H.M. Jones, *The Decline of the Ancient World*. London: Longman 1966, 100–101).

'Celt' and 'German' are words with respectable classical pedigrees: 'Celt' derives from Greek *Keltoi* (the Romans called these people *Galli* or Gauls); 'German' from Latin *Germani*. 'Slav', however, does not appear until the sixth century, in the form *Sclaveni*. But the modern usage of 'Celt', 'German' and 'Slav' derives from the usage of philologists from the eighteenth century onwards. The Celts are those who speak one of the Celtic languages (of which the modern speakers are to be found among the Bretons, Welsh, Irish and Scots); the Germans are those who speak one of the Germanic languages (which in modern times includes Dutch, German, the Scandinavian languages including Icelandic and English); and the Slavs are those who speak one of the Slavic languages (today Russian, Polish, Czech, Serbian and so on). Thanks to nineteenth-century nationalism (and racism) historians have had a tendency to use these linguistic terms as if they represented biological groups, or races. But 'Celtic-speaking' means no more than that. Celtic-speaking peoples were to be found across much of western Europe, probably arriving in Ireland, Britain and elsewhere as a military elite who taught or otherwise persuaded the local inhabitants to speak their language. Speaking a Celtic language is not a sign that someone belonged biologically to a 'Celtic' 'race', even though a century ago it would have been easy to find scholars who believed that it did.

In this period, therefore, 'Celts' would not have thought of themselves as Celts, or 'Germans' as Germans, although they *might* on occasion have identified themselves as 'non-Romans', or as barbarians. In this book I shall try not to refer to Germans or Celts or Slavs, but, if I have to, to Germanic-speakers, Celtic-speakers and Slavic-speakers.

Some people have asked why, if I am so touchy about the usage of 'Celt' and 'German' (with a tendency to launch into a tirade, for instance, if an unfortunate student starts using a nonsensical term like 'the Celtic Church'),[7] I use the politically incorrect term 'barbarian'. There is a simplicity to it, of course, which cannot be matched by any other possible word; and is certainly more elegant than saying 'non-Roman' all the time. In 2003 Hans-Werner Goetz defended the retention of the word 'Germanic' in a book he had edited on the grounds that to substitute 'barbarian' for 'German' 'would only mean adopting another Roman ideology which, in the final analysis, is as inadequate as "Germanic".'[8] I cannot agree. Quite apart from the fact that by no means all barbarians were Germanic-speaking, the word 'Germanic', 60 years after the defeat of Hitler, still has racial connotations; the word 'barbarian' does not. For Romans, 'barbarian' could certainly be a derogatory term; on the other hand, unlike modern racists, Romans believed that barbarians could be civilized, and had been, frequently, in the past. (By AD 212, when Caracalla gave the citzenship to all free inhabitants of the Empire, most Roman citizens were descended from peoples early Romans had regarded as barbarians.) Whether one uses 'barbarian' or 'Germanic', of course, one has to remember that generalizations about the groups that are labelled that way are almost impossible; there was quite as much difference and contrast within the barbarian world as there was between the barbarians and the Romans.

There is nothing necessarily politically incorrect about the word 'barbarian', particularly if we do not share the prejudices of the Romans and of our own much more modern ancestors. If, in a post-colonialist world, we reject the imperialist project and the imperialist ideology of cultural or racial supremacy, then we can start recognising and valuing non-imperial cultures and using 'barbarian' with pride: it is analogous to the recovery of the word 'queer' by the gay community. 'Barbarian culture' or 'barbarian civilization' are not oxymorons, as Romans would have thought; we can now appreciate the aesthetic values of the material culture of the barbarians, even though we can only guess at the wealth of barbarian oral culture from what survives from much later periods. The semi-abstract swirls of animal interlace on early medieval jewellery or manuscripts seem attractive to generations brought up to appreciate abstract art (while, conversely, the excesses of Mussolini or Stalin have caused us to distrust the self-conscious grandeur of official Roman art).

There is also, one must confess, a certain dark romance to the word 'barbarian', at least in northern Europe. It is an appeal that the Nazis tapped into, with their cult of the Nordic race and their adulation of Wagner's version of ancient Germanic mythology. But it has an appeal beyond northern Europe. Contemporaneous with the rise of Nazism, but in Texas, Robert E. Howard was writing the various short stories about Conan the Barbarian, which made a similar appeal to roots, to old-fashioned values (like patriarchy) and to simplicity – such as the simplicity of settling disputes by violence rather than by reason or negotiation. The romantic image of the barbarian is one of the sources of the huge popularity of fantasy fiction, much of which stems from the almost diametrically opposed tap-roots of Robert E. Howard and J.R.R. Tolkien. Professor Tolkien, of course, found his inspiration not in inchoate popular images of the barbarian (as Howard did), but in the literature of real barbarians, above all Anglo-Saxons and Icelanders.

The modern obsession with the barbarian goes back in uninterrupted continuity to the Age of Discoveries, with the renewed European contact with peoples who were seen as 'primitive'. It is worth quoting Claude Rawson's description of his own book on *God, Gulliver, and Genocide*.

This book is about how the European imagination has dealt with the groups which it habitually talks about killing, and never quite kills off, because the task is too difficult or unpleasant, or the victims are needed for their labour, or competing feelings get in the way. It is concerned with the imaginative resonances of the idea of the savage, the 'other', not as simply noble or ignoble, but as a figure through whom we confront our own selves in an anguished self-implication too complex and 'conflicted' to be amenable to the customary reductive categorizations. We are obsessed with 'barbarians'. They are the 'not us', who do not speak our language, or 'any language', whom we despise, fear, invade, and kill; for whom we feel compassion, or admiration, and an intense sexual interest; whose innocence or vigour we aspire to, and who have an extraordinary influence on the comportment, and even modes of dress, of our civilized metropolitan lives; whom we often outdo in the barbarism we impute to them; and whose suspected resemblance to us haunts our introspections and imaginings. They come in two overlapping categories, ethnic others and home-grown pariahs.[9]

The cultural complexity of 'the barbarian' in the modern era is nothing new. It colours all our ancient sources too and may, if we are not wary, confuse and mislead us.

'Barbarian' is a word that goes back to the very beginnings of Greco-Roman culture.[10] The word *barbaros* itself, meaning no more than 'someone who did not speak Greek' (but spoke instead meaningless sounds resembling *barbar*), became more common, it has been argued, after the Persian invasion of Greece. It is used extensively by the Greek tragedians of the fifth century BC, who rewrote Greek myths to make place for barbarian stereotypes. The image of the superior Greek facing the inferior barbarian had become so common that in the second half of the century Euripides could offer the spectacle of barbaric Greeks and noble barbarians, which Edith Hall has called 'an ironic and sophistic reversal of the accepted premise';[11] it is the precursor of Rousseau's noble savage.

Hall remarked that she could have called her book *Inventing the Hellene* rather than *Inventing the Barbarian*,[12] since the purpose of inventing stereotypes of barbarians with undesirable features was in large part to define the qualities which the Hellenes (Greeks) themselves admired. Hellene/barbarian became a binary opposition which reminded Greeks of other oppositions: reason/instinct; logical/emotional; male/female; human/animal; control/chaos; order/disorder; and, of course, civilized/uncivilized.

It was long common to think of the barbarian in deliberately negative terms: as someone who was deprived of most or all of the benefits of civilization. In the sixteenth century Montaigne described the Tupinamba of Brazil:

This is a nation, I should say to Plato, in which there is no kind of commerce, no knowledge of letters, no science of numbers, no title of magistrate or of political superior, no habit of service, riches or poverty, no contracts, no inheritance, no divisions of property, only leisurely occupations, no respect for kinship but the common ties, no clothes, no agriculture, no metals, no use of corn or wine. The very words denoting lying, treason, deceit, greed, envy, slander, and forgiveness, have never been heard.[13]

One can easily see how one's personal preferences, or one's immediate social or political context, could make it possible to see Montaigne's cannibals as the epitome of barbarism, and on the other hand (or simultaneously) as the hint of a real utopia. Thomas More's *Utopia* (1516), which was so heavily influenced by the news of the discoveries in the Americas, was a product of a long tradition of seeing the satiric possibilities of contrasting our own 'civilization' with the customs of the 'Other'.[14] From the time of Euripides at least there was this dichotomy in Greco-Roman views of the barbarians. The barbarians can stand for the worst that mankind is capable of, but they can also remind Greeks and Romans of the purity and simplicity which they themselves have lost.

Since the barbarian is to a large extent an imaginative construct, there was inevitably no single geographical vision of the barbarian world. For some Greco-Roman writers, the most distant barbarians were the most noble. Strabo, for instance, reckoned that those who lived furthest from the Greco-Roman world were as a consequence not – yet – tainted by the vices of civilization:

We regard the Scythians the most straightforward of men and the least prone to mischief, as also far more frugal and independent of others than we are. And yet our mode of life has spread its change for the worse to almost all peoples, introducing amongst them luxury and sensual pleasures and, to satisfy these vices, base artifices that lead to innumerable acts of greed.[15]

For other writers, the further away barbarians were from the fount of civilization, the more barbaric they were. This is sometimes expressed in the concept of cannibalism, a touchstone for barbarism then as now. Strabo said that the Irish were cannibals, and did not have an incest taboo. Few people cite the conclusion to this much-quoted passage, however: 'I am saying this only with the understanding that I have no trustworthy witnesses for it.'[16] St Jerome, in the early fifth century, did not add such a postscript to his bald comment that in northern Britain the Attacotti (perhaps a confusion with the Scotti, the inhabitants of Ireland) were cannibals.[17] There are those modern anthropologists who doubt that cannibalism has ever existed, that it is always an accusation levelled at one's enemies or inferiors.[18] But this is in one sense irrelevant; the interesting observation is that, in ancient as in modern times, cannibalism is regarded as the custom of the most degraded of all barbarians.

Not all barbarians were the same, therefore, for Roman writers. Most Romans, however, did probably think that those barbarians who were living settled lives, with agriculture and with trade, were closer to civilized beings. Nomads, who had not learned the arts of agriculture, were lower down the scale. Incessant mobility, by horse or by camel, was a reflection of the troubled state of the soul.[19] As a result, some barbarians were described as nomadic who were clearly not; their nomadism is much more a reflection of their perceived position in the hierarchy of peoples than anything resembling accurate ethnographic observation.

It must be emphasized again that for the Roman the barbarian was not inferior in the sense that, for modern racialists, the Slav or the African was inferior. The African cannot change colour, and nor, a racialist would say, the genetic code which determines his inferiority. A Roman, on the other hand, for whom colour does not seem important,[20] would say that barbarians could change: they could become civilized, and indeed they could become Roman citizens. To quote Yves Dauge, the acknowledged authority of Roman attitudes to the barbarian:

> For the Roman, the barbarian is not a different species, but an inferior *state* of man, whether collective or individual, a type of being who is defective, unfinished, incomplete – not definitive, but variable. The barbarian, like the civilized person, is always subject to change and can always evolve: access to *humanitas* is always possible, and so is falling, or falling again, into barbarism.[21]

Romans remembered that they too had once been barbarians. Gallo-Romans in the fourth century, say, were perfectly well aware that their Gallic ancestors had once been barbarians, and that, after their conquest by Julius Caesar, they had became integrated into the Roman world. For Vitruvius, barbarism resulted from disequilibrium, either from excess or from lack. Balance could be supplied by civilization. 'The logical consequence was that the barbarian world, powerless because incomplete, could only find its fulfillment by entering into Roman civilization.'[22] Some peoples had passed through the state of barbarism (although they could slip back again); others were still living in barbarism (but could emerge from it). And indeed, in each of us there is something of the barbarian. As Themistius proclaimed to the Senate of Constantinople in 370, 'There is in each of us a barbarian tribe, extremely overbearing and intractable – I mean temper and those insatiable desires, which stand opposed to rationality as Scythians and Germans do to the Romans.'[23]

To Romans – which is shorthand for 'the members of the Roman literary elite who provide us with almost all our ideas about Roman opinions' – barbarism remained a constant threat. If anything, it was not so much 'real' barbarians living outside the frontiers of the Roman Empire who were feared; Romans for the most part felt that they could deal with them. The barbarians within, Rawson's 'home-grown pariahs', were the real problem. Cicero regarded Greeks as barbarians, because they had been weak-willed enough to submit to Rome; but Romans thugs such as Catiline, Dolabella or Mark Antony were worse than barbarians. Juvenal too saw barbarism as a threat: but what he meant by that was that he feared contamination by corrupt, effeminate, luxury-loving, hedonistic and vain Greeks and Orientals.[24] The fourth-century Latin Panegyrics, which often celebrate imperial victories over barbarians, and which give the impression of hordes about to submerge the Empire were it not for the constant vigilance of the emperors, nevertheless express at several points a preference for the uncivilized peoples of the North, who were fierce and energetic, over the soft, idle and effeminate peoples of the Roman East.[25] But for Tacitus home-grown pariahs were not just in the Eastern Empire: they were everywhere. Slaves, peasants, urban mobs and even soldiers were all as bad as barbarians, and the Roman Empire itself might well be bringing the known world back to barbarism rather than forward to civilization. 'A regime which encourages adulation and servility will deprive the Roman gradually of his soul, making of him a "subject", in the Asiatic manner.'[26] The concept of the barbarian, therefore, was a way by which the Roman elite could assure themselves of its own superiority, not only in the *oikumene*, the known world, over the rest of humanity, but also within the hierarchy of imperial society. At the same time these Romans could remind themselves of those values which they needed to maintain in order to secure that superiority.

Romans did not necessarily see all non-Romans as barbarians. Although the Greeks regarded the Persians as barbarians *par excellence* – it was after the Persian invasion of Greece that Greeks developed their concepts of Hellene superiority over the barbarian – the Romans did not, or at least did not do so consistently. The Persians were generally regarded by Romans as superior to the idle and effeminate Asians of the Roman Empire, above all because the Persians had created a multi-ethnic empire which could be the military match of Rome. The most famous Persian victory against the Romans was the battle of Carrhae in 53 BC. It was said that the victorious Persian king was watching a performance of *The Bacchae* by Euripides when the Roman general Crassus's head was brought to him:[27] a Greek might well have thought him more 'civilized' than Crassus.

In Crassus's time Persia was usually referred to as Parthia, as it was under the control of the Parthian dynasty of the Arsacids; in AD 226 the Arsacids were replaced by the Persian dynasty of the Sassanids. But both dynasties regarded themselves as the successors of the Achaemenid dynasty (who had led the invasion of Greece in the fifth century); and both referred to their ruler as the Shahinshah, and their country as Iran. Sassanid Persia is of importance in the history of the European barbarians, even if it will barely be mentioned again, for if it had not been for the frequent military threat which the Sassanids posed throughout much of the period of this book, the Roman emperors might have been able to offer a more effective military opposition to the barbarians.

It should be clear by now that the barbarian came weighed down with so many cultural meanings that the reality of the barbarian may often be wholly obscured. Nor should we forget the political meanings of the barbarian within Roman political discourse. One of the most common images of the barbarian in Roman art, in stone or in the metal of coins, was the figure of the barbarian warrior being trampled under the feet of an emperor's horse. The emperor's whole purpose was to protect the lives and livelihood of Romans from attack by the supposedly savage hordes from across the imperial frontiers. The bulk of the taxes that were wrested from Roman peasants were directed to the maintenance of the Roman army, and it was in the interests of the Roman emperor and his apologists to emphasize the barbarian threat. If an emperor needed a victory to impress his subjects, a quick raid across the frontier (ostensibly to punish a prior raid in the other direction) was a common ploy. 'What better reminder to the Roman public that barbarians were being kept firmly in line than odd bits of decomposing barbarian king hung up for public display?' Only, perhaps, as Peter Heather added, the sight of Sarmatian prisoners being fed alive to animals in the circus.[28]

John Drinkwater has suggested that the Franks and Alamanni were no real military threat to the Empire in the fourth century, but merely occasionally violent irritants.

> The Franks and Alamanni may have been used to excuse the maintenance of a large military force in Gaul and along the Rhine, and thereby to justify the continued maintenance of the whole imperial system in the west . . . the leaders of the civil population, educated to believe in the German menace along the Rhine, impressed by imperial *busy-ness*, and open to imperial persuasion through their desire for imperial generosity and imperial office, were happy to give this structure their full support, and to reinforce it in their panegyrics. . . . The 'Guard on the Rhine', which the imperial establishment sold so successfully to contemporaries, and to later historians, was a sham, an artefact . . . a 'stage-show.'[29]

The image of barbarians looming threateningly all along the 4,000-kilometre Roman frontier in Europe, found in much modern historiography, may thus be in part a witness to the persuasiveness of Roman imperial propaganda – and a warning, if we needed one, always to question our sources.

We shall look later (in Chapter Five) at the problems of defining and identifying different groups of barbarians. But it is worthwhile emphasizing at the beginning that knowing precisely who was a barbarian and who was not during this period is by no means easy for the historian, and probably was not easy for a contemporary, either. Was the great Roman general Stilicho, the son of a Vandal military officer and a Roman

Plate 1 An ivory diptych depicting the general Stilicho, with his Roman wife Serena and his son Eucherius. Stilicho had two daughters: Maria (married the Emperor Honorius in 395; died 407/8) and Thermantia (married Honorius in 408). Stilicho was executed on Honorius's orders in 408; the execution of Serena, the murder of Eucherius and the divorce of Thermantia followed not long afterwards. (Museo del Duoma, Monza).

mother, a barbarian? Given that some Late Roman sources use the word *barbarus* to mean simply 'soldier', how can we distinguish 'Roman' from 'barbarian' in the Roman army (and in Syriac the word for 'soldier' can be either 'Goth' or 'Roman').[30]

The Sources

We not only have to reckon with conscious or unconscious bias in our sources, but also with considerable ignorance. Descriptions of how the barbarians lived, such as we find in the account of Priscus, who was on an embassy sent to meet with Attila, king of the Huns, in 449 (see below, p. 68), are very rare. Although there must have been other Roman ambassadors who went to negotiate with barbarians, let alone many Roman merchants who must have travelled through barbarian territories, their observations were either not written down or else simply did not survive. An able commentator like the historian Ammianus Marcellinus (writing towards the end of the fourth century) was perfectly familiar with barbarians, having served alongside them in the Roman army, but even he might have hazy ideas about the barbarians beyond the frontiers. Less careful writers may be doing no more than repeat rumours or received opinion.

A few words are necessary about the written sources, for those not familiar with the period. The most common writing material in this period was probably papyrus, a kind of paper produced from a reed that grew by the banks of the Nile. However, papyrus is fragile, and while some papyrus documents do survive, in the dryness of the Egyptian desert or the relative dryness of certain archives and libraries, the great bulk is lost. The small cache of letters found at Vindolanda on the northern British frontier, at Hadrian's Wall, are written on postcard-sized sheets of wood. This is likely also to have been a very common writing material – perhaps more common than papyrus in the West, which was far removed from the Egyptian sources of papyrus – although it is only under very special circumstances that they are going to survive. The Vindolanda letters show the very considerable use even ordinary Romans made of writing, at least in the first century AD, and also demonstrate how massive our losses have been. It has been estimated that in the first three centuries of the Empire 225 million pay-records would have been produced for the army; and just 3 survive, at this damp spot on the edge of the Roman world.[31]

Stone inscriptions survive very well, of course; it takes effort to break them up. They are still being found, although they are seldom found in the context in which they were originally placed, since they were often reused as building material or foundations. They have become an invaluable source of local information for classicists, although the biographical detail found on memorial stones from the early Roman Period thins out drastically by the later Empire. There are funerary inscriptions for barbarians found inside the Roman Empire (defined either by their personal name, or sometimes by mention on the inscription of the barbarian group to which they belonged); but this evidence has so far not been gathered together from around the Empire and analysed.

The bulk of our surviving written material is found on parchment: the prepared skins of animals, primarily cattle or sheep. Letters or legal documents might be written on single sheets of parchment; longer documents would normally consist of several or numerous sheets of parchment sewn together into rolls, or into codices, that is, books as we would recognize them. It is only in the last century or two of the Roman Empire that the use of the parchment codex took over from the papyrus scroll or codex. But most of our documents relating to the fourth or fifth century – histories, collections of letters, laws, theological treatises and so on – do not survive in contemporary codices of the fourth or fifth century, but in later parchment manuscripts, often from the ninth century or later. Sometimes crucial texts only survive in summary form, or in fragments, copied into some encyclopaedic work. Frequently the texts that do survive are copies of copies of the original, and the first task is to work out what errors have occurred in the copying process and to publish a good edition of what the editor believes to be the author's original text. For most texts, editions have been produced in the last two centuries which are perfectly satisfactory for most purposes, and increasingly they are becoming more accessible and amenable to processes such as word searches: some of the more important series of published texts, such as the *Monumenta Germaniae Historica* and *Patrologia Latina*, are now available online, although sometimes at a price that only a few universities can afford.[32] The body of surviving evidence is becoming better known and better exploited all the time, while new written sources are discovered very rarely indeed. Here is a great difference with archaeology, where new finds are being discovered weekly. Indeed, unless the structures of archaeology change radically, discoveries will continue to take place far too rapidly for archaeologists properly to process and publish the results. The two most important archaeological finds from barbarian England took, respectively, 25 and 54 years to see publication, but many excavations never reach full publication at all.[33]

The history of 'barbarian archaeology' – I put it in inverted commas, as the category does not exist; it hides away in 'late Roman', 'early medieval' and 'Migration Period' archaeology – is instructive. It begins in 1653, with the discovery in Tournai (now in Belgium) of the grave of the Frankish king Childeric (d. *circa* 481). But it took until the early nineteenth century before all other graves, of lesser wealth but similarly containing weapons, items of personal ornamentation and vessels, were recognized as being from the fifth, sixth and seventh centuries. Cemetery excavation dominated 'barbarian archaeology' until the second half of the twentieth century. Because early medieval cemeteries frequently contained artefacts such as weapons, buckles, brooches and vessels, they were relatively easy to spot, as nineteenth-century engineers drove canals, railway lines and roads across the countryside, and laid sewers and water- and gas-pipe lines everywhere, and as nineteenth-century house-builders extended villages and suburbs. Many of the objects found their way into museums and private collections, and every now and then a local antiquary, often a doctor or priest, took the task of excavation seriously. In the twentieth century a good deal of the impetus towards more professionalism came from museums rather than universities, partly because the barbarian period for the most part fell in the gap between the interests of classicists and medieval historians. It was no accident that the most influential archaeologist in the early twentieth century dealing with the barbarian invasions of Britain was E.T. Leeds, the curator of Oxford University's Ashmolean Museum and not a teaching member of the university. What was probably the most important single discovery from the period in the twentieth century, the ship-burial at Sutton Hoo (Suffolk, UK), was discovered (in 1938) by an amateur. Right across Europe, amateurs (in the best sense of the term, since many of them were highly skilled) were important contributors to the archaeological enterprise.

The second half of the twentieth century brought great changes. More and more universities acquired Departments of Archaeology, and more people with excavating skills were being produced, right across Europe. One result of this – and of the growing complexity of excavation and post-excavation techniques – was that, gradually, professionalization squeezed out the amateur. The impact of the amateur now is most obvious within the hobby of metal-detecting. Still viewed with suspicion by many archaeologists, because of a history of pillaging sites and failing to report finds, the metal-detecting fraternity is credited now for bringing to light sites and artefacts that would otherwise never have been found. More Anglo-Saxon metalwork is now found in England by metal-detectors than by archaeological work; and that only relates to the finds that metal-detectors report.

Among the new professionals, 'barbarian archaeology' advanced in particular in northern Europe: in Germany, the Netherlands, Britain and the Scandinavian countries. And there was a shift away from cemeteries.

For the first time settlement sites were discovered and excavated: sites which by their nature were difficult to detect and to investigate, since structures were usually of wood and often left no more than some discolouration in the soil to indicate their presence. In more recent years, legislation in several countries in Europe has forced developers to allow archaeologists time to excavate before development. This means that much archaeological effort has been devoted to towns (and sometimes to strips of countryside, along projected motorways). Rescue archaeology – excavating, sometimes in haste, before mechanical diggers removed all traces of the past – took attention away from the possibility of conducting research excavation into sites of strong academic interest. More significantly, the exponential increase in the rate of discovery, and the increase in costs of both excavation and post-excavation work, has meant that a high proportion of sites excavated over the last generation have not actually been properly studied yet, let alone published. However, archaeologists became much more sophisticated in their analysis of the material remains themselves (developing all kinds of scientific techniques) and in their consciousness of the theoretical problems that the analysis of these remains entails. Through most of the twentieth century, for instance, very simplistic assumptions about the ethnic or religious identity of a person buried in a grave could be put forward; nowadays there is rather less conviction that archaeology can provide answers, as opposed to a series of plausible hypotheses. It is, however, still capable of finding out a great deal more than we know at present. New sites are being discovered all the time, by accident or by deliberate survey; and new questions and new techniques applied to well-known material still produces new results, as it does for historians.

It is relatively easy to contrast historians and archaeologists, in terms of the types of material that they are looking at and the types of conclusions that they can reach. But there are a number of generalizations that one can make which apply to both disciplines.

The first generalization is about *generalization*. Archaeologists when they excavate a site or historians when they analyse a text are looking at just one site or just one person's idea of what happened. It is very difficult to generalize from the particular, because in the state of our knowledge about the barbarian period we have so few points of comparison. Is what Sidonius Apollinaris tells us about barbarians in any way representative of how other Gallic aristocrats regarded barbarians in the later fifth century? (Which, of course, ignores the vexed problem of whether we *really* even know what Sidonius himself thought or meant when he wrote his poems and letters.)

The second is about *survival*. Both historians and archaeologists have constantly to bear in mind that they are looking at what happens to have survived, and in both cases some types of material survive better than others. Theological texts from the late Roman Period survive better than pornography, for instance, as most Latin and Greek texts are preserved because they have been copied by medieval monks and preserved in medieval monasteries: there was a conscious censorship (if only because of the cost of parchment), and hence a destruction not just of pornography, but of ostentatiously pagan or heretical texts as well. Moreover, monastic archives have considerable survival characteristics, and royal or aristocratic archives do not, so that day-to-day items produced by a secular bureaucracy have usually disappeared without trace. Survival on an archaeological site may depend largely on material durability. We can say quite a lot about the oil or wine trade, because the containers survive, even when the contents do not; we can say almost nothing, from archaeology, about the grain trade or the slave trade. I remember my York colleague Philip Rahtz demonstrating the survival of items in a grave by getting a student to lie on a table while other students assessed the durability of his clothes. His ear-ring and watch would survive most conditions, but his clothes would only be traced by the eyelets on his shoes and the rivets and zip on his jeans. Only exceptional qualities of the soil, above all permanent wetness, would preserve textiles, and perhaps even body-parts such as hair. If the English did bury the dead wearing their jeans, no doubt archaeologists in the far future would divide between those who argued for a massive invasion and/or migration of England in the late twentieth century from North America, and those who adhered to theories of trade and/or cultural diffusion.

The third generalization is about *context*, the context in which the artefact was produced and preserved, which will determined the way in which it is interpreted. A high proportion of known archaeological artefacts from this period were buried with the dead, for instance: they cannot be assumed to be items of everyday use, for they may have been manufactured as grave-goods. Which artefacts were deliberately deposited in the ground, and which were the product of accidental loss? What occasioned the writing of a particular text, and of its preservation on parchment (for everyday texts that were written on papyrus or wax-tablets have largely disappeared)? To what extent (*pace* those literary critics who deny the author's existence) has the motivation which produced a particular text shaped that text in ways that are (to us) misleading and deceptive?

The Book

There are two parts to this book. In the first part (Chapters 2–4), using largely the written sources, I trace what is known about the history of the barbarians and their involvement with the Roman Empire, dividing this enquiry up into three chronological periods. The first is from roughly the first century BC up to the first time that a barbarian people came into the Roman Empire and stayed there: that is, 376, when one group of Goths crossed the Danube. The second goes from 376 to what has frequently been taken as the end of the Western Empire, exactly a century later, when a barbarian general in the Roman army deposes the last western emperor. The third takes the story from 476 through to the end of the sixth century and slightly beyond. In the second part of the book (Chapters 5–12), I deal with a number of themes and problems in relation to the barbarians, in which archaeology becomes much more important. I have placed these in roughly chronological order, starting with definitions and moving then from the time in which the barbarians and Romans were separated by the imperial frontier to the time in which barbarians established kingdoms within the former Roman Empire.

chapter two

THE BARBARIANS
BEFORE AD 376

⟨ornament⟩

Classical Ethnography

By the time that the Roman Empire was established, a generation before the birth of Christ, Greeks and Romans had known barbarians for a long time, and had been describing them, and indeed attempting to explain them. The treatise *Airs, Waters, Places*, written in the fifth century BC and ascribed (probably wrongly) to the great medical writer Hippocrates offers both an environmental and a cultural explanation of the differences between peoples.[1] Asians live in a hot climate, and are ruled by despots; these factors both contribute to their indolent, soft and cowardly nature. Europeans endure a more varied and extreme climate, and do not have kings; they are therefore more independent in spirit, hardier and more belligerent. The most belligerent peoples tend to be tall and blond; the most cowardly are shorter and dark. Greece offers the ideal climate (Latin writers would later say the same of Italy). Benjamin Isaac comments 'it seems to be the first work in Greek literature, or any literature for that matter, which consistently describes peoples in terms of stereotypes that are said to cover all of the individual members of the group it describes'; a crucial document in the development of racialism, therefore.[2]

This European view of Asians survived into modern times; it is at the root of the Orientalism described by Edward Said.[3] Romans frequently included Greeks among the Asians – encouraged no doubt by the large number of Greeks and Greek-speakers who were to be found in Asia Minor, and increasingly, after the time of Alexander the Great, in the rest of the eastern Mediterranean. Greeks were famous for their levity (*levitas*), which was the opposite of the *gravitas* admired by the Roman elite, and Romans looking at Greeks were able to tick many of the boxes which made up the category 'oriental'.

For both Greeks and Romans the barbarians *par excellence* were the Celts, *Keltoi*, whom the Romans called Gauls, *Galli*. They were formidable fighters: they had sacked Rome in 390 BC, and would have nipped the very embryonic Roman Republic in the bud, we are told, had it not been for the vigilance of Juno's sacred geese.[4] There was an extensive war between Celts and Romans towards the end of the third century BC: these were the Celts of what Romans called 'Cisalpine Gaul', that is, 'the land of the Gauls on this side of the Alps', in other words, northern Italy. At that time there were Gauls in north Italy, in Gaul (a somewhat larger area than modern France), in Galicia in north-west Spain, in Britain and Ireland, in much of the land that later came to be known as Germany, and even in Asia Minor (the Galatians to whom St Paul wrote). In describing this war, Polybius uses ideas about the Gauls which were to become stereotypes, easily transferable from 'Celt' to 'German': they were courageous, impulsive, fickle, fond of booty and alcohol and had no staying power in battle. Strabo tells how the traveller Posidonius, early in the first century BC, had seen at first hand the Celtic habit of decapitating the heads of their enemies in battle and nailing them to the porches of their houses (embalming and preserving the heads of the most famous); at first Posidonius had been nauseated, but he had grown used to it.[5] The classical characterization of Celts has had a powerful influence on the archaeological and historical study of the Celts ever since; it is only now that it is beginning to be questioned.[6]

Julius Caesar's well-known *Gallic War* gives an account of his conquest of Gaul, from 59 BC, but also of his expedition across the Rhine into Germany in 55 BC, and of his two expeditions to Britain, in 55 and 54 BC. In his literary treatment of the Gauls, he generally follows the Polybian line, although he does add distinctions between one group of Gauls and another. The Belgae, for instance, were better fighters than other Gauls. Caesar gives three reasons for this: most of them were Germans, who had migrated westwards across the Rhine;[7] they were furthest away from Rome and civilization (and hence the merchants 'who import the wares that induce effeminacy' seldom visited them); and they were close to and influenced by the even more courageous and barbaric Germans.[8] The Belgic tribe of the Nervii were the best fighters of all, because they refused to accept imports of wine and other enervating luxuries.[9] The later geographer Strabo (see below, p. 24) does not say that the Belgae themselves were Germans, although he does say that the Nervii and Ubii had come into Gaul from across the Rhine, fleeing from the powerful Suevi.[10] Recently the geneticist Stephen Oppenheimer has suggested that the Belgae were indeed German-speaking (citing the almost total lack of Celtic-derived place-names in Belgic Gaul), and posited the idea that the presence of Belgic tribes in Britain, attested by Caesar, may have paved the way for the rapid spread of the English language in the post-Roman period.[11]

It was Caesar who first gave the peoples east of the Rhine the name of 'German' (a word which is itself probably of Celtic origin). He intimated that the Cimbri and Teutones, who had attacked the Roman world around 100 BC, had been Germans too, thus reminding his readers that the Germans were a people to fear. He was very concerned to stress their differences from the Gauls.

> The Germans differ much from this manner of living. They have no Druids to regulate divine worship, no zeal for sacrifices. . . . Their whole life is composed of hunting expeditions and military pursuits; from early boyhood they are zealous for toil and hardship. . . . For agriculture they have no zeal, and the greater part of their food consists of milk, cheese, and flesh.[12]

They do not have private ownership of land, said Caesar, both to avoid settling down and thus losing their warrior habits, and the wish to distribute wealth evenly in order to avoid envy. They frequently attacked their neighbours, aiming in particular to establish a wide unpopulated area between them and their neighbours, to avoid the possibility of sudden attack. Once upon a time, he added, the Gauls had been superior to the Germans militarily, but the Gauls had been weakened by their contacts with civilization, and had become used to defeat, and thus giving up their claims to be superior.[13]

Caesar intended to give several clear indications about the Germans: that the Rhine was a natural frontier between Gauls and Germans (which is certainly wrong); that the Germans were primitive barbarians, who had little of value worth plundering (which is probably wrong); and that trying to conquer them – they live in the almost limitless Hercynian Forest – would be pointless and really rather difficult (which is possibly right). He had his own very clear political ideas for coming to these conclusions: namely, that he had completed his conquest of the Gauls, and that extending his campaigns across the Rhine would have no purpose except to postpone his political ambitions south of the Alps.

The difficulty of conquering the Germans was not something with which Caesar's successor Augustus apparently agreed. In AD 4 his son Tiberius reached the mouth of the Elbe with his army and fleet. But the expedition led by Augustus's general Varus, which ended in AD 9 with the slaughter of his three legions at the battle of the Teutoburg Forest, inclined most Romans to Caesar's view. The disaster was one of the worst that Roman armies ever experienced. Their opponent was Arminius, from the Cherusci (Hermann, the hero in much later German legend). There were few Roman survivors; the remains of some have now been found by German archaeologists at Kalkriese, north of Osnabrück, in a low area of marsh between two rivers.[14] All the weapons found, with one single exception, were Roman, which has led to a recent suggestion that it was not a clash between Rome and the barbarians, but essentially a Roman military revolt.[15] Even at this early stage of relations with Germanic-speaking barbarians, loyalties were complex. Arminius himself had once served in the Roman army, and his brother Flavus continued to serve there throughout Arminius's war. Flavus's son Italicus for a time lived in Rome. Arminius's brother-in-law was opposed to Arminius's anti-Roman stance, but stayed among the Cherusci, while his son became a Roman priest in Cologne.[16]

The official policy after the defeat of Varus was one of caution, and few people imagined major advances into Germany. The geographer Strabo was one exception: at one point he notes that the Romans 'have not *yet* [my italics] advanced into the area beyond the Elbe'.[17] But military minds were in reality content with little more than a few advance posts east of the Rhine, particularly in the area of the Lower Main River. Arminius was not long afterwards murdered by his own people – the debates between pro-Roman and anti-Roman groups within a barbarian people were probably ubiquitous and occasionally bitter – and for a long time thereafter the Romans found it relatively easy to prevent any alliances among the barbarians that could prove to be a similar threat.

Strabo, writing at the time of Augustus, was very aware that some of the peoples who had been recently conquered and incorporated into the Roman Empire were little better than barbarians. For Strabo there was no clear dividing-line between barbarism and civilization, but degrees along a continuum.[18] The Cantabrians of Roman Spain, for instance,

> live on a low moral plane – that is, they have regard, not for rational living, but rather for satisfying their physical needs and bestial instincts – unless some one thinks those men have regard for rational living who bathe with urine which they have aged in cisterns, and wash their teeth with it.[19]

Gaul too was full of still semi-barbaric peoples, grouped as Aquitani, Celtae and Belgae. These were now at peace (having been 'enslaved' by the Romans), and he declared that he would describe them as they used to be, before the Roman conquest, and he could do this by drawing on his knowledge of the Germans, 'for these peoples are not only similar in respect to their nature and their government, but they are also kinsmen to one another.' (Caesar stressed the differences, Strabo the similarities.) Strabo said that the Gauls lived simply, enabling them to migrate easily, 'for they move in droves, army and all, or rather they make off, households and all, whenever they are cast out by others stronger than themselves'.[20] They were simple, witless, boastful and high-spirited; 'and by reason of this levity of character they not only look insufferable when victorious, but also scared out of their wits when worsted'.[21] Across the Channel, the Britons were very similar, although even 'more simple and more barbaric'. Barbarism increased the further one moved from the Mediterranean, so the Irish were even more savage than the Britons: they were cannibals, who not only ate their fathers when they died, but had intercourse with their mothers and sisters.[22]

In Book 7, Strabo looked at the world beyond the Rhine and Danube, and he repeated his opinion that the Celts and Germans are very similar, apart from the fact that the Germans were wilder, taller and had yellower hair. Indeed, Strabo suggested that the Romans called them *Germani* to indicate that they were 'genuine Gauls', since, he claimed, *germani* meant *genuine*.[23] Some of the peoples Strabo enumerates are well known, such as the Suevi and the Langobardi; others (the Lugii, Zumi, Butones and so on) are much more obscure. Strabo regards them all as semi-nomads:

> It is a common characteristic of all the peoples in this part of the world that they migrate with ease, because of the meagreness of their livelihood and because they do not till the soil or even store up food, but live in small huts that are merely temporary structures; and they live for the most part off their flocks.[24]

Others, he says, are still more indigent; and he names a group of peoples most of whom would seem to have joined together in the third century as the Franks, on the Middle and Lower Rhine: the Cherusci, Chatti, Gamabrivii, Chattuarii, Sugembri and Bructeri – the last of whom had been defeated by the general Drusus in a naval battle. Of the people beyond the River Elbe, Strabo says, he knows nothing, and this ignorance extends to the people who are known to be east of the northern Germans: the Iazyges, Roxolani, Hamaxoikoi ('wagon-dwellers'), Bastarnae and Sauromatae (Sarmatians). Things were slightly clearer about who lived east of the southern Germans, north of the Danube: the main peoples were the Getae, the Dacians and the Thracians. But much of the rest of Book 7 was concerned with disputing with other authorities, complicated by the fact that Strabo concerned himself with the whole ethnic history of this region, from the time of Homer onwards.

Sometimes classical ethnographers were actually informed by their own personal experience. The encyclopaedist Pliny, for instance, writing in the middle of the first century AD, had come across the Chauci while serving in a campaign against them in AD 47.[25] They lived in the far north, on the edge of the North Sea, between the Frisians and the River Elbe. They lived on raised hummocks above the flood plains (these are generally referred to as *terpen* or *Wurten* by archaeologists: see below, p. 137). There were no trees, so they had to burn peat; they had no flocks or cattle, and they lived on fish, washed down by rainwater collected from ditches. Some of them had been enslaved by the Romans; others were punished by Fortune, and remained in wretched and sordid freedom. There was no nobility among these savages; there was nothing that they could teach Romans. They lived in an impermanent world, on the margins of the Ocean, which indeed penetrated and dominated their territory; they lived no better than animals, in a landscape which was like primordial chaos.

As an ethnographer of barbarians, Tacitus (writing *c.* AD 100) was far more influential than either Strabo or Pliny. First, in his study of his own father-in-law, Agricola, governor of Britain between AD 78 and 84, he writes about the barbarians of Britain. He admitted that he did not know their origins, although he suggested that their appearance offered clues. The Caledonians in the north had reddish hair and large limbs, like the Germans; the swarthy faces and dark curly hair of the Silures in the west suggested a Spanish origin; the bulk of the people in the south were so like the Gauls in appearance and in customs that they had surely come to Britain from across the Channel.[26] The Britons who had been conquered by the Romans after Claudius's invasion of AD 43 had come to tolerate the obligations imposed on them by government, although they could not tolerate abuse: 'their subjection, while complete enough to involve obedience, does not involve slavery'.[27] It is the first hint that Tacitus shared with Strabo what we might think of as an unorthodox attitude to barbarians, whereby he admired them the more they preserved their independence from Rome. His view became much clearer when he was talking about Agricola's programme of Romanization. Agricola encouraged the building of temples and public buildings, the learning of Latin and the wearing of the toga, 'and little by little the Britons went astray into alluring vices: to the promenade, the bath, the well-appointed dinner table. The simple natives gave the word "culture" to this aspect of their slavery.'[28] According to Tacitus, Agricola thought that it would be useful to conquer not only all northern Britain but Ireland too (which he reckoned could be reduced and held with one legion), so that the Britons would not have any sight of liberty.[29]

It is, however, Tacitus's *Germania* which should concern us most: it is the only surviving ethnographic treatise from the ancient world concerned solely with the northern barbarians. Its modern influence has been immense partly because it painted a picture that modern German nationalists could accept. Statements like 'I agree with the views of those who think that the inhabitants of Germania have not been tainted by any intermarriage with other tribes, but have existed as a distinct and pure people, resembling only themselves'[30] had obvious appeal in the twentieth century, for instance, among those obsessed with racial purity. His frequent generalizations about 'the Germans' too, as if all the Germanic groups were really one people, also had a clear appeal in the years before and after the unification of Germany in the days of Bismarck. But Tacitus did recognize the problem of knowing who the Germans were. He did not use the criterion of language, as modern scholars have done; instead, he seemed to use economic, social and geographic criteria. 'Germania was separated from the Gauls and from the Raeti and Pannonii by the Rhine and Danube rivers, and from the Sarmatians and Dacians by mutual fear or mountains.'[31] There were some groups in the east who were difficult to categorize, like the Peucini (also known as Bastarnae), the Fenni and the Venedi; the latter had intermarried with the Sarmatians, but nevertheless should be categorized as Germans 'because they have fixed homes and bear shields and take pleasure in moving fast by foot: all these things are at odds with the Sarmatians, who live on wagons and horses'.[32] As we have seen, in the Roman hierarchy of barbarism, those who have settled homes are closer to civilization than nomads. Recent scholars have identified the Venedi as Slavs, and the Fenni (Finns) as Lapps, but neither identification is certain.

Tacitus's picture of the Germans is best known for its moral generalizations. The Germans do not particularly value silver or gold; they do not dress ostentatiously; they are very strict monogamists, and adultery is very rare 'for no one there is amused by vice, nor calls the corruption of others and oneself "modern life" ';[33] their children are not pampered; they are unfailingly generous and hospitable; they do not have professional entertainers; they do not raise freedmen above their natural station; they do not practise usury; they are not ostentatious about funerals, nor do they build high monuments of stone to the dead.[34] In saying such things, of course, Tacitus was reminding his audience or readership that all those things which Germans did not do, the decadent Romans did. We should certainly not assume the Tacitus really *did* admire the Germans; nor, indeed, can one assume that he is being ironic in his apparent delight at German deaths. When he reports that the Bructeri were completely wiped out by a coalition of neighbouring tribes, he says 'more than sixty thousand fell, not by Roman army and weapons, but something more magnificent, for the delight of Roman eyes', and he adds that fortune could grant Rome nothing greater than discord among its foes.[35]

He spends 23 chapters generalizing about the Germans, treating them effectively as if they were one people with a consistent set of characteristics – an approach which certainly some of those who have read him have been content to follow. But the last 20 chapters deal with the

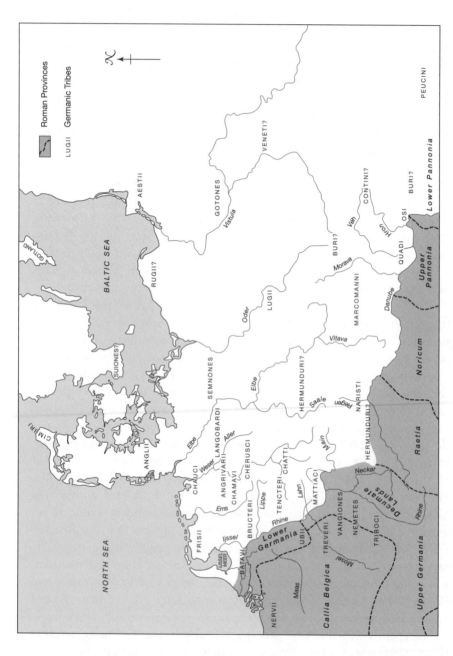

Map 2 The possible locations of the barbarian peoples in Tacitus' *Germania* (after J.B. Rives, *Germania*, xii–xiii).

various Germanic peoples one by one, moving from those nearest the Rhine to those furthest away, and moving to ever greater levels of barbarism on the part of the Germans and of ignorance on his own part. In the process, he shows that some, at least, of his generalizations in the first part of the book do not hold water. There is in fact little uniformity among the Germans: there is variation not just in appearance and dress, but in worship and styles of government. Sometimes we can actually confirm what Tacitus says: the knot in which Suebian men tie their hair, for instance, has been found archaeologically.[36] But we do have to remember that the further away are the peoples he is describing, the less likely is his information to be reliable. Beyond the maritime Suiones (in Scandinavia?) are the Aestii (on the Baltic?), who collect amber on the beaches, although, as typical barbarians, they have no curiosity about its origins. Beyond them, at the very edge of the Germanic world, are the Sitones, among whom women rule: 'so much do they sink not merely below freedom but even below slavery'.[37] Nevertheless, it is the way Tacitus generalizes about the Germans which is the most memorable part of his ethnography. If what Patrick Geary declared 20 years ago is true – that 'the Germanic world was perhaps the greatest and most enduring creation of Roman political and military genius'[38] – then Tacitus should be given some of the credit.

There is an interesting shift of usage in the later use of the word *Germanus*. As we have seen, Tacitus used the expression of almost all those peoples he saw living east of the Rhine, and the early usage of the word was similar. In the first and second centuries AD, victories over any of the Germanic peoples earned an emperor the title *Germanicus*.[39] The one exception was with a people which did not appear in Tacitus's list and which was perhaps not immediately associated with the Germans further west: the Goths. Thus, in the later third century, we have Claudius *Gothicus*, and several of his successors take the same title. In the fourth century more distinctions come in: Diocletian takes the name *Carpicus* (the Carpi were related to the Goths); Constantine II and his successors take the name *Alamannicus maximus*; Julian *Francicus maximus*. All of these emperors also called themselves *Germanicus maximus*. (We can make no further distinctions, since these ethnic titles were not used between 378 and their revival by Justinian in the sixth century.) It seems clear that in the fourth century 'German' was no longer a term which included all the western barbarians. And this is borne out by other sources too. Ammianus Marcellinus, in the later fourth century, only uses *Germania* when he is referring to the Roman provinces of Upper Germany and Lower Germany; east of *Germania* are *Alamannia* and *Francia*. The author of the *Historia Augusta*, contemporary to Ammianus, specifies that the Alamanni were *once* called *Germani*;[40] a poem by Claudian speaks of Stilicho defeating the 'Germans and also the Franks';[41] and, writing from Bethlehem around the year 400 to add to the confusion, St Jerome noted that *Germania* was now called *Francia*.[42]

The Empire and the Barbarians to 250

After the loss of Varus's legions, the Romans undertook occasional expeditions to put down troublesome Germanic peoples, like the Bructeri and the Chatti on the Lower Rhine, but the main effort undertaken by the imperial government was the construction of defences along the *limes*. The Roman *limes*, it is now generally agreed, was not a frontier in a modern sense, a line on a map which designated a clear linear boundary. Even if there was a river, or a wall like Hadrian's Wall in northern Britain, the frontier was a zone as much as a line. There were forts beyond the line inside Barbaricum (the word commonly used of the land beyond the *limes* in the later Roman Period),[43] and there were forts within the Empire, providing defence in depth. Moreover, the defence of the Empire consisted not only of fortifications and troops, but, much more, of constant diplomacy, aimed at making barbarians willing partners of the Roman world by persuasion and by ties of economic dependence.

Two barbarian territories were added to the Roman Empire in Europe after Augustus: the lands of the Britons and of the Dacians. We have already mentioned the conquest of Britain, as seen through the eyes of Tacitus. Sadly, there was no Tacitus to write about the Dacians, for Dacia was an intriguing kingdom. Under the kings Burebista and Decebalus, this proto-state north of the Middle Danube, which brought together two ancient peoples, the Getae and the Dacians, was more of a state along Roman lines than most barbarian polities. Dacian and Getic were possibly the same language (belonging to what some scholars categorize as the Daco-Thracian branch of Indo-European), but the language only survives in a few dozen words in modern Romanian. The fate of Dacia was in part sealed by the demands of Roman internal politics: Trajan wanted a triumph to his name, and he secured it in a series of vicious campaigns (AD 101–6), proudly celebrated in relief on Trajan's Column in Rome, which destroyed the Dacian kingdom and added a new province to the Empire.

After AD 106 the Empire's frontiers did not expand, and they were kept secure from barbarian attack not so much by defences as by diplomacy backed by overpowering force. The extent of the influence that Roman emperors could exert on neighbouring barbarian peoples can be seen by looking at the Marcomanni and the Quadi, two Germanic-speaking peoples to the north of the Middle Danube (in Lower Austria and Bohemia).[44]

The difficulty of studying Roman policy arises in part from the fact that we know much more about periods of unrest and tension than we know about periods of quiet normality, which are much less newsworthy. But it would seem that for the most part the Marcomanni and Quadi lived in *amicitia* (friendship, alliance) with the Empire. Tacitus commented on the lucrative commerce that was carried out by Roman merchants in Bohemia under the Marcomannic king Maroboduus,[45] and this is confirmed by archaeology. The seriousness of the treaties was indicated by the fact that the Emperor Domitian attacked these peoples to punish them for not helping him against the Dacians. Far more telling, however, is an episode from the second century, early in the reign of Marcus Aurelius, when the Quadi asked Roman permission to install their new king, Furtius. When Furtius was eventually expelled and replaced by a king who did not have Roman approval, the new king was captured by the Romans and exiled to Alexandria. As Pitts said, 'By the mid-second century, then, Rome's right to choose the leaders of the tribes beyond the Danube was apparently firmly established; like other friendly kingdoms the area was looked upon as an extension of the Empire.'[46] Marcus Aurelius was even said to have been contemplating a new province of *Marcomannia*.[47]

In 166 the so-called Marcomannic Wars interrupted this relatively peaceful coexistence.[48] They started with an invasion of Pannonia by Langobardi and Obii, which was put down by one of Marcus's generals. In 168, Marcus himself went north, where this time the Marcomanni and the Victuali were causing problems. Apparently they were both being hard pressed by aggressive peoples from the north, and begged for admittance into the Empire. This was refused. But the real trouble came in 170/1. Marcus Aurelius, attacking across the Danube, was defeated (in obscure circumstances), and barbarians – mostly Marcomanni and Quadi – crossed the Danube and the Alps and besieged Aquileia in northeast Italy. There were attacks on other fronts too. The Roman general Claudius Fronto was defeated near the Danube; the Costoboci swept into the Balkans, reaching southern Greece and sacking the shrine of Eleusis.

Marcus started some serious diplomatic activity in late 171. He managed to detach the Quadi from the 'conspiracy', and they promised to release thousands of captives and deserters. They were not given the right to attend markets in the Empire, as they wished, because Marcus feared that Marcomanni or others would pass themselves off as Quadi and obtain provision in the Empire as well as spy out the land. Some of the barbarians were sent off on campaigns elsewhere on behalf of the Romans; others were given land within the Empire, even in Italy – although Marcus changed his mind about the wisdom of that after some barbarians settled in north-east Italy tried to seize Ravenna. Marcus also managed to obtain an alliance from the Astingi (who were later to be regarded as part of the Vandal people). Campaigning continued in 172, with victory going to Marcus, but the wars dragged on for some years after that. Various barbarian groups, including the Quadi, broke their agreements; the Iazyges in particular proved difficult to subdue.

The Marcomannic Wars had involved most of the barbarians ranged along the frontiers, and, for the barbarians themselves, it was a disruptive period. All along the frontiers new peoples and new groupings formed in the course of the next few generations. The Alamanni appeared in the area between the Upper Rhine and Upper Danube, incorporating some of the Suebi and other Germanic peoples (although the Suebi or Sueves were to emerge again as a separate group in the fifth century, and the area called Alamannia in the sixth and seventh century is now called Swabia). North of the Alamanni, various peoples like the Bructeri and the Chatti became known as the 'Franks': a federation of peoples, never fully united until the beginning of the sixth century. East of the Alamanni, on the Upper Danube, the Langobardi or Lombards established themselves, and on the Lower Danube powerful groups of peoples came to the fore who would by the third century be known as the Goths.[49] As Southern notes, these new 'peoples' did not abandon their old 'tribal' roots, and we should not necessarily trust Romans when they use these labels; they were almost never dealing with the entire group, and may not have been sure with whom they were dealing. These confederacy names all express the same vagueness: they are 'the people of one law' (Suebi), or 'human beings' (the Goths), or 'the free' or 'fierce' (both possible meanings of 'Franks'), or they were even 'all men' (Alamanni).[50]

As Pitts shows, the close relationship between the Romans and the Marcomanni and Quadi seems to have renewed after this war, and Roman domination continued. Rome's approval was again demanded for their choice of leaders, and under Commodus they were allowed to have regular assemblies, but only if a Roman centurion was present. Even so, it does not look as if they paid any regular tribute, and only occasionally were they required to provide troops for the Roman armies. We might even think of these peoples as being partially 'Romanized': some of them took Roman citizenship, served in the Roman army and settled in the Empire, and archaeology shows the depth of trade relations, and even such things as the Roman style of the buildings used by the barbarian aristocracy. While further away in Barbaricum we find Roman goods being used largely by the well-off, here on the frontier Roman pottery is found in the humblest of barbarian homes.

The Third-Century Crisis

In 250, the Emperor Decius sent troops to the Greek kingdom of Bosporos, in the Crimea, apparently to find out about the movements of Scythians in that area. Unfortunately, 'Scythian' is a classical literary term, hiding the real name of the people concerned (but also illustrating, perhaps, Roman ignorance of barbarian realities). Writing around 500, Zosimus said that the peoples who had invaded the Roman Empire between 253 and 259 were the Borani, Goths, Carpi and Ourougoundoi. The Carpi are also mentioned by a contemporary source; but most historians have assumed that the people who brought Decius's downfall were the Goths, partly because Jordanes (writing in the sixth century, like Zosimus) says that an early king of the Goths was Cniva, and that is the name of the 'Scythian' leader.[51] (The first attested mention of the word 'Goth' itself was in 208, in an inscription recording the name of a unit of Roman auxiliaries defending an Arab fortress, although some scholars would argue that the 'Goths' were the same people as Strabo's *Gutones* or Ptolemy's *Guthones*.)[52] Whoever these 'Scythians' were, in 250 they broke through the frontier, and defeated Decius and his army; the emperor was killed. St Cyprian of Carthage was prompted to write that the end of the Roman world was at hand, or even the end of the world.[53]

This was really the beginning of the so-called 'third-century crisis', in which the Empire was beset by invasions of barbarians and of Persians, but, even more seriously, by a host of Roman usurpers, some of whom aspired to be rulers of the entire Empire while others seemed to have wanted merely regional authority. It is clear that for some parts of the Roman Empire – but by no means all – there was a serious economic crisis as well: there was a decline in the number of inhabited settlements in the Rhineland and in parts of Italy, even while North Africa and Syria seem to have experienced considerable prosperity.[54] The political problems allowed invading barbarians greater opportunities. 'Scythians' or Goths even took to ships: in 252 they sailed through the Bosphorus into the Aegean and raided along the coast of Asia Minor, destroying the celebrated Temple of Artemis at Ephesus. In 258 another group sailed across the Black Sea and ravaged Pontus and Cappadocia in Asia Minor. The Emperor Valerian led troops north from Antioch, but failed to deal with them. Valerian's next move was even less impressive: he fought the invading Persian ruler Sapor I, and was captured by him. The later story that Valerian was flayed alive can probably be discounted; somewhat more credence can be given to the story that he was kept as a slave in the Persian palace, until his death, when his skin was hung in a temple.

A fascinating insight into the effect of these invasions on life inside the Empire is afforded by the *Canonical Letter* written by Gregory Thaumaturgus, bishop of Neocaesarea, in Pontus (north-eastern Asia Minor).[55] He is concerned with the sins committed by Romans in the wake of the invasions. He is not worried about the eating of meat sacrificed to idols, as he says all were agreed that the barbarians did not sacrifice to idols while in the Empire. But he is concerned about those who took advantage of the turmoil to do some robbery of their own; about those who kept any discarded booty of the barbarians, or who kept as slaves those who had escaped from barbarian captivity; and about those who joined with the barbarians,

> forgetting that they were men of Pontus, and Christians, and have become so thoroughly barbarized as even to put to death men of their own race by the gibbet or noose, and to point out roads and houses to the barbarians, who were ignorant of them.[56]

Taking advantage of this crisis, the Germanic-speaking Juthungi invaded Italy (Zosimus called them 'Scythians' too). An inscription from Augsburg records their defeat, and the freeing of thousands of their prisoners, by an army sent from the provinces of Raetia and Germania.[57] Perhaps in response to this crisis, Postumus, the Roman governor on the Rhine frontier, declared himself emperor in 260. He seems to have shown no interest in going outside Gaul and claiming the whole Empire; he was content to rule an empire in Gaul, from his capital at Cologne. His writ may have run into the Alps and the Upper Danube frontier; it may be that it was the struggles between his troops and those of the Empire, rather than barbarian attacks, that led to the abandonment in these years of the Agri Decumates (see below, p. 39) and Raetia.[58]

The 'Scythians' invaded again in 268 or 269, apparently led by the Herules (*Eruli*) this time, and again involving sea-borne activity. The new emperor, Claudius II, managed to defeat them in 269, gaining his nickname of 'Gothicus'. But this was not the end of the attacks. Both the Juthungi and the Vandals invaded Italy in 270, in two separate attacks; and a further attack by the Goths led to the abandonment of the province of Dacia. That spur of territory north of the Danube had been held only since Trajan's victory in 106, but it had already been thoroughly Romanized. The withdrawal of Roman administration, however, did not necessarily bring an end to the Roman way of life in the province. It is one of those oddities of history (that has become a matter of nationalist controversy) that this province, held by the Romans for less time than any other, should be the one whose people today – Romanians – speak a language that is linguistically very close to Latin.

The Emperor Aurelian (270–5) finally restored some order and unity to the Empire, ending the so-called Gallic Empire and repelling another invasion by the Juthungi; but not long afterwards was murdered by his own senior officers, for reasons which are obscure.[59] Indeed, much of what happened in the period 275 to 284 is obscure. According to the unreliable *Historia Augusta* barbarians occupied Gaul after the death of Aurelian. It was under Probus that the Franks were pacified and the Burgundians and the Vandals dealt with, according to Zosimus.[60] There seem to have been attacks by the Sarmatians and Goths on the Danube provinces. Some barbarians were quietened, it seems, by settlement within the Empire, although that did not always work. The Franks asked for a place in which to live and, according to Zosimus, they were settled somewhere in the East. The much more contemporary Panegyric to Constantius recalls what happened next, when:

> a few Frankish captives in the time of the deified Probus, who, seizing some ships, plundered their way from the Black Sea right to Greece and Asia and, driven not without causing damage from very many parts of the Libyan shore, finally took Syracuse itself, . . . and, after travelling on an immense journey, entered the [Atlantic] Ocean, . . . and this showed by the outcome of their boldness that nothing is closed to a pirate's desperation where a path lies open to navigation.[61]

Perhaps the most pernicious legacy of this period, from the point of view of the emperors, was a catastrophic decline in the trust which Roman citizens had in the ability of Roman emperors to defend them. We not only find for the first time the appearance of 'local' emperors – Postumus in Gaul in 260, and Carausius in Britain in 286 – but also the occurrence of local uprisings, of so-called 'Bacaudae'. The question of who precisely these people were, and whether there is any continuity between their appearance in the third century and their reappearance in the fifth, has been a matter of strong controversy. They have been interpreted as 'peasant rebels'[62] – social revolutionaries in a Marxist sense – while for the Roman authorities they were bandits; in the third century, at least, we should probably think of them as 'dislocated peasants who sought security in the leadership of second-order figures of authority'[63] – 'lesser aristocrats, yeomen or even visionaries or bandits'.[64] In the fifth century they may have played as significant a role in the collapse of imperial authority in some parts of the Western Empire as the barbarians themselves.

The repercussions of the 'third-century crisis' are unmeasurable, but probably considerable. They not only set in train a reorganization of the Empire, which involved both a large increase in the size of the Roman army and also in the scale of the taxation needed to sustain it, but they also, almost certainly, produced changes of attitude. All Roman citizens became aware of the fragility of the Empire; they also learned, perhaps, a new attitude towards barbarians. Now that the Empire was on the defensive, and no one expected an expansion across the frontiers, the barbarians shifted from being people who, one day, would be incorporated into the Empire and 'civilized', to people who were hostile. As Sherwin-White put it, the 'sense of *Romanitas* has been sharpened by the conflict with the German peoples'.[65]

As is well known, the recovery of the Empire led by Diocletian after 284 was predicated on a restoration of order and an attempt to maintain that order by a system of two senior emperors and two junior emperors: the Tetrarchy. Maximian, who became the senior emperor in the West in 286, was almost immediately celebrated by a panegyric which praised him for his victory over various barbarian peoples who crossed the Rhine, and for installing a client king called Gennobaudes over the Franks. The Latin panegyrics of the late third and fourth centuries – written in praise of various emperors and recited publicly at court – are a major source for Roman relations with the barbarians. Given the context, however, what these 'relations' consist of for the most part was stories of imperial victories. What is perhaps remarkable is the joyful fervour with which they celebrate the slaughter of barbarians (although one might optimistically detect a concern for animal welfare . . .).

> Countless numbers [of Bructeri] were slaughtered, and very many captured. Whatever herds there were, were seized or slaughtered; all the villages were put to the flame; the adults who were captured, whose untrustworthiness made them unfit for military service and whose ferocity for slavery, were given over to the amphitheatre for punishment, and their great numbers wore out the raging beasts.[66]

It is possible that these sentiments represent a new implacability as regards imperial policy towards barbarians. We have discussions of the possibilities of genocide as a solution to the problem;[67] we have the more frequent use of the wholesale transfer of populations as a means of controlling 'lesser peoples'.[68] Thus, in 280, the Emperor Probus settled numerous Bastarnae in Moesia, and this once powerful barbarian people, known to Greco-Romans since the third century BC, disappeared from history.[69]

The authors of the Latin Panegyrics seem to be all from Gaul, hence their interest in particular in those barbarians who are on the Rhine frontier. In fact in the period covered by these Panegyrics, the very end of the third century to the middle of the fourth, the most significant military campaigning was actually at the other end of the European frontier. In 328 Constantine built a bridge across the Danube, and in that year and the following two he fought campaigns against the Goths.[70] In the peace that ensued Constantine not only demanded that the Goths

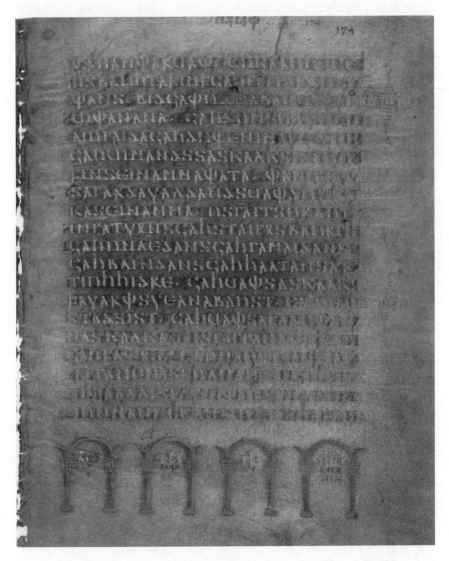

Plate 2 A page from the Codex Argenteus, written in silver and gold lettering on purple-stained parchment, containing part of the Bible which Ulfila translated into Gothic. The manuscript was probably produced in the Ostrogothic capital of Ravenna, around 520; only 188 of the original 336 pages survive.

send men for the Roman army, but he (or his successor Constantius II) appointed Ulfila to be bishop of the Goths. Ulfila, who had been brought up among the Goths (the son of Roman captives) worked among the Goths for several years, before being exiled – in a reaction to what had apparently been a fairly successful missionary effort. His most lasting achievement was the translation of parts of the Bible into Gothic: it was said that he decided not to translate the Books of Kings in the Old Testament, since the Goths were warlike enough without offering them further encouragement.[71] This was the first time, as far as we know, that an extensive text had been written down in a Germanic language, and in a script devised for it; hitherto all that survives is very short inscriptions in the runic alphabet that Germans had devised for themselves. Speakers of a Germanic language today, like English, can even now make out some of Ulfila's text. The opening words of the Lord's Prayer, for instance, read 'atta unsar þu in himinam, weihnai namo þein', where 'namo þein very clearly translates as 'thy name'. The letter þ (thorn) was introduced by Ulfila into the Gothic alphabet to represent the sound 'th'; it survived in English until the end of the Middle Ages (when typesetters often substituted 'Y' – whence 'Ye Olde English Tea-Shoppe'), and in Icelandic to this day. The Gothic Bible remains extremely important for philologists in their investigations of the development of the Germanic languages. Its best-known exemplar, the Codex Argenteus, today occupies pride of place in the University Library in Uppsala, Sweden, lying in a room gently lit by amber light, reminiscent of the late Roman mausoleum of Galla Placidia in Ravenna (north Italy).

The Barbarians in the Later Fourth Century

We have two invaluable snapshots of the barbarians on the eve of the 'barbarian invasions', which unfold in the years after 376. They are of very different kind and quality. The first is a mere list of barbarians, known as the Verona List, which is thought to come from the middle of the fourth century. It names the barbarian peoples in rough geographical order along the Roman frontiers, starting in the far West with the Scoti (the Irish) and ending in the East, with the Goths and Venedi by the western shores of the Black Sea. These are the peoples known to Roman diplomats and Roman soldiers in the generation before 376:

> Scoti. Picti. Caledoni. Rugi. Heruli. Saxones. Franci. Chattuarii. Chamavi. Frisiavi. Amsivarii. Angrivarii. Flevi. Bructeri. Chatti. Burgundiones. Alamanni. Suevi. Iuthungi. Armilausini. Marcomanni. Quadi. Taifali. Hermunduri. Vandali. Sarmatae. Sciri. Carpi. Scythae. Gothi. Venedi.[72]

The list continues with the peoples of the East: the Armenians; the Isauri (a wild and 'barbaric' people from southern Asia Minor, who had in fact been part of the Empire for centuries); and the Persians. The list alone illustrates the problems faced by Roman authorities, who had to try to gather intelligence on all these peoples (with a great range of linguistic variation) and to keep track of the complex internal and external policies of each, in order to be alert to any imminent danger. And these are only the peoples closest to the frontier.

Our second snapshot – or whole series of evocative sketches – comes from the *History* written by Ammianus Marcellinus, a Greek by birth, who wrote in Rome in the 380s. The surviving part of his *History*, Books 14 to 26, constitutes an account of the Empire in the 25 years from 353 to 378; it is by far our most important narrative source for the later Roman Empire. What makes Ammianus so valuable is not just his skill as an historian, but the fact that he knew many of the people he wrote about personally. He had himself been involved, as an officer in the Roman army, in campaigns both in Gaul and on the Persian frontier. He appears as a character in his own narrative between Books 14 and 19, and again between Books 23 to 25. Indeed, Momigliano accused him of displaying an 'almost indecent readiness to speak about himself'[73] – something for which we may be truly grateful. We must not imagine that he is utterly reliable: he had his own axes to grind, and he can be caught out in acts of embellishment, and indeed outright fabrication. He was a conservative, and hostile to Christianity, and therefore inclined to offer rather a jaundiced view of what was happening to Roman society. The quality and quantity of information in his work is almost certainly superior to any other historian of the later Roman Empire, even if, as John Drinkwater and others have pointed out, we would be advised to 'concentrate on his description of events while eschewing his analysis of them'.[74]

We may start our roundrup of Ammianus's barbarians with the Alamanni or Alamans.[75] There is no set-piece description of the Alamans, as there is for the Huns, but there are altogether 19 sections dealing with Roman relations with the Alamans, and a good deal of incidental detail about them. There are several Alamannic tribes mentioned, such as the Bucinobantes, who lived in the northern part of the Alamannic world, just to the west of the Middle Rhine and south of the River Main, and the Lentienses, who lived near Lake Constance (and whose name is preserved in the modern district name of Linzgau). Unlike most Germanic groups, they already lived in a post-Roman world. Their territory was what Tacitus called the Agri Decumates, the triangle between the Upper Rhine and the Upper Danube which the Romans annexed in the 70s and abandoned in the 250s.

There is a good deal of evidence of destruction on excavated sites in this area, above all evidence of burned buildings, though one has to recognize that dating this destruction to the middle of the 250s can lead to circular arguments: archaeologists date their destruction to this period because of the historical evidence, and then historians refer to the excavations as independent support for the destructions which the sources claim to have happened at this period. Moreover, it is not only barbarians who can be destructive. The destruction of Niederbieber, for instance, the westernmost fort on the Upper German *limes*, may be the work of Roman rebels against Gallienus in the early 260s.[76]

In the fourth century the Alamans lived in a landscape marked by ruined Roman towns, roads and villas. Ammianus said that they avoided the towns as if they were 'tombs encircled by nets', whatever that means.[77] The Emperor Julian thought of recovering seven ruined towns in the Middle Rhine area; the Emperor Valentinian II once travelled to the ghost town of Lopodunum (Ladenburg), and saw the ruins and read the inscriptions.[78] Sometimes these Roman ruins may have been reused by the Alamans: Ammianus refers to Alamans in the Main valley living in houses 'carefully built in the Roman style'.[79] Matthews compares this with the small Roman villa of Ebel bei Praunheim, near Frankfurt, which had been extended by dry-stone walling in the fourth century, by some Alamannic landowner, who was buried there with his weapons and various vessels of Roman and Germanic origin.[80] Ammianus's Alamans were clearly agriculturalists; apart from anything else, he describes how Roman raiding parties would destroy their crops. They lived in fragile wooden buildings (easy for the Romans to torch). Archaeologists have shown us that in the third and fourth centuries the Alamans also sometimes lived in reoccupied prehistoric hill forts; it is probable that the attack of Valentinian on a hill-top position, which Ammianus describes, is an attack on such a fortification.[81]

The Alamans' two most distinctive customs, for Ammianus and other Roman writers, were their long hair and their love of drink. They were not politically united, but were a confederation of tribes under their own kings. When Chnodomarius faced Julian at Strasbourg, there were six other Alamannic kings with him; and they did not join him out of obedience to an overlord, but for pay and for promises of mutual support. At other times we see Alamannic kings in dispute with each other, often over the question of their friendship or enmity towards the Romans. Several stories show the touchiness of these kings, and their determination to hold on to their dignity and status. When in 374 Valentinian wanted to avoid Alamannic attack, he decided to placate Macrianus personally, and summoned him to a meeting near Mainz.[82]

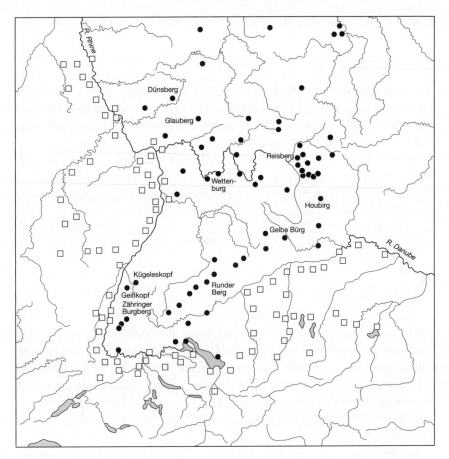

Map 3 The frontier between Alamans and Romans: Alamannic hill-forts (full circle) and Roman camps (squares). (After Brather, 'Acculturation and ethnogenesis', 156).

Macrianus was so won over by the emperor that he remained loyal to the last: which in his case meant attacking the Franks on behalf of the Romans and dying in an ambush laid by a Frankish king, Mallobaudes.

One of the most impressive descriptions of an individual barbarian is that of the Alamannic king Chondomarius, who led the Alamannic forces against Julian in 357 at the battle of Strasbourg. 'a huge figure wherever the heat of battle was looked for; erect on his foaming steed, he towered with a lance of formidable size'.[83] Julian's great generalship, according to his loyal fan Ammianus, was too much for the Alamannic leader, however. Chondomarius tried to escape through the piles of Alamannic corpses, but was eventually recognized, and surrendered, 'and his attendants (*comites*), two hundred in number, with three of his closest friends, thinking it a disgrace to survive their king, or not to die for their king if an emergency required it, gave themselves up to be made prisoners'.[84] Chonodomarius was taken to Rome, and he eventually died there, a prisoner. He had a nephew, called Agenaric originally; but Agenaric's father Mederic had been kept as a hostage in Gaul and had there been initiated into the oriental cult of Serapis, and changed his son's name to Serapio. Serapio led the right wing at the battle of Strasbourg, but Ammianus does not record his fate.[85]

Serapio is a useful reminder that the Alamans lived close to the Romans, and not just geographically. The Romans impressed them. When King Macrianus went with his brother and with another Alaman, Vadomarius, to Julian's camp, Macrianus

> was amazed at the variety and splendour of the arms and the forces, things which he saw then for the first time . . . but Vadomarius, who was familiar with our affairs (since he lived near the frontier) did indeed admire the equipment of the splendid array, but remembered that he had often seen the like from early youth.[86]

Vadomarius indeed would have had long familiarity with Rome. He had been persuaded by the Emperor Constantius to invade Gaul to keep Julian busy;[87] he had made peace with Julian in 359, but in 361 attacked the Empire again, and was sent by Julian to Spain. Some time after that, he was made *dux* of Phoenicia, and was sent by the Emperor Valens to recover Nicaea from a rebel. He is last heard of in 371, fighting the Persians.[88]

Vadomarius was by no means the only Alaman to be found in Roman service. Several Roman regiments listed in the *Notitia Dignitatum* bore the names of Alamannic cantons, from where the soldier had been first recruited; there was a troop of Alamans, under Alamannic command, stationed in Britain. And sometimes the closeness of relations could be exploited by both sides, as when Julian sent a military tribune called Hariobaudes to Alamannia on an intelligence-gathering mission, because he could speak the language, or when the Alamannic Lentienses learned about imperial troop movements from a rather garrulous member of the imperial guard who was home on leave.[89]

The abandoned Roman frontier to the east of Alamannia, partly an earthwork fortified by a wooden palisade and partly a stone wall with towers probably served as the frontier between the Alamans and their neighbours, the Burgundians. 'Members of this warlike people, rich in a countless number of strong warriors', know, says Ammianus, that they are descended from Romans;[90] Valentinian seems to have exploited this fictitious link in order to recruit them to fight the Alamans on his behalf.

In the fifth century Orosius repeats the idea, and adds that they are called 'Burgundians' because they take their name from the fortified places along the Roman frontier called *burgi*. The origins of the word *burgus* are in fact still disputed, some suggesting a Germanic origin, and others a Greek one.[91] (Whichever the origin, it comes into modern English, via Old English *burh*, as 'borough'.) That the Burgundians were Germanic-speaking is beyond doubt, however. The most intriguing comment about them from Ammianus makes this clear. He says that

> In their country a king is called by the general name *hendinos*, and, according to an ancient custom, lays down his power and is deposed, if under him the fortune of war has wavered, or the earth has denied sufficient crops; just as the Egyptians commonly blame their rulers for such occurrences. On the other hand the chief priest among the Burgundians is called *sinistus*, holds his power for life, and is exposed to no such dangers as threaten the kings.[92]

This has caused much discussion, as the only known example of so-called 'sacral kingship' among the early Germans; customs like this can be paralleled in other Indo-European cultures, from Ireland right across to ancient India. But here it is worth noting that the words *hendinos* and *sinistus* are clearly Germanic, and relate closely to the words used in the Gothic Bible of, respectively, Roman officials like Pontius Pilate and of the elders (as in the phrase 'chief priests and elders').[93]

Ammianus tells us much less about the Franks, who lived east of the Middle and Lower Rhine, north of the Alamans. Like the Alamans, they were not a united people. He tells us of one group, the Salii (Salians), who had settled within the Roman Empire, in Toxandria (near the mouths of the Rhine); another group, the Chamavi, like the Salii, would make irritating (but not militarily threatening) raids into Gaul. In 358 Julian subdued both of them; in 360 he defeated another troublesome group, the Atthuarii, who are presumably the same as Tacitus's Chattuarii. These skirmishes had been going on for decades; and, like the Alamans, many Franks were prepared to cooperate with the Romans. Ammianus notes that 'the Franks were at that time [355] numerous and influential in the palace';[94] and by the end of the fourth century a number of Franks had risen to the highest positions in the imperial service, and indeed had a greater influence at high level than any other barbarian people at the time. It is not really clear why this should be, save that the first few to be established may have been adept at finding posts for their relatives. There were two Franks called Merobaudes: one of whom was *magister militum* in the West from 375 to 388, and seems to have been nominated consul for the third time – a great honour – just before his death, while the other was commander of the army in Egypt.[95] The same name recurs two generations later: this last Merobaudes, who may be a descendant, had become thoroughly Romanized, and surviving fragments of the panegyrics he composed for the general Aetius in the 430s show us his skill in literary Latin.[96] In the years on either side of 390, the commanders of the Roman forces in the East and in the West were Richomer and Arbogast respectively, who were both Franks, and uncle and nephew. Arbogast may have been the son of another Frankish *magister militum* in the West, Bauto, whose daughter Eudoxia married the Emperor Arcadius.

Ammianus made his comment about Frankish influence in the course of his discussion of the rise and fall of Silvanus.[97] Ammianus is not the only source to mention Silvanus, although he provides more detail. He was a Frank, we are told; but his father was called Bonitus – a Roman name like his own – so if a Frank then clearly a very Romanized one. In 355 a hostile faction plotted to discredit him, circulating forged letters that implicated him. Two other well-placed Roman officials, also both Frankish in origin, tried to declare his innocence, but they were ignored, and Silvanus was summoned to court. Silvanus was very disturbed by this news, and rightly so, for if Ammianus is to be believed Emperor Constantius was paranoid about possible conspiracy and inclined to act upon suspicion alone. Silvanus thought of fleeing to the Franks; but another Germanic military official 'assured Silvanus that the Franks, whose fellow countryman he was, would kill him or on receipt of a bribe betray him'.[98] Silvanus saw no alternative, therefore, but to proclaim himself emperor. Constantius heard of this, and sent Ursicinus, Master of the Cavalry, to settle the matter; Ursicinus took with him a number of staff officers, including Ammianus himself. They were disturbed to find that Silvanus was very popular among the army in Cologne, and was seen as a potential saviour by some disgruntled soldiers, who urged an immediate invasion of Italy. Ammianus was sympathetic towards Silvanus, and very hostile to the brutal and suspicious Constantius, but orders were orders . . . Ursicinus and his group bribed some soldiers to break into the palace, and had Silvanus taken from sanctuary in a church, and killed. He had been emperor for 28 days. The next emperor of Frankish birth was Charlemagne, crowned in Rome on Christmas Day 800.

The last major Germanic group of barbarians described by Ammianus was the Goths. Until his last book they make little impact. Julian was advised to attack them, since they were a deceitful and treacherous people, but Julian commented that there was no point; just leave them to the mercy of Galatian slave-traders, he says, who sell Gothic slaves all over the Empire.[99] Goths raided across the frontier in 364, after the accession of Valentinian I, but, then, most self-respecting barbarians did: Alamans attacked Gaul and Raetia; Sarmatians and Quadi attacked Pannonia; the Picts, Saxons, Scots and Attacotti attacked Britain; various Moorish tribes attacked Africa; 'and predatory bands of Goths were plundering Thrace and Pannonia'.[100] Before that time, and since their defeat by Constantine the Great, the Goths had in fact been relatively docile. Not long after the Alamanni had occupied the Agri Decumates, in the middle of the third century, one group of the Goths had moved into the province of Dacia (roughly modern Romania, with parts of Moldavia): these were the Tervingi or Thervingi. Further to the north and, it seems, beyond the River Dniester, were the other main group, the Greuthungi. Ammianus was confused by the situation, however. He described how Valens attacked the Tervingi in 367 and 368, and in 369 launched a much more extensive expedition, crossing the Danube near its mouth. 'After continuous marches he attacked the warlike people of the Greuthungi, who lived very far off',[101] and defeated their king Athanaric. But we know, from elsewhere in Ammianus, that Athanaric was the chief of the Tervingi, so there is clearly something wrong here. What it is does indicate, however, is that Valens launched three attacks against the Goths, and the one against the distant Greuthungi must have been a major expedition.

One difference between the two parts of the Gothic people may be more apparent than real. Ammianus refers to the leader of the Tervingi as the *iudex* (judge) and the leader of the Greuthungi as the *rex* (king). But both institutions seem to be hereditary, and to have involved the leading of armies, and our sources do not allow us to say whether there was any difference in political reality. The hereditary principle was certainly strong among the Greuthungi, because when Vithimir died fighting the Alans, his son took over, although he was a minor and had to be under the regency of two Gothic notables. The Goths next appeared in Ammianus's account crossing into the Roman Empire in 376, and thus appear in my next chapter; when they crossed the Danube as a result of the arrival of the Huns in the lands to the north of the Empire.

Ammianus's last book starts with various omens of doom, and moves immediately into his most famous ethnographic description, of the Huns, who 'exceed every degree of savagery'. They scar the cheeks of their children at birth, to prevent the growth of beard later on. They 'are so monstrously ugly and misshapen that one might take them for two-legged beasts'. They do not cook their food, 'but eat the roots of wild plants and the half-raw flesh of any kind of animal whatever, which they put between their thighs and the backs of their horses, and thus warm it a little'. 'They dress in linen cloth or in the skins of field-mice

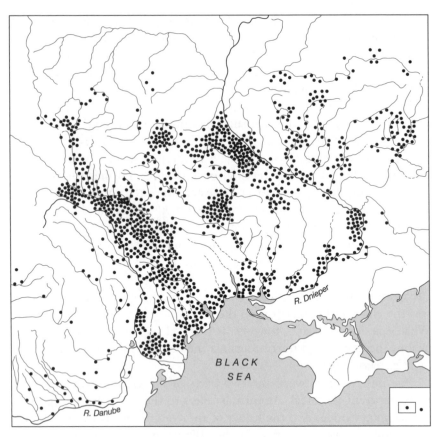

Map 4 Sites of the Černjachov and Sîntana–de–Mureş culture north of the Black Sea. There is no way to distinguish between the sites of the two groups of Goths, the Tervingi and the Greuthungi. (From Brather, *Ethnische Interpretation*, 263).

sewn together.' They have poorly made shoes, and thus seldom walk; 'they are almost glued to their horses' and 'from their horses by day or night everyone of that nation buys and sells, eats and drinks', and sleeps and dreams. 'They are all without fixed abode, without hearth, or law, or settled mode of life, and keep roaming from place to place, like fugitives, accompanied by wagons in which they live . . . Like unreasoning beasts, they are utterly ignorant of the difference between right and wrong; they are deceitful and ambiguous in speech, never bound by any reverence for religion or for superstition.'[102]

The Huns are not the last barbarian people to make their appearance in Ammianus's work. Immediately after this description he talks about the *Halani*, whom we would call the Alans, who roam around a wide tract of country, from the Black Sea to the Ganges. They somewhat contravene the usual ethnographic rules of the ancients, by which the further away from the centre the more savage peoples are, since the Alans are not as bestial as the Huns. But they are very similar. They are nomads, subsisting on flesh and milk. They live in their wagons, but they are all skilled at riding from an early age. Unlike the Huns they are tall and handsome. They consider dying of old age to be shameful; they regard men who die in battle as happy, and they consider killing other men to be the greatest achievement; when they have done so they tear off the heads of those they kill, and hang their skins from their horses. They do not have temples: they worship the god of war in the shape of a naked sword fixed in the ground.[103]

It is, of course, difficult to know what to make of set ethnographic descriptions like these. We would probably be right to think that the incidental details about Alamans scattered through Ammianus's *History* are much more reliable than these descriptions of Huns and Alans, largely compiled from ethnographic stereotypes found in many previous authors. The assumed link between pastoralism and extreme barbarity goes back to Herodotus, and no doubt a lot earlier.[104] Indeed, Thomas Wiedemann went so far as to suggest that Ammianus was just going through the motions that his audience would have expected from him.[105] They would, Wiedemann has suggested, have been disappointed that there was only one reference to cannibalism – that expected vice of the most barbaric of barbarians – in all the surviving books.[106] It is also true that archaeology suggests that Ammianus could be either wrong, or not sufficiently well-informed. That the Huns did not cook their food would seem to be belied by one of the most characteristic finds from Hunnic sites: large copper cauldrons. And that the Huns may have been just as 'barbaric' as Ammianus suggested, but in a totally different way is indicated by the artificially deformed skulls that are found in the various parts of Europe influenced by the Huns. It seems that they bound the heads of their young children so that the skulls would grow out elongated almost into cones; had Ammianus known of this, he would surely have mentioned it.[107]

What is clear about the Huns, and their Alanic allies, is that they were new and they were different. They were not Germanic-speaking (their language was probably related to the language of later Asiatic nomads who settled in Europe, like the Magyars and the Khazars). And their military techniques, above all using cavalry and the bow, were astonishingly effective. Their arrival in the area of the Black Sea in the second half of the fourth century was, arguably, the catalyst that upset much of the settled world of the European barbarians and therefore a very significant contributing factor to the collapse of the Western Empire, as we shall see in the next chapter.

However, it is perhaps salutary to end this chapter with a reminder that, in the years immediately before 376, some Romans were much more worried about other kinds of barbarians. Romans in Britain experienced the worst barbarian attacks since the creation of the province. In 360, according to Ammianus, 'the savage tribes of the Scots and Picts, who had broken the peace that had been agreed upon, were laying waste the regions near the frontiers, so that fear seized the provincials, worried as they were by a mass of past calamities'.[108] This is the first time that the pairing of 'Picts and Scots' is to be found in our sources. 'Picts' is the replacement for *Caledonii*, the word formerly used for the inhabitants of the far north of Britain; the *Scotti* are the inhabitants of Ireland. Clearly the Irish attacks were maritime expeditions; in all likelihood the attacks of the Picts were as well, if only because there were a number of British peoples north of Hadrian's Wall who would have had to have been dealt with before that land frontier was reached. The Picts were truly barbarous, Romans agreed. They were so called because their bodies were *picti*, or 'painted': the Greek historian Herodian said that the barbarians of Britain (presumably including the Picts) used to 'tattoo their bodies with various patterns and pictures of all sorts of animals', and used to go naked so as not to hide the pictures.[109] The Picts are best known archaeologically for their 'symbol stones', from perhaps the seventh and eighth centuries – which depict various patterns and pictures of all sorts of animals.

According to Ammianus, the Picts and Scots attacked again in 364, but this time alongside the Attacotti (whom St Jerome claimed were cannibals)[110] and the Saxons. The most serious attack came in 367, however: which was a *barbarica conspiratio*, that brought 'Britain into a state of extreme need'.[111] Romans believed, at least, that various and very disparate barbarian peoples had conspired together in planning a simultaneous attack on Britain from all sides: the Picts, Scots and Attacotti from the north and west, and the Franks and the Saxons from the south and east. A Roman general in charge of coastal defences was killed, and many Roman soldiers deserted. There was, however, a good reason for Ammianus to exaggerate the scale of the disaster.[112] He was writing in the reign of the Emperor Theodosius I, and it was Count Theodosius, the emperor's father, who had restored order, 'leaving the provinces [of Britain] dancing for joy'.[113] One can almost sense Claudian, the panegyrist of the Emperor Honorius, dancing for joy too as he recalled the triumphs of Count Theodosius, Honorius's grandfather: 'The Orkneys were drenched with slaughter of the Saxons; Thule was warm with Pictish blood; and icy Ireland wept for the heaps of Scottish dead.'[114] Traditionally, archaeologists have been happy to ascribe layers of charcoal and signs of burning to this episode; more recently it has been suggested that there is no certain evidence of destruction at all.[115] But there is other evidence for attacks by Picts and Scots, and better evidence for the fifth century. And there is no doubt at all that the Saxons – a generic word used in Latin sources for maritime Germanic-speakers of all kinds (including Jutes, Angles and Frisians) – were attacking Britain in the fifth century, and settling there.

chapter three

THE BARBARIANS FROM
376 TO 476

Between 376 and 476 the authority of the Roman emperor in the Western Empire was gradually replaced by that of various barbarian rulers, and the equilibrium of the barbarian world was disturbed just as dramatically as that of the Roman one. The period saw apparently dramatic movements of barbarian peoples: the Visigoths, for instance, moved from north of the Lower Danube to the banks of the River Garonne in south-west Gaul between 376 and 418/419, via Italy and Spain, while between 407 and 439 the Vandals moved from the Rhine to the city of Carthage in North Africa. The historian today finds it almost as difficult to keep track of all the local crises, and their wider implications, as Roman authorities did. The collapse of Roman power often makes more sense in a regional context: thus we have good modern accounts of the end of the Roman Empire in Britain (the first province in the West to fall beyond Roman control), in Spain and in Gaul. We also have accounts of the individual barbarian peoples who played a part in the downfall of the Empire: the Angles and Saxons, the Franks, the Goths, the Huns and the Vandals. But to understand the whole process by which the barbarians made their impact on the history of Europe, it is more useful to try to look at events chronologically across Europe. Events on one side of Europe often had an impact on the other: just to take an obvious point, the Gothic threat in Italy which led to the sack of Rome in 410 directly led the Emperor Honorius to leave Britain to its own devices, a decision which soon led to the domination of south-eastern Britain by barbarians from across the North Sea.

There are many problems with trying to write a full history of these years. There is no reliable contemporary historian, like Ammianus; we have extracts from historians, preserved in later accounts; brief chronicles or annals, often summarizing the events of a year in a few laconic sentences; and moralistic treatises from Christians disguised as historical commentary. Our written sources, of course, tell us much more about the Roman Empire than about the barbarians; archaeology, which is so valuable for discerning long-term trends in matters such as settlement history or technology, can tell us very little about political events.

The Gothic Threat: 376–406

The period between 376 and 406 is sandwiched between the two major incursions of barbarians into the Roman Empire: groups of Goths in 376 and groups of Alans, Sueves and Vandals on the last day of December 406. The common factor in those two incursions, historians such as Peter Heather have argued, was the Huns.[1] The evidence that the Huns pushed the Goths into the Empire in 376 is clear; that they propelled barbarians across the Rhine in 406/7 is purely conjectural.

Before their crossing of the Danube, there were basically two groups of Goths: the Tervingi, closest to the Danube frontier, and the Greuthungi further north. The Tervingi were divided, however; with the support of the Romans, Fritigern (an Arian Christian) defeated King Athanaric, who had been persecuting Christians. Partly because of their internal problems, the Goths were in no position to cope with the sudden arrival of the Huns from the north-east. The Huns overran the territory of the Greuthungi, and then moved south. Many of the Tervingi who survived the initial onslaught moved to the Danube, and early in 376 petitioned the Roman authorities for permission to cross the river and take refuge inside the Empire. Emperor Valens eventually gave permission for his former ally Fritigern to enter the Empire with his people; but permission was denied both to the other Tervingi, under Athanaric (who had been active but ultimately unsuccessful in trying to resist the Huns), and to the Greuthungi. Fritigern's Tervingi eventually crossed the Danube, though the ferrying operation took several days, and was hampered by the spring rains; numerous Goths drowned.

Valens had ordered that the Goths be given food in the first instance, and then land which they could cultivate. But the Roman authorities had probably underestimated the numbers who would cross; and food supplies soon ran out. Goths sold their own people into slavery in exchange for dog flesh, says Ammianus, while Eunapius and Zosimus claim that Roman commanders raced each other to acquire sex slaves and agricultural labourers.[2]

By the following year, the refugee Goths showed signs of rebellion, and Roman troops moved them some 100 km south-east to Marcianopolis. While these troops were engaged on this operation, the Danube was relatively unprotected, and the Greuthungi were able to cross the river. Many or most of the Greuthungi joined up with Fritigern, whose army rapidly swelled through the recruitment of various other groups – Goths who had been in the Empire earlier, groups of Asiatic barbarians (Alans, Huns and Taifals), disgruntled Roman miners and slaves and deserters from the Roman army. This group, nominally controlled by a Tervingian king, can by this stage clearly no longer be called Tervingi: indeed, Ammianus now substitutes either *Gothi* or *barbari* for the term *Tervingi*. Modern historians have often used the term 'Visigoths', but this is technically anachronistic (see below, p. 120), and the use of the term implies more unity in this ragtag army than it merits. Fritigern's barbarians, a 'heterogenous agglomeration of ethnicities', in Noel Lenski's happy phrase,[3] were a new people or were *potentially* a new people. There was a superfluity of kings and leaders, who seem at times to have overruled Fritigern, until his name disappears altogether in 382. In all likelihood this group seldom operated as a single entity, and this perhaps made it more of a threat to the Roman authorities. The area south of the Danube was raided constantly in 377 and 378, even up to the suburbs of Constantinople, by relatively small and mobile groups, against which the Romans seemed powerless.

When Valens heard how the situation had deteriorated, he petitioned his western colleague Gratian for reinforcements, and came to Constantinople, arriving there at the end of May 378. He was met by rioting, and abuse at the circus (the traditional venue for encounters between emperor and people); the populace resented his failure to protect the city from the Goths. He left 12 days later, promising punishment on his return, and made for Adrianople. Negotiations got nowhere, and skirmishing between the two sides seems to have escalated into a full-scale battle before they could be completed. Gratian's troops had not yet arrived, but Valens went into battle anyway, possibly misled by his scouts into thinking that Fritigern's army was much smaller than it actually was. By the end of the day's battle, two-thirds of the Roman soldiers had been killed, and the Roman cavalry had fled. The emperor himself died on the battlefield. Later on it was accepted that he had been burned alive in a house in which he had taken refuge; but Ammianus offered an alternative: that he fell in the melee, and his corpse was never identified.

The battle of Adrianople on 8 August 378 was the greatest defeat inflicted by barbarians on the Roman army since the defeat of Varus in AD 9. Unfortunately the surviving part of the *History* by Ammianus breaks off not long after his description of the battle, so we are deprived of detail. Indeed, as Thomas Burns has suggested, that fact has had its own consequences. Ammianus leaves the reader with a sense of total crisis:

'By ending when he did, Ammianus unintentionally elevated the significance of the defeat [at Adrianople] beyond what even he himself believed to be the case.'[4] Noel Lenski, on the other hand, believes that Ammianus wanted to show that Adrianople was *not* a turning point: Rome had had setbacks before, and they had been overcome. Ammianus's advice on

> the need to keep the borders impenetrable through fortifications and defense, to starve out barbarians rather than engage them, to kill them through treachery where possible, to settle them only in small groups of *dediticii* and to exterminate them the moment they caused trouble, all constitute his plan for how to prevent another Adrianople. Ammianus believed that the Roman Empire was eternal, that it could never be challenged in a way that would threaten its existence.[5]

And, of course, Ammianus wrote some 20 years after Adrianople, and had seen for himself that, to a large extent, the Empire *had* weathered the storm.

It might seem surprising at first that the Goths did little to exploit their superiority. But the facts remain that their military forces (almost certainly no more than 50,000 strong) were not a match for what Rome could put together; that they did not have the ability to take the walled towns of the Roman Empire; and that they had to spend much of their energy foraging for food not just for themselves, but for the women and children they had brought with them across the Danube. The peace that was eventually agreed in 382 was portrayed by Romans as a victory, and perhaps it was. The Goths gave up their ambition for a kingdom of their own in Thrace; Thrace continued as a tax-paying Roman province, and the Goths were granted land scattered through several of the Balkan provinces. The Romans thus split the Goths up, and declined to recognize any single leader of the people; the disappearance of several Gothic leaders at this time, including Fritigern, might have been the price paid by the Goths for this peace.[6] Ammianus greatly approved of the means adopted by Julius, commander of troops beyond the Taurus. When Julius heard of Adrianople, he called all his own Gothic soldiers together under the pretext of handing over their pay, and had them all put to death: 'this prudent plan was carried out without any confusion or delay, and thus the eastern provinces were saved from great dangers'.[7]

An insight into this settlement is provided by an imperial propagandist, Themistius, who praises Valens's successor Theodosius the Great for this coup. Theodosius brought the Goths to surrender, and thus could do what he wanted with them. He could have killed them; but he spared them.

Was it then better to fill Thrace with corpses or with farmers? To make it full of tombs or living men? To progress through a wilderness or cultivated land? To count up the number of the slaughtered or those who till the soil? . . . I hear from those who have returned from there that they are now turning the metal of their swords and breastplates into hoes and pruning hooks.[8]

It is likely that Theodosius only resorted to Christian mildness because he was in no position to wipe out the Goths; indeed, possibly, he too had suffered defeat although no doubt not as disastrously as Valens had. Themistius seems to have been responding to those who *had* wished to wipe the Goths out, and was making the best of a bad job of the situation. But if Theodosius could persuade the Goths to settle down within the Empire, supplying him with soldiers and farmers, then potentially that was indeed much better than filling Thrace with corpses.

For a while, at least, the treaty seems to have been maintained. In return for their land, the Goths had agreed to send contingents to assist the Roman army when called upon to do so. Theodosius used Goths against the British usurper Magnus Maximus in 387/8, and against the pagan usurper Eugenius in 392/3. However, on both occasions the Goths felt that they were being used as 'cannon fodder'; in the crucial battle against Eugenius they were put into the front line and suffered many losses. A generation later, the historian Orosius noted that the ten thousand Gothic allies lost in battle by Theodosius 'was certainly a gain, and their defeat a victory'.[9] Goths revolted against their commanders on both occasions, and when Theodosius died in 395, the Goths chose as their leader the man who had led these revolts: Alaric. He took the Gothic army on a pillaging expedition down to Athens and up the Adriatic coast, in an attempt to force the Romans into a new peace. The dominant minister in 397, the eunuch Eutropius, gave the Goths what they wanted (settlement in Moesia and Macedonia), but he was eliminated in 399, and the agreement with the Goths was annulled. A Roman general of Gothic origin, Gainas, was an important figure in Constantinople in that year; but an alleged conspiracy by him was foiled, and thousands of Goths resident in Constantinople, including many women and children, were slaughtered.

It is unclear to what extent popular Roman animosity to Goths was responsible for the downfall of both Eutropius and Gainas. However, the *De Regno* of Synesius survives as an example of anti-Gothic rhetoric. Its 'Scythians' have often been taken to be a reference to Gainas and other influential Goths at court, although Heather has argued that he was referring to Goths who presented a much great potential danger: Alaric's Goths.[10] It is an extraordinary admonition to the young Emperor Arcadius.

The Roman emperor should uphold the noblest Roman traditions: not the obscene luxury that fetters you, but the simple manliness that won the empire. . . . Arming peoples who have been raised under different laws, of whose loyalty you lack that guarantee, is like mixing in wolves with your sheep dogs. . . . Our present course is suicidal. . . . The first step will be to ban these skin-wearing foreigners from the Roman civic honours they insult. It is absurd to let the same race govern us as provides our meanest slaves. . . . The foreign infection must be purged from the army before it spreads.[11]

Arcadius, of course, paid no heed to the utopian suggestion of removing all Goths from military service and replacing them with Romans. If this piece was written in around 398, then by the end of the following year three of the five eastern *magistri militum* were Goths: Gainas, Fravitta and Alaric himself.[12]

Alaric eventually gave up any hopes of settlement with Constantinople, and he brought his Goths into Italy to try his luck with the western emperor, or, rather, with the man who had been the real power in the West since Theodosius's death in 395 – the barbarian Roman general Stilicho. Alaric campaigned in Italy in 401 and 402, but Stilicho did not yield, and Alaric returned to the East. His fortunes only revived when a new crisis threatened to unseat Stilicho: further barbarian incursions. The first was led by Radagaisus, whose own origins are somewhat obscure, although if our sources are to be believed he too was a Goth, and a leader of Goths. In 405 he led a large force across the Alps into Italy, possibly from Pannonia, and caused considerable disruption and destruction before he met his end at Fiesole, above Florence, in August 406. On the last day of that year, an even larger force of Alans, Sueves and Vandals crossed over into Gaul. Gibbon noted that this was 'in a season when the waters of the Rhine were most probably frozen' (a comment which many later historians have turned from conjecture into fact).[13] An immediate reaction was three successive usurpations in Britain, each of these risings caused, says Zosimus, both by fear of the barbarians who had come into Gaul and also out of a desire to do something about it. According to Zosimus, the third usurper, Constantine, crossed into Gaul, defeated numerous barbarians and made the Rhine frontier secure once more.[14]

From the Sack of Rome to the Fall of Africa: 407–435

The most famous event in the history of the 'barbarian invasions' was the sack of Rome by the Goths in 410. It was the first time in 800 years that the city of Rome had fallen to barbarians. But it turned out to be an event of little real strategic significance.

The sack of Rome in 410 was at the second attempt. In 408, the Gothic leader Alaric's army had been swollen by the barbarian auxiliaries of the assassinated Stilicho – 30,000 of them according to Zosimus, infuriated by the way in which Roman troops had massacred barbarian women and children in the wake of Stilicho's death.[15] They laid siege to Rome in that year. There was a severe shortage of food in the city, and epidemics; the bodies of the dead could not be buried in the usual cemeteries outside the walls, as Alaric's troops controlled the gates. Alaric demanded 'all the gold and silver in the city, as well as all movable property and the barbarian slaves', and when he was asked what he would leave the citizens of Rome, supposedly replied, 'their lives'.[16] The population of Rome turned to pagan gods in their despair, and the city prefect asked Pope Innocent I to ignore pagan sacrifices, as long as they were done in private. But if this to some extent placated those Romans with a nostalgia for the old gods, the next decision did not: in order to pay Alaric what he was demanding, the gold and silver statues of the gods were taken out of their temples. The pagan historian Zosimus regarded this as the beginning of the end for Rome: 'whatever bravery and virtue the Romans possessed disappeared, as experts in religion and ancestral worship had foretold'.[17] Alaric was promised 5,000 pounds of gold, 30,000 pounds of silver, 4,000 silk tunics, 3,000 scarlet skins and 3,000 pounds of peppers. When he had been paid part of this, he opened up several gates of the city to allow the inhabitants to supply themselves with food: it was an opportunity for his soldiers to sell food at very high prices.

Alaric withdrew from Rome then, but continued negotiations. Alaric asked for annual payments of money and grain, and homes for his people in Venetia, Noricum and Dalmatia; and the Roman ambassador reported back to Honorius that Alaric would probably accept less if he got the title of *magister militum*. Honorius agreed on the money and grain, but refused the title. Alaric advanced on Rome again, although still continued to negotiate, this time modifying his demands. According to Zosimus, he sent 'the bishops of each city as ambassadors to urge the emperor not to allow a city which had ruled the greater part of the earth for more than a thousand years to be destroyed by barbarian flames, but to make peace on reasonable terms'.[18] He had ceased to demand Adriatic provinces in which to settle, but only the two Noricums on the Danube which, as pointed out to the emperor, were not a great loss, since they were 'subject to continual incursions, and pay little tax to the treasury'.[19] What happened next, however, suggested that Alaric was still engaging in Roman politics rather than leading a barbarian army intent upon destruction. He demanded that the senate replace the Emperor Honorius by a leading Roman senator, Attalus – who showed his willingness to cooperate with the Goths by converting from paganism and being baptized by Sigesar, an Arian bishop of the Goths.[20] Diplomacy was not successful, however. Honorius offered to recognize Attalus as his imperial colleague; Attalus refused. Honorius responded by ordering the count of Africa to stop the corn supply to Italy. When Attalus also refused Alaric's suggestion to send troops to North Africa, the Goth deposed him. Alaric again tried negotiating with Honorius, but he was attacked by Honorius's troops, and turned back to complete the sack of Rome. The historian Zosimus, a pagan, places all the blame for what follows on Honorius and his advisers: 'so blind were the minds of those in charge of the state at that time in the absence of the gods' care'.[21]

On 24 August 410, the actual sack of Rome began, and continued for three days. Alaric had managed to get into the city: according to some he had the help of some Gothic slaves inside the city. It was said a century after the event that when the Emperor Honorius, safe in his stronghold in Ravenna, was told of the death of Rome, he broke out into wailing and lamentation, but calmed down when it was explained to him that it was the *city* of Rome that had met its end, and not 'Roma', his pet rooster.[22] But a more normal reaction was from St Jerome, writing from Bethlehem:

> A dreadful rumour reached us from the West. We heard that Rome was besieged, that the citizens were buying their safety with gold . . . The city which had taken the whole world was itself taken; nay, it fell by famine before it fell to the sword.[23]

The City of God, which St Augustine of Hippo began in 413, was another direct response to the sack of Rome: he needed to show to pagans why the sack of Rome was not a result of the abandonment of the pagan Gods, but he needed also to reassure Christians, who could not understand why suffering was inflicted even on them. As a commentary on the events of 410 it is almost contemporary, and it does not minimize the violence. Women were raped; so many people were killed that many corpses lay around unburied; many people were taken prisoner.[24]

Late Christian writers were keen to play down Gothic barbarity, and instead emphasized Gothic piety: even as Arians they showed reverence for the Christian God (more than pagan Romans did, but even more than Catholic Romans whose lack of reverence was being punished by God). Alaric ordered his men not to violate the sanctuary of the basilicas of St Peter and St Paul, for instance, where many Romans sought refuge.[25] One woman fought off her would-be Gothic rapist, and provoked him almost into making a martyr of her; but the Goth relented and led her into sanctuary at St Peter's.[26] Another Goth entered a house of religious women, and demanded gold and silver: the things that were shown to him were liturgical vessels belonging to St Peter. The Goth reported this to Alaric, and Alaric had them ceremoniously restored to the basilica. If Orosius is to be believed, Alaric was able to create a wonderful ceremony symbolizing the union between peoples under Christ: 'The pious procession was guarded by a double line of drawn swords; Romans and barbarians in concert raised a hymn to God in public.'[27]

This view of the sack of Rome probably owes more to the rhetorical example of the noble barbarian than to historical reality. We find a similar rhetoric later on in the fifth century, in the writings of Salvian of Marseille (see below, p. 201). Enough evidence survives to indicate that the three days' sack had a more than merely psychological impact. Even Orosius admits that there were still burnt-out buildings to see in Rome in 417, although he adds hastily that rather more fires were started by lightning (a visible sign of God's displeasure) than by the Goths.[28] The house of Sallust the historian was still half-ruined in the mid-sixth century, according to Procopius.[29] In the 430s, Emperor Valentinian III paid for the replacement of a silver *fastigium* (a canopy structure over the altar), allegedly weighing 1,610 pounds, which had been taken from the Lateran basilica by the barbarians.[30]

Not only was there material damage, but also a great deal of social disruption. Numerous prisoners were taken by the Goths, including clerics and even Galla Placidia, the emperor's sister. Many others abandoned their possessions and fled Rome and, as Goths moved south from Rome, Italy itself. The biblical scholar Rufinus complained peevishly, with the single-mindedness and self-centredness of the true scholar, that

> in front of our eyes, the barbarians burnt Reggio; the narrow stretch of sea which separates Italy from Sicily was our only protection. In these conditions, how can I find the tranquillity of mind I need in order to write and above all to translate?[31]

At the other end of the Mediterranean, the scholar Jerome, Rufinus's bitter enemy, had to abandon his *Commentary on Ezechiel*, distracted by the arrival of 'numerous slaves, men and women, from the city which was once mistress of the world . . . Bethlehem the holy receives every day, reduced to beggars, guests of both sexes, who were formerly noble and wealthy'.[32] Augustine was not so sympathetic when he witnessed the arrival of refugees in Carthage, and remarked that despite the fact that the whole world was in mourning for their tragic fate, all they could think about was going to the theatre and enjoying themselves.[33]

For Procopius, writing in the sixth century, it was not just Rome which was seriously affected by the entry of the Goths, but much of Italy.

For they destroyed all the cities which they captured, especially those south of the Ionian Gulf, so completely that nothing has been left to my time to know them by, unless, indeed, it might be one tower or gate or some such thing which chanced to remain. And they killed all the people, as many as came in their way, both old and young alike, sparing neither women nor children. Wherefore even up to the present time Italy is sparsely populated.[34]

This seems confirmed by what Rutilius Namatianus wrote in his poem which describes his journey in 416 from Rome back to his home in Gaul. He went by ship largely because the Goths had damaged the Via Aurelia, the western coastal road of Italy, and in particular its bridges.[35]

The sack of Rome was only one in a series of disasters at this time. A Gallo-Roman chronicler writing of the events of around 408 to 410 recorded an invasion of Britain by the Saxons, the ravaging of Gaul by the Vandals and Alans, the loss of Spain to the Sueves and the sack of Rome by the Goths, and concluded: 'as the host of enemies grew stronger, the powers of the Romans were weakened to their very foundation'.[36]

Almost no one on the Continent, one suspects, worried about the British, whom a letter from Honorius in 410 told to defend themselves from their enemies. But Gaul was a different matter: it was relatively densely populated, and thus paid large amounts of tax, and it contained numerous influential Romans. It was prey to those barbarians who had invaded in 406/7, but there were other problems too. Rutilius Namatianus in that poem cited above mentions a relative called Exuperantius who had just apparently put down a slave revolt, freeing slave-owners from slavery to their former slaves.[37] It was bad enough to have bands of barbarians who were escaping Roman control, but there was the problem that the only real resistance to these barbarians came from a usurper, Constantine. Emperors had learnt from bitter experience that usurpers were more of a problem than barbarians. They could lose their throne and lives to Roman usurpers but barbarians were responsible for just three imperial deaths: Decius and Valens, killed by the Goths, and the special case of Valens's elder brother Valentinian I, killed by the Quadi – in the sense that the demands of Quadi ambassadors in 375 were such that he dropped dead in apoplectic rage.[38]

Constantine was the third Roman soldier based in Britain who had proclaimed himself emperor in 406–7, although he was the only one to survive more than a few weeks. The army in Britain, which always (rightly) felt itself to be overlooked and underfunded, was prone to revolt, and, as in the case of Constantine, a revolt in Britain was frequently succeeded by an invasion of Gaul. Constantine III apparently established himself relatively easily in Gaul and Spain, probably a sign that those provinces resented the way in which the Empire's *de facto* ruler, Stilicho, was doing little to protect them from the invading barbarians. Constantine established his base at Arles, in southern Gaul, and troops under his rule seem to have fought a number of successful campaigns against the invaders. The result was quite satisfactory from the point of view of those in Gaul, but less so for those in Spain; the invaders slipped across the Pyrenees, and began the process of plunder and living off the land all over again.[39]

The amount of destruction caused by these marauding barbarians, in both Gaul and Spain, may have been considerable. Even allowing for literary exaggeration (like Orientius's oft-quoted 'All Gaul was filled with the smoke of a single funeral pyre'),[40] we have to reckon that for two years Gaul was subject to attack by these invaders, and for a further two years Spain suffered in the same process. Spain, not a frontier province, had never had many Roman troops stationed there, and there were no forces to protect the population. Even so, it was not just the barbarians who caused havoc; Hydatius, a contemporary Spanish chronicler, also instanced pestilence, famines (which drove women to cook and eat their own children) and a loss of wealth in the cities thanks to 'the tyrannical tax-collector'.[41] The situation eased in 411, when the barbarians in Spain decided to make peace and to settle: the Asding Vandals took over part of Gallaecia, while the Sueves took over the rest; the Alans got Lusitania and Carthaginiensis, and the Siling Vandals had Baetica. 'The Spaniards in the cities and forts who had survived the disasters surrendered themselves to servitude under the barbarians, who held sway throughout the provinces.'[42] But despite Hydatius's doom-laden pronouncements, the evidence is that many people probably rarely saw barbarians. Severus, a rich heretical priest from Huesca, thought he was going to be perfectly safe when he took a journey in around 417, carrying various valuable books with him. When he was mugged by some barbarian book-thieves, they at first tried to sell the books, and then when they realized that they contained heretical and magical texts, they surrendered them to the Catholic bishop of Lleida.[43] These were clearly barbarians well adapted to live in the Roman world.

Zosimus, writing long after the crisis of 406/7, adds an intriguing few lines to his description of the invasion:

[The barbarians] reduced the inhabitants of Britain and some of the Gallic peoples to such straits that they revolted from the Roman Empire, no longer submitted to Roman law, and reverted to their native customs. The Britons, therefore, armed themselves and ran many risks to ensure their own safety and free their cities from the attacking barbarians. The whole of Armorica and other Gallic provinces, in imitation of the Britons, freed themselves in the same way, by expelling the Roman magistrates and establishing the government they wanted.[44]

It is tempting to relate this to the slave revolt in Armorica that Rutilius Namatianus's relation Exuperantius put down, as we have just seen. If so, it is a reminder that one person's 'slave revolt' might appear to others as a local self-defence league. But we must remember that in 410 Honorius wrote to the Britons telling them to look to their own defence, so we may simply be seeing a rather jaundiced description of a process that had actually been sanctioned by the emperor. It was around this time that a not wholly reliable Gallo-Roman chronicler said 'the British provinces were laid waste by an invasion of Saxons'; in 442, the same chronicler asserted, 'the British provinces . . . were subjected to the authority of the Saxons'.[45]

Not long after Gaul had been cleared of these barbarians (and the Emperor Honorius had rid himself of Constantine), Alaric's Goths arrived in Gaul. They were no longer led by Alaric, who had died in Italy in 411, but by his brother-in-law Ataulf. He seems to have had even grander ambitions than Alaric. He too set up a puppet emperor: Attalus, the same man Alaric had made and unmade as emperor. But he also married Galla Placidia, the daughter of the Emperor Theodosius the Great (d. 395) and sister of the Emperor Honorius, the most illustrious of the captives that Alaric had led out of Rome in 410. They were married in the house of a leading Roman citizen in Narbonne, according to the historian Olympiodorus.

> There Placidia, dressed in royal raiment, sat in a hall decorated in the Roman manner, and by her side sat Ataulf, wearing a Roman general's cloak and other Roman clothing. Amidst the celebrations, along with other wedding gifts Ataulf gave Placidia fifty handsome young men dressed in silk clothes, each bearing aloft two very large dishes, one full of gold, the other full of precious – or rather, priceless – stones, which had been carried off by the Goths at the sack of Rome. Then nuptial hymns were sung, first by Attalus . . .[46]

When their child was born, they named him Theodosius, after his grandfather; and given that Honorius was without children, for those wedded to the hereditary principle (as some Romans were), here might be the next emperor. It seemed to some that an apocalyptic moment had arrived; surely this was the marriage of the daughter of the king of the south with the king of the north, as predicted by the prophet Daniel.

We do have an idea of Ataulf's ambitions, if we are to believe a high-ranking Roman official, who told Jerome, in an audience which included Orosius, that many times Ataulf had said that once he had intended to replace Romania by Gothia, but that he had realized that the Goths were too barbarous to follow laws and had decided instead to sustain 'the Roman name by the power of the Goths, wishing to be looked upon by posterity as the restorer of the Roman Empire, since he could not be its transformer'.[47] It sounds rather too much like what a Roman would have wanted a Gothic king to say; but perhaps Ataulf said it for that very reason.[48]

Honorius's able general Constantius put an end to any ambitions Ataulf might have had. He blockaded him in Narbonne, and forced him to go south, where he was murdered in Barcelona by one of his own men. His successor Wallia made peace with Constantius, and 'in the name of Rome Wallia, the king of the Goths, inflicted a vast slaughter upon the barbarians within Spain'.[49] If we are to believe Hydatius, all the Siling Vandals in Baetica were wiped out; and the Alans suffered such losses that the few survivors joined the Asding Vandals. Constantius may have been worried by Wallia's success; he recalled him and his Goths, and settled them in the Garonne valley, between Toulouse and Bordeaux. One Roman aristocrat, Paulinus of Pella, was pleased: he had suffered greatly under Ataulf, but this new peace 'remains unregretted, since already in our state we see many prospering through Gothic favour'.[50]

This settlement – traditionally dated 418 but now often placed in 419[51] – was significant only in hindsight, since attempts to settle the Goths had been made before. What makes the event special was that it effectively laid the foundation of a kingdom in Gaul that was to last for another 90 years and would be the basis for a kingdom in Spain that lasted until the arrival of Islamic forces from North Africa in 711. There has been considerable historical controversy about why Constantius organized this settlement, and what were its terms. Was it to protect Gaul's landowners from the threat of peasant rebellion, or from further barbarian invasion, or was it simply a desire to stabilize the situation by tying the Goths down? Were the Goths given land on which to settle, or were they given revenues from land, or even the right to collect taxes from that land? The latter questions will be dealt with later, in Chapter nine. And the former set of questions might be answered by considering the consequences and aftermath. The Goths remained in that part of southwest Gaul for nearly a century.[52] They forged good relations with the Romans and in particular with the Roman aristocracy in the area. As their power grew (a process which in part went hand in hand with the decline of imperial power), they provided stability, government and a source of patronage for the Roman population of the area. Their armies successfully protected the area from any further barbarian incursions, at least until the time that the Franks overthrew their power in the south-west in 507. If the power of the Gothic kings of south-west Gaul grew to eclipse and to take over from the Empire in that area, this was not necessarily against the will of the Roman population, and owed more to imperial weaknesses and failures than anything else. To call the policy which produced these kind of settlement, as Walter Goffart did, 'an imaginative experiment that got slightly out of hand'[53] is perfectly reasonable – even though now Goffart is tempted to change these 'brash lines' and suggest that it was not experimental, and neither did it get out of hand.[54]

The Goths – or, as these particular Goths would come to be known, the Visigoths – were settled on Roman land in return for military service, primarily in Spain. But the most significant development in Spanish history at this time was the departure of the Vandals and their allies. This was the consequence of a bold decision by Geiseric, who became king of the Vandals on the death of his half-brother Gunderic in 428 (driven mad by a demon after his capture of Seville, according to Hydatius).[55] In May 429, Geiseric gathered all his people, the Vandals and Alans, with their wives, children and dependents, at a port near Gibraltar, and organized their migration to North Africa. There were said to be around 80,000 involved in this sea-crossing.[56] They began the long 2,000-km trek from Tangiers across the North African coastline until they reached the three densely populated Roman provinces of Numidia, Proconsularis and Byzacena. They arrived at the town of Hippo in June 430: famously, at the time when the man who had been its bishop for 35 years, Augustine, perhaps the greatest theologian in the history of the Church, was on his deathbed. Hippo was taken after a 14-month siege, and the Romans made peace with Geiseric in 435.

The Age of Aetius: 435–54

Aetius was one of the most significant Romans of the last century of the Roman Empire in the West; by default, in part, because those who held the title of emperor in his day were not an impressive crew.[57] For Procopius, writing a century after his death, he was 'the last of the Romans'.[58] He was born around 390, and as a teenager was in the Roman army. Between 405 and 408 he was a hostage with the Gothic king Alaric, and at some time after this was a hostage with the Huns. Much later the Gallic aristocrat and poet Sidonius Apollinaris claimed that he had learnt the art of war from the Huns.[59] Around 424 he was sent by the usurper John on an embassy to the Huns, in order to obtain their military help, and returned with a large force: too late, for John had already been defeated. It looks as if he might have acquired a promotion as a reward for arranging for the Huns to be sent back out of the Empire. In the years following this he established a considerable military reputation: he relieved a siege of Narbonne by the Goths; regained territory from the Franks; defeated Alamans in Raetia; and wiped out a group of

Visigoths near Arles. His ambition was considerable; it was alleged that he murdered Felix, the leading Roman general in the West, in 430, at the instigation of Galla Placidia; and he became embroiled in a power struggle with Bonifatius, the commander in Africa, which ended in a battle near Rimini in which Bonifatius was fatally wounded. Aetius still had enemies, however, and there was an attempt on his life in 432/3. Aetius fled to his friends the Huns; it was with their help – somehow or other – that he regained office, and further promotion. From 435 until his death in 454 he was *magister militum* in the West, and in 435 he secured the coveted title of *patricius*.

For 20 years Aetius dominated the political and military scene in the West. But his military activities rarely extended beyond Gaul. In 436 he defeated the Burgundians in Gaul; and in the following year sent his Hunnic allies against them (an episode dimly remembered in the later medieval *Nibelungenlied*); in 438 he won a major victory against the Visigoths; in 440 and 442 he arranged for groups of Alans to be settled near the River Valence and in Armorica; and in 443 he settled the surviving Burgundians west of Lake Geneva. His greatest triumph undoubtedly was in 451, when he assembled an alliance of Visigoths and others to meet the attack on Gaul by Attila and his Huns. The battle of Chalons was a disaster for Attila, and the beginning of the end of the great Hunnic 'Empire' north of the Danube. Three years later Aetius was assassinated in the imperial palace at the orders of the Emperor Valentinian III; in the following year, in 455, Valentinian was himself assassinated, by two of Aetius's own bodyguards (both of whom had Gothic names).

Aetius's name is remembered by historians of Britain for a single mention in an obscure and difficult source. Gildas's *The Ruin of Britain* was a tract written towards the middle of the sixth century, which attempted to lay the blame for Britain's woes on the sins of its rulers and clerics. In the course of this moral treatise, Gildas briefly recapitulated the history of the previous century, in order to make his somewhat depressing point: that when people are prosperous and happy, they tend to sin, and that brings down the wrath of God. Gildas wrote about the attacks of the Picts and the Scots on the British, and about how Saxons were recruited from Germany in order to protect the British – a standard Roman procedure. However, these Saxons revolted, and began to attack the British themselves. And sometime after Aetius's third consulship, that is, between 446 and his death in 454, he received 'the groans of the Britons'. 'The barbarians push us back to the sea; the sea pushes us back to the barbarians; between these two kinds of death, we are either drowned or slaughtered.'[60] The Britons appealed for troops, but as far as we know

Aetius did not send any; Britain had been effectively abandoned by the Empire for a generation by that stage.

The traditional date for the arrival of the Angles and Saxons in Britain is 449. That is a date given to us by Bede, who in his *Ecclesiastical History of the English People* tried desperately to make chronological sense of Gildas's account (which gives us no dates at all) and, like most historians who have followed him, he failed. The year 449 is almost certainly too late for the arrival of the barbarians in Britain. What we can say, from archaeological evidence, is that in the time of Aetius there is some evidence of the survival of life along Roman lines, especially in the west of Britain, but that there is much impoverishment and, possibly, depopulation. By the end of the fifth century most of the south-east corner of Britain seems to have been settled by Angles and Saxons, and in the west the descendants of Romano-Britons, organized into several kingdoms, managed occasionally to win battles. One of their leaders might have been called Arthur (the man whom later romancers turned into the most famous king of all).

The Britons had appealed to Aetius in vain. But they were not the only ones to appeal in vain; Hydatius was on an embassy to Aetius in 431, fruitlessly begging for help against the Sueves, who (after the departure of the Vandals to Africa) were aggressively pushing beyond their settlement in Gallaecia.[61] We may doubt whether Aetius actually deserves his reputation as 'the last of the Romans'. Although his panegyrist Merobaudes in 446 credited him with bringing peace from Spain to the Don and from Libya to the 'polar region of Scythia',[62] the reality was rather different. Aetius largely ignored the problems of Spain and Africa; he betrayed the provincials there for the benefit of his friends, the Gallic aristocrats. J.R. Moss agued that he had twice betrayed the Empire for personal gain before he achieved ultimate power.[63] Valentinian III killed him as a traitor in 454; 30 years too late, perhaps. Even so, for some Romans Aetius appeared as a powerful saviour, and some were even prepared to credit him with achievements that were not his; some believed, for instance, that he had successfully arranged the assassination of Attila.[64]

For most of the period of Aetius's domination, there were just two Roman emperors – Honorius (395–423) and Valentinian III (425–55) – both of whom were largely ineffectual, becoming emperors as children and usually remaining victim either to their advisors' ambitions or to events themselves. Three barbarian rulers, on the other hand, were outstanding: Theoderic I of the Visigoths (419–51), who presided over the establishment of his people in south-west Gaul and the making of the Gothic army into an essential support of the Roman Empire; Geiseric of the

Vandals (428–77), whose extraordinarily long reign saw the move from Spain to North Africa and the establishment of a great west Mediterranean power base; and Attila of the Huns (434–53), whose military dominance briefly stabilized the barbarian world north of the Danube.

The achievement of Theoderic I of the Visigoths was, above all, to survive. His three predecessors had lasted just seven years between them (one was murdered after seven days). Theodoric completed the arrangement begun under Wallia to settle in Aquitania, and established a regime stable enough to allow him a reign of 32 years. Little is known of him, save for his involvement in a number of campaigns: he fought the Romans on a number of occasions, but seems to have fought for them as well. According to Jordanes, Attila urged him to abandon his alliance with Rome in 451; instead he commanded probably the largest contingent in the coalition put together by Aetius. He led his Visigoths in the battle of the Catalaunian Fields, in which Attila was defeated, and he himself died on the battlefield. A significant figure in his life would appear to be the Gallic senator Avitus, although this may simply be because Sidonius tells us of Avitus (his father-in-law) at some length. Avitus persuaded Theoderic to raise his siege of Narbonne in 437; he negotiated a peace treaty with Aetius in 439, thanks to the good offices of Avitus; and he allowed Avitus to direct the education of his son Theoderic.[65] It was Avitus, apparently, who persuaded him to fight against Attila; and after the king's death in battle it was his son Theoderic II (453–66) who was the main support of Avitus in the latter's successful but short-lived career as emperor (455–6). The willingness of the two Theoderics to cooperate with the still very powerful Gallo-Roman aristocracy was surely a major reason for the success of the Visigothic kingdom in the fifth century.

The second great figure of the mid-fifth century was Geiseric, king of the Vandals, whom we have already seen establishing himself in North Africa. This book, concentrating as it does on barbarians in Europe, will not have much to say about the African kingdom of the Vandals, but its significance on the fortunes of the Roman Empire in the West should be emphasized, and indirectly, therefore, its significance on the history of European barbarians too. Geiseric was by most measures the most successful of all the barbarian kings who wielded power within Roman territory.

In 439 Geiseric broke out of Mauretania, and attacked Carthage, the second most important city of the Western Roman Empire, and essential port for the supplies of corn and oil that kept the city of Rome going at its usual strength. Quodvultdeus, the bishop of Carthage (who spent the last 15 years of his life in exile in Naples) lamented the horrors that were being afflicted on the Carthaginians – not only the slaughter of pregnant women and babies, but some kind of social revolution: 'the impious power of the barbarians has even demanded that those women who were once mistresses of many servants have suddenly become the vile servants of barbarians'.[66] A huge expeditionary force was assembled in Sicily, which would have been due to sail to Carthage in spring 441. It never sailed; the threat from the Huns proved to be too worrying, and a treaty was made in 442 ceding much of North Africa to the Vandals. Geiseric was recognized as an 'allied king and friend' of the Empire, and his son Huneric, who had been sent as a hostage, was betrothed to Eudocia, the daughter of Valentinian III. Never before had such an alliance between barbarian and imperial family been contemplated as part of official policy. It was to have very long-term consequences, as well. Huneric himself became king in 477; on his death in 484 he was succeeded by his nephew. In 523 Hilderic, the son of Huneric and Eudocia, finally came to the throne. He was overthrown and imprisoned in 530; and the invasion of North Africa by the imperial forces, and the overthrow of the Vandal regime, came, ostensibly, as revenge for this injury done to the grandson of a Roman emperor.

Imperial propaganda put a brave face upon the treaty of 442. Geiseric had been made a friend, officially. The grain tribute to Rome seems to have been restored. Imperial forces were free to face a much more serious threat to the north. And it was not as if Geiseric did not have his own problems: there was a serious conspiracy against him in 442 (financed or inspired by the imperial government), and many Vandals were put to death. Geiseric was another of the fifth century's greatest survivors, however; he survived the huge naval attack sent by the western emperor in 460, and by good luck captured most of the Roman fleet; he survived the disastrous naval expedition sent from Constantinople in 468 (allegedly by bribing its leader); and he survived the Western Roman Empire itself, dying in 477.

The third member of our mid-century trio is the best known of all: indeed Attila the Hun is probably the only barbarian from this period that is known throughout Europe (particularly to film buffs, who will remember Anthony Quinn as Attila, with Sophia Loren playing Honoria). For some, his name epitomizes barbarian savagery; in Hungary, he is a national hero, and 'Attila' is a name one might give to one's son.

Attila's predecessor as king of the Huns had been Rua, who had initiated the policy of blackmailing Roman emperors out of large sums of money by threatening to invade. For 10 years, from around 435, Attila shared power with his brother Bleda; in 445, according to Roman writers, fratricide brought him sole power. It is difficult to know the full extent of his ambitions. He was certainly very successful in forcing emperors to give him gold. Previously the eastern emperors had agreed to pay the Huns 350 pounds of gold per annum; from 438 the demand went up to 700 pounds per annum. In 447 Attila invaded, and threatened Constantinople; he claimed all the territory within five days' journey south of the Danube, and demanded 2,100 pounds of gold per annum, and 6,000 pounds in arrears. It has been estimated that by the time the emperor ceased payments the Huns had been paid over 9 metric tons of gold.[67]

His four great invasions were, first, into the East, advancing on Constantinople in 442 and deep into the Balkans in 447, and, in the West, into Gaul in 451, which was defeated by Aetius's confederation of barbarian troops, and into Italy in 452, which was halted, probably not miraculously despite the legend, by the intervention of Pope Leo I ('the Great').[68] When Attila got to Milan, Priscus recorded, he saw a painting of Roman emperors on thrones, with dead Goths at their feet: and he ordered a painter to paint him on a throne, with emperors pouring out sacks of gold at his feet.[69] His ambitions may have involved more than mere extortion, however, although it is difficult to know whether we should believe him to be serious in regarding the appeal for help by Valentinian III's sister Honoria as a signal that she was betrothed to him, or whether he really demanded the Western Empire as her dowry. If he had such ambitions, he failed. The Roman Empire, despite all its problems, did still have remarkable staying power: it was able to defeat his great invasion of Gaul in 451 in a pitched battle, and turn away his invasion of Italy in 452. The following year Attila died. He had a nosebleed while celebrating with his concubine, it appears; although some said that she had murdered him, and others that Aetius had bribed one of Attila's bodyguards to kill him.[70] However he died, within a very short space of time the empire he had built up vanished.

For Attila we have a text which is one of the most fascinating of all texts relating to Rome and the barbarians: the account by Priscus of Panium of an embassy to Attila's court in 449. It survives as a long fragment copied into the tenth-century Emperor Constantine Porphyrogenitos's book on embassies. Priscus accompanied the senior ambassador Maximinus on the mission. It is a vivid account of the state of mind of the ambassadors, dependent on an interpreter whom they did not trust, lost among the court intrigues, forced to wait for days for a useful meeting, endlessly going over conversations to try to find out what they meant. Priscus describes the wooden palaces in Attila's kingdom, one of which had a stone bathhouse in Roman style, built by a Roman slave who had hoped in vain for freedom as his reward. Attila himself was supplied with Roman secretaries, and was able to get them to read out from a papyrus document the names of the Hunnic fugitives among the Romans whom he wanted returned. Indeed, Attila was so angry with the ambassador for not having handed ever the fugitives already that he said 'he would have impaled him and left him as food for the birds if he had not thought that it infringed the rights of ambassadors'.[71]

It was at his second meeting with Attila that Priscus was greeted by someone in Greek. He had met Greek-speakers among the Huns before: prisoners, easily recognizable by their tattered clothes and filthy hair. But this man looked like a well-dressed Scythian, with trimmed hair. He said that he was a Greek merchant from a town on the Danube; he had been enslaved, but had fought for the Huns and earned his freedom. He now had a barbarian wife, and children, and lived a much better life than before, he claimed. Priscus corrected this unpatriotic sentiment, and his 'acquaintance wept and said that the laws were fair and that the Roman polity was good, but that the authorities were ruining it by not taking the same thought for it as those of old'.[72] Priscus's text implies Priscus won the argument, but one of Attila's men made a similar point to him. Indeed, the anonymous Greek's main message was shortly afterwards repeated to Priscus by a Hun: 'slavery to Attila is preferable to wealth among the Romans'.[73] Priscus and Maximinus finally made their way home, not without witnessing some signs of Attila's strict laws in practice: an impaled spy, and slaves who had been arrested for killing their lords in battle.

A lengthy commentary could be made on this text, if there was space. No other text from the period gives so much detail (and fairly reliable detail, perhaps) on the mechanics of an embassy to the barbarians, on life among the barbarians and on the complex multi-faceted nature of relations between Romans and barbarians.

The Ends of Empires: 453 to 476

Within a short space of time three crucial figures were removed from the scene. Attila died in 453, and the Hunnic Empire broke up shortly afterwards; Aetius was murdered in 454; and Valentinian III was murdered in revenge in 455. The Venerable Bede, writing in the eighth century, was of the opinion that with the death of Valentinian III the Western Empire came to an end,[74] and there is some merit in that point of view. Although there were vigorous emperors in the West in subsequent years, notably Majorian (457–61) and Anthemius (467–72), they were seldom able to impose their will over more than portions of the Western Empire, and sometimes seem to have had little authority outside Italy. A number of other emperors were no more than figureheads, installed by their barbarian generals, presiding over an empire in which military and political power were increasingly held by barbarians, mostly acting in the name of a Roman emperor (or a Roman usurper) but often in reality chasing their own ambitions.

Before we follow generations of historians and blame barbarian generals for the collapse of the Western Empire, it is worth noting that in the East one barbarian general did rather a good job at holding the Empire together. This was Aspar, who was a significant figure in imperial politics in the East from 431 until his eventual murder four decades later in 471. He was an Alan; his father, Ardabur, had led Roman troops against the Persians with great success. Aspar was present at the deathbed of Theodosius II, and was no doubt instrumental in the appointment of Marcian, a member of his own household, as emperor. He was given the title of *patricius* in 451, and got his own candidate Leo proclaimed as successor to Marcian in 457. One source claims that he himself was offered the imperial throne, although this seems unlikely.[75] Leo proved too independent for him, however. Aspar relied on his Gothic federates; but Leo turned to the Isaurians. Aspar failed in an attempt to assassinate Leo's Isaurian general Zeno in 469, and two years later Leo had Aspar and his son Ardabur murdered.[76] Three years later Zeno – whose unfamiliar Isaurian name has been mangled in the manuscript tradition[77] – became emperor: a barbarian himself in the eyes of many Romans, even if Isauria was within the Empire. The difference between East and West was not so marked; both imperial courts fell under the control of barbarian generals.[78]

The collapse of the Hunnic Empire caused some chaos in the barbarian world, particularly in the Middle and Lower Danube area, where Goths, Gepids, Herules, Rugians, Sueves, Skirians and others, all of whom had been under Hunnic domination for probably two generations or more, now fought for survival and independence. The Gepids were among the winners: they led a coalition against surviving Hunnic groups, defeated them in a battle by the River Nedao in Pannonia, and emerged as the major force in that area. Numerous cemeteries from the late fifth and sixth century in the Tisza valley and in eastern Hungary have been identified as Gepid.[79] Other groups finding themselves independent territories on the Danube were the Lombards and the Herules. But perhaps the most significant result of the disappearance of the Huns was the re-emergence of those Goths who had been under Hunnic domination, and who would become known as the Ostrogoths. They will be discussed in the next chapter.

Towards the end of the century with which we are concerned here, one ruler of a barbarian people stands out: Euric, king of the Visigoths

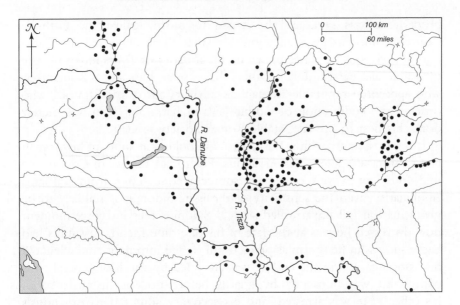

Map 5 Late fifth- and sixth-century finds within the Carpathian basin. Those west of the Danube belong to the Lombards, and those east of the Tisza to the Gepids: there seems to be a no–man's–land between the two. (After Curta, *Making of the Slavs*, 198).

in south-west Gaul (466/7–484). The standard picture of Euric in our books[80] ultimately derives from Jordanes. As Andrew Gillett has pointed out, Jordanes 'compresses all the ills leading to the collapse of the western empire . . . into Euric's times'. He and Geiseric are 'boldly-drawn literary figures whose purpose is to advance the plot of decline'.[81] But there is in fact no evidence that Euric made any changes to Visigothic policy. He continued to attack the Sueves and stop their expansion outside Gallaecia, just as the Empire had persuaded his late brother to do. There are no signs of hostility towards the Empire until 471, when Euric sent an army into Provence, which was followed in 473 by attacks on Spain, Provence and even Italy. In 475 he gained Auvergne (the capital of which was Clermont, whose bishop would be Sidonius Apollinaris); he achieved this by exchanging it with Arles and Marseilles, although he won those back in 476. By then, if not by some time earlier, it was not at all clear who the legitimate ruler of the Western Empire was.

That at some point a few years after his accession Euric began to expand aggressively into territory formerly an acknowledged part of the Empire is undoubted. It is his motivation that is unclear. Some scholars have portrayed him as essentially anti-Roman: he could not even speak Latin properly, it was said, and he began to move against the Catholic Church. (Sidonius gives an impression that Euric neglected the Catholic Church; this was later blown up by Gregory of Tours into a picture of wholesale persecution.) Others have seen him as a Romanizer, who appointed reputable Romans as advisors and administrators, who ordered the codification of Gothic laws in Latin and who was merely doing his best to preserve stable Roman society in Gaul.

It is worth approaching Euric through looking at some of his Roman contemporaries. There was Arvandus, Praetorian Prefect of Gaul in the mid-460s, for whom our main source is one letter from Sidonius Apollinaris; given the sensitivity of the issue Sidonius is unlikely to be giving us the full unvarnished story.[82] Sidonius tells his correspondent how distressed he was at the fate of his one-time friend. Arvandus had had a successful first term as prefect, but he fell into debt, and alienated his associates, 'till in the end he was encircled by a wall of general antipathy, and was burdened by guards before he was disburdened of his office'. He was arrested, and his secretary admitted to Arvandus's authorship of a letter addressed to Euric,

> insisting that the Britons settled to the north of the Loire should be attacked, and declaring that the Gallic provinces ought according to the law of nations to be divided up with the Burgundians, and a great deal more mad stuff in this vein.

Sidonius and other friends intervened on his behalf, and although he had admitted his guilt his death sentence was commuted to exile. Sidonius's letter was written in late 468 or 469, and seems to suggest that Sidonius did not know how Euric would react to Arvandus's suggestion: in other words, that Sidonius at least did not think of Euric as inherently anti-Roman.

A particular bugbear of Sidonius's was Seronatus, although it is not easy to tell from Sidonius's diatribes exactly what his position was within the Visigothic kingdom. He was greedy, brutal, arrogant, insulting, irreligious. 'Each day he crowds the woods with fugitives, the farms with barbarian occupants, the altars with accused persons [seeking sanctuary], the prisons with priests . . . He tramples on the laws of Theodosius and issues laws of Theodoric.'[83] The people of Javols go pale with terror at his approach: 'he sometimes drains them dry with unheard-of kinds of imposts or again ensnares them in the tortuous guile of false accusations; and not even when they have paid him an annual tribute does he allow the poor wretches to return home'.[84] Worst of all, he seems to have been involved in the negotiation with the Empire that brought Sidonius's own Auvergne under Euric's control in 475.[85] Sidonius's complaint over the 'enslavement' of his Arverni – sprung, like the Romans, from the blood of Trojan exiles, he adds imaginatively – has been called 'the epitaph of the Western Empire'.[86]

Seronatus was eventually tried for his crimes, and executed. But we must not take Sidonius's 'epitaph' too seriously – it is not even consistent with the views expressed in his other letters[87] – and nor must we think of Seronatus as typical. There were other, much more respectable, Roman supporters of Euric's regime, such as Namatius, whose literary interests are attested by a letter asking Sidonius to lend him works by Varro and Eusebius, and whom Euric appointed to command the fleet which was to protect the Atlantic coast of Gaul from attack by Saxons. There is in fact evidence that very senior figures in Gaul were looking to the strong Gothic king for leadership, rather than to an ineffectual Roman emperor. It is probable that it was Gallo-Roman desires for stability and order which persuaded Euric to pursue an expansionist policy in the 470 s, not any supposed latent barbarian aggression. Sidonius complained loudly about the loss of Auvergne. But even he, and certainly many of his aristocratic colleagues, had accepted that the barbarians were there to stay.[88]

On the Danube

A very different picture of life in a Roman province at precisely this time comes from the *Life of St Severinus*. This was written by Eugippius, who became abbot of a monastery near Naples some 30 years after the events; but he knew Severinus – 'one of those prodigious, if unsavory, ascetics about whom medieval men love to read'[89] – and had visited him in the territory in which he spent the latter years of his life. Scholars have generally regarded this *Life* as a largely accurate reflection of life in a frontier province at the very end of the Roman Empire in the West.

Very few late Roman or early medieval saints' lives give us such a clear picture of the political world in which the saint lived. The narrative even starts with the political setting: 'At the time when Attila, king of the Huns, had died, the two Pannonias and the other districts bordering on the Danube were in a state of utter confusion.'[90] Severinus spent his active career in Noricum Ripense, whose northern border on the Danube ran from just upriver of Vienna westwards to Passau. Much of the province was in present-day Austria; most of the arable land was near the Danube itself. By the time Severinus arrived, to establish and run a monastery at Favianis, Noricum barely functioned as a Roman province. There was a small contingent of Roman soldiers at Favianis, and an even smaller one garrisoning Batavis. They were seldom paid, and when some soldiers from Batavis went south into Italy to collect their pay, they were massacred by barbarians or bandits. When the barbarian leader Hunumundus brought a few barbarians to Batavis most of the inhabitants were out gathering the harvest, and there were only 40 soldiers defending it, all of whom were killed. The towns that were able to survive did so by making agreements with barbarians, particularly with the Rugians, who lived just the other side of the Danube. The countryside lay open to the depredations of bandits and barbarians. Indeed, the only time we hear of Romans who are not living behind the shelter of their town walls, they are being enslaved by the wicked Giso, the Rugian queen. After the death of their protector Severinus in 482, and on the orders of Odoacer (who was by then king in Italy), the entire Roman population of the province was (according to Eugippius) ordered to emigrate to Italy in 488, and thus they were 'freed of a life that was daily threatened by the robbery of the barbarians'.[91] There was some continued occupation of Roman sites; but there is no evidence of the survival of Roman institutions.[92]

Life was clearly very difficult for the Romans in Noricum during Severinus's time. There were food shortages, and constant raiding by the Rugians and the Alamanni. One night the Herules came to Ioviaco unexpectedly, 'laid the town waste, took most of the people prisoners, and hanged the priest on a cross'.[93] Yet for some life went on. There was a good deal of travelling and letter-exchange with the Mediterranean world, despite the dangers. There was trade: the Rugians held weekly markets north of the Danube, and the Romans frequented those markets – crossing the frozen Danube on foot in the winter. Roman merchants in Batavis begged Severinus to try and get a trading license for them from the Rugian king (although Severinus gloomily asked them what the point was, since 'the time has come near when this town will lie abandoned like all the upper forts which have been deserted by their inhabitants').[94] In the shelter of towns, Noricans farmed, bred cattle, kept bees and cultivated fruit and vines.[95] If we are to believe Eugippius, such stability as there was resulted from Severinus's leadership and ability to create friendship. He befriended the young Odoacer, who was on his way to Italy; he befriended Flaccitheus, the king of the Rugians, and his son and successor Feva (although not Feva's wife Giso – who, apart from any possible character defects, was a fervent Arian). The Rugians demanded tribute; but in return they did apparently try to protect Noricum from other barbarian peoples, such as the Alamanni, the Herules and the Thuringians. The king of the Alamanni negotiated with Severinus through an intermediary, perhaps an interpreter, but we never hear of an interpreter being present when Severinus negotiates with Rugian kings: presumably they speak Latin. Even so, Severinus's efforts ultimately come to nothing; more and more of Noricum fell into barbarian hands, until Odoacer wiped out the Rugians, and then evacuated the Romans. 'To Eugippius, this was a happy ending,' suggests Walter Goffart, who thinks the *Life* may be a warning to those in Italy who collaborate with barbarians.[96]

This story of gradual barbarian encroachment was repeated in other frontier regions, at other points along the Upper Danube, and along the Rhine. These are the areas – as, indeed, was the whole of Roman Britain – where Latin-speakers were eventually to be replaced by Germanic-speakers, a process that must have involved the death, migration or simple domination and enslavement of the Roman population. Indeed, Noricum and the much larger Danube province immediately to the east, Pannonia, had fates that may not have been dissimilar to parts of Britain. There was considerable disruption to the structures of the Empire; there was barbarian settlement, and widespread evacuation by Romans. And there is great debate about whether and in what form Roman life might have continued. Did surviving natives actually think of themselves as Roman? Did town life survive, or was it merely life in towns (that is, scattered habitation in the empty shells of what were once towns)?[97] There is certainly archaeological evidence from Pannonia suggesting that despite the evident disruption some form of continuity with the Roman past survived into the sixth century. Most later Lombard cemeteries are within 2 km of Roman sites, particularly forts and towns; and there is archaeological and historical evidence (as in Britain) for the survival of the Church, the institution which was responsible for passing on so much of Roman civilization to the medieval world.

chapter four

THE BARBARIANS AFTER 476

The 'End of the Western Empire'

The year 476 has often been seen by historians of western Europe as a turning point in world history.[1] It was the end of the Roman Empire in the West; it was the ultimate victory of the barbarian over the Roman.

What actually happened was that Julius Nepos had been sent to be emperor in the West by Leo, the eastern emperor. Orestes, the *magister militum* (and former secretary to Attila), had refused to accept Leo's choice, and nominated a young man with the ironically suitable name of Romulus (the last emperor recalling the name of the founder of Rome). Nepos fled to Dalmatia. Orestes' barbarian troops, under their leader Odoacer, demanded that Orestes give them land in Italy; Orestes refused, and was killed, and Odoacer deposed Orestes' puppet Romulus. This was the event – or the non-event – of 476. The legitimate western emperor Julius Nepos continued to rule in Dalmatia, although with little or no authority in the West. When Julius Nepos died, in 480, Odoacer continued to administer Italy, theoretically in the name of the eastern emperor, and did not bother to appoint another western emperor. This was just a recognition of the fact that for a generation emperors had been fairly irrelevant to most people in the West.

The historian responsible for promoting 476 as a turning point seems to have been Marcellinus Comes, an Illyrian, who had gone to Constantinople in *c.* 500 to seek his fortune, and became one of Justinian's court officials.[2] He wrote a Chronicle in Latin, and there he records that the Western Empire came to an end with the death of Aetius in 454, but also that it came to an end in 476, when the empire of Augustus was dissolved by the deposition of Augustulus, as Romulus was derisively nicknamed.[3] Thanks to Marcellinus this idea eventually became firmly established in western historiography.

It was in fact perfectly easy for most people in the former Western Empire not to notice that anything had changed in 476. In Britain, the descendents of Roman leaders in Britain were still holding out against the barbarian invaders of eastern Britain. Even in the mid-sixth century we find British kings (or, as the Angles and Saxons would call them, *Welsh* kings) calling themselves by names such as Constantine and Aurelian. By 476 most of Spain had already fallen into the hands of the Visigoths, still ruling from their base in the Garonne valley of south-west Gaul, although the Sueves still clung to Gallaecia in the north-west. North Africa was controlled by the Vandals: in 476 Geiseric, who had brought them there nearly 50 years before, was still alive, just. The military power in Italy was in the hands of Odoacer.

The Burgundians

The situation in Gaul was more complex than any other part of the former Western Empire except Britain; but with Gaul we have better sources. In 476 King Euric of the Visigoths, who had already managed to extend his authority over most of south-west Gaul, took advantage of the fact that the emperor had disappeared to annex Provence in the south-east. To the north of Provence were the Burgundians. They had crossed over the Rhine in the wake of the invaders of 406 and established a kingdom in the area of Mainz. This first kingdom was destroyed by Aetius's Huns in 436, and in 442/3 the Burgundians were settled by Aetius in Sapaudia: not the later Savoy, but probably just the area between Geneva and Lyons. It was a small-scale and inauspicious beginning for a kingdom which, by the end of the fifth century, had become quite powerful. It is interesting to note how closely connected the Burgundian royalty were to the Empire in the second half of the fifth century. In the early 460s one of the members of the Burgundian royal family, Gundioc, was *magister militum* in Gaul; he was brother-in-law to Ricimer, the barbarian emperor-maker who dominated imperial politics in the West from his defeat of Emperor Avitus in 456 through to his death in 472. Gundioc's son, Gundobad, took up a position with his uncle Ricimer in Italy: he killed the Emperor Anthemius in 472 at Ricimer's behest (according to the *Gallic Chronicle of 511*), and, after Ricimer's death, persuaded Glycerius to take the imperial throne. Gundobad's brother Chilperic probably received his titles of *magister militum* and *patricius* at this point, from Glycerius himself. In 473/4 Gundobad abruptly abandoned imperial politics and returned to Gaul, probably because his father had died and the kingdom of the Burgundians was going to be divided up between his three brothers. Gundobad then stayed in Gaul, and shared power with his brothers, finally becoming sole ruler in 500. He did much to keep his kingdom together, and his legislation for the kingdom still survives. He became convinced of the truth of Catholicism, says Gregory of Tours, but decided not to announce this publicly to his Arian followers, despite pressure from his eloquent bishop Avitus, who told him, 'You are afraid of your people. Do you not realize that it is better that the people should accept your belief, rather than that you, a king, should pander to their every whim?'[4]

The evidence suggests that Gundobad (474–516) and his successor Sigismund (516–23) ruled over a kingdom in which a successful *modus vivendi* had been established between Romans and barbarians. Sidonius Apollinaris poked fun at his senatorial colleague, Syagrius, for learning the Burgundian language; but it is more significant that he calls Syagrius 'a new Solon of the Burgundians in discussing the laws'.[5] It looks as if this Gallo-Roman aristocrat was drafting legislation for the Burgundians, presumably in Latin; at the same time (in the 470s) Sidonius referred to Euric of the Visigoths as drawing up laws too, which may well be the compilation known as the *Codex Euricianus*.[6] What little of it survives in later compilations shows that it was largely a rewriting of Roman law. Everything suggests that in the two south Gallic kingdoms, those of the Visigoths and the Burgundians, new systems were being set up which were 'post-Roman' or 'sub-Roman' rather than 'barbarian' in character.

Britons and Franks in Northern Gaul

In north-west Gaul, in Armorica, the dominant force was the Britons, who had been, and still were, emigrating from southern and western Britain in order to seek more security on the Continent. Armorica changed its name as a consequence to *Britannia*, or Brittany: in the Middle Ages it became known as Lesser Britain, and its larger partner Great Britain, so that the two Britains would not be confused. The Britons in Gaul established a military presence of some importance, and the name of one of their military leaders is known: Riothamus. He had led his army against Euric at the emperor's request, and had to take refuge among the Burgundians; later he was addressed by Sidonius Apollinaris, who asked for his help in returning some slaves who have been 'enticed from [their owner] by underhand persuasions of certain Britons'.[7] Riothamus has been claimed by some as the original 'King Arthur': he certainly does seem to have been a successful military leader, like his contemporary Ambrosius Aurelianus, who was active in Britain – but there is no contemporary evidence that Arthur ever existed.[8]

To the west of the Gallic Britons (not quite Bretons, yet) were the Franks, although it is a matter for scholarly dispute how much of north-eastern

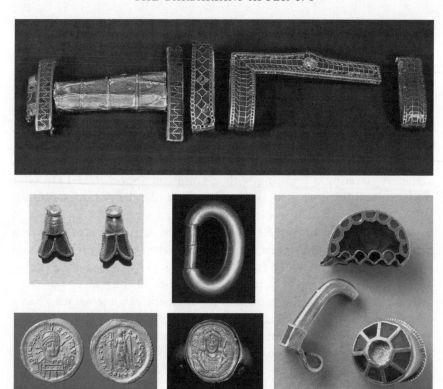

Plate 3 What survives of the items buried with King Childeric around 481 in Tournai. The seal-ring (middle bottom) is based on copies taken before most of the treasure was stolen from its home in Paris in 1831. Two of the bees (?) from the horse harness can be seen on the left. (Cabinet des Médailles, Bibliothèque Nationale, Paris).

Gaul they actually dominated by 476. We are reasonably well-informed about the Franks of the sixth century thanks to the writings of Gregory, bishop of Tours from 573 to 594. However, it is only when he himself is contemporary with the events that Gregory is really detailed; his account of how the Franks came to dominate northern Gaul is scanty, and full of problems. The first Frankish king of whom he tells us very much is Childeric, whose death was (if we are to believe Gregory on this) around 481.[9] In some ways we know more about Childeric's death than his life, in that his grave in Tournai, although excavated unscientifically in 1653, still provides us with fascinating information.

How one interprets it is a matter for individual preference, in the sense that it is remarkably ambiguous. Is it the grave of a barbarian, or a Roman official? He was buried surrounded by pits containing horses, presumably sacrificed as part of his burial ritual, as much more recent excavations have shown.[10] He was buried with all his weaponry and finery, which included a considerable amount of gold. This appeared unusual in a Roman context, but it was unusual in a Frankish context too as early as 481; it was more like some of the great princely burials of the Hunnic Empire, and indeed the gold-and-garnet decoration of his weapons and other items was also part of that international style popularized among the barbarians at the time of the Hunnic domination. But he was buried in a Roman cemetery, wearing a seal ring with a Latin inscription (CHILDERICI REGIS), and he wore a brooch on his cloak like that worn by Roman officials and generals. The earliest contemporary reference to him is in a letter written by Bishop Remigius of Reims at the time of his death to his son Clovis, noting that the latter had taken on the administration of the province of Belgica Secunda, which his *parentes* had done before him, and advising him to follow the counsel of his bishops.

It makes more sense, of course, to see Childeric as someone who had a foot in both the barbarian and the Roman worlds; and, indeed, perhaps as someone who would not make that distinction at all, as we tend to do. Perhaps he was not too different from his southern contemporary, the Burgundian Gundobad, although his own connections with imperial politics were not at such an exalted level. Gregory of Tours says little about his battles or about the fact that he was able to dominate a large territory in northern Gaul (which is implied by the *Life of St Genovefa*). He simply tells us a folk tale about Childeric being thrown out of his kingdom by his subjects because of his habit of seducing their daughters. Childeric remained in exile with King Bisinus of Thuringia (east of the Rhine), and when he returned after eight years he came back with Bisinus's wife, who bore him his son Clovis. There is one interesting element in the story, however: when Childeric went into exile 'the Franks unanimously chose as their king the same Aegidius who . . . had been sent from Rome as commander of the armies'.[11] Aegidius had been appointed by the Emperor Majorian, probably in 456/7; there is just time to fit in this notional eight-year reign over the Franks before Aegidius's death in 465. He left a son called Syagrius who, in the 480s, still seems to have been commanding a Roman army in the north: Gregory calls Syagrius *rex Romanorum*, 'king of the Romans'. What we are to make of this idea of a Roman general being elected king of the Franks is very difficult to know, but perhaps it suggests that Gregory knew of the close relations between Franks and Romans in northern Gaul at this time, or had heard of Frankish soldiers being commanded by Aegidius, and made what seemed to him a logical extrapolation.

Childeric's son Clovis is generally taken to be the 'real' founder of the Frankish dynasty later known as the Merovingians (from the semi-mythical founder of the family, Merovech). What we know of him comes very largely from Gregory of Tours, writing 70 or more years after Clovis's death in 511. Gregory gives us a very tidied up and almost certainly simplified picture, and whenever we can check a date against another source Gregory seems to be wrong. Clovis's main achievements are fairly easy to list, however (not in chronological order): the defeat of the Thuringians and the Alamans, the two main neighbours of the Franks; the destruction of the Visigothic kingdom of Toulouse; the violent removal all other Frankish kings and the establishment of his descendants as the only royal dynasty (and one that preserved the monopoly for 250 years); and the choice of Catholicism rather than Arianism as the brand of Christianity to convert to. As a reward for his defeat of the Visigoths (or perhaps for his baptism as a Catholic), the Emperor Anastasius, in Constantinople, bestowed an imperial title on him, probably an honorary consulate. Gregory depicts Clovis standing in St Martin's church in Tours, clad in his purple tunic and wearing a diadem, and then riding through the streets of Tours from St Martin's to the cathedral, showering the crowd with gold and silver coins, in consular fashion.[12]

It is often said that one of Clovis's greatest achievements was the winning of the loyalty of the Gallo-Roman majority, thanks in part to his choice of their religion, Catholicism. If Gregory is correct, on his Visigothic campaign Clovis played the religion card: he presented his campaign as a crusade against Arianism, presumably in an effort to win over the Catholic Romans of the Visigothic kingdom. Relevant here is a strange passage in Procopius, which talks about the Franks (whom he calls Germans) and their neighbours, the Arborychoi (who are presumably the Armoricans, of north-west Gaul). Through intermarriage they became one people, he says, and the Roman soldiers in Gaul joined with them.

> For even at the present day [the 550s] they are clearly recognized as belonging to the legions to which they were assigned when they served in ancient times, and they always carry their own standards when they enter battle, and always follow the custom of their fathers. And they preserve the dress of the Romans in every particular, even as regards their shoes.[13]

Some of this – like other passages relating to barbarians in Procopius – may be wholly fanciful. However, the idea that surviving Roman troops willingly incorporated themselves into the Frankish armies is perfectly plausible, and helps to account for the success of the Frankish armies through the first half of the sixth century. The Frankish kings, particularly after their conversion to Catholicism, could be seen as the natural successors of the Roman emperors. They did little to upset the spiritual monopoly of the Romans in the Church: they seem generally to have supported the rights of Roman landowners and of the Church, and their considerable military success brought much wealth into the country and almost certainly reduced the tax burden of the average Gallo-Roman.

Military success lasted for at least a generation after Clovis. Clovis was succeeded by four sons, and those four sons (under the pressure of Clotild, perhaps, the mother of the three youngest), divided the kingdom among themselves in 511.[14] Under Clovis's sons, the Frankish conquest of Gaul continued, with the incorporation of the kingdom of the Burgundians. Their armies went east, and fought the Saxons several times, although – unless this is pure propaganda, relayed by Gregory of Tours – they only did so when the Saxons refused to pay the annual tribute which they had agreed upon. It is probable that the Thuringians, Alamans and Bavarians were, initially, in a similar position as tribute payers. Frankish armies also had some success in Spain and in Italy. To understand Frankish involvement south of the Alps we need to turn to what had been happening in Italy since 476, when Odoacer had deposed Romulus and declared himself king.

The Goths in Italy

In the late 460s, the Goths who had been settled in Thrace seem to have been doing well. They were recognized federates, with an annual subsidy, and Thrace was near Constantinople, which gave them some influence there. However, the Emperor Leo was falling increasingly under the influence of Zeno, an Isaurian general (see above, p. 70), and in 471, fearing that they were going to be cut out, the Thracian Goths, under Theodoric Strabo, decided to revolt. Only two years later the Goths established in Pannonia decided to move towards Thrace: presumably Thiudimer, their main leader, wanted to share in the benefits of Theodoric Strabo's Goths. Leo came to agreements with both groups of Goths, settling Thiudimer's in Macedonia, and renewing the subsidy for Theodoric Strabo and making him *magister militum*.

In 474, Leo died; and his son-in-law Zeno became emperor. Theodoric Strabo backed a coup led by Leo's widow, and her brother Basiliscus was put on the throne. However, Zeno had his Isaurian troops, and late in 476 he won back power. He persuaded the new leader of the Pannonian Goths, Theodoric, to attack Theodoric Strabo's Thracian Goths. It soon became clear that what Zeno wanted was the two groups of Goths to wear each other out. To confound his plans, the two Theodorics agreed to a peace; and Theodoric Strabo forced Zeno to renew his title and his people's subsidy. When Theodoric Strabo was killed in a bizarre accident (his horse threw him onto a spear-rack), the other Theodoric managed to get himself accepted by most Goths as the leader of a newly united people. Zeno rewarded Theodoric with titles and a subsidy in 483.

Their alliance did not last long; by 485 Theodoric was rebelling, and moving towards Constantinople. What happened next depends on whether one believes the western sources or the eastern. Western sources give Theodoric the initiative, and say that he went to Italy to rule in his own name; eastern sources say that Zeno sent Theodoric to Italy to drive out Odoacer and to rule as Zeno's deputy.

Theodoric arrived in Italy in 489, defeating an army of Gepids who tried to bar the way. He inflicted two major defeats on Odoacer, in 489 and 490, but each time Odoacer was able to retreat to the former imperial capital of Ravenna, well defended behind its marshes and walls. Theodoric blockaded Ravenna by land and sea, and in 493 the two leaders entered negotiations. Theodoric agreed to share power with Odoacer; and shortly afterwards he (allegedly) killed Odoacer with his own sword, at a banquet, and had most of Odoacer's followers massacred.

It was not an auspicious opening to his reign, perhaps. But for the next 33 years Theodoric 'the Great' not only ruled Italy remarkably successfully, but he stamped his presence on much of the former Western Empire.[15] A contemporary wrote:

> Whatever he did was good. He so governed two races at the same time, Romans and Goths, that although he himself was of the Arian sect, he nevertheless made no assault on the Catholic religion; he gave games in the circus and the amphitheatre, so that even by the Romans he was called a Trajan or a Valentinian, whose times he took as a model; and by the Goths, because of his edict, in which he established justice, he was judged to be in all respects their best king.[16]

As Peter Heather has pointed out, Theodoric's Italy was the most 'Roman' of all barbarian states, and in his official correspondence he was suitably obsequious to the emperor in Constantinople. Yet, argues Heather, 'Theodoric's Roman-ness was a consciously adopted pose, and his deference to Constantinople a sham.'[17]

One could certainly agree that the 'Roman-ness' or *Romanitas* was consciously adopted; but it would be hard to prove that it was merely a pose. This is, of course, partly because we know about Theodoric largely from his propagandists: from the man who drafted most of his letters (Cassiodorus) and from those who minted his coins. As in the Roman

Plate 4 The so-called Senigallia Medallion, depicting the moustachioed Theodoric the Great. The reverse has the inscription 'King Theodoricus *victor gentium* [victor over foreign peoples]'. *Gentes* normally means 'barbarian peoples': it is a suggestion that Theodoric was more Roman than barbarian himself. (Sopratindenza Archeologica di Roma.)

Empire, minting a new coin-type was the easiest way to spread a political message throughout one's territory.

Romanitas as Theodoric saw it was not necessarily a quality which would have been appreciated by Zeno's successor in Constantinople, Anastasius. It seems to have involved Theodoric claiming near-parity with the emperor himself. It was in Anastasius's time (probably in 509) that Theodoric issued a gold medallion, in imperial style, depicting himself in imperial pose, holding in his left hand a globe on which stands the goddess Victoria: on the reverse is Victoria again, with the legend REX THEODERICVS VICTOR GENTIVM, 'King Theodoric, conqueror of nations'. The slogans and the imagery – all except for Theodoric's hairstyle and his very obvious moustache – are drawn directly from imperial models. Theodoric might well have said that this was devout imitation: in his letter to Anastasius of 508, which figures as number 1 in Cassiodorus's letter collection, he says that 'Our royalty is an imitation of yours, modelled on your good purpose, a copy of the only Empire.'[18] And indeed the way in which Theodoric imitated the emperor probably did much to win loyalty from the Italian elite and bring him prestige among the other barbarian kingdoms. He took care to foster good relations with the Senate in Rome (whose members were made up of the economically dominant class in Italy); he took care to have good relations with the Catholic Church as well, despite the fact that he was an Arian heretic. Catholic churchmen appealed to him to settle a disputed papal election, and they acclaimed him (in a ritual chant, repeated 30 times) at a meeting of a Roman synod in 499 whose minutes happen to have survived. They did not mention the emperor once;[19] perhaps they thought of Theodoric as, in some sense, their emperor. Theodoric himself never used an imperial title; but just one inscription survives from the Appian Way outside Rome, in which a Roman senator called him 'victor and conqueror, ever augustus, born for the good of the state, guardian of liberty and defender of the Roman name, tamer of foreign peoples'. The phrase *semper augustus* is the most obviously imperial phrase, but apart from the use of the word *rex* for Theodoric the whole inscription is indistinguishable from one established in honour of an emperor.[20]

It was only in his last years that relations with his Roman subjects deteriorated, and Theodoric's suspicions led to the execution of two senators and politicians, who also happened to be scholars of repute: Symmachus and Boethius. (The book which Boethius wrote in prison before his execution, *The Consolation of Philosophy*, was for centuries the most widely read philosophical work in the Latin West.) Not long afterwards Theodoric threw Pope John into prison too. His plans for his succession had gone awry; his far-reaching foreign policy plans had come to nothing. Had he not died in 526, he might have rescued the situation. As it was, his daughter Amalasuntha, in the name of his 10-year-old grandson Athalaric, found it difficult to hold things together after his death; and she was murdered in 535. In the following year, allegedly to avenge her murder, the Emperor Justinian launched the reconquest of Italy.

Theodoric's quasi-imperial policy is revealed above all in his foreign policy, and it is in the light of that that we should read his letter to Anastasius in 508. On the face of it, the letter is a gesture of respect. Reading between the lines (as one should in all diplomatic correspondence) one can see it as a rebuke to Anastasius. That year, in alliance with the Franks, the emperor had sent ships to attack the coasts of Italy. The emperor should not have chosen the Franks as his ally, Theodoric says; they should have chosen Theodoric himself, ruler of the one state in the West which was trying to sustain *Romanitas*. 'In so far as we follow you do we excel all other nations.'[21]

Theodoric's imperial attitude may be echoed in the language he – or his minister and secretary Cassiodorus – used when writing to other barbarian kings. He offered two clocks to Gundobad of the Burgundians, and suggested that these clocks might bring him and his people to civilization. Civilized people live ordered lives, and need clocks, but 'it is the habit of beasts to feel the hours by their bellies' hunger'.[22] It is an astonishingly arrogant gesture, but very revealing of attitudes. For Cassiodorus, at least, Theodoric had transcended his origins, and was now in a position to teach other barbarians how to leave their barbarism behind.

Theodoric's ambitions led him towards imperial territory in the direction of the Danube; he defeated the Gepids and an imperial force under Sabinianus. At this point he came into contact with one of the fascinating figures who crop up in the sources for these years: Mundo, or Mundus.[23] This man was born the son of a Gepid king on the Danube, who had died around 480 when Mundo was still young. He came under the protection of the new king, his uncle Trapstila. When Trapstila died, around 488, Mundo was either banished (as a failed claimant to the throne) or else decamped (as someone who feared elimination by the new king, his cousin). He gathered around himself a band of freebooters or brigands. They distinguished themselves in taking on the Roman army under Sabinianus, the *magister militum* in Illyricum, defeating him, in alliance with Theodoric. Mundo then joined Theodoric and served him for around 20 years. On Theodoric's death Mundo returned to his people in the Danube region, and then, in 529, offered his services to Justinian, who was trying hard to defend the frontiers against the Slavs. He became a loyal and successful Roman general, initially as *magister militum* in Illyricum (the successor of the Roman general he had helped to defeat 25 years earlier). He succeeded Belisarius as leader of the troops on the Persian frontier, and was instrumental in suppressing the Nika riots in Constantinople. He was eventually killed in Dalmatia, in the opening stages of Justinian's war against the Ostrogoths, while trying to avenge the death of his own son Mauricius in a skirmish with the Goths.

The period around 507–8 was crucial in Theodoric's foreign policy. Theodoric had set up a series of marriage alliances in the former Western Empire in order to extend his influence. He himself had married Clovis's sister (a recognition, perhaps, of the singular importance of the Franks), and he had established marriages with Burgundian, Vandal and Visigothic royalty. The marriage alliance with the Vandals was a particularly aggressive one. It followed a defeat inflicted by his troops on the Vandals in Sicily; and in about 500 Theodoric's sister went off to Carthage to marry King Thrasamund, not only with a dowry but with 'a thousand of the notable Goths as a bodyguard, who were followed by a host of attendants amounting to about five thousand fighting men'.[24]

These troops were clearly intended to do rather more than simply protect Theodoric's sister.

We are lucky that Cassiodorus began working for Theodoric in 506, and so we have the various letters of 507 and 508 which relate to a crisis point in Theodoric's foreign relations. He clearly knew that Clovis was about to attack his fellow Goth Alaric II, king of the Visigothic 'kingdom of Toulouse'. He wrote to both Clovis and Alaric, urging them to settle their trivial differences by negotiation, and he wrote to the kings of the Burgundians, Thuringians, Herules and Warni, asking them to restrain Clovis if they could.[25] In the end Theodoric sent troops in 507; but they arrived too late. Clovis destroyed Alaric's army; Alaric died on the battlefield. Theodoric's army stopped the advance of the Franks and their Burgundian allies towards the Mediterranean and supported the claims to the Visigothic kingdom of Theodoric's own nephew Amalaric. (Alaric, like the Vandal Thrasamund, had married one of Theodoric's sisters.) Amalaric was still a boy, and Theodoric ruled in his name. Theodoric now ruled a kingdom which included the whole of Italy and most of Spain, and those two territories were joined by a land-bridge under Theodoric's control: the whole Mediterranean coastline of Gaul.

It may have been that initially Theodoric hoped to retain this whole territory, and to unite it and the two branches of the Gothic people. According to Procopius, 'the Goths and Visigoths, as time went on, ruled as they were by one man and holding the same land, betrothed their children to one another and thus joined the two races in kinship'.[26] If that was his plan, it fell apart, as did much else, in the last years of his life. Opposition to Ostrogothic rule in Spain, it seems, led him to appoint a deputy in Spain, Theudis, an Ostrogoth and one of Theodoric's closest supporters. But Theudis 'went native', establishing his own power base in Spain and, a few years after Theodoric's death, he became king of the Visigoths (531–48).[27]

If Theodoric made an attempt to unite the Goths, he seems to have been uninterested in trying to integrate the Gothic and Roman populations of his kingdom. This was no doubt deliberate. It suited Theodoric to have an identified group, separate from the population at large, who could be used for administrative and military duties. It seems that there must have been a register of Goths kept centrally, since all adult male Goths received a monetary payment in return for their (potential) military service. We shall look later (p. 206) at the modern historical controversy surrounding the settlement of the Goths, but it is possible also that the Goths were given land on which to live. Their military function gave them some sense of identity, as did the fact that they continued to live under their own laws, with their own legal system. We might, of course, see this as Theodoric's attempt to preserve the centuries-old traditions of the Goths. But, as we shall see in the next chapter, it may be that actually what Theodoric was doing was trying to forge a relatively new nation together from the ethnically very diverse group of people who came with him to Italy.

One of the things that bound the Goths together was, it seems, their Arian brand of Christianity, which underlined their separateness from the Roman community. The dualism of Ostrogothic life can still be experienced, to some extent, when visiting Ravenna, main residence of late Roman emperors and Ostrogothic kings. The modern tourist can visit the church of Sant' Apollinare Nuovo, which was formerly the Arian cathedral of St Anastasia; nearby is the Arian baptistery. Towards the other side of town is the Catholic (or Neonian) baptistery, which was near the Catholic cathedral (destroyed in 1733). Each cathedral had its own attendant bishop and clergy. It is probable that the liturgy in the Arian churches was in Gothic, and that the Bible translated by Ulfila in the fourth century was used. The text of the Gothic Bible known as the Codex Argenteus (see above, p. 37) was probably copied in Ravenna, around 520. There is a papyrus document, also from Ravenna, which lists the clergy belonging to St Anastasia. Most of them had Gothic names, and four of them signed their names with the Gothic letters designed by Ulfila for his Bible.[28]

As has been noted before, some at least of Theodoric's edifice crumbled in the three or four years before his death in 526. In Burgundy Theodoric's daughter died, and her son, the heir to the Burgundian throne, was executed by the king. In 523 Thrasamund died in North Africa, and his successor Hilderic massacred the Gothic troops who had apparently been stationed in Carthage for 20 years, ever since Thrasamund's marriage to Theodoric's sister. She was imprisoned, and died in jail.

When Theodoric died, Italy went to one grandson, Athalaric, and Spain to another, Amalaric. Almost immediately the nascent unification between Ostrogoth and Visigoth was broken. Amalaric agreed a treaty with Theodoric's daughter Amalasuntha, the chief regent, in which the tribute paid by Spain to Italy was ended; the Visigothic treasure retained by the Ostrogoths was returned; and those Goths who had intermarried were allowed their choice of ethnicity and allegiance.[29] Amalaric married the daughter of Theudebert of the Franks: the first of several disastrous marriages between the Frankish and Visigothic dynasties. His ill-treatment of his wife (who refused to give up her Catholicism) led to the invasion of Spain by the Franks, and the defeat and subsequent death of Amalaric.

It is interesting to note that the first sign of crisis after Theodoric's death revolved around the control and education of the 10-year-old king Athalaric. A group of Goths claimed that educating him like a Roman (as Amalasuntha was trying to do) would unman him (see below, p. 200). Amalasuntha dealt with the situation (according to Procopius, who like most early medieval writers instinctively thought the worst of women in power) by murdering her three strongest critics. In 534, however, there was a more serious crisis: Athalaric died, and Amalasuntha (as queen-mother) lost her reason for continuing power, was imprisoned and then killed.

The Gothic Wars

The invasion of Italy, launched by the Emperor Justinian in 536, was ostensibly to avenge the death of Amalasuntha. In reality it was a natural extension of his invasion of Vandal Africa in 533, which had ended, within six months, in the reincorporation of Africa into the Roman Empire. Italy, however, was a very different proposition: the war in Italy lasted, with gaps, for precisely 25 years.

The details of the war need not concern us: they are very well known, thanks to the closeness of the historian Procopius to Belisarius, the general who launched the attack on Africa and was in command in Italy from 536–40 and from 544–8. Athalaric's successor Theodahad, the last of Theodoric's line, was murdered by some of his own men after the fall of Rome in late 536. Wittigis kept the war going until the loss of Ravenna in 540, when he was taken prisoner. The Goths were without a single leader for a while until Totila achieved predominance in 541. After Belisarius's second recall in 548, Totila went on the offensive, taking Rome early in 550, and attacking Dalmatia, Sicily and even some Greek islands. But Justinian was still able and determined to respond, and he defeated the Gothic navy in 551, and sent an army under Narses into Italy in 552. Totila was defeated and killed in battle in 552; his replacement Teias also died in battle in the same year. After that it was a question of a few lesser Gothic leaders sparking off essentially local revolts against Roman power: the last, in Venetia, was quelled in 561.

Byzantine propaganda stressed that this prolonged war was designed to free Italy from the rule of a tyrant. Some modern commentators have suggested that actually there were many Romans who supported the Goths in their stand against invasion by 'Greeks'.[30] Most Romans probably tried to maintain a low profile, particularly since support of the Goths could lead to Roman reprisals (as in Belisarius's sack of Naples) and sometimes active support of the Romans could lead to reprisals by the Goths (as in the Gothic sack of Milan, which ended, Procopius claimed, with the killing of 300,000 males and the enslavement of all the women).[31] The elites suffered greatly, as members were taken as hostages and then killed when hostilities resumed. And the general population suffered too, as any late antique or early medieval population was going to when in the way of armies on the move. It is difficult to know, however, whether the decline in the population (most obvious in the towns) was a direct result of the war, however, because during the quarter-century of warfare the first great epidemic of what has come to be called the 'Justinianic Plague' arrived in western Europe.

Procopius's description of the bubonic plague in Constantinople in 542 has become nearly as famous as Boccaccio's of the Black Death in Florence in 1348. At its height, Procopius wrote, more than ten thousand a day were dying, and the bodies were carried down to the wharfs, 'and there the corpses would be thrown upon skiffs in a heap, to be conveyed wherever it might chance'.[32] It has always been presumed to be bubonic plague, though recent work on the later Black Death has suggested this may be a wrong diagnosis.[33] Whatever its epidemiology, it spread (as in the 1340s) through the ports of the Mediterranean, and it continued to be endemic for decades. There is dispute about its impact upon late antique and early medieval society, but it would seem likely that it was a major factor in the undoubted decline of towns, a decline which may have started earlier, but which (arguably) became very obvious after the mid-sixth century.[34]

Much more controversial is the possible effect of the Event of 536.[35] Did this event happen at all, and if so, what was it: an asteroid strike, or a volcanic eruption? The argument of certain scientists, based on deep-core sampling and on tree-ring analysis, is that the Event had an effect like a nuclear winter, hiding the sun behind clouds of dust, bringing widespread crop failure and famine and, perhaps, contributing to malnutrition which could have helped make the plague of the 540s more devastating than it might otherwise have been. The problem (as far as many historians are concerned) is that the historical evidence for such a catastrophe in the Greco-Roman sources is pretty thin. There are some sources, though. Cassiodorus notes that the sun shone for the whole year so feebly that the crops had been deadly sick; both he and Procopius noted that it was like an eclipse lasting for a whole year, 'for the sun gave forth its light without brightness'.[36] Contemporaries were hardly in a position to know what the global effects of this phenomenon might be, any more than we are at present. But for Procopius, at least, it was a turning point. 'From the time when this thing happened men were free neither from war nor pestilence nor any other thing leading to death.'[37]

The long-lasting war in Italy had profound effects right across Europe. The Reconquest brought North Africa and Italy back into the Roman Empire, and no doubt gave some barbarian kingdoms the feeling that their turn might be next. Indeed, Roman troops did land in Spain in 552, and maintained a foothold in the south-east until 621.[38] It is possible that the revolt of Hermenigild against his father King Leovigild of the Visigoths in 582 was financed by Constantinople, as, apparently, was the contemporary revolt of Gundovald in southern Gaul.[39] Gundovald had actually spent a number of years in exile in Italy and Constantinople, and landed in Gaul with a large treasure, almost certainly provided from imperial coffers. In hindsight we can see that the Reconquest had probably overstretched the Empire, and we know that after the rise of Islam two or three generations later Byzantium (as we should probably call the Eastern Roman Empire from the seventh century onwards) had no spare attention for the West. But in the later seventh century an emperor briefly re-established his capital in Italy, and indeed the Persian and Islamic conquests in the seventh century inspired a flood of Greek-speakers to seek refuge in Italy. One of them – Theodore of Tarsus – even found himself, no doubt in a state of some bemusement, being sent by the Pope to became Archbishop of Canterbury, in the barbarous north (where he was a very effective organizer of the English Church for 21 years, from 669 to 690).

The war also provided opportunities for other barbarian peoples, as the Byzantines hired them in to help them against the Ostrogoths, or vice versa. The Lombards or Longobards were brought in by Narses in 552, for instance – 2,500 warriors with 300 armed retainers – although Narses soon thought it better to pay them to go away, so lawless had they been, 'setting fire to whatever buildings they chanced upon and violating by force the women who had taken refuge in the sanctuaries'.[40] The most problematical allies, however, were the Franks.

Gregory of Tours said that the Franks initially got involved in Italy because they were so angry at the murder of Amalasuntha, the daughter of Theodoric but also the granddaughter of their own great king Clovis. Clovis's sons threatened to seize Italy from the Goths if they were not paid compensation for her death, and they received 50,000 gold pieces.[41] 'Family honour' was often invoked by the Merovingians as an occasion for war; it is very difficult to know whether this was merely a cloak for other more pressing and material reasons. In 536 the Frankish kings were given Provence by Vitigis in return for their support: this gave them access to the Mediterranean, and to the tolls paid by merchants, particularly at Marseille.

Gregory of Tours in fact knew very little about Frankish involvement in Italy, although he did note that 'those regions are apparently very unhealthy'.[42] For him, invading armies usually lost to dysentery and other ailments rather than to enemy action. Gregory does not hide the basic characteristic of Frankish involvement, which was certainly stressed by the Byzantine sources: duplicity. Neither Goths nor Romans could trust Frankish promises; they were not genuinely interested in helping allies so much as in taking booty and territory for themselves. Although Alamans and Burgundians, both under Frankish authority at the time, invaded Italy in 538, it was not until 539 that King Theudebert led an army south himself, with his Alaman and Saxon allies. Procopius claimed that there were one hundred thousand altogether. The small number of cavalry, he said, grouped around the leader; the best were foot soldiers, armed with sword, shield and axe. 'Now the iron head of this weapon was thick and exceedingly sharp on both sides, while the wooden handle was very short. And they are accustomed always to throw these axes at one signal in the first charge, and thus to shatter the shields of the enemy and kill the men.' This is the famous *francisca*, a term normally applied to the type of throwing-axe commonly found in many graves in north-east Gaul from the late fifth to the mid-sixth century: so named not in any Frankish source, but in Isidore of Seville's *Etymologies* (early seventh century), where he says that this is what the Spanish called them.[43] Agathias, a Greek source, does not mention the throwing-axes, but he does talk about another typically Frankish weapon, also found in graves in north-east Gaul: the *ango*, a barbed spear, used not only to inflict severe wounds, but also to incapacitate an opponent's shield, for if the *ango* impaled the shield it could not be hacked free, as the whole upper part of the weapon was encased in iron.[44]

Gregory says that Theudebert was eventually driven back by disease, which is confirmed by Marcellinus Comes, writing in Constantinople: 'Theudebert, king of the Franks, advanced with an enormous army and devastated the whole of Liguria and Aemilia. He subjugated and looted the town of Genoa located on the shore by the Tyrrhenian Sea.'[45] According to Procopius the Goths rejoiced at the news that the Franks had arrived to help them; but as they advanced towards Pavia, being allowed to cross the Po unmolested,

> the Franks began to sacrifice the women and children of the Goths whom they found at hand and to throw their bodies into the river as the first-fruits of war. For these barbarians, although they have become Christians, preserve the greater part of their ancient religion; for they still make human sacrifices and other sacrifices of an unholy nature, and it is in connection with these that they make their prophecies.[46]

The Franks defeated the Goths, and for good measure defeated their own Roman allies as well. But all the Franks had to eat and drink were cattle and Po water; and Procopius thinks that as much as one-third of

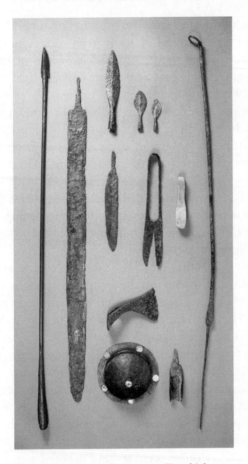

Plate 5 The equipment from a sixth-century Frankish grave at Wiesbaden-Biedrich. From left to right one can see an ango, a long-sword, a spear-head, a knife, two arrow-heads, shears, the head of a throwing-axe, a shield-boss, and a spit for roasting meat. (From *Die Franken*, fig. 568).

the Frankish army succumbed to dysentery. Belisarius advised Theudebert to retreat, and he did.

Theudebert invaded again at least twice more before his death in 548, and the Franks seem to have occupied parts of northern Italy.[47] In 552 the Romans under Valerian besieged the Goths in Verona, and the Goths thought of surrendering, but 'the Franks who were keeping guard in the towns of Venetia [. . .] tried with all eagerness to prevent it, claiming the right to take charge of the land as belonging to themselves'.[48] In the reign of Theudebert's son Theudebald, there was an invasion by a general called Buccelin, who, Gregory of Tours claims, conquered the whole of Italy, and Sicily too. Agathias provides some information about this episode, including the little detail (entirely omitted by Gregory) that Narses wiped him out in 554 at River Volturno. Almost all the Franks and Alamans were killed, with, supposedly, a loss of just 80 Romans: 'scarcely, I imagine, have past ages produced another example of such signal and overwhelming victory', said Agathias.[49]

The chaos of the Gothic wars might have died down in the 550s had the Franks not been willing to intervene and to fan the flames, but it ended for good in 561. Many of those who had been defeated in the final stages were deported to the east. There may have been a few Ostrogothic aristocrats who survived, but very few. Effectively the Ostrogoths had been wiped out. The Roman general Narses restored the Italian towns to their 'former splendour' according to one source; but there is no archaeology to support that claim.[50] And there was, basically, not enough time.

According to Paul the Deacon (whose *History of the Lombards*, although written at the end of the eighth century, is often based on earlier written sources), King Alboin led his Lombards out of Pannonia in April 568.[51] They crossed the Alps into north-east Italy, taking Friuli, and moving into Venetia, taking Vicenza and Verona, and making their way to Milan, a former imperial capital. The nearby town of Pavia (much smaller and more defensible) was the first to put up any sustained resistance. But by the time it was taken, after a three-year siege, much of the rest of northern Italy had fallen into Lombard hands. After the deaths by treachery of both Alboin and his successor Cleph, the Lombards did not choose another king, but were ruled by dukes for 10 years. Oddly, perhaps, some of these dukes seem to have devoted a good deal of energy not to consolidating their hold on the rest of Italy, but to invading Gaul. These invasions were described by Gregory of Tours in some detail, although there is no independent Italian source for the events.[52] He claims that Saxons had invaded Italy along with the Lombards, and that they joined with the Lombards in attacking south-east Gaul across the Alps. Initially they had been very successful, but then they met with an army led by a patrician newly appointed by the Frankish king Guntram (grandson of Clovis). This was Eunius Mummolus, one of the few Romans of whom we hear who had military command under the Frankish kings. His fellow Roman, Gregory of Tours, may have been exaggerating his skills, but he is portrayed as one of the most successful of the military leaders of the sixth century (though he ended his career in supporting what, from Gregory's account, appears to be the futile rebellion by the Merovingian pretender Gundovald).[53] He defeated these invaders, and forced the Saxons home (to Saxony?) and the Lombards back to Italy. 'They were all terrified by the prowess of Mummolus.'[54]

The Danube Region and the Balkans

The activities of the Franks, Visigoths and Ostrogoths in western Europe are well known to historians, and our sources are relatively good. Much less is known about what happened in the Danube region and the Balkans, even though the sixth century is perhaps even more crucial for the later history of eastern and south-eastern Europe than for western Europe. This is partly because of the relatively sudden appearance of the Slavic peoples in our written sources.

The early story of the Slavs has often been seen through the eyes of modern Slav nationalists. There has been an attempt, for instance, to contrast the brutal Germanic invasions with the slow peaceful takeover of land by the Slavs. 'Infiltration' and 'penetration' were words commonly used. But more recently it has been pointed out that Slavs seem frequently to have returned north of the Danube after their 'infiltrations', and so words like 'invasion' and 'raid' are being used more often.[55] Political considerations have also played a part in the search for the 'homeland' of the Slavs. Borkovsky suggested an origin in Bohemia, which angered the Nazi authorities in Bohemia at the time. Others – Russians and Ukrainians – identified the early Slavs with the Cherniakhov culture, or with the Kiev culture. The Polish archaeologist Józef Kostrzewski linked them with the later phases of the Przeworsk culture, which occupied roughly the area of modern Poland. In the 1950s, some Yugoslavians proposed a homeland in Pannonia.[56] Florin Curta has commented recently that 'The more radical the reaffirmation of Slavic antiquity becomes, the more writing about the history of the Slavs takes on the character of a mere description of the history of humans living since time immemorial in territories later inhabited by the Slavs.'[57]

Procopius is the first author to refer to a Slavic raid south of the Danube: it was an attack of the Antes, 'who dwell close to the Sclaveni', and probably dates to 518.[58] These two peoples are clearly closely related, and many scholars generally regard both Antes and Sclaveni as Slavic.[59] Procopius has a short ethnographic digression on them.

> These nations, the Sclavini and the Antes, are not ruled by one man but they have lived of old under a democracy, and consequently everything that involves their welfare, whether for good or for ill, is referred to the people. It is true that in all other matters, practically speaking, these two barbarian peoples have had from ancient times the same institutions and customs.

They worship one god, the god of lightning, and they sacrifice cattle to him, but they worship other spirits too. 'They live in pitiful hovels which they set up far apart from one another, but, as a general thing, every man is constantly changing his abode.' They have the same 'utterly

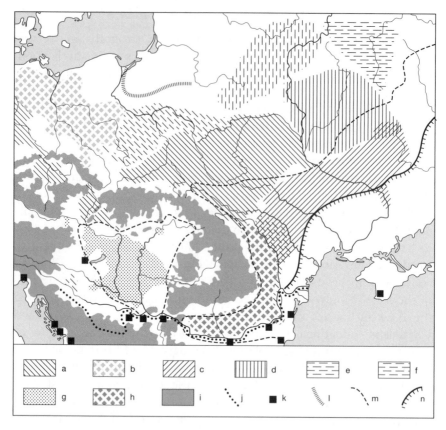

Map 6 Slav groups in the sixth century from the archaeological record. a: the Prague culture (Sclaveni). b: the Sukow–Dziedzice group (Sclaveni). c: Penkovka culture (Antes). d: Kototchin culture. e: Tuchemlya culture. f: Moschino culture. g: Avars. h: Slav sites. i: mountains. j: frontier of Roman Empire. k: important Byzsntine centres. l: south-west limits of Balts. m: northern limit of forest steppes. n: northern limit of steppes. (After Kazanski, *Slaves*, 84).

barbarous' language, and the men of both peoples are exceptionally tall, strong and hardy. They are

> at all times covered with filth; however they are in no respect base or evil-doers, but they preserve the Hunnic character in all its simplicity. . . . They hold a great amount of land; for they alone inhabit the greatest part of the northern bank of the Danube.[60]

No other Greek writer describes these Slavs in as much detail as Procopius, although his view of the state of anarchy in which they lived is corroborated by the anonymous writer known as the Pseudo-Caesarius, writing around 560: the Sclaveni were so lacking in discipline that they would kill their leaders, 'sometimes at feasts, sometimes on travels'.[61] The *Strategikon* attributed to the Emperor Maurice adds that their leaders were so much at odds with each other that it was easy to persuade or bribe them to attack each other. But he does think that they were kind and hospitable – and their women so sensitive that when their husbands died they smothered themselves . . .[62]

Procopius's second, oblique, reference to these people, is in his account of Chilbudius, *magister militum per Thraciam* between 530 and 533, who crossed the Danube (the first Roman general to do so since Valens) and attacked the barbarians there; three years later, on a similar raid, he lost his life. Thereafter, Procopius claimed, 'the river became free for the barbarians to cross all times just as they wished, and the possessions of the Romans were rendered easily accessible'.[63] In his *Secret History* – his diatribe against Justinian and Theodora, in which there is a good deal of exaggeration and invention – he elaborated:

> the Medes, Saracens, Sclaveni and Antes and other barbarians . . . omitting no season of the year, made raids in rotation, plundering and harrying absolutely everything without a moment's pause . . . No settlement, no mountain, no cave . . . remained unplundered, and many places had the misfortune to be captured more than five times.[64]

Despite Chilbudius's death, Justinian added *Anticus* to titles like *Vandalicus* and *Africanus*. He does not seem to have launched any further strikes against these barbarians; but, over the next 20 years, he did put an enormous effort into renewing and establishing fortifications in the Balkans. Later in the 530s it looks as if Justinian may have applied the usual 'divide and rule' policy to the Slavs: the Antes and the Sclavini were occupied in fighting each other. According to Procopius, one of the Antes captured by the Sclavini at this point claimed to be Chilbudius, who had not been killed in battle after all: he sustained his claim by speaking fluent Latin, which is an interesting pointer to the degree of contact the Antes had already had with the Empire at that point.[65] Even this internecine warfare, however, did not necessarily bring peace to the Romans; Procopius said that during this war the Antes attacked the Empire again and brought back many Romans as slaves.[66] In 545 the Sclavini did the same.

Thereafter the attacks by Slavs upon the Balkan provinces were almost unceasing. In 548 Sclavini reached Dyrrachium (Dürres, in modern Albania); in 549 Sclavini crossed the Danube and, splitting into two groups, attacked Thrace and Illyricum, capturing fortresses as they had never done before. For the first time they took a city: Topeiros, near Abdera. Procopius describes the atrocities in detail: they killed around 15,000 men by impaling them on stakes, or else by burning them alive in huts, and they enslaved all the women and children.[67] In 550 Sclavini crossed

the river again and attacked Thessalonica; the Roman defence was effective, so they moved west into Dalmatia, and there for the first time they
wintered within the Roman Empire, 'as if in their own land and having
no fear of the enemy'.[68] In 551 another group of Sclavini, carrying a
large amount of plunder, were found near Adrianople by a Roman army;
the Romans were annihilated, and the generals barely escaped with their
lives. The Sclavini moved towards Constantinople, where, however, they
were defeated and many of their Roman captives released.[69] At that point,
there seems to have been a lull in Slav attacks; there are no known raids
between 552 and 577. This does, however, coincide roughly with the
disappearance of Procopius as our major source, and so the apparent
lull could just be an absence of evidence. However, it would seem to
be partially confirmed by the absence of any Roman coins dating from
between 545 and 565 north of the Danube in Romania.[70] And it could
be a direct result of the huge programme of fortress building which
Justinian undertook between the 530s and the 550s, which is celebrated
by Procopius in his *On Buildings*. Procopius claimed that the emperor
built or restored over 600 forts in the Balkans.

If the building programme was successful in containing the Sclavini
for a while it could do little against a new military threat, which arrived
on the imperial frontier at this time. The Avars, like the Huns two
centuries before them, migrated from the Central Asian steppe. The
Romans became aware of them in the 550s; around 560 the Avars
settled to the north of the Danube, and presumably overwhelmed those
Slavs who were there. They attacked further westwards in the 560s, reaching the borders of the kingdoms of the Franks (and being defeated by
Clovis's grandson Sigibert). Under their ruler or *khagan* Bayan, they
defeated the Gepids on the Tisza, in alliance with King Alboin of the
Lombards,[71] and then in 568 settled in the Carpathian Basin, forcing
the Lombards to migrate from Pannonia into Italy. As Florin Curta has
noted, 'Some historians go so far as to regard that year as marking the
beginning of the Middle Ages, the East European equivalent of 476,
with Bayan conveniently replacing Odoacer as the first barbarian ruler
after the end of Antiquity.'[72]

By the end of the sixth century the Avars had gained a dominant
position in central Europe, from which they could threaten both East
and West. And by 626, it has been estimated, the Avars managed to extract
tribute from the Roman Empire in excess of 27 metric tons of gold –
and that is not counting what they gained in raiding and from the sale
of slaves.[73] They remained a significant power until Charlemagne's 796
campaign, which destroyed their capital and removed enormous quantities of booty (which, it has been argued, did much to fund the church

building and endowment that supported the so-called Carolingian Renaissance). News of it even reached Northumbria, where a monk recorded with awe that early in the campaign 15 wagons left for the West so loaded with gold, silver and silk that they each needed 4 oxen to drag them.[74] 'Not one Avar survived,' wrote the author of the earliest Russian chronicle, around 1100. 'There is to this day a proverb in Russian which runs "They perished like the Avars".'[75]

Byzantine writers are fascinated by Avar hair. John of Ephesus described them as 'an abominable people, who, from their long hair, are called Avars'.[76] Agathias described it as unkempt, dry, dirty and tied up in a knot; but Menander, describing the visits of the Avars to Constantinople in 558 and 565, writes of their hair ornaments (which have also been found in their graves), which suggests that Agathias is not actually describing them, but situating them in a hierarchy of barbarism.[77] Their hair even figures in Corippus's description of their reaction to Byzantine court ceremonial, designed to impress all but the most cynical barbarians:

> [The Avars] believed that the Roman palace was another heaven . . . But when the curtain was drawn aside and the inner part was revealed, and when the hall of the gilded building glittered and Tergazis the Avar looked up at the head of the emperor shining with the holy diadem, he lay down three times in adoration and remained fixed on the ground. The other Avars followed him in similar fear and fell on their faces, and brushed the carpets with their foreheads, and filled the spacious halls with their long hair and the imperial palace with their huge limbs.[78]

They were nomads, of course, and that immediately ranked them among the lowest. Greek writers frequently referred to them as Scythians, thus placing them in a long line of supposedly nomadic barbarians north of the Danube, like the Huns, the Goths before them, back to the Scythians of Herodotus's day. The Emperor Maurice thought them treacherous and foul: 'They prefer to prevail over their enemies not so much by force as by deceit, surprise attacks, and cutting off supplies's[79] – precisely the tactics Maurice recommended that Romans should use against barbarians . . .[80]

For a long time thereafter the history of the southern Slavs – the only Slavs to appear in our written sources until the seventh century – is bound up with that of the Avars. The first impulse of the Byzantine emperors was to use one group to rid themselves of the other. In 578 the Avars were asked to attack the Slavs on the Lower Danube frontier; they did so, very successfully, but then the Avars entered the Empire, and attacked the Romans too. After a three-year siege, Sirmium fell to the

Avars in 582. The shaky writing of one of the besieged Romans has been found on a tile: 'God Jesus Christ, save our city, smash the Avars, and protect the Romans and the one who wrote this.'[81]

In the 580s and especially the 590s there were numerous raids, which reached right into the Balkans; and in the wake of the Avars came more Slav raiders and settlers. John of Ephesus, writing in the mid-580s of the events only two or three years earlier, said that the accursed Slavs burnt and looted, and

> overcame the country and settled it freely and without fear as if it were their own, and strange to say to the present day inhabit it . . . without fear or cares, plundering, murdering, and burning, enriching themselves and robbing gold and silver, herds of horses and much weaponry, and they have learnt to conduct war better than the Romans.[82]

At times our sources refer to the Slavs as being 'ordered' by the Avar *khagan* to attack the Romans; at other times they seem to be acting independently. Certainly the Roman authorities in the later sixth century treated them as separate problems: they bribed the Avars to go away, and they tried dividing the Slavs and getting them to fight each other. The difference in tactics may have been a result of different circumstances: the Avars seem to have been a relatively united people, ruled autocratically by their *khagan*, while the Slavs consisted of much more loosely organized groups. In the early sixth century, Slavs only appear *en masse* in our sources, without apparent leaders; later in the sixth century Byzantine authors talk of the Slavs having many kings, and for the first time we hear the names of their rulers; and not long after that we hear about the names of some of their tribal groups. The author of Book II of the *Miracles of St Demetrius* talks about the Drugubites, the Sagudates, the Berzetes, Baiunites and Belegezites: all these groups lived south of the Roman frontier.[83] The name 'Antes' disappears around this time, however; in 602 the Avars attacked the Antes, and they are not heard of again.

In the early seventh century Avar raids tended to be directed against the Adriatic coast, and between 612 and 614 many towns were taken. Between 614 and 616 Avars turned their attention to Thessalonica. Over in Spain, the *Chronicle of 754* recorded that in the fourth year of the Emperor Heraclius (615), 'the Slavs seized Greece'.[84] In 626 large numbers of Slavs were involved in the joint attack by Avars and Persians on the city of Constantinople. The attack failed, and turned out to be the last major attack by the Avars on the Empire. The Persians were far more successful: they conquered Egypt and Syria in 614–17, only to lose both before the assaults of Emperor Heraclius between 622 and 627, and to lose their complete independence before the Arab onslaught of 637–41. But those cataclysmic events are outside the scope of this book.

In the first half of the seventh century the Byzantine Empire seemed to have been able to do little to hold back Slav settlement in the Balkans. Some major coastal towns on the Adriatic and the Aegean remained in Roman hands, but much of the countryside – probably already heavily depopulated by the mid-sixth century – was in Slav hands. The *Miracles of St Demetrius* give us a vivid picture of Thessalonica in the early seventh century as a Greek island within a largely Slavic world; and surviving only because of the interventions of the saint.[85] From the middle of the seventh century emperors like Constans II and Justinian II did try to restore imperial control over area they had lost, and with some success; but this policy did not so much involve trying to remove the barbarian settlers as trying to impose authority over them. By the end of the seventh century, John Fine argues, the Balkans were effectively lost to the Roman Empire: it held on only to 'most of Thrace, a few walled cities along the Dalmatian and Greek coasts, and many islands'.[86]

The chronological account of the barbarians of Europe could of course continue beyond the rough date of AD 600. There were new 'barbarian' groups to come into Europe, such as the Arabs, the Magyars, the Khazars, the Turks and the Mongols. The story of the development of the barbarian states in western Europe could continue to the fall of the Visigothic kingdom of Spain in the early eighth century, or to the re-emergence of Frankish power under the Carolingian royal family in the eighth century. But the new barbarians who invaded Europe entered at the margins and – apart from the Magyars and the Turks – did not become the founders of peoples or polities that lasted into the modern period.

chapter five

ETHNICITY, ETHNOGENESIS AND IDENTITY

Very often in the three narrative chapters that precede this, words like 'Angle' and 'Frank' have been used as if they mean something precise, even though I have at times pointed out the problems of our written sources, and the shifting meaning of ethnic labels such as these. Before looking in more detail at barbarian society, in the rest of this book, it is important to look more closely at the problem of ethnicity or identity in this period. The whole question of *ethnogenesis*, the origin of peoples, has been much discussed by scholars in recent decades, and is central to the modern view of Europe's barbarians.

The Debate

It is hardly surprising that recent debate on the origins of barbarian peoples should have been so lively. What constitutes an 'Angle' or a 'Frank' is, after all, a question very close indeed to the question of what constitutes the 'English' or the 'French', and those questions, and other national equivalents, have become, again, an important part of public debate. In the UK the useful word 'British' is often used to encompass immigrants, because of a feeling that some have that those of, say, Nigerian or Jewish parentage cannot comfortably regard themselves as 'English' or 'Welsh'; 'British' is also a reminder of the political entity 'the United Kingdom of Great Britain and Northern Ireland', which, since 1922, has attempted to keep the four main ethnicities of these islands under one flag.[1] France has no alternative to 'French', which may be one of the reasons why there has been a recent rebirth of racial politics in France, and why the French government thought it necessary to ban the 'un-French' custom of the wearing of headscarves by Muslim girls in schools. In Germany it was only in 2000 that some of the difficulties faced by immigrants who wished to acquire German citizenship were removed; before this, being German had legally been a question not of residence, but of 'blood'. Protagonists of the European ideal may once have dreamed that nationalism would ultimately lose its emotional content; but events in the former Yugoslavia and elsewhere in the last two decades have demonstrated that nationalist feelings can be as strong as ever. The question of the origins of nations therefore has acquired renewed topicality; and is bound up inextricably with the question of the nature of nations.

The academic debate about nationality has continued for a very long time. It could be agreed that nations were communities of language, custom, law and birth, but different scholars emphasized different elements. There were philologists who regarded language as a primary factor; there were anthropologists who regarded physical distinctions as more significant. Before the Second World War, racial explanations of European diversity and European history were common. Skull measurements were used to distinguish brachycephalic (broad-headed) peoples from dolichocephalic (long-headed) peoples, and these were associated with political or national groupings. For the French anthropologist Paul Topinard (a supporter of the French Republic) the dolichocephalics were the aristocracy; the brachycephalics 'constitute the laborious, sober, farsighted, peace-loving and patriotic population', and he concluded that the future belonged to them.[2] Georges Vacher de Lapouge, on the other hand, thought that the brachycephalics were born slaves, seeking out new masters when they had lost their own, 'an instinct which is common only to brachycephalics and to dogs'. He predicted chillingly in 1887 that 'in the next century people will slaughter each other by the million because of a difference of a degree or two in the cephalic index'.[3] Similar ideas can be found, for example, in the works of the English zoologist and Darwinian Sir Arthur Keith (d. 1936), and in the American scientist Madison Grant (d. 1937). In the words of Grant's *The Passing of the Great Race* (1916), 'the great lesson of the science of race is the immutability of somatological or bodily characters, with which is closely associated the immutability of psychical predispositions and impulses'.[4]

These theories, as it happens, were supported by many of the written sources from the Middle Ages, which defined peoples in terms of common descent. No one believes now, as they did in the later Middle Ages, that the Franks were descended from Francus or that the British were descended from Brutus (both of them, not coincidentally, being Trojan princes of the same rank as Aeneas, whose ancestry of the Romans was celebrated in Virgil's *Aeneid*). But in the past scholars would have seen these ideas as some unconscious recognition of a people's common ancestry. It was also generally thought that Germanic peoples emerged from the Nordic world, or, as Jordanes called it, *Scandza*, somewhere around the time of Christ's birth, 'as from a hive or races or a womb of nations'.[5] And so, from an explanation which involved the *nature* of peoples, we come to an explanation of historical process. These communities of people, tied together so strongly by biological as well as cultural bonds, had to be treated as unchanging historical entities. If, say, the Vandals originated in Scandinavia and moved to the Danube frontier and thence to Spain and Africa, there must be a wholesale movement of a people: hence the centrality in traditional German historiography of the Migrations (*Völkerwanderung*), which for many scholars gave and still gives its name to the entire period: *die Völkerwanderungszeit*, the Migration Period.

These beliefs conditioned much of the modern study of the period right up to the post-war period. The belief in the immutability of races extended to the 'sub-races': the Germanic race, for instance, was divided up into various peoples, such as the Goths and Vandals, and these too were seen as biological entities. Few doubted that someone described as a 'Vandal' in the sources was of 'German blood', whose ancestors had originated in the Nordic world. There were few worries among archaeologists about determining the ethnicity of the inhabitants of the cemeteries which were turning up in their hundreds from the mid-nineteenth century onwards. The presence of grave-goods, including items of personal dress, was enough to show that they were Germans (since, it was axiomatic, Romans did not have this type of burial practice); and the type of brooch or other surviving metal accoutrement enabled them to denote the inhabitant of the grave as 'Frankish' or 'Alamannic'. There was often the unstated assumption that a brooch-type could somehow be an ethnic indicator or badge, as if early medieval jewellery were like the regional rural costumes that were invented in the nineteenth century (like the clan-related Scottish kilts or the sometimes highly localized versions of Swedish *folkdräkt*).[6] The idea that *Tracht* – the surviving (hence largely metal) items of costume – was an ethnic indicator did, however, become an article of faith for some archaeologists, notably German archaeologists such as Hans Zeiss and Joachim Werner.[7] If a particular brooch-type was found largely in an area of known Thuringian settlement, for instance, it was assumed to be exclusively 'Thuringian', rather than simply the product of a workshop or group of related workshops that happened to operate in that area. It was assumed that different peoples had made a conscious choice to use artefacts that denoted their own ethnicity; which stemmed in part from a belief strongly held in the nineteenth century and later that one's unchanging ethnicity was the most important part of one's identity (as opposed to, say, kinship, gender, rank, profession, class and so on). Of course, even when one has moved to a position that ethnicity *is* changeable and culturally determined, one can still stay with the idea that people chose a particular brooch-type deliberately as an assertion of ethnicity. This is a position recently adopted by John Hines, for instance, in a discussion of brooch-types in the Elbe–Weser triangle, the known homeland of the Saxons.

> The coincidence of distinctive brooch-types and the particular area is itself sufficient and compelling evidence for us to read this feature of material culture as an expression of Saxon identity; . . . we can go so far as to argue that the use of this category of material for such symbolism can be interpreted as a *purposeful* assertion of a particular ethnic identity.[8]

I do not find it easy myself to see how we can say, when a woman wears a type of brooch manufactured locally, as worn by her family and neighbours, perhaps the only type of brooch readily available to her, that she is making a 'purposeful assertion' of ethnicity.

Certainly if one takes our sources at face value, it is easy to think of barbarian peoples as quite separate groups with their own traditional and (perhaps) unchanging ways of doing things. Jordanes, in his description of the battle of the Nedao in 454, wrote of

> the Goths fighting with lances, the Gepid raging with the sword, the Rugian breaking the missile in his wound, the Suevian daring on foot, the Hun with the arrow, the Alan ordering the line of battle in heavy armour, the Herul in light armour.[9]

But such descriptions are best explained in terms of classical literary commonplaces rather than observations, and they are not even consistent; Claudian describes the young Emperor Honorius as playing with Suevian bridles, which hardly corresponds to Jordanes's daring Suevian footsoldiers.[10]

What moved historians away from the position of unchanging biological ethnicity more than anything else was a strong reaction, after 1945, to anything that resembled the ideology of the Nazi party. The reaction, however, was slow to come. In 1958 Eugen Ewig published a study which demonstrated the fluidity of ethnic labels, and the importance of territoriality rather than descent for the development of ethnic identities: in other words, if someone lived in a territory called *Francia* and was ruled by *reges Francorum*, one was likely to develop a sense of being a Frank regardless of biological descent.[11] Generally regarded as more important was the publication in 1961 of Reinhard Wenskus's *Stammesbildung und Verfassung* (*Tribal Formation and Political Organization*).[12] The Germanic peoples, he said, were defined by their language, but developed their ethnic consciousness through encounters with the Celts and the Slavs, but above all with the Romans. The Romans treated the various German peoples as separate peoples, quite distinct from their own universalism, and the Germans learned from this. But the Romans, or the existence of the Roman Empire, also changed the nature of Germanic social structure, and enabled new groups or peoples to form, because of the continued existence of large-scale warfare. A successful military leader gathered a group of warriors around himself. The core of his army might be gathered together from his own people, but he might also recruit warriors from many other peoples. New peoples – with new names, or with old names but in a very different guise – would emerge from a successful military confederation, as people descended from very different backgrounds learned to identify with the new political grouping.

Wenskus did, however, cling on to aspects of the old theories, which allowed a version of the 'migration from Scandza' idea to survive. These peoples all possessed a *Traditionskern*, a 'kernel of tradition', that gave them their identity as Goths or whatever. This kernel of tradition was preserved by the leaders and elites, and presumably could in theory consist of legends and stories that went back many generations – and might contribute to the earliest written origin stories, such as those preserved in the *Getica* or *Gothic History* by Jordanes. Adherence to these tribal legends gave the tribe its identity. And then, as Thomas Noble put it, 'new peoples, in a sense, were invited to enter the story of older, or of other, peoples'.[13]

Wenskus has been cited, criticized, condemned and even occasionally read,[14] ever since publication.[15] But his former Vienna colleague, Herwig Wolfram, has become much more widely known, partly because several of his works have appeared in translation in English and other European languages. He has developed Wenskus's ideas both himself and together with a number of his research students (of whom the best known is Walter Pohl). He moves further away from the biological explanation of Germanic peoples (an idea that is still preserved implicitly in Wenskus; even Wenskus's notion of the *Stamm*, or 'tribe', has racial implications), and he is much more open to the idea that traditions can be invented rather than have, somehow, to be based on an historical truth. But he adheres to the idea that a *Traditionskern* is an essential part of a people's identity, and that this is something preserved by the elite; he even wants to allow for the possibility that the tradition of a Scandinavian origin of a people like the Goths preserves an element of truth.[16] A people cannot exist without the 'kernel of tradition'; and he suggests that the 'kernel' will come into place about a generation before the people in question emerge in the (Latin or Greek) historical sources. It is not a point that he proves; indeed, almost by definition he cannot, because we cannot know very much at all about the political life of a people before they have emerged into the (Latin or Greek) historical record.

It is with Wolfram that we see the emergence into the discussion of this period of a word borrowed from anthropology: ethnogenesis. It is a word much used subsequently, even if one might have disagreements with both its implications and its meaning. There was an exchange between Giorgio Ausenda and Ian Wood at a conference in 1995 that illustrates the problems well. Ausenda noted that both halves of the term are ambiguous. What is an *ethnos*? The words 'race', 'people', 'ethnic group', and other possible translations, are all 'ill-defined and ambiguous terms'. As for *genesis*, or origins, it implies not only that there *is* a definable beginning, but that what comes into existence has a stable reality: in other words, *genesis* implies the existence of a something which has an origin. 'It would be more correct to talk about population or group dynamics in a given period, forgetting altogether the implication of "origin".'[17] Ian Wood's response was that ethnogenesis was a useful word even if people had different ideas of its meaning: his own definition – 'studies of literary sources to see how stories of origin are developed'[18] – proves the point about people having different definitions, because it is a far narrower definition than most people adopt. Ethnogenesis for most scholars (including Wolfram) has not been about literary stories of origin, but about origins. But, as Charles Bowlus complained, 'like "the Middle Ages" and "feudalism", the noun "ethnogenesis" can be used either to convey a rigid model, a straight jacket into which data must be forced, or it can be employed so vaguely that it is totally devoid of meaning'.[19]

Jordanes and the Goths

We can better understand the controversy that still surrounds Wenskus and Wolfram if we look at a key text: the *De origine actibusque Getarum* (On the Origin and Deeds of the Getae), by Jordanes, usually called the *Getica*. The Getae are a people well known to classical writers; they are a steppe-people like the Scythians. But the word (like the word 'Scythian') is often used in late Antiquity to refer to the Goths – perhaps to imply antiquity, but also to avoid neologisms in one's Latin or Greek writing – and Jordanes's text is in fact a history of the Goths, from their origins until 551, when King Vitigis of the Ostrogoths was defeated by Justinian – when, as Jordanes puts it, 'this glorious race yielded to a more glorious prince'.[20] Jordanes was a Goth himself, as he announces at the very end – 'know that I have followed the writings of my ancestors' – but he stresses in his final paragraph that he has not invented anything to glorify those ancestors, but only repeated what he had 'read or learned from inquiry'.[21] That might give some credence to his account as a record of the Gothic *Traditionskern*. However, at the very beginning of the *Getica* he had noted that he had been urged by his friend Castalius to 'condense in my own style in this small book the twelve volumes of Senator on the origin and deeds of the Getae from olden time to the present day'.[22] But he was only allowed access to these twelve volumes for three days, by Magnus Aurelius Cassiodorus Senator's steward.

> The words I recall not, but the sense and the deeds related I think I retain entire. To this I have added fitting matters from some Greek and Latin histories. I have also put in an introduction and a conclusion, and have inserted many things of my own authorship.[23]

Much of the controversy about Jordanes – and, in a sense, about ethnogenesis itself – has revolved around this statement. Jordanes is the earliest writer of Germanic-speaking background concerned with the origins of a Germanic-speaking people. Is he actually doing no more than summarizing a Gothic history by Cassiodorus Senator? And if so, does he reproduce him accurately, or reassemble the facts to make them say something quite different from what was intended?[24] If Jordanes does no more than repeat Cassiodorus, then how well informed was Cassiodorus?

Cassiodorus was a much more important figure in the late antique world than Jordanes, and a much better-known one. He was born about 490 (possibly around the same time as Jordanes), from a reasonably wealthy southern Italian background, and he served as a senior bureaucrat for four successive Ostrogothic rulers, beginning with Theodoric the Great. Letters he wrote in the name of those rulers, and on his own behalf when Praetorian Prefect of Italy, were collected in 12 books, known as the *Variae*. When he retired from secular life into a monastery he had founded on his ancestral land, he wrote the *Institutions of Divine and Secular Learning* as a guide to his monks and, as it happened, to many future generations. He was an apologist for the Goths, and eager to make them acceptable to the Italian aristocracy of his day.

Two poles of opinion on the value of Jordanes are represented by two poles of opinion on ethnogenesis: Herwig Wolfram and Walter Goffart. For Wolfram, Jordanes represents a window into Gothic tradition, even though he assumes that when we read Jordanes we are really reading Cassiodorus; as Goffart notes, the fact that Cassiodorus had written the *Gothic History* at Theodoric's behest 'spurs Wolfram to the daring inflation that Theodoric personally dictated the Gothic past to Cassiodorus'.[25] It is certainly disturbing to find that Wolfram makes far more references to the supposed title of Cassiodorus's work (the *Origo Gothica*) than to Jordanes's *Getica*.[26] He has no high opinion of Jordanes, but at no point in his *History of the Goths* grants any discussion to the author of his most important single source.

Goffart's contribution to the debate in 1988 was quite differently posed, and that partly because of the context: he was not writing a history of the Goths, but attempting to explain the four main 'narrators of barbarian history': Jordanes, Gregory of Tours, Bede and Paul the Deacon. In each case he looked at the probable motives for writing their very different 'barbarian histories'; but in the case of Jordanes, of course, he has to try to reconstruct the motives of Cassiodorus as well, for writing a history that is (despite Wolfram's assumptions) lost. We do have a clue to Cassiodorus's motives, in the speech which King Athalaric made to the Senate in Rome: it is written by Cassiodorus himself.

> He [Cassiodorus] extended his labours even to the ancient cradle of our house, learning from his reading what the hoary recollections of our elders scarcely preserved. From the lurking place of antiquity he led out the kings of the Goths, long hidden in oblivion. He restored the Amals, along with the honour of their family, clearly proving me to be of royal stock to the seventeenth generation. . . . In consequence, as you have ever been thought noble because of your ancestors, so you shall be ruled by an ancient line of kings.[27]

His *Gothic History*, therefore, was a celebration of the antiquity of the Goths, and especially of their Amal dynasty (to which Theodoric had belonged), but it was addressed not to the Goths so much as to the Roman Senate, whose acquiescence in and support of barbarian rule was (in Cassiodorus's mind) essential for the stability of Italy and, perhaps, for their own survival. Cassiodorus does not claim he took dictation from Theodoric, but, rather, that he had found out things about the Goths from books that even the Goths had forgotten. One is reminded of the way in which the British in India were keen to show their superiority by teaching the Indians about Indian cultural and historical achievements. The Curator of the Museum at Lahore in *Kim* – based on Kipling's own father John Lockwood Kipling – is Cassiodorus's literary descendant.

Goffart argued that Jordanes's motives for producing his *Getica* were quite different. He was writing after the disaster that Cassiodorus had hoped to prevent; he was not celebrating the Goths so much as the emperor who brought them to heel. Nor, as an historian, was he likely to have been content to be a mere copyist of Cassiodorus: Goffart argues that his two-part *Romana*, a history of Rome from the beginnings to around 550, was actually quite original. It helps Goffart to his conclusion, that 'all in all, Jordanes seems to tell us that he blended one main source and a series of minor ones into a basically new work, much as he did in the *Romana*'.[28] The result was, 'with its colorful legends, glaring blunders, and vast omissions, [. . .] a carefully structured piece of literature'.[29] It deliberately demoted Theodoric into an 'authentically untrustworthy barbarian'[30] – presumably a long way from Cassiodorus's public opinion of his royal patron – and placed him in a prolonged story of Roman triumph. Goffart reminds us that it was written alongside the *Romana* – in the opening lines Jordanes tells Castalius that he was interrupting his work on Roman history to write about the Goths – and the three books together constitute an explanation of the success of the Romans and the failure of the Goths. It was designed, Goffart suggests, to comfort the Italians and to reassure them that the destruction of Gothia and restoration of Romania was in their best interests.

In short, Wolfram is prepared to accept some statements found in Cassiodorus/Jordanes as representative of Gothic oral tradition, while Goffart is inclined to doubt that genuine oral traditions ever reached the safety of a parchment page. Indeed, Goffart goes further (and, one might suggest, goes much too far) in asserting that the Germanic barbarians never had significant oral traditions at all. 'Does the distant past impinge on the Invasion Age Germans?' he asks.[31] And his answer is, not much.[32] He admits that the barbarian peoples had praise songs: Ammianus tells us at one point that when the Goths heard a Roman war cry they responded by singing the glories of their forefathers.[33] But it is more likely, Goffart says, that these Goths were remembering new heroes rather than old ones.[34] Jordanes does indeed refer to the songs of the Goths; but, as a recent study by Arne Søby Christensen of the whole Cassiodorus/Jordanes debate points out, Jordanes's description of the battle of Adrianople in 378 is clearly a narrative of a Roman defeat and not a Gothic victory, and therefore cannot be using Gothic songs for its material.[35] Peter Heather shows that Jordanes knew nothing of the important Gothic ruler Eormanric except what he found in Ammianus.[36]

These two positions held by Wolfram and Goffart do not just offer us a different perspective on our sources, they also lead directly to two different ideas of the nature of the barbarian migrations; see Chapter Eight for a discussion of this. But, from the point of view of ethnogenesis, Wolfram adheres, ultimately, to the traditional picture of the Migration Period, where peoples, or perhaps merely 'cores of tradition', migrate across Europe over a period of centuries, eventually ending up in their ultimate home, whether inside or outside the former Roman Empire. In their ultimate home they use those ancient traditions to help them construct an identity both for themselves and for all those people of different origins (other Germanic groups, Roman provincials, slaves and so on) who have tagged along. Goffart's position is that the folk memory is a short one, but that this hardly matters: in practice most of the barbarian peoples we see in our sources were born from the political entities that were, for the most part, created in the full glare of our historical sources. It was the very process of moving into the Roman Empire and being settled within the Empire, under kings, that was the process of *ethnogenesis*. Most of the peoples we see in our historical sources in this period are *new* peoples, with invented traditions.

A study by Patrick Geary on 'ethnic identity as a situational construct' has had a considerable impact on this debate. Geary noted that after the revolution in thought led by Ewig and Wenskus, scholars still shared a number of assumptions about early medieval ethnicity: that it was closely related to law and language; that everyone had a specific identity; that this should be recognizable by contemporaries (so that a person should not appear as an Alaman in one source and a Frank in another); that ethnic identity could only be changed over several generations; and that ethnic identity was a source of friction in society.[37] He suggested that none of these things were necessarily true. Ethnic identities are labels that are applied to people, or to some people, for specific political or social purposes: ethnicity 'is a code which must be deciphered in order to understand the process of social change'.[38]

Some degree of agreement has been reached, in part, through the assimilation of debates that have been happening outside this period. Historians of modern Europe have shown how tradition can be invented. Anthropologists and sociologists have done much to illustrate the shifting nature of 'ethnicity' and how 'new' ethnic groups can come into existence. Some have realized that 'ethnicity' can be a code word for 'race', and have suggested that instead we should think in terms of 'identity' rather than 'ethnicity'.

Archaeological Approaches to Ethnicity

It is worth looking at how attitudes to race and ethnicity have changed in recent years among archaeologists. The difference between the two, and the possibilities archaeology offers to ethnic studies, was clearly outlined by the prehistorian Gordon Childe back in 1935:

> Culture is a social heritage; it corresponds to a community sharing common traditions, common institutions and a common way of life. Such a group may reasonably be called a people . . . It is then a people to which the culture of an archaeologist must correspond. If ethnic be the adjective for people, we may say that prehistoric archaeology has a good hope of establishing an ethnic history of Europe, while a racial one seems hopelessly remote.[39]

There are problems with this model. There is the assumption that a 'people' does indeed have a common way of life, although one might easily imagine, for instance, an upper class which borrowed its way of life (recognizable, perhaps, archaeologically in terms of imported artefacts) from a socially or politically superior neighbour. There is the assumption that a community sharing common traditions will be a 'people'; but a 'people' is also to some extent a political construct, and politics need not necessarily pay mind to a community of shared artefact types, settlement patterns or burial practices. Childe's picture is essentially static, assuming a largely homogeneous society. Modern archaeological approaches to ethnicity regard it as 'an aspect of social organization often related to economic and political relationships, and in particular inter-group competition'; archaeological studies of ethnicity look in particular at 'the relationship between material culture and ethnic symbolism' and 'the role of ethnicity in the structuring of economic and political relationships'.[40]

In the nineteenth century both French and German excavation reports frequently gave as much prominence to the skulls found in cemeteries as to the grave-goods: they were seen as important indicators of ethnicity, and cemeteries were therefore extremely significant signposts to the presence of (mostly) Germanic invaders and/or migrants. This was put on a stronger theoretical footing by the work of Gustaf Kossinna, whose 'true greatness is perhaps not fully appreciated in this country', wrote Gordon Childe, because of 'certain nationalistic idiosyncrasies in his speculation'.[41] In fact Kossinna's *siedlungsarchäologische Methode* and Childe's cultural archaeology were not that different, except that Childe preferred to look at material assemblages rather than individual artefact types, and preferred a cultural rather than an ethnic interpretation.[42] Kossinna's ethnic approach led very easily to a political reinterpretation under the Third Reich, and his theories lay behind the work of the SS-Ahnenerbe, Himmler's archaeological storm troopers.[43] The expansion of the German world at the time of the barbarian invasions could be traced through its very direct traces in the soil.

That barbarians could be detected from the appearance of their grave-goods was an assumption, rather than a proposition to be proved, since the very existence of grave-goods was seen as something that proved their possessors to be barbarians. The most characteristic aspects of these graves seemed to settle it: if a male was buried with vessels and items of any complexity, he was usually also supplied with weapons – generally a spear and a dagger, but sometimes a bladed weapon (a long-sword or a single-edged *scramasax*), an axe or some arrows. Given the connection between the barbarians and warfare, not to mention stereotypes of violent barbarians, identification seemed certain.

The debate thus usually revolved around the question of what kind of barbarian was represented in the grave, and this was generally settled by the geographical origin of the grave-goods, itself shown by the density of finds on distribution maps. It was often forgotten, or at least not emphasized, that distribution maps do not provide a visual image of where objects were manufactured, but only the points at which those objects formed part of a burial ritual. Before the relatively recent excavation of settlement sites (which do not always provide many artefacts) distribution maps of artefact-types were in reality distribution maps of burial practices. It is hardly possible, therefore, to look at a distribution map of a particular type of brooch, as used to be done, in order to trace 'the march of the Vandals' from the Danube to Spain.[44] Indeed, nowadays such maps reveal problems.[45] 'Silver-foil brooches' (copper alloy bow-brooches with silver overlay) have more recently been associated with the Visigoths. They are to be found in the northern Meseta of Spain, where the so-called Visigothic cemeteries are located, but they are also to be found on the Middle Danube and on the Hungarian Plain, where Visigoths are not known to have ever been located, as well as on the Middle Rhine and the Upper Rhône valleys, where, historically, Visigoths also did not stray. One response would be to suggest that the archaeological evidence shows the historical evidence to be false. But it is probably simpler to assume that these particular brooches are not Gothic at all, in the sense of being used by people of only one ethnic or political group.

If one cannot with any certainty relate artefacts to specific ethnic groups, we might more safely relate specific cultural customs. In Spain, for instance, cemeteries with grave-goods (if we can so lump together non-perishable items of dress, such as brooches and buckles, with items having no connection with the body, such as glass or pottery vessels) are found almost exclusively on the inhospitable plateau of the central northern Meseta. This is a type of burial practice that is not found earlier in Spain, or elsewhere than here, but is clearly closely related to the type of burials found commonly in the northern barbarian world. So if these cemeteries do indicate where the Visigoths settled, as many archaeologists have assumed, why had this conquering military elite not chosen more desirable and profitable land? One answer might be that the Visigoths who settled in areas of more dense Roman settlement adopted Roman styles of burial, and are thus largely invisible archaeologically. But another answer may be that these cemeteries are not exclusively Visigothic at all. Most of the cemeteries were excavated a long time ago, and poorly recorded, but Gisela Ripoll López has looked exhaustively at the site of El Carpio del Tajo (in the hinterland of the main royal residence of the Visigothic kings,

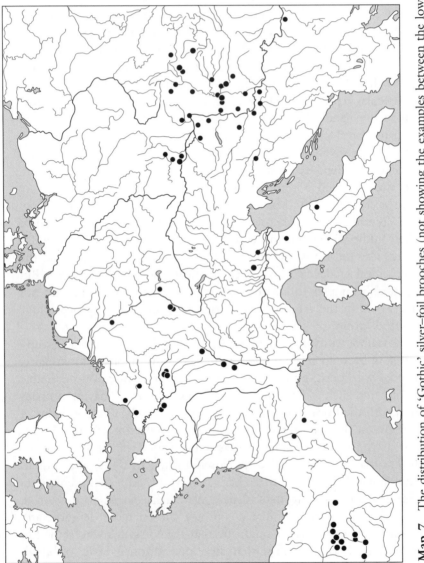

Map 7 The distribution of 'Gothic' silver-foil brooches (not showing the examples between the lower Danube and Crimea). Some of them are found in areas settled by Goths (Crimea and Spain) but others, particularly those in the Carpathian basin, are not. (After Brather, *Ethnische Interpretation*, 266).

Plate 6 The jewellery found in a grave at Vicq, near Paris. The two large silver-foil bow-brooches and the belt buckle are typically Visigothic. The two bird-brooches, however, are Frankish, and the bow-brooches were worn on the chest, in Frankish fashion, and not on the shoulders, as among the Visigoths, which suggests that these items were booty brought back from Spain by a Frankish army and worn by a Frankish woman (from *I Goti by Palazzo Reale di Milano, Electa*).

in Toledo), for which a good deal of evidence survives, and concludes that 'it was a cemetery that should be identified as representing a mixed, Visigothic and Roman, settlement site, rather than one exclusively used by Visigothic leaders and their followers, as traditional historical works would claim'.[46] On the other hand, it has recently been suggested by Andreas Schwarcz that the appearance of 'Visigothic' cemeteries in the northern Meseta of Spain in the sixth century is nothing to do with the settlement of Visigoths at all, but rather the result of the migration of much less Romanized Ostrogoths into northern Spain during the period of the Ostrogothic domination of Spain under Theodoric the Great.[47]

Probably these distribution maps are most useful when the artefacts appear as exotic in that particular region, and where there was other corroborative evidence. For instance, in the coastal area of northern France, around Boulogne and in Calvados, there are a number of cemeteries, probably from the sixth century, which contain graves with artefacts which are very similar, or identical, to those found in southern England. Some place-names in that area have close parallels among the Anglo-Saxon place-names of southern England: thus Alincthun (= Allington) and Offrethun (= Offerton) (both Pas-de-Calais).[48] Here we might suggest that the archaeology gives us some insight into the processes of migration and settlement; that we have solid evidence to back up the otherwise faintly implausible story found in Gregory of Tours's *History* that there were Saxons in the region of Bayeux, whom Queen Fredegund ordered to dress up as Bretons, with Breton haircuts, in order to support the Bretons against the Franks without letting her royal Frankish brother-in-law suspect what she had done.[49] (That anecdote is, incidentally, one of the very few written testimonies to the idea that people of a particular ethnic group might look different from another.)

There are good reasons to associate 'furnished' cemeteries with the barbarian newcomers. They are found in the areas that one would expect from the historical sources. Cemeteries like these are found predominantly in the north of Italy, for instance, in the areas where the historical sources suggest that the Ostrogothic and Lombard barbarian settlements were made. They are found in the north-east of Gaul, closest to the Frankish homeland, again in the areas in which Franks were most likely to have settled: cemeteries in other parts of Gaul which can be dated to the Frankish period are almost all deprived of grave-goods, and have usually been ascribed to the dominant Roman population (although, of course, cemeteries deprived of grave-goods have often to be dated by guesswork rather than actual evidence). The mechanisms for dating the various types of artefacts placed in graves are getting better all the time,[50] and it is fairly clear that these new methods of burial were being initiated within the former Roman Empire at around the time that barbarians arrived or established their dominance. In Gaul there seem to be relatively few furnished graves from the fifth century; it had not become the fashion at that time, which means that there is in effect no archaeological evidence at all for the presence of the Visigoths in south-west Gaul at the time of their 'kingdom of Toulouse' (418–507) and that the appearance of the Franks in the archaeological record on a large scale does not come until around the end of the reign of Clovis (d. 511).

There is some connection between the appearance of new burial customs and the appearance of barbarians on Roman soil. But there is increasing doubt about whether we can say that with every 'new style' burial we have a Germanic-speaking barbarian (nor, indeed, that when we come across a grave without grave-goods that we have discovered a Roman). To begin with, a 'new style' grave in most cases is just that: it is not the importation of a custom found in the homeland, wherever that is. East of the Rhine, the Franks did not bury their dead fully dressed. It is possible, therefore, that the new burial custom, for the Franks, is the expression of a *new* idea of what Frankishness means. That idea seems to have accompanied the idea of weapons as a status symbol.

It is certain that the end of the Roman Empire saw a rapidly increasing militarization of society.[51] This may have had very little to do with barbarians, and everything to do with the increasing insecurity of society. Under the Romans one could be a socially important civilian; in the post-Roman world churchmen were the only important civilians, and secular leaders had to be warriors, or at least had to command warriors. Even in parts of the Roman world unaffected by barbarian settlement (like Wales) secular power came to mean military power. There seems little doubt that the appearance of weapons has to do with the display of social status: hence the placing of swords and other weapons (either adult-sized, or miniaturized) in the graves of small boys. We must probably imagine that funerals were public affairs, and that the placing of particular objects in the grave had some recognizable symbolic value. Some graves are more lavish than others, particular those of mature adult males, those with a social position that might be inherited.

> . . . perhaps indicating that their funerals were important in demonstrating the heirs' right and ability to succeed to this social status. . . . [T]he conclusion is reached that burial with grave-goods represents a society where local power is open to competition, and thus somewhat unstable.[52]

There is, however, no reason to believe that those who took part in this social competition, and in this newly militarized society, were all biologically barbarian by descent. But it may mean, nevertheless, that these graves are of those who, regardless of biological descent, have adopted the ways of the new military elite, and who thus take on the identity of the people ruled by their new ruler. As I argued back in 1979, in relation to the Franks, the appearance of new well-ordered cemeteries (*Reihengräberfelder*, or row-grave cemeteries) coincided with the reorganization of disrupted Roman estates under new Frankish ownership, and new burial habits were adopted by the dependents of their new Frankish lords.

Thus the typical row-grave cemetery loses much of its importance as an indicator of the expansion of Frankish settlement within Gaul; but as a clue to the way in which the Franks extended their political and economic hold over northern Gaul it gains new significance.[53]

If we turn to the Alamans, with the excellent guidance of Sebastian Brather, we find more problems.[54] We know from Ammianus that the Alamans were living in what is now south-west Germany, particularly in the territory on the Upper Rhine and Upper Danube which had been abandoned by the Romans in the third century (see above, p. 39). It is very difficult to detect them archaeologically until the emergence of row-grave cemeteries in the late fifth century – although this is precisely the time when they were falling under the domination of Clovis's Franks. There are distinctive brooches; it is possible to say that Frankish graves have more spear-heads and axes, and the Alamans more short- and long-swords (saxes and spathas); there is more wheel-made pottery and glassware in Frankish areas (but this is a distinction that goes back to Roman times, and is to do with areas of distribution). There are no clear ethnic markers, unless one wants to argue that women's brooches are ethnic markers. There is an emergence of a clearer archaeological culture later in the later sixth and seventh century, but this is as much, Brather argues, a matter of 'communication, traffic and (after the incorporation of the region into the Merovingian kingdom) politically drawn boundaries, not an ethnic identity'.[55] Archaeological maps show connections with the Elbe region of north Germany and the Alamannic territories, but these indicate not so much migration as another cultural area, involving interactions in both directions, rather than a migrating flow from north to south. Brather concludes that although Alamans might have chosen some sort of ethnic indicator or indicators that separated them from their neighbours, such as the Franks or the Thuringians, these are not apparent to archaeologists.

> On the one hand, nearly any part of material cultural *could* have demonstrated 'ethnic identity'. And on the other, it is possible that no *material* sign was important; *habitus* and people's actions could have been the only relevant way that an *ethnos* differentiated itself from its neighbours.[56]

Archaeological cultures are created and defined by archaeologists – they represent less a reality than a convenient way of categorizing a mass of disparate material – while the cemeteries investigated by archaeologists are a location of *social* difference or distinction within the community which supplies the dead to the cemetery.

Not all archaeologists are quite so pessimistic on the issue of ethnicity as Brather, and the debate continues. Indeed, Brather's massive monograph on ethnicity in early medieval archaeology has produced furious rebuttal within the German-speaking archaeological community.[57] Heinrich Härke's work on Anglo-Saxon weapon-graves has been equally controversial. He notes that the peak of frequency is in the first half and middle of the sixth century (almost exactly the same as with the Franks). Frequency of weapon-burial has nothing to do with the frequency of warfare:

> few of the men buried with weapons in the first half of the sixth century are likely to have been involved in battles, whereas the majority of the warriors of the seventh century (let alone the eighth century) must have been interred without their arms.[58]

He notes that by no means all of those buried with weapons were warriors: they include children, men with severe osteo-arthritis, and, most convincingly, a man from Berinsfield (Oxon) with spina bifida. There are others who have sword wounds who were not buried with weapons. On the other hand, there is a clear correlation between being buried with weapons and height: in a sample of earlier graves, those with weapons were between 2 and 5 cm taller than those without. He then notes that Anglo-Saxon immigrants were on average 4 cm taller than native Romano-British: his conclusion is that those buried with weapons were 'almost entirely Germanic'.[59] This has seemed to some a controversial conclusion, but it is actually the corollary that is more interesting: that many people buried in 'Anglo-Saxon' cemeteries – those buried *without* weapons – may have been 'Romano-British' rather than 'Anglo-Saxon', at least by descent. In the future, perhaps, it might become clearer whether men with weapons are, on average, taller because of their genetic inheritance, or because of the better diet that one might expect with members of a military elite.

Some Case Studies

How are we to apply these ideas to specific peoples and to specific contexts? It would be logical to start with the Goths and, *pace* Wolfram, to ignore Jordanes. We know from Ammianus (see above, p. 45) that there were two main groups of Goths when the Huns arrived on their borders, in the 370s: the Greuthungi and the Tervingi. It used to be assumed that the Greuthungi were the group who became known as the Ostrogoths, and the Tervingi the Visigoths. But it does not seem to have been nearly as simple as that, and the words 'Ostrogoth' and 'Visigoth' are used very much less frequently in our sources than modern usage would imply. The word *Ostrogothi* appears for the first time in Claudian's poem *In Eutropium* from 399 (although in the form *Austrogothi*), and although it is subsequently used by Sidonius Apollinaris it is not actually used in contexts where we might expect it: in sixth-century Byzantine sources, for instance, or in Cassiodorus's collection of letters written in the name of the (Ostro)Gothic kings.[60] There is no evidence that any 'Ostrogoth' ever called him- or herself an Ostrogoth (although Theodoric the Great did apparently name a daughter Ostrogotho).[61] And the word *Visigoth* makes its first appearance in the title of a letter written by Cassiodorus, in Theodoric's name, to King Alaric, *Alarico regi Wisigotharum*. Presumably he wished to distinguish the Visigoths not from the *Ostro*goths, but from Theodoric's own people, the Goths. Sidonius Apollinaris, who ended his days within the 'Visigothic kingdom of Toulouse', never uses the word 'Visigoths', referring to them as 'Goths' or, more poetically, as Getae and Scythians – although he does occasionally use the word *Vesi*. It would seem, therefore, that we might think of the ethnogenesis of the Visigoths as something that occurred well after their entry into the Roman Empire. Perhaps there was an elite among the Visigoths who could trace their ancestry back to the Tervingi in their former homes north of the Danube. But there is no evidence for it, and it is quite likely that such people were outnumbered by those others who swelled the ranks of the Tervingi: members of other barbarian groups, former Roman soldiers, disaffected Roman civilians and escaped slaves. Over the course of the fifth century, one may imagine, these groups came to accept, first, the name Goth, and then the new name Visigoth: it was not until that last name was generally accepted among the Visigoths that a new people could be said to have emerged.

The ethnogenesis of other barbarian peoples took different tracks, and happened at different times, although almost invariably so obscurely, as far as our sources are concerned, as to be largely invisible. One of the problems is that of point of view. We can trace, for instance, one stage by which the Franks began to emerge as a people by looking at when the Romans stopped referring to the inhabitants of the area to the east of the Lower Rhine as Bructeri, Chamavi, Cherusci and so on, and started using the generic 'Frank'. But even though the word is of Germanic origin, we cannot assume that this is when the Chamavi themselves started thinking of themselves as Franks. It is not impossible that from the point of view of the ordinary Frank the Franks emerged as a people at the beginning of the sixth century, when Clovis destroyed the power of other Frankish kings and united the people under his rule. He was now *rex Francorum*, and those who accepted his authority could choose to call themselves Franks – or not, as the case may be. But 'tribal' consciousness may have long outlasted this Frankish ethnogenesis: Charlemagne (king of the Franks, 768–814) issued the *Lex Francorum Chamavorum*, a law-code for his Chamavian subjects.[62]

It was probably from the time of Clovis, that some of his Roman subjects (that is, mostly, the descendents of the indigenous inhabitants of Gaul) began thinking of themselves as 'Franks'. It may have been no more than a political identification at first, meaning 'subject of the Frankish kings', and no doubt identity was still also expressed, as in the Roman period, by the name of the *civitas* of birth: people were Arverni (from Auvergne) or Turonenses (from Tours). But by the seventh or eighth century, particularly in northern France, the descendants of Romans were calling themselves *Franci* without any consciousness of having been descendants of Romans at all. Even in the area of Trier – a highly Romanized area where, for instance, the custom of erecting Latin tombstones lasted for much longer than elsewhere in the north-east – those who were clearly descendants of Romans, bearing Roman names, were referred to as 'senators of the Franks' in one source.[63] A marginal note in a ninth-century manuscript of the *Liber Historiae Francorum* shows that one Frank, at least, could only imagine one way in which everyone in northern Gaul (except the Bretons) had become Frankish:

> Clovis exterminated all the Romans who then lived in Gaul, so that scarcely one could be found. And the Franks at this time are seen to have learnt the Roman language, which they still use, from those Romans who lived there. What their national language was before this is unknown in these parts.[64]

Roman processes of negotiation and alliance could help create peoples; and the Franks took over that role north of the Alps in the sixth century. The origins of the Bavarians are obscure, but the Franks do seem to have been involved. The Bavarians were first mentioned by Jordanes, and at almost the same time the Frankish king Chlothar I offered a Lombard princess (to whom he had briefly been married) in marriage to one of his followers, Garibald, duke of the Bavarians. Garibald may have been a Bavarian; he may have been a Frankish appointee over this conquered territory on the Upper Danube. The members of the ducal family, the Agilolfings, later took on near-regal trappings; and perhaps their own people considered them kings, but the Frankish remained determined to keep them in a subordinate position. The Bavarians or *Baiovarii*, were the 'people from Baiaheim', wherever that was. In all likelihood they were a 'people' assembled from very varied groups, from Sueves, perhaps from Marcomanni, Lombards, Thuringians and other barbarian groups, but also from the remnants of the Roman population of Raetia and Noricum.[65]

The way peoples get named can be almost accidental. The Saxons were a well-known and (to Romans) stereotypically barbaric people in the fourth and fifth centuries. They had been raiding the coastal areas on either side of the Channel, and the defensive system set up by the late Roman authorities was known as the *Litus Saxonicum*, 'the Saxon Shore'. When the province of Britain was overrun by Angles, Saxons and Jutes (along with others such as Frisians, Franks and perhaps even Swedes), everyone – in Ireland, Wales and the Continent – gave these newcomers the generic name 'Saxons'. The Irish for 'England' is still *Sasana*, or 'Saxony', and to the Scots the English are Sassenachs. Even in England this terminology can be found: according to the early eighth-century author of the *Life of St Wilfrid*, St Wilfrid speaks to Pope Agatho, referring to himself as a 'humble and unworthy bishop of *Saxonia*' – despite the fact that, according to Bede, the northern part of England over which Wilfrid presided as bishop of York was solidly Angle.[66]

So why do the English now refer to themselves as 'English' (*Angli*) rather than 'Saxons'? Patrick Wormald addressed this question in a characteristically brilliant way in 1983, and came to a surprising but logical conclusion.[67] When talking about all the various newcomers to Britain in his *Ecclesiastical History* Bede uses the generic *Angle* rather than *Saxon*. But he was not the first to do so: St Boniface, West Saxon missionary to Germany in the early eighth century, appealed to all God-fearing *Angli* to help convert the *Saxones* on the Continent. Both Bede and Boniface had read the works of Pope Gregory I 'the Great', who was responsible for the first missionary expedition, under St Augustine of Canterbury, to the newcomers in Britain. Gregory invariably describes the targets of his mission as *Angli*: even when writing to Æthelberht, king of the Jutes of Kent, he calls him *rex Anglorum*. Subsequently, Canterbury sources always talk of the new church as the Church of the *Angli*. In the voluminous correspondence of Pope Gregory, the earliest reference to *Angli* is to the Angle slaves which he instructs his agent to buy in Gaul. The later famous story about him personally meeting slaves in the marketplace makes it clear they are indeed Angles ('not Angles but angels'): they come from Yorkshire, indeed, from the kingdom of Deira (which Gregory vows to save *de ira Dei*, from the wrath of God).[68] Even Bede had his doubts about the veracity of this story. But if these slaves really were *Angli* it offers the explanation: Gregory falsely extrapolated from this to conclude that all those who had come to Britain were *Angli* (one of several signs of his ignorance of the state of affairs in Britain) and such was his influence that even the Saxons eventually came to accept this. Thanks to Pope Gregory's ignorance, one might say, I was born in England rather than in Saxony.

One has to add another sensible reason for the adoption of the term 'English': 'Saxon' would have caused some confusion, given the prominence of the Saxons on the Continent (the same confusion as was created by the existence of a *Britannia* in the north-west of Gaul). In an attempt to avoid this, the term 'Anglo-Saxon' was coined in the eighth century by writers on the Continent, to distinguish the insular Saxons from the Saxons of north Germany. Bede himself called these latter people the *Antiqui Saxones*, or Old Saxons.[69]

What recent studies emphasizing 'identity' rather than 'ethnicity' have suggested is that people may express their identity in different ways depending on the social context. Bede probably thought of himself as an Angle in the sense of a member of the Church of the Angles; when he came across a Saxon he may have thought of himself as an Angle in the narrower sense, or as a Northumbrian. The fact that when he uses the word *Nordanhymbri* he usually adds 'that is, those people who dwell north of the river Humber' suggests that this is a relatively new ethnic coining, emerging after the union of the kingdoms of Bernicia and Deira (the inhabitants of which must have been largely British rather than Anglo-Saxon). Of course, if he met someone from Deira he might well have thought of himself as a Bernician; and above all he might have identified himself as a Christian, loyal to Rome and its teachings. As a monk, he had (in theory) abandoned his family; but many Angles might have identified also with their kinship group, which might well be seen as the basic social unit of barbarian society.

On early English ethnicity, Bede is a dominant source; but he writes long after the complex process of migration and the establishment of new polities in England had been completed. It is interesting to compare his picture with what archaeology reveals. The Angles and the Saxons seem to have been distinct archaeologically before the migration; cremation is much more common among the Angles, for instance, and there are different brooch-types. These differences are not necessarily immediately apparent after the migration, but the contrasts in material culture between what Bede thought of as Saxon areas (Wessex, Essex and Sussex) and those that he thought of as Anglian (East Anglia, the Midlands and the north) do become more apparent in the late fifth and sixth centuries.[70] The Anglian areas show the development of a distinctive material culture, above all in female dress jewellery, involving wrist-clasps, girdle-hangers and particular types of brooch; in Saxon areas different types of brooch are developed. If we believe that ethnicity is expressed in dress, then we have new ethnicities being born in Britain, rather than the importation of ethnicities from north Germany.

Some recent studies on the Burgundians offer other perspectives on ethnicity and ethnogenesis. Ian Wood starts in the ninth century, with the complaints of Bishop Agobard of Lyons about the Burgundian lawcode he calls the *lex Gundobadi*. He objects to the practical difficulties created by people in his day being judged by the law of whichever ethnic group they claim to belong to, but also, more specifically, he detests the Burgundian law because of its use of trial by battle, which ensured not justice but the dominance of the strongest.[71] This refers to clause 45 of the Burgundian lawcode (the *Liber Constitutionum*), a clause ascribed to Gundobad, although it exists within the lawcode established by his son Sigismund in 517. Agobard's text is a prime text for the idea of the principle of the personality of the law, where the law one is judged by depends on one's ethnicity, as opposed to the modern principle of territoriality. But in the centuries before Agobard, Wood points out, there is really very little evidence of the survival of Burgundian ethnicity. There is also no agreed tradition of Burgundian ethnogenesis. In the Carolingian period the *Passio* of King Sigismund (regarded as a martyred saint because of his murder by the Franks) said that the Burgundians left Scandinavia shortly after the birth of Christ, and moved to the Rhine, where they lived in the *burgi* (fortified settlements) which gave them their name. The tradition about Scandinavia was probably added at this time (on the principle that *all* barbarians came from there), but it was accepted by many modern scholars partly because of the similarity of the Burgundian name with early forms of the name of the Baltic island of Bornholm. Wood suggests that the Burgundians of the kingdom established in south-east Gaul in the middle of the fifth century had relatively little to do with earlier Burgundians, such as the *Burgundiones* mentioned by Pliny. He notes that the two most common synonyms for *Burgundiones* in the *Liber Constitutionum* are *barbari* and *populus noster*, 'our people'. There are two legal groups: Romans and non-Romans, and all the non-Romans or barbarians are called Burgundians. Some of these were no doubt descended from those people already settled in the Rhineland in Ammianus's day, but the Burgundians had suffered considerable disruption since then, and had probably been augmented by other barbarians, such as the followers of Ricimer who joined Gundobad after Ricimer's death (see above, p. 77).

According to Paul the Deacon's *History of the Lombards*, Saxons entered Italy with the Lombards (as we know also from Gregory of Tours), but they left Italy and moved into Gaul because the king of the Lombards would not allow them to live under their own law. If Paul's information is correct, the king of the Lombards wanted to treat all barbarians in his kingdom as Lombards; it is a parallel situation to that in the Burgundian kingdom. Wood concludes that at the time of the *Liber Constitutionum* the Burgundian people were still in a process of formation or transformation. They were the non-Roman subjects of a new state. By the seventh century, however, the term 'Burgundian' seems to be used territorially, to designate all the inhabitants of the region.

More recently Patrick Amory nuanced Wood's views, without departing too far from his conclusions. He looks at the two law-codes from the Burgundian kingdom, the *Liber Constitutionum* and the *Lex Romana*. The latter never uses the words 'Burgundian' or 'Roman', while the former uses them in inconsistent and contradictory ways, although usually the *Burgundiones* are those who were settled in Roman territory under specific legal and financial conditions. *Populus noster*, on the other hand, can be used to mean 'Burgundian' (reflecting the king's own ethnicity), but was 'beginning to mean the people of the territory subject to the king and the government'.[72] When Sigismund refers to *obtimates populi nostri* (the aristocrats of our people) he is clearly referring to people of both Roman and barbarian ancestry. *Barbari* in earlier laws can be the same as *populus noster*, but in later laws means not so much 'non-Roman' as 'non-Burgundian'.

Amory subverts the traditional dichotomies Roman/barbarian or Roman/Burgundian still more in his study of names in the Burgundian kingdom. The traditional view is that the ruling classes were split 'into two ethnic groups, barbarian warriors grouped around the king, and the Gallo-Roman senators who monopolized education and the offices of the Church'.[73] All but one of the counts have Germanic names, and all but one of the bishops have Greco-Latin names, which seems to confirm the traditional view very neatly. But the German-named people that we know much about seem culturally indistinguishable from Romans. Ansemundus, the good friend and correspondent of Bishop Avitus of Vienne (who praised him for his piety), a great patron of monasteries, a devoted citizen of Vienne, which is repeatedly called 'our city' in his will, appears indistinguishable from any late Roman aristocrat; it is only his name (undoubtedly linguistically Germanic) which 'proves' his barbarian origins. The names of the counts who subscribe to the *Liber Constitutionum* are mostly solidly Germanic. Amory relates this not so much to ethnicity, as to the military nature of the office of count: the military, like the Roman aristocracy, had its own traditions and its own naming habits, and (like the aristocracy) was a hereditary caste. It is by no means certain that a military official with a Germanic name was actually of Germanic birth: indeed, the laws themselves refer to 'all counts, both Burgundian and Roman'.[74] And, to take an examples from outside Burgundy, the only military man known from the family of Gregory of

Tours, which had many connections with the Church on both his father's and mother's side, was his mother's uncle, who bore the Germanic name of Gundulf;[75] while among the Lombards the historian Paul was a cleric, and his brother, with the Lombard name of Arichis, inherited the family estates.[76] The society of the kingdom of Burgundy in the late fifth and early sixth century was, Amory concludes, a late antique society, with nothing distinctively 'barbarian' or 'Germanic' about it. 'In trying to understand the complexities of this society, the concept of an ethnic dichotomy between barbarian and Roman, or a cultural dichotomy between Latin and Germanic, can only be a hindrance.'[77]

One conclusion we might reach is that we – the tribe of European historians, the inheritors of a powerful racialist ideology, whether we like it or not – have a more black-and-white view of ethnic difference than the Romans or barbarians. For some contemporaries, it would seem, ethnic difference was not that important. Gregory of Tours, writing in Gaul in the later sixth century, rarely mentions ethnic differences, and seldom comments on the fact that one person is a Frank and another is a Roman. Normally the only time when he might make the distinction is when the person in question is exotic in a particular context: for instance, he is very specific about 'Childeric the Saxon', who is first seen active in the region of Poitiers, and was then made duke of the territory south of the Garonne (later Gascony): both of them areas where Saxons were presumably rare.[78] And he uses other words in a context that is perhaps surprising. For instance, he once uses the phrase 'the custom of barbarians', in the context of the observation of the flight of birds as an omen. But the man who is doing this has the very Roman name of Claudius, and it is clear in the context that *barbarus* here meant 'pagan' and not 'barbarian'.

Changing concepts of what was 'Roman' and what was 'barbarian' can be investigated through sixth-century writers in Constantinople too, particularly Procopius.[79] Procopius is certainly interested in the *genos*, or birth-identity, of those he writes about; though he is just as likely to pick someone out as an Egyptian, Cappadocian, Thracian or Isaurian as he is to mention their Gothic or Herule origin. And sometimes he makes clear the distinction between birth-identity and acquired-identity. Thus Sisifridus, 'though a Goth by birth (*genos*), was exceedingly loyal to the Romans and the emperor's cause';[80] while Paul, although acting as an interpreter for the Persian king, 'had been reared in Roman territory and had gone to an elementary school in Antioch, and besides was said to be by birth of Roman extraction'.[81]

By the sixth century, of course, many barbarian groups had been in the Roman Empire for a long time, and so their exact ethnicity can be in doubt, not only to us, but to contemporaries. Greatrex has singled out the case of Vitalianus. He rebelled against the *magister militum* in Thrace because he and his troops had not been paid. He made several attacks on Constantinople, and generally emerged successfully from his encounters with imperial troops. Perhaps this was because he had friends in high places; two prominent figures refused to lead troops against him. Eventually he got the title of *magister militum* in Thrace from the emperor, and indeed held the consulate in 520. His father was called Patriciolus, so one might assume that he was a Roman: Vitalianus was another good Roman name. But Vitalianus used Gothic military tactics (using wagons in defensive formations), and he named his three sons Coutzes, Bouzes and Venilus, the first two of which were Thracian or Dacian names. Was he a Roman rebel or a barbarian leader? John of Antioch, who provides the most detail about Vitalianus, calls him a tyrant, and his followers were *barbaroi*. Victor Tonnensis also called Vitalianus's soldiers *barbari*; but Marcellinus Comes said that they were Romans.

Contemporary explanations were also subtly different from those of modern historians. In modern times we have, for instance, tended to think of Justinian reconquering North Africa from the Vandals and Italy from the Ostrogoths. But for Justinian, Africa and Italy were parts of the Roman Empire which had temporarily been taken over by illegitimate rulers: tyrants. So Belisarius was not sent against the Vandals, but against the tyrant Gelimer, and he seems to have thought that some Vandals would support him.[82] Justinian was not trying to remove Vandals from the Empire; he was simply restoring legitimate government to all the people of the province, regardless of their *genos*. It was loyalty to the emperor, concludes Greatrex, that 'was the determining factor as to who was Roman and who was not in the sixth century'.[83] Conversely, one might say, it was the emperor's loyalty to his troops and his ability to pay them which determined whether or not they might continue to be regarded as Roman. In Justinian's wars in Africa and Italy, there appears to have been little or no ethnic solidarity: troops switched loyalty with bewildering ease.

There seems to have been relatively little ethnic prejudice revealed in the Greek sources in the sixth century, although a considerable amount of religious prejudice. Here ordinary people may have been more prejudiced than pragmatic emperors. In 575, the Emperor Tiberius recruited a large force of barbarians to fight on the Persian frontier, and their wives took up residence in Constantinople during the campaign. They petitioned to have an Arian church for their own use, and Tiberius was happy to refer this to the patriarch. But the people of Constantinople refused to accept this, and seem to have accused Tiberius of being an Arian for even contemplating this. Barbarians who accepted orthodox Christianity had accepted *Romanitas*, and could be treated with respect; but not those who persisted in their heresy. Greatrex quotes an inscription from the other side of the former Empire to make his point: a tombstone from Lyon, which states *germine barbarico nati, sed fonte renati*, 'born of barbarian stock, but reborn in the font'.[84]

Many scholars working in this period now accept that being a barbarian, or a Frank, or a Goth, or a Hun was not a question of belonging to a descent group which was easily identified by dress, appearance or custom. To begin with, self-identification would not necessarily result in the same label as external identification. And self-identification would not necessarily have been a matter of making an assumption based upon parents or grandparents. It may have been a result of belonging to a particular army, accepting the authority of a particular king or other ruler or even of assuming the identity of one's neighbours or associates.

chapter six

THE BARBARIANS AT HOME

In this chapter we shall look at the barbarians of Barbaricum: that is, at the barbarians before they moved into the Roman Empire, and at the very many barbarians who did not move at all. Our primary evidence here is archaeological, since (with the exception of Ireland) our written sources almost all come from within the Empire, or are centuries later, and can only be used very speculatively to try to reconstruct the barbarian society of the fifth century or earlier.

Burial and Cemeteries

Almost the only thing that all the varieties of barbarians discussed in this book have in common is that they are dead. And their deaths – or at least the aftermath of their deaths, in terms of disposed bodies, graves, funeral monuments and gravestones – are in some ways what we know best about them. It is with burials and cemeteries that barbarian archaeology began. Burials containing weapons, pottery and glass vessels and items of personal adornment (perhaps even made of precious metals) easily attracted the attention of the nineteenth-century maker of roads, canals and railways, as well as the layer of pipes or the excavator of cellars. They were dug up in their tens of thousands, and the artefacts commanded ready money from antiquaries and collectors. An early medieval settlement typically reveals few artefacts that would have been of interest to nineteenth-century antiquaries, but, more importantly, would never even be noticed in the course of public works. Only careful and relatively large-scale excavation will reveal the trace of houses and other settlement features, which often consist of no more than discolorations in the soil, the only remains of long-rotted timbers.

A cemetery can – when fully investigated and published – give us an idea of the size of the community which used it, its state of health and mortality, its links with the outside world as reflected in the artefacts buried with the dead and the particular burial practices demonstrated on the site and perhaps some idea of rank and status within the community, as well as, obviously, on its notions about appropriate burial practices. Not all barbarians disposed of their dead in such a way as can be easily investigated by archaeologists. The Irish, for instance, like indigenous peoples within Britain at this time, did not bury artefacts within the grave, making their cemeteries both difficult to identify and to date. This is true of some of the Germanic-speaking peoples as well, before their move into the Empire; the graves of the Franks in the third and fourth centuries, for instance, are very little known.

In Barbaricum most burials, whether of peoples who might be regarded as 'German' or as 'Slav', were cremations in the early period (up to the fourth century or beyond). Only in southern Scandinavia were inhumations at all common, apart from some exceptional elite burials, distinguished by the deposition of luxury Roman imports, in north Germany. Within the Roman world inhumation had slowly begun to replace cremation from the first century AD onwards, and it is possible that these elite burials were made in partial imitation of Roman burial. Most of these burials are of men, and almost none of them contained weapons (although an arrangement of three silver arrow-heads may be seen as a symbolic deposition of weapons). German archaeologists have distinguished two groups of these rich ('princely', 'royal', 'elite') burials:[1] the Lübsow type (named after a place in Polish Pomerania), from the first two centuries AD, and the Haßleben-Leuna group, named after two sites in central Germany, from the third century. Most of these graves were at some distance (over 200 km) from the Roman frontier, and they have little in common with each other, except that they are inhumations in societies where cremation was still the norm, and that they had a range of Roman artefacts, above all vessels, of glass, silver and bronze, but also coins and even furniture. As Hines has pointed out, 'the range of material ritually used in the burials – dress-accessories, weaponry and riding equipment, and special feasting utensils – places particular emphasis on a particular, prestigious, *life*-style', but he warns that we should not think of these princely graves as a 'simple, uniform phenomenon'.[2] Nevertheless, the more recent of these graves seem to share more characteristics than the older ones: Brather suggests that 'this increasing "homogeneity" may perhaps indicate a more intense communication between barbarian elites, as well as augmented connectivity and conflict with the Roman world'.[3] Even if some of these 'Roman imports' may have been made in Barbaricum (see below, p. 146), the fact remains that Roman-ness was a powerful symbol for barbarian elites, and perhaps for most barbarians.

Some of the cremation cemeteries contained several thousand graves. The ashes would usually be gathered together in an urn or some other container and placed in a pit, although there were other ways of doing it: in the east, for example, in modern Poland, there are cemeteries where there are no individual graves, but the ashes and offerings are spread over the ground and covered with a layer of soil.[4] In the individual assemblages there are often grave-goods: a pottery vessel, a piece of jewellery, a knife and traces of food-offerings. Mostly the cemeteries seem to cater for whole communities, although there are cemeteries in northern Germany which seem to be all-male or all-female, while, as in the later inhumation cemeteries, there are far fewer infants than there should be, so these are presumably disposed of elsewhere.

In the first centuries AD cemeteries might contain a few inhumations, which are often placed separately, either singly or in a small group, apart from the main cemeteries. But from around 400 there appear right across Barbaricum, from the Crimea across to France, a series of very wealthy inhumation burials, containing large amounts of gold, made into jewellery, ornaments, harness-fittings and decorations for weapons, as well as luxury Roman items. It is this which heralds the emergence of what became the characteristic cemetery form for barbarians of the Migration Period and beyond: the *Reihengräberfelder* or 'row-grave cemeteries'.

The 'gold of the barbarian princes', to use the title of an exhibition catalogue relating to these rich graves of the fifth century,[5] gives a startling impression of the wealth of the barbarians at the height of the Migration Period, as well as of the considerable degree of standardization in princely fashion across the barbarian world. It has been suggested that the Hunnic Empire was responsible for this degree of standardization: it bestrode the entire barbarian world in the middle of the fifth century, bringing most other continental barbarian peoples within its orbit. The most characteristic feature of the gold-work was its polychrome style (see below, p. 150). As an example we may take the two so-called princes' graves from Apahida (east of Cluj, Romania). The first one was found in 1889, and dates from the last quarter of the fifth century. Like the grave of Childeric at Tournai – which is near contemporary – it contained a gold cloak-brooch of the type used by Roman officials, and a Roman-style seal ring (although with a monogram rather than with a portrait and name, as with Childeric's seal-ring (see above, p. 80). It also had a gold finger-ring with a personal name on it: OMHARUS. In addition there were gold-and-garnet buckles and fittings from a horse-harness, and two silver jugs of Roman manufacture, decorated with maenads and satyrs.[6] The second prince's grave, some 500 m away from the first, was one of the most spectacular assemblages of this polychrome jewellery; it dates from slightly earlier and, because it was found in 1968, had a much better level of post-excavation survival. The prince was buried in a wooden coffin. The upper part of the grave had been disturbed by a mechanical digger, but much of it remained intact. The contents included numerous gold-and-garnet buckles, although some of the most spectacular pieces in terms of their craftsmanship, such as a pair of gold-and-garnet eagles, in fact belonged to the saddle and harness of the prince's horse. This grave too had a Roman artefact which had clearly been highly prized: part of a not very special Roman glass beaker, which had been carefully repaired with gold-leaf fixed to the glass by 17 tiny rivets.[7]

The relationship between these wealthy barbarian leaders and the Roman Empire would appear to be close, and if only we had any similar graves of Roman military leaders we might find even closer similarities. The glittering display which we can see in these high-status graves was not necessarily so unlike the way Roman generals would have shown themselves. This was the international military style of the fifth century, which may have transcended any idea of ethnicity. Some of the finds north of the Danube even seem to show that some barbarian leaders had decided, presumably consciously, to attire themselves like emperors. Four hoards or graves – those of Szilágysomlyó II (now Şimleul Silvanei) and Pietroasa (Romania), and Ostrovany and Michalovce (Slovakia) – contained items that have been called *Kaiserfibeln* (imperial brooches), large disc brooches with pendant stones or pearls, such as are worn in a depiction of the Emperor Theodosius I on a great silver dish, or by Justinian on the mosaics at San Vitale, Ravenna. In some cases, these *Kaiserfibeln* may have been imperial gifts. According to Agathias, in 522 Justin I bestowed various items of regalia on King Tzathes of the Lazi, including a 'clasp, resplendent with jewelled pendants and other kinds of ornament, with which the cloak is fastened'.[8] But, Schmauder argues, the example from the Pietroasa hoard was clearly made in a barbarian workshop, and therefore may represent an attempt by a barbarian chief to place himself, as Theoderic the Great did, not above the emperor, but at least on the same level.[9]

This generation of high-status graves in the later fifth century preceded the much wider spread of what German archaeologists have called the *Reihengräberzivilisation*, the 'row-grave civilization': that is, the culture distinguished by burial of the dead, fully dressed and with accoutrements such as weapons and vessels of various kinds, in cemeteries distinguished from the more higgledy-piggledy Mediterranean type by having the graves laid out in rows. These inhumation cemeteries are seldom as large as the largest of the cremation cemeteries, and often contain only a few hundred graves at most – which, if the cemetery lasted from the sixth through to the eighth century, would suggest a very small-scale rural settlement. Arguably, however, the row-grave custom has little to do with the 'barbarians at home', at least in its origins: it may well have originated within the Roman Empire, perhaps in cemeteries that were used by barbarians settled within the Roman Empire in return for military service.[10] I look at some of its implications on p. 210.

Central Places

Our understanding of barbarian societies has increased immeasurably in the last generation by the excavation of settlement sites of various kinds. Barbarian societies – by definition, a Roman would have said – did not have towns at this period, except when they began to live in or resettle former Roman towns. But they did have what archaeologists have called 'central places', which in some instances resemble 'proto-towns'.

On the Danish island of Funen, the sites of the Gudme complex were excavated in the 1980s and early 1990s.[11] The complex is spread out:

Figure 1 A gold bracteate from the Gudme area: the large head, raven (?) and horse (?) are typical iconographic elements. There is a brief runic inscription. (From Hedeager, 'Asgard reconstructed', 477).

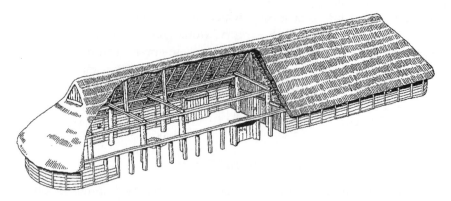

Figure 2 A reconstruction of the great hall at Gudme, the largest wooden building excavated on any barbarian site. (From Hamerow, *Early Medieval Settlements*, 13).

one could say that its various proto-urban functions were separated geographically rather than being concentrated in one place. Gudme itself is some 4 km inland; Lundeborg is an associated port; while Møllegårdsmarken was the cemetery. Gudme itself was occupied from *c.* 200 to *c.* 600 AD, and at its height consisted of some fifty small fenced farmsteads and two larger houses, one of which was a huge wooden hall, perhaps of two storeys, nearly 50 m long. In and around this settlement have been found many hoards, some containing scrap silver, scrap bronze (part of a Byzantine statue) and even some scrap gold, and some with locally made golden jewellery, necklaces and so on, as well as the enigmatic items known as 'bracteates', of which more later. The single finds included Roman coins of gold and silver and the gilded fragments of a Roman helmet. The largest of the hoards found at nearby Borholm consisted of four kilos of gold jewellery. There is enough of the debris of metal- and glassworking, including drops of melted gold, to indicate that Gudme was a production site for luxury goods. Similar evidence from Lundeborg showed that it too was a centre of production, as well as of trade. There are tools as used by carpenters, goldsmiths and blacksmiths, as well as those working with amber, bone and antler. It has been suggested that iron ingots had been imported from Poland; the finds of over 8,000 broken or unused iron rivets from ships suggest that shipbuilding and/or ship repairs took place on site. Finally there was the cemetery at Møllegårdsmarken, which was remarkable for its size (around 2,300 graves). It was predominantly a cremation cemetery. The cremation urns contain objects along with the ashes, including many Roman objects; but there are no traces of weapons.

One possibility is that Gudme was a sacred site. Several place-names in the surrounding area have names that have religious connotations; Gudbjerg ('hill of the gods'), Albjerg ('hill of the shrine') and Galbjerg (possibly 'hill of magic'). Gudme itself means 'home of the gods'. Karl Hauck, who has written extensively on the iconography of gold bracteates, suggests that the Gudme bracteates indicate that there may have been a cult of the god Odin/Woden here.[12] But it might be more significant that it seems to be an early example of the 'central places' which become more common in Scandinavia later in the early Middle Ages, including such familiar Viking-Period sites as Ribe, Kaupang, Helgö ('Holy Island'), Birka, Gamla Uppsala and others. A number of these places are similarly a few kilometres inland, with a connected port. Hedeager suggests that 'such central places served as a basis for some form of political or religious control exercised over a larger area; the radius of their influence went well beyond the site itself'.[13] As the earliest such place, however, Hedeager suggests that Gudme may have been special. She links it (tentatively, and with all due caution) to Icelandic literature of the twelfth and thirteenth centuries, which provides us with most of our earliest Scandinavian literature and our clearest ideas of pre-Christian Scandinavian religion. In this literature, smiths, especially those who work precious metals, are regarded as people with high status, as people who are at the same time close to the gods and removed from ordinary human society. In this literature too, gold appears as something of very high value, and in particular as a medium for the ritualized gift exchange which was central to the social relations, particularly perhaps at the level of the social elite. The hall at Gudme is apparently surrounded by workshops, which has seemed strange to some archaeologists; it would be the equivalent, perhaps, of siting a parliament building on an industrial estate. But Hedeager points out that this would not have seemed strange in early Scandinavian society. In Icelandic tradition, Odin's hall at Asgard, called Gladsheim, is close to the forge where his smiths worked: 'Highly skilled metalwork was not merely a craft; it was an integral part of political and religious power, and something closely linked to ideals of royal authority.'[14] In this picture of the world, Lundeborg performed an important function too. It was a portal to the world outside, through which flowed exotic goods, from the Roman world and elsewhere, which gave the elite status in the same way that gold objects did.

Similar 'central places' are known from elsewhere in the barbarian world. One example is Uppåkra, some 5 km south of Lund in southern Sweden.[15] It covered some 40 ha, with much of the site being occupied simultaneously over several centuries (the settlement layers are some 2 m thick), making it the largest known settlement in southern Scandinavia in the first centuries AD; there seems to have been continuous occupation there throughout the first millennium AD. Near the centre of the site is a wooden building of not excessive size (13 by 6.5 m) which was used over several centuries for the deposit of valuable objects, of gold, glass and other materials; around the building were further deposits, of deliberately damaged weapons and of (sacrificed?) animals. Such deposits of damaged weapons (deliberately bent swords, for instance) are known from bogs in Scandinavia,[16] but this is the first instance of such things on a settlement site, and indicates Uppåkra's importance, perhaps, and certainly suggests that this building was some kind of holy site.

Another 'central place', in a very real sense, is the Hill of Tara, in the centre of one of the five ancient provinces of Ireland, Meath, from whose modest heights (on a good day) the other four provinces can all be seen. 'Here sat in days of yore kings with golden crowns upon their heads; warriors with brazen swords in their hands; bards and minstrels with their harps; grey-bearded ollamhs; druids with their oak-leaf crowns,' enthused Oscar Wilde's father William.[17] Sadly, the idea that Tara was the seat of the high king of Ireland from prehistoric times was an invention of those from the seventh century onwards with aspirations for a unified Ireland.[18] But the Hill of Tara was clearly an important site, for burial and perhaps for religious ritual, from early days: the earliest of its 30 visible monuments is Neolithic. Later traditions suggest that some of the sites were connected with royal inauguration, or with regional meetings: the earthwork known as the Rath of the Synods (largely destroyed by the British Israelites in their search for the Ark of the Covenant)[19] was traditionally associated with meetings of the early Church. The site was used in the period covered by this book, probably sporadically rather than throughout the year, and probably mostly because of the presence of many much older monuments. This phenomenon was common throughout the barbarian world: many cemeteries and other sites seem to have been deliberately situated close to prehistoric burial mounds or other similarly visible monuments, perhaps because by doing so one laid claim to the landscape of one's ancestors.[20] Tara is thought of as a seat of kingship; but just as important in terms of its function as a central place may be its role as a cemetery. As Howard Williams has argued, cemeteries have been 'central to the ways in which world-views, identities and memories were built and maintained'.[21]

Settlements and Fortifications

The founding moment of burial archaeology in the period was the discovery of the Frankish king Childeric's grave in 1653; the comparable moment for settlement archaeology was the excavation of Ezinge, in Frisia, by A.E. Van Giffen, between 1923 and 1934. It was a *terp* or *wierde* (*Wurt* in German): 'a settlement mound made of turves and dung raised in flood-prone coastal regions'.[22] They exist in their thousands along the North Sea coast from the Netherlands to the Jutland peninsula.[23] Ezinge showed evidence of settlement from *c.* 500 BC to *c.* AD 500. Other significant excavations since the Second World War include Feddersen Wierde, a *Wurt* from Lower Saxony; Wijster, in Drenthe (Netherlands); Vorbasse (central Jutland); and, in England, Mucking (Essex) and West Heslerton (Yorks).[24]

I follow here Helena Hamerow's division of the discussion into buildings and settlement structure. The most significant of the buildings found on these rural settlements was the timber longhouse (German: *Wohnstall-haus*): normally an east–west oriented building with living quarters at the west, a central entrance hall with an entrance in the middle of each long side and space for farm animals at the east. There is a transition, happening in different regions of the north Germanic world at different times, between the longhouse, where the roof was supported by numerous internal timber posts, and the hall, where the load-bearing posts were in the wall (and from which animals seem to have been excluded). For reasons that are not entirely clear, the long sides of the hall buildings were frequently bowed, so that the centre of the hall was wider than the ends; this type emerged right across the North Sea region, from the Netherlands to southern Scandinavia, which would seem to indicate close connections within this whole area. There was much more variety (although rather less systematic excavation) elsewhere, in southern Germany or in Francia. In all these areas, however, alongside the larger buildings, is to be found what is often called the *Grubenhaus* (French: *fonds de cabane*) which has been 'anglicized' as 'grub-hut', but which is now generally known by Philip Rahtz's coinage of 'sunken-featured building' (SFB).

When SFBs were first excavated in England, by E.T. Leeds at Sutton Courtenay (Berks), they were regarded as symptomatic of the squalid living conditions of barbarians. Lethbridge and Tebbutt found some in 1933, at St Neots (Cambs):

> We have here people living in miserable huts in almost as primitive a condition as can be imagined. They had no regard for cleanliness and were content to throw the remains of a meal into the furthest corner of the hut and leave it there. They were not nervous about ghosts, since they did not mind having a skeleton sticking out of the wall of one of their huts.[25]

These buildings consisted of a hollow dug into the ground, with a roof supported by two gable-posts, four corner-posts or else a combination of those two. There is evidence of various types of walling: wattle-and-daub, planks, turf and, in France, stone; there is evidence that the bottom of the hollow was the floor in many cases, but it seems that sometimes planks made a floor on ground level, and that the above-ground structure (almost invariably lost, of course) could have been quite substantial. In most cases (despite Lethbridge and Tebbutt) the SFBs were probably not used as dwellings: loom-weights and spindle-whorls are commonly found, for instance, suggesting a use as weaving-huts; indeed, Pliny had noted that 'in Germany, the women carry on this manufacture [of linen] in caves dug underground'.[26] Tacitus had claimed that Germans used sunken buildings as crop stores, and that too has been confirmed by archaeology, as at West Heslerton in North Yorkshire.[27] The excavator there, Dominic Powlesland, believes that the presence of loom-weights, animal bones and so on were the result of them being used as rubbish pits later on, and that many of them were constructed as grain-stores, with under-floor ventilation.[28] In other cases, however, grain-stores were probably raised on stilts above ground, and traces of sturdy posts which might have supported these buildings have been found at Feddersen Wierde. SFBs that are found in Slav territories as well are similar, although mostly with one structural difference: the presence of a stone oven in one corner of the building, which indicates that here at least the buildings were used as dwellings. Whether the oven is an ethnic distinction or a regional one is unclear; both have been suggested. The oven was, however, a fairly effective means of heating these houses during winter months. Experimental archaeology at Březno near Prague has shown that the internal warmth of these buildings is increased considerably by sinking the floor below ground level. It also suggested that these houses would normally have accommodated a family of five or less, which indicates that, despite theories to the contrary, the basic social unit was the minimal family, and that the average settlement may have consisted of between 50 and 70 people.[29] But, of course, we have to be careful about assuming the house-types necessarily relate to ethnicity. Are the SFBs found in north-east Gaul in the fourth century, for instance, signs of barbarian presence, or part of the trend there, from the early fourth century, to abandon traditional Roman masonry and to build in wood?[30] The Anglo-Saxon village at West Heslerton, Powlesland believes, with its continental-style SFBs, was first settled in around 400, some time before the traditional date for the Anglo-Saxon invasions; although he thinks its inhabitants are mainly local, alongside people from elsewhere in Britain and (based on trace elements in the bones) some settlers from southern Sweden.[31]

Several decades ago, as each new excavation of a settlement revealed a new type, it could be thought that there were no generalizations to be made about the structure of settlements. Now a loose typology can be proposed:[32] we find row settlements (where farmsteads are aligned along a road or waterway); grouped settlements (where farmsteads are located around a central space or building); polyfocal settlements (where clusters of buildings are linked together to no obvious plan); perpendicular settlements (where track-ways divide farmsteads up into a roughly 'checkerboard' pattern); and single farmsteads. In practice these plans are often difficult to ascertain, even assuming very large-scale excavations. The subdivisions of settlements are not always clear, particularly

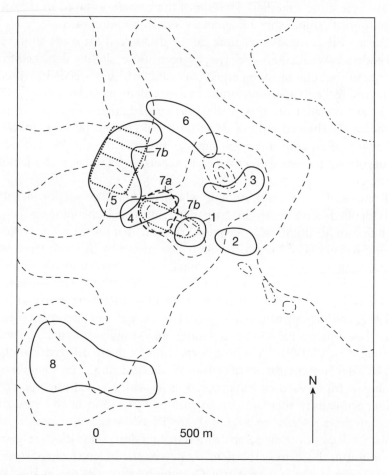

Map 8 The wandering village of Vorbasse (Jutland). Area 1: 1st century BC. Area 2: 1st century AD. Area 3: 2nd century AD. Area 4: 3rd century AD. Area 5: 4th–5th centuries AD. Area 6: 6th–7th centuries AD. Area 7a: 8th–10th centuries AD. Area 7b: 11th century AD. Area 8: the village after the 11th century. (From Hamerow, *Early Medieval Settlements*, 55).

if dividing fences cannot be located, and it is not easy to discover how many of the farmsteads would have been used at any one time. One of the features of these settlements that emerged from excavation, however, which had not been anticipated, was that the location of settlements shifted over time. This is clearest at Vorbasse, where eight separate settlement locations have been discerned over the period of the first millennium.[33] This has now been recognized as a common phenomenon, which however came to an end around the end of the first millennium AD. It may represent shifting patterns of social organization, or perhaps is related to the need to cultivate new agricultural sites, given that fields and settlements were close together. Sometimes the cemetery stayed in the same place, until the final shift of cemetery site to a churchyard.

Certain other trends over time can be discovered. At some sites, such as Feddersen Wierde and Vorbasse, a larger house, slightly detached from the rest of the settlement, emerged over time, which has been interpreted as the residence of a leading family in the settlement (a *Herrenhof*). One might extrapolate from this to suggest that barbarian society in this part of the world showed an increasing hierarchicization, perhaps linked to the ability of an elite to exploit luxury imports from the Roman world – but, of course, it is dangerous to generalize on the basis of a handful of sites.

There is also a certain amount which we know about fortifications and fortified settlements in barbarian Europe. Depending on one's definition of 'fortification', one might conclude that these were most common in Ireland. The 'ring-fort', often also known by the Irish term *ráth*, seems to have been a largely early medieval phenomenon (though this is based on a relatively limited number of excavations): an estimate of their number was made (on the basis of Ordnance Survey maps) back in 1902, and the estimate was 30,000; but more recent surveys of smaller areas (based particularly on aerial photography) suggest that the true number might be 60,000.[34] The ring-forts come in many different varieties. Mostly they are circular fortifications made of a single, or sometimes a double or triple, earthen bank, occasionally with a raised earth platform inside. Sometimes they are constructed of stone, and in this case they are sometimes referred to as *caiseal* (anglicized as *cashel*) or *cathair*; this probably does not indicate any different function, since they are generally found in those areas (particularly in western Ireland) where stone is rather more available than earth. One might also consider in the same category the monument known as a *crannóg*, which is an artificial island built in a lake or a bog. All these sites are clearly defensible, to a limited extent, but their primary function seems to have been as farms. If, as has been estimated, around 10,000 might have been in use at any one time, they clearly do not belong to a very exalted rank of person (even allowing for the presence of 150 kings at any one time in early historic Ireland). The internal arrangement of these ring-forts is sometimes, even after excavation, a matter of conjecture. It has even been suggested that in some cases the whole internal area of the ring-fort was roofed, making one large circular building.[35] It is more likely that there were a number of round or square buildings, such as have been found in some excavations; often, however, there were no substantial traces inside the walls at all.

Whether ring-forts were really fortifications is open to question. One can perhaps compare them to Irish monasteries of the first Christian centuries, which were often enclosed by a circular ditch-and-bank:[36] here it is likely that the enclosure was symbolic or legal rather than defensive in nature. Much more obviously military in nature are the walled settlements on Öland, which form one of the most remarkable archaeological landscapes of barbarian Europe.

Öland, even without its early medieval monuments, already forms a unique landscape. It is an island 137 km long, lying off the south-east Baltic coast of Sweden; although it is 16 km wide at its widest point, much of the island is considerably narrower. It was fertile land, and, although well situated to participate in coastal Baltic trade, it was also exposed to seaborne raids. It was for this reason, it seems, that a series of fortresses was built all along the island.[37] There are at least 16, and perhaps as many as 20; the earliest predate the Migration Period, and some were used right into the Viking Age, but the majority seem to have been built and occupied in the fourth and fifth centuries. They are mostly roughly circular in shape, and vary between around 40 m in diameter (Treby) to nearly 200 m (Gråborg). The stone walls were between 4 and 6 m broad, and the best preserved remains (at Gråborg and Ismantorp) show that they could have been between 4 and 6 m high, and perhaps with stone crenellations.[38] Eketorp had two broad gates and one narrow one; there are grooves cut in the walls which might indicate the presence of a portcullis, which almost certainly indicates Roman influence on the construction.[39] Ismantorp had nine gates altogether, which would seem far too many for a purely defensive site, and suggests that this and other sites might have served as central meeting places as well as occasional refuges or fortresses in times of war. On the other hand, we must not assume that defences were all of the stone type: through much of the year the gates of Eketorp could only have been reached by a shallow-draft boat, across the marsh which almost surrounded the fort.[40]

Ismantorp – one of the most impressive surviving monuments from barbarian Europe – also has the substantial remains of 88 houses inside

Plate 7 The fortified settlement of Ismantorp (Öland, Sweden) from the air, showing clearly the foundations of the 88 houses within the walls. The fortification has a diameter of around 125 metres.

the perimeter: 45 are placed so that their back end wall is formed by the fortification itself, while the rest are grouped in 4 blocks in the centre of the fortification. Eketorp seems to have held 13 farmsteads and a chieftain's hall. But the forts were not on the best agricultural land: they were peripheral, beside lakes or hidden within marsh or forest. The forts are well-spaced out along the island, with no more than 8 km between each fort in the south and centre, and no more than 18 km in the north. The largest forts are those in the centre of the island, the broadest part of the island. Everything suggests that these forts were not individual enterprises, but were built as part of a communal strategy to defend the whole island from external attack. The people who lived on Öland (the Öningi), may have been around 9,000 strong, giving a military potential of some 1,800 troops, adequate for defending the forts in Näsman's view.[41] It is perhaps at Gråborg, the largest fort, in the centre of the island and in the centre of the most fertile area, and opposite the main crossing to the mainland (by modern Kalmar), that the chieftains who organized and controlled this defensive system lived.

On the Continent, a number of significant fortifications were constructed – or reoccupied – during the fourth and fifth centuries. The best-known group of these is in the Alamannic region in south-west Germany, where there were a whole series of hill-forts just east of the Rhine frontier, apparently facing the comparable Roman fortifications.[42] Some of these seem to have been headquarters of military operations, such as Geißkopf, where the finds were almost exclusively those of military equipment. Just to the south of this, at the Zähringer Burgberg, barely 20 km from the Roman frontier-fortress of Breisach, there were large terraces and apparently extensive buildings which imply the residence of an Alamannic chief or king (there was a similar site at Runder Berg near Urach, which was very much further from the frontier).[43] All these hill-top sites showed evidence of industrial production, although most of it was military and domestic, with evidence of jewellery production only at the obviously residential sites.[44] At some sites there were scales and weights, and silver ingots, suggesting that trade was carried out there. Brather suggests that these hill-forts could have been Roman outposts east of the frontier, manned perhaps by federates, as has also been suggested for the site of Kreutzwertheim-Wettenburg, on the River Main, at some distance from the frontier, rather than fortifications designed to defend the territory against the Romans. It is perhaps even more likely that alliances between Romans and different groups of barbarians changed so frequently, that the strategic function of a particular hill fort might itself be in constant flux. But studies show that occupation on all these hill-top military sites ended around the middle of the fifth century, at precisely the same time as Roman forts in the area were abandoned: nothing can more clearly show the reciprocal relationship of the two defensive networks.

Merchants and Exchange

We might get some idea about trade contacts by looking at language. The Latin word *ganta* or 'wild goose', for instance, seems to have come from Germanic dialects; indeed, Pliny says that it did, and adds that the wild geese of Germany provided much valued down for stuffing cushions.[45] Pliny also uses the word *glaesum* to refer to 'amber', which came mostly from the Baltic region; this too seems to be a Germanic word, although later, when it provided Germanic-speakers with their word for 'glass' a new word had to be found for amber (like the modern German *Bernstein*). The Latin word *sapo* also seems to be of Germanic origin; it was a hair-dye or hair-wash imported from the Germanic world: it later designated 'soap'.

The process worked in the other direction too, of course, as did the trade. One of the most important trade-goods for the Germans was the Latin *vinum*, which was adapted to modern German *Wein* and English *wine*. Oddly enough archaeologists have found very few traces of the standard transporting vessel for wine, the amphora, and other possible vessels such as barrels or skins would not normally survive archaeologically. But the Germanic use of wine – and the Roman customs associated with wine-drinking – is strongly suggested by the discovery of Roman wine-sets: which include a scoop with a built-in sieve (to catch the lees) and vessels for mixing heavy wines with water.[46] Terms for measures were taken from the Latin: the Latin *pondo* (which faded out in favour of *libra*) gave us the English 'pound'; *uncia* provided 'ounce'. Dennis Green suggested that we may even get an idea of the level of Roman trade from the words that were borrowed. Latin *mango* gave the Germans various words for 'trade' and 'trader' (as in later English '-monger'); but in Latin it could mean something like 'deceitful huckster', but also 'slave-trader'. The Latin *caupo* also meant something like 'huckster', and also 'publican' or 'wineseller', but in the Germanic languages it came to mean something more respectable. In Old English *ceapmann* ('chapman') is a standard word for a merchant; it survives in the London street-name Cheapside.

When we look at the archaeological evidence for trade between the barbarian and Roman worlds, it is almost entirely one-way: that is, evidence of trade with Rome survives in Barbaricum but almost nothing of barbarian trade survives within the Roman world. No doubt this is partly, at least, to do with survival. Even if we found the feathers stuffing a Roman cushion (which we haven't), we would not be able to say they came from Barbaricum. What was possibly the most significant item of trade from Barbaricum to Romania in financial terms – slaves – is not going to show up archaeologically, either. We know little about the slave trade, although it is likely that it became increasingly less common in the early medieval period, above all when Christianity spread across the barbarian world and the Church had more success in persuading people that enslaving fellow Christians was wrong. By the ninth and tenth centuries, the still pagan Slavs became the great slave-suppliers, not just to the Christian world, but also to Islam (which prohibited the enslavement of Muslims or of those Jews or Christians who paid taxes to Muslims). Hence it was that the word Slav gave English (and other western languages) its word 'slave', while in Arabic too *saqlabi* or *saqaliba* (derived from the Greek *sclavenoi*), meant both 'Slav' and 'slave'.[47] Tacitus also mentions an internal fur trade within Barbaricum, although it is not clear whether this trade, so important to the northern economy in later centuries, extended into the Empire; there is no archaeological evidence.[48] The same question of invisibility applies to some of the Roman imports into Barbaricum, no doubt: food, spices and textiles will all be largely invisible.[49]

One object of trade has both archaeological and historical evidence for its existence. Tacitus said that the Aestii, on the Baltic shores, collect amber, 'and gape at the price they are paid'.[50] There are objects of amber surviving in the Roman world which is evidence of this trade (almost all European amber comes from the Baltic); but even more significant is the large number of Roman coins found around the Samland peninsula.[51]

Very little is known about the mechanisms of trade across the frontiers. One Roman trader is known, from his funerary inscription, found at Boldog in Slovakia: Quintus Atilius Primus.[52] He worked among the Quadi, north of the Danube, around the year 200. He had been an interpreter and centurion in the Roman army, and had apparently turned his skills and contacts to good effect by setting up business among the Quadi. Tacitus had referred disapprovingly to Roman merchants among the Marcomanni settling down and 'going native'.[53] Later in the second century the Marcomanni were keen to recover their right to go to markets within the Empire as part of the peace negotiation at the time of the Marcomannic Wars, which is an indication (and one of the few) of the importance of trade to the barbarians themselves. As Erdrich has shown, in the first three centuries of Empire trade with Rome, as measured in imported goods, fluctuates over time, depending on circumstances.[54]

We ought also to distinguish between distant parts of Barbaricum and those which were close to the Roman *limes*. As C.R. Whittaker has reminded us,[55] we must not think of the *limes* as a line drawn on a map, along which armoured Romans could eyeball skin-clad barbarians. The frontier was not a line: it was a zone, which stretched for some distance on both sides of the river. In particular, a river-frontier, the Rhine or the Danube, was not a barrier, but a convenient thoroughfare, particularly for the large quantity of supplies which the frontier troops needed. Such was the economic effect of the stationing of troops that a frontier zone, archaeologically, appears more prosperous and densely settled than areas further away in the Empire, and the prosperity seems to have extended beyond the frontier too. The barbarians along the frontier may have supplied grain for the frontier troops as part of their tribute to the Romans; but they may have supplied it for cash or for other goods. Sadly, the fourth-century waxed tablet found on a Dutch *terp* called Hatsum, which seems to be receipt handed over by a Roman soldier for the purchase of a cow from the Frisian farmer Stelus, is a unique find.[56] Are the Roman-style houses north of the Middle Danube the homes of Romanized barbarians, or were they Roman outposts?[57] Such was the level of permeability in some frontier zones that distinguishing between 'Roman' and 'barbarian' may not have been at all easy.[58]

Recent excavations at Haarhausen in Thuringia revealed another problem, which had hitherto not been suspected. It is likely that large quantities of apparently Roman pottery was not imported from the Empire, but made in Barbaricum. At Haarhausen three pottery kilns of Roman design were found, together with workshops and a large drying shed.[59] This pottery produced wheel-made pots of utilitarian Roman style; it has been suggested that a team of between 25 and 30 workers could have produced up to 80,000 vessels a year here. It seems to have been operational in the last 30 years of the third century, and Dušek suggests that it could have been founded, and even manned, by Romans leaving the Empire in the turmoil of the 'third-century crisis', when it is known that many potteries in the Empire ceased production. Pottery made at Haarhausen has been found on around 170 sites all across the Thuringian plain. Haarhausen and some other Thuringian sites also show the presence of larger-size Roman cattle; further evidence of 'technology transfer' between the Romans and the largely friendly Hermunduri (the precedessors of the early medieval Thuringians). It has been suggested that the wheel-made pottery of the Sîntana de Mureş culture, north of the Danube, associated with the Goths, was similarly made by Romans, perhaps prisoners-of-war; there is even one pot with a Greek inscription on it. But the balance of opinion seems to be that in that part of the barbarian world, that kind of pottery was purely indigenous;[60] although some examples from southern Romania may be evidence for the survival of a Romanized population in the former Roman province of Dacia.[61] But there are other signs of Roman innovation north of Danube. Along the coast of the Black Sea, right up to the Dnieper, are fourth-century sites with stone-built buildings. At Sobari, more than 400 km away from the frontier, archaeologists found a porticoed house, with roof tiles and glass windows, and imported objects in one of its rooms.[62]

The one area of trade and technology transfer which the Roman authorities did try and control was that which concerned war supplies, which included not just weapons, but also grain, oil and iron. Selling arms to barbarians was to be regarded as an act of treason, punishable by death.[63] The most explicit law on this was issued by Marcian in 456; a century later it was still being enforced.[64] On the other hand, there is plenty of archaeological evidence the Roman weapons *did* reach barbarians, although perhaps not through trade. Roman swords are found throughout Barbaricum, and in considerable quantity in ritual weapon-deposits in Denmark, such as Illerup Ådal.[65] One fascinating text throws additional light on Roman fears. In 419, Asclepiades, bishop of Chersonesus, petitioned the emperor on behalf of people accused of passing on boat-building techniques to barbarians; Theodosius II pardoned them, but decreed capital punishment in future cases of this kind. Chersonesus is at the southernmost tip of the Crimea, 500 km from Constantinople on the other side of the Black Sea; this text is our only evidence that it was regarded as part of the Roman Empire at this time, but it also suggests that the inhabitants of this town were in close relations with the various barbarian groups who lived in the surrounding countryside (Goths, Alans and others).[66]

What survives of Roman manufacture in Barbaricum shows that the extent of trade must have been considerable. Bronze vessels of all kinds, manufactured in Gaul or the Danube provinces, have been found in large numbers. Glassware, also in large quantities, reached as far as Sweden. Distribution maps of finds show that glasses decorated with cut facets arrived even in Sweden from the Black Sea area, via Poland, in the fourth and fifth centuries; other types of glass reached Sweden (and England) from the Rhineland in the later fifth and sixth centuries. From the mid-sixth century there are finds of claw-beakers, made in the Rhineland or possibly in Anglo-Saxon England, which are found in Scandinavia. One has to be careful in suggesting that imports of glassware began or stopped at particular periods, because until fairly recently the distribution maps were made up largely from finds in graves, and thus survival depended on burial fashion rather than actual level of importation. Increasingly, small fragments of imported glass are being found on settlement sites in Scandinavia, even in places and at times when they are not found in graves, which suggests that the importation of glass from the Roman world was fairly continuous.[67]

Silver vessels represent the most costly items found within Barbaricum: they are generally found as single items in the most richly furnished graves, like those of the Lübsow group from the early Imperial Period. The finest silver plate of all was found in a hoard of around 70 silver items, at Hildesheim: it seems to consist not of a set, manufactured at the same time, but a collection of items received over a series of dates from the late first century BC to the mid- to late first century AD.[68] The Hildesheim hoard reminds of the danger of putting all this kind of material together in a subsection headed 'trade'. It is unlikely (though never impossible) that the Hildesheim pieces were actually *bought* in the Empire or from some travelling Roman merchant. Indeed, we can rarely tell from the archaeological evidence (most usually from graves) whether specific items got there as a result of trade. As Philip Grierson reminded us many years ago,[69] individual items can reach their recipient as gifts and as booty as well as via trade. It is rather more plausible to imagine the very high quality silverware from Hildesheim as the result of a succession of diplomatic gifts from the Roman Empire to the court of some barbarian ruler.[70] And the find-spots of such high-status gifts are now realized to go far further east than had previously been realized. In the early Empire, for instance, barbarians in the Lower Don valley were being buried with silverware and bronze vessels not only from the Black Sea area but from the heart of the Roman Empire.[71] There is a chieftain's grave on the Middle Don at Tretyaki which contains Roman imports, but also metalwork from Han China.[72]

We can only speculate upon the significance of these exotic items within barbarian society in the Roman Period. But it would be reasonable to assume that the display of high-status objects of Roman manufacture gave prestige to those barbarians who were able to afford them. We can see this most obviously in a number of very rich graves, discussed above (p. 130) which have been found deep within Barbaricum from the early centuries AD. This can be seen also in the way in which Roman gold medallions (*multipla*) – finely made objects, invariably depicting the emperor – were prized by barbarians. Around one hundred *multipla* are known today.[73] They are found mostly in central Europe, stretching from the Lower Danube to southern Scandinavia, and most of them are from the fourth century; they may well have originated as gifts from the emperor, and no doubt many Germanic leaders were as pleased to receive them as King Chilperic was to receive gold medallions, weighing a pound each, from Tiberius II.[74] Almost all those which have been found were fitted with suspension loops by barbarian goldsmiths, and showed more wear on the reverse than on the obverse, showing that the items were worn with the imperial portrait displayed. Bursche has argued that the evidence of the suspension loops suggests that the medallions were sent from the Empire to a major power centre within Barbaricum, where the loops would have been fitted and the medallions distributed further afield.

Barbarian Art

These *multipla*, or else Roman coins (also frequently found used as pendants), formed the model for the barbarian artefacts known as bracteates, around 900 of which are known, mostly from Scandinavia, but also from Germany and England. The oldest ones are clear imitations of Roman coins: the design on bracteates of type A in particular are modelled on depictions of the heads of Roman emperors. The largest group, however (around 400 items), are the C-bracteates, which have a human head, together with a four-legged animal and often a bird. (Animals or birds are the main motifs of the second largest group, named D-bracteates by scholars of the nineteenth century who first studied these objects.) The scholar who has dominated the study of the iconography of these bracteates, particularly the C-bracteates, is Karl Hauck.[75] He sees the figure on these bracteates as Odin, and that the animals which accompany him are evidence of this: the horse, the boar (on A-bracteates in particular) and the bird (a raven?) are all associated with Odin. Even when the animal in question is shown horned and bearded, Hauck argues that it is a horse – wearing ritual horns; and that the 'bearded horse' is not actually Thor's goat. The horse is often depicted on its back, or with twisted legs: rather than seeing this as part of the problem of portraying an animal on an object often no more than 2 cm across (by craftspeople not familiar with realistic representation), he interprets the scene as Odin curing a sick horse.[76] Tyr appears as well, with his hand in the mouth of the Fenris-wolf, and Balder in the act of being killed with the branch of mistletoe. The concentration on Odin, however, fits into the idea that royal families (later) frequently chose Woden/Odin as their ancestor; it is a politically appropriate symbol. These objects may have been distributed by kings to their retainers; and indeed Elmer Seebold and others have suggested that the human bust that figures on so many of them is not Odin, but a king, surrounded by symbols illustrating his sacral powers. Axboe suggests, however, that the weight of the evidence supports Hauck's religious interpretation of the iconography, though he argues that their actual function does not have to be too closely defined. 'The bracteate users hardly saw any contradiction between "amulet", "status symbol", "gift" or "ethnic marker".'[77] As Märit Gaimster notes, there also has to be some explanation of why they are so often found as pendants in women's graves. Does it 'challenge our current understanding of kingship based on a warrior ideology', or does it merely fit in with the custom of women wearing amulets, coins or bracteates as part of a bead necklace which is widespread across the northern barbarian world.[78] Axboe suggest that one function for bracteates was precisely to be 'deposited in graves and hoards', where they 'played a role in the leading classes' communication with the Other World'.[79] Many of these gold hoards, Axboe speculates, were sacrifices made by the elite on behalf of their community, and that some at least of them may have been buried to propitiate the gods at the time of the frightening darkness that followed the Event of 536 (see above, p. 90).

Bracteates are one example of the way in which barbarian artists and craftsmen drew on Roman models in order to produce something highly distinctive. Unfortunately our understanding of 'barbarian art' is probably extremely limited, above all if we restrict ourselves to the period of this book. We have examples of Pictish sculpture, of Viking wood-carving and textiles and of highly decorated manuscripts, all of which might qualify as 'barbarian art', but all these are from a century or several centuries after AD 600. For our period, there are no wood-carvings or textiles from the barbarian world which would qualify as 'art', yet these might be precisely the media within which barbarians produced their greatest masterpieces. There are no examples of painting; there are no fragments of tattooed skin from Pictland; there is very little carved antler or whalebone. 'Barbarian art' resolves itself, in practice, into metalwork.

Barbarian decorative gold-work, in particular, could be highly accomplished technically, and there is an indication that the Romans themselves appreciated this work. The Latin term *barbarica* was used of a certain type of gold jewellery, and it was from this term that we have *barbaricarii*, who were prized craftsmen working in the Roman Empire, producing jewellery, but also such things as decorated armour. In the fourth century there were three *praepositi* who looked after the 'barbaricarii or silver-smiths' of Gaul, in the state factories at Arles, Rheims and Trier.[80]

Buckles or brooches or horse-harness might not be the places to find 'high art', but we should at least remember that, in the earliest surviving poetry, gold, particularly as worked into ornament, was of the highest prestige in barbarian society, and represented a high investment of skilled labour. A garnet cut into a complex shape might well take a skilled craftsman a day and a half to create; the cutting and polishing of the 4,000 garnets from the Sutton Hoo ship-burial may represent 6,000 person-days' work, before the goldsmithing itself started.[81]

The two main barbarian art-styles are usually referred to as polychrome art and animal art. To some extent they transcend ethnic divisions: polychrome art is found right across the Continent, and although animal art has its origins in the Germanic-speaking world it had its own forms in the Celtic-speaking world, and in so-called Hiberno-Saxon art, from the late seventh century onwards, animal art reached its pinnacle in such works as the Lindisfarne Gospels and the Book of Kells.

Polychrome art, essentially gold objects inlaid with precious or semi-precious stones, had its origin in the art of eastern nomadic peoples such as the Scythians; it seems to have come into the barbarian world in this period through the Goths, and spread westwards and northwards with the help of the Hunnic Empire. The metalwork from Childeric's grave offers fine examples. Polychrome art was predominantly a southern style in its origins. Sometimes rounded stones (cabochons) are set into the surface of the gold; at a later point, slices of semi-precious stone, particularly garnet, were attached to the surface within cell walls (cloisons) and sometimes worked into complex designs: this technique is known as 'cloisonné'.

Animal art derives, almost certainly, from late Roman art; the interlace which often figures likewise possibly derives from the geometrical
interlace patterns found frequently on late Roman mosaics. But its main
development was in northern Europe, and in Scandinavia in particular
it remained popular right through the Viking Period into the eleventh

Plate 8   A sword hilt and scabbard from Snartemo (Norway). The hilt is
covered in gold leaf. And the opening of the scabbard is in silver. It is all
decorated in Style I animal ornament: disembodied and stylised paws, and
jaws can be discerned. (Oslo, Universitetets Oldsaksamling).

century. On late Roman metalwork, animal art often consisted of fairly naturalistic animals or animal heads, sometimes in friezes along the edge of an artefact. In the hands of barbarian artists, these animals disintegrate and reintegrate, and appear in disjoined and distorted elements to cover the surface of the artefact; sometimes it takes a trained eye to recognize them as being animals at all. In 1904, the archaeologist Bernhard Salin published his study of animal art, which divided it into three different styles, largely in order of chronology: the terms Salin Style I, Style II and Style III are still widely used, even though some have refined them further.[82] The style I have just described is Style I, which predominated through the later fifth and sixth centuries. In the seventh century, Style II dominated: the animals were not disjointed, but they were elongated and interlaced together, in an often complex and highly symmetrical way.

The finest examples of Style II metalwork are to be found in Scandinavia and in England. With some of the Sutton Hoo cloisonné work, in fact, we get a fusion of the polychrome and animal styles, with Style II animals being created by the goldsmith with the help of expert garnet cutting, the translucent garnets being set over hatched gold foil, which adds glitter to the astonishingly intricate designs.

Whether Style II was used in wood-carving, or in painting, we do not know. But it was taken up by the illustrators of parchment manuscripts in Britain and Ireland in the course of the later seventh century, fusing with elements drawn from earlier 'Celtic art' (spirals and other curvilinear motifs) and with ideas drawn once more from the Mediterranean, to produce the great achievements of Hiberno-Saxon art in the eighth century, the Lindisfarne Gospels and the Book of Kells.

Barbarian Civilization

If one is trying to assess barbarian 'civilization', and to compare it with 'Roman civilization', we may note that many barbarians had some of the attributes that Romans would have considered as part of civilization, but not all. Most of the barbarians practised agriculture; but they did not have towns. They did not build major public works (except for defences). They did have a developed legal system, and probably a developed literary culture, but these do not seem to have been written down. They did, however, have writing, even though it seems to have been in its infancy as an instrument of self-expression or record-keeping.

The two main non-Roman systems of writing that were developed in the barbarian world were *ogham* (pronounced 'ome') in Ireland and those parts settled by the Irish in the Migration Period, and, in the Germanic-speaking world, runes. Both systems used letters built up of rectilinear lines, ideal for scratching into wood or onto stone: as far as is known, neither were used for writing extended texts. Epitaphs, labels indicating ownership and what are probably magical formulae were the commonest uses, as far as is known. Since at a later time runes were regarded as having magical properties, it is possible that they originated within a priestly caste. But they may have been used more widely, and Ulfila seems to have been familiar enough with them in the mid-fourth century to borrow some letters from the runic alphabet when he came to invent his own alphabet for his Gothic translation of the Bible.[83] Heather suggests that it is not impossible that barbarian states on the Rhine or Danube, which were running tribute systems and increasingly complex military systems, had developed record-keeping to some extent: 'it would be unwise to insist too fiercely on the non-existence of records.'[84]

Those barbarian peoples who adopted Christianity – mostly those people who lived nearest the frontiers – soon developed literacy in Latin or Greek. Indeed it is likely that many barbarians developed some functional literacy in Latin or Greek in the course of their communications with the Empire, whether inside it or outside. Nevertheless, earlier systems of writing continued, even within a solidly Christian context. The Ruthwell Cross, carved and erected in Northumbria in the eighth century, probably for a monastic community, was covered in inscribed texts in both Latin and runic scripts, with the runes being used to express Old English. At some distance from the Empire, as in Scandinavia, runes continued to be used exclusively for centuries. In Sweden there are many runic inscriptions, mostly epitaphs, from the Viking Period, especially from the eleventh century, and in Norway excavations in Bergen found hundreds of runic inscriptions on wood, in domestic contexts. In Sweden runes were commonly used in rural communities in the nineteenth century, and even into the twentieth, for such things as farmer's almanacs and calendars. It is easy to see how Olof Ohman, a Swedish farmer in Minnesota in the late nineteenth century, could have forged the Kensington runestone that has convinced so many Americans that Viking barbarians reached the mid-West long before any other European settlers.

This concentration on writing, of course, is to accept the prejudice that 'civilization' inevitably involves writing. As far as we can see, early barbarians in Ireland or in Barbaricum did not use writing very extensively; but they both had very lively oral traditions. This is most clearly seen in Ireland, whose 'learned classes' do not seem to have had any parallel in continental barbarian societies. There were two main types of learned individual in early Ireland: the *druí* (druid) and the *filí* (bard). Druids figure in the descriptions of pre-Roman Celtic society: they are described as philosophers as well as priests. Part of their power rested in their ability to forbid Gauls to go to the regular festivals held in the territory of the Carnutes (Chartres), which were organized by them and where legal and political issues were discussed.[85] The Irish equivalent of this may have been the *óenach*, or assembly, of Tailtiu.[86] There seems little doubt that druids had considerable power in Ireland before the conversion, and the *magi*, as Christian texts tend to call them, were the principal opponents of the Church in the early years.

The order of druids disappeared once Christianity established itself in the fifth and sixth centuries; but the order of *filid* survived, and indeed may have taken over some of the characteristics of the druids. (Others, perhaps, such as the power of prophecy, were inherited by Christian saints.) The *filid* were made equivalent to churchmen: an eighth-century law-tract gives them seven grades, with three subgrades, exactly equivalent to the canon law prescription of the *Collectio Hibernensis*, which gives seven clerical grades, with three subgrades.[87] The most senior of the grades of *filid*, the *ollamh*, has (like a bishop) the same honour-price as a king.[88] As in the Church, the gradation reflected degrees of proficiency and learning. Even though the *filid* were probably consciously imitating the Church by the seventh and eighth centuries, there is little reason to doubt that they were preserving some of the functions of the pre-Christian learned classes: to preserve and pass on the oral traditions of poetry and genea-logy, to write poems of praise and of obloquy (their satirical poems could bring humiliating shame) and to pronounce on matters of law. There were schools where they learned their craft, and (like churchmen) they could move anywhere in Ireland for employment.

These men were, as can be seen, the ideal bearers of Wenskus's 'kernel of tradition' from one generation to another. The question is, did continental barbarians have any similar groups, or was the 'Celtic' tradition unique among European barbarians in this respect? All we have is a few scattered references in our sources. There is more documenta-tion from a later period: there is, for instance, the reference in Einhard's *Life of Charlemagne* to his king directing 'that the age-old narrative poems, barbarous enough, it is true, in which were celebrated the warlike deeds of the kings of ancient times, should be written out and so preserved', which indicates the existence of a vernacular oral tradition.[89] Two cen-turies earlier, the Italian poet Venantius Fortunatus complained about the barbarian songs he heard among the Franks, sung to the strumming of a harp, and that some of these are (like the poems of the *filid*) praise-poems is clear from the words of a poem addressed to Duke Lupus, while staying at the court of the Frankish king Sigibert in 567/8: 'let the Roman applaud you with the lute, the barbarian with the harp, the

Greek with epic lyre, the Briton with the crowd [*crwth*].'[90] The translation of words for musical instrument is fraught with problems, as is their
reconstruction from archaeological remains. The harp found in Sutton
Hoo Mound 1 is now reconstructed as a lyre;[91] some say that it was very
similar to the medieval *crwth*. But crucially, stringed instruments are found
in high-status tombs in this period, suggesting that musical skill is something which is prized – and, as suggested by the story of Cædmon (who
had to go and hide when the *cithara* (harp?) passed his way at a party
and he was expected to do his turn) was widespread among ordinary
laymen.[92]

The Anglo-Saxon vernacular tradition, older and more voluminous than
any other except for the Irish, gives us more of an idea of the role of
the bard in barbarian society.[93] Three sources are of particular interest:
the poems *Beowulf, Widsith* and *Deor*, all of which are difficult to date
and all of which survive in unique manuscripts from the beginning of
the eleventh century.[94] A court poet (*scop*) is mentioned four times in
Beowulf. In one case the *scop* is also a *thegn*, a royal warrior:

> Meanwhile, a thane
> Of the king's household, a carrier of tales,
> a traditional singer deeply schooled
> in the lore of the past, linked a new theme
> to a strict meter. The man started
> to recite with skill, rehearsing Beowulf's
> triumphs and feats in well-fashioned lines,
> entwining his words.[95]

He told the story of Sigemund, the dragon-slayer. This *gleoman* (elsewhere
a synonym for *scop*) is in effect telling Beowulf that great deeds like dragon-
slaying (which Beowulf later carries out) bring great fame; but only if
those deeds are remembered thanks to the skill of *scopas*.

The poem *Widsith* is specifically about court-poets. Widsith himself
is depicted as a poet who has travelled around the barbarian courts of
Europe: but this would seem to be symbolic, as he mentions the names
of kings who are not contemporary, from Eormanric (mid-fourth-
century Gothic king) to Ælwine (Alboin), the late sixth century king of
the Lombards. He receives treasure from all his royal employers, and the
narrator poet ends by reminding his listeners that poets should be
treated generously: if it was not for Widsith these great heroic kings of
the past would have been forgotten. 'So, as in *Beowulf*, panegyric is a
mechanism for the generation of historical tradition.'[96]

Finally, there is the poem *Deor*, where a *scop* bemoans the loss of his
position at court among the Heodeningas (a small people of northern

Germany) when Heorrenda – who appears in later German tradition as a 'sort of Germanic Homer'[97] – turns up and takes his job. The poet had been given land, as part of his lord's retinue, but he lost the land when he lost his position. Like the other two poems, the setting is primarily northern Germany and southern Scandinavia, and although the historical context is clearly the Migration Period for all three, one clearly has to wonder in what way they might function as evidence for the Migration Period itself, which is half a millennium earlier than the date of the manuscripts.

chapter seven

BARBARIANS IN ROMAN
EMPLOYMENT

Barbarians were found within the Roman Empire at all social levels, from slaves, prisoners-of-war and merchants to ordinary soldiers in, or allied to, the Roman army, right up to commanders-in-chief of the army and imperial advisors. To what extent had this led to a 'barbarization' of the Empire (and/or a Romanization of the barbarians) even before the wholesale settlements of the fifth century? What was the relationship, if any, between this 'infiltration' and the subsequent collapse of the Western Empire? And, just as important, what effects did the close proximity of the Roman Empire have upon the development of barbarian societies themselves? This chapter will also incorporate, as a mirror image, the question of Romans who were in barbarian employment, either unwillingly (as enslaved captives) or not.

Slaves

Since most accounts of barbarians in the Roman Empire concentrate on soldiers, it is probably worth starting instead with slaves. As with soldiers, the real problem here is the question of numbers. We have no idea of the proportion of slaves to free persons in the later Roman Empire, nor do we have any idea of the scale of the slave trade. A.H.M. Jones believed that agricultural slaves were almost always home-born, and that the various imperial services which used slaves – weaving mills, dye-works, mints, the post – used hereditary slaves rather than buying them in the market.[1] He puts together some evidence that these domestic slaves were common: a law of Constantine suggesting that every non-commissioned officer had his slave batman, and the fact that St Martin, when in the army, was regarded as ascetic because he only had one slave (and was regarded also, no doubt, as subversive, since he was so humble that he used to wait on his own slave and clean his boots).[2] Libanius, bewailing the low status of teachers in Antioch in the late fourth century, noted that teachers might only have two or three slaves, and that these were often insolent, because their masters were unused to dealing with servants.[3] But Jones reckoned that these domestic slaves were also home-bred, and allows for just one exception: eunuchs. Castration was forbidden within the Empire, and consequently eunuchs were imported especially from Persia and the Caucasus region. According to Procopius, most of the eunuchs at Justinian's court were from the pagan barbarian tribe of the Abasgi, at the eastern end of the Black Sea. He tells us, implausibly, that their kings used to make eunuchs of the best-looking boys and then kill their fathers so that they would not take vengeance on the kings. Procopius does not tell us where the court got its eunuchs from after the Abasgi converted to Christianity (and Justinian sent one of his Abasgian eunuchs to tell the kings to stop the practice of castration) though he does say that when they learnt what their kings had been doing, they dethroned them, and now 'seemed to be living in a state of freedom'.[4]

However, Jones also provides the evidence that there was indeed a slave trade with the barbarians. Themistius claimed that on the frontiers the ordinary troops were deprived of weapons and even clothing, but 'the commandants and officers act[ed] as merchants, even slave traders, this being their sole employment – to buy and sell as much as possible',[5] and the senator Symmachus in Rome, wanting 20 stable boys, commented that 'on the frontier slaves are easy to come by and the price is usually tolerable'.[6] The same senator complained bitterly when the 29 Saxon prisoners-of-war he had bought for his son's quaestorial games in 393 throttled each other rather than face almost certain death in the amphitheatre.[7]

In the late fourth century the words *Gothus* and *Skuthos* became equivalent to 'slave'; Synesius said that every household, however humble, had a Scythian (i.e. Gothic) slave, because they were well adapted for serving Romans.[8] It is something which is confirmed by Ammianus, who reported that in 362 Julian had told his counsellors that he wanted a better enemy than the Goths: 'for the Goths the Galatian traders were enough, by whom they were offered for sale everywhere without distinction of rank'.[9] Zosimus alleges that Emperor Constans bought handsome young barbarians to have around him at court, 'provided that they would allow him to corrupt their youth'.[10] The life of St Severinus makes mention of some brigands who raided slaves from the Rugians in the later fifth century. The saint warned the Rugian king not to cross the Danube in pursuit of the brigands: the clear implication is that the brigands (whether Roman or barbarian) were acquiring slaves whom they presumably would sell off in the Empire.[11]

The Theodosian Code has a number of references to barbarian slaves. One law makes a clear distinction between 'barbarian' slaves and 'provincial' slaves, in the context of a contract to buy, to the extent that it says that the law should apply to both groups.[12] Another equally enigmatic distinction occurs in a law giving privileges to teachers of art, who shall be free of tax assessment on their own account, but also on behalf of their wives, children and 'barbarian slaves'.[13]

Barbarians may have been seen as natural suppliers of slaves to the Romans; but barbarians would themselves enslave Romans whom they captured on raids on imperial territory. Perhaps the most famous incident was the capture and enslavement of the Romano-Briton Patricius by Irish barbarians, on a raid on the western coasts of Britain: 'as a youth, indeed almost a boy without any beard, I was captured', writes St Patrick.[14] Gildas tells us that many Romano-Britons were enslaved by the Saxons too, later in the fifth century. Some of the 'wretched survivors' of Saxon attacks, indeed, went voluntarily into slavery: 'their spirit broken by hunger, [they] went to surrender to the enemy; they were fated to be slaves for ever, if indeed they were not killed straight away, the highest boon'.[15]

Again, we have no idea of the quantities of Romans who were enslaved. But it is perhaps significant that there were a number of imperial edicts directed to the wellbeing of such people. If Romans returned to their lands after a period of barbarian captivity, they should be allowed to reclaim their heritage 'since this question only shall be asked, whether a person was with the barbarians voluntarily or through compulsion'.[16] 'No one shall detain against their will persons of different provinces, of whatever sex, status, or age, who have been led away through barbarian savagery under the compulsion of captivity, but those who desire to return to their own homes shall have the unrestricted right to do so.'[17]

In the absence of statistics, individual cases of hardship tell evocative stories. There was Maria, for instance, a young girl who was enslaved by the Vandals in North Africa, and sold, together with her own slave, to Roman merchants. Maria's slave knew her place (or so the story runs); she went on washing her mistress's feet and making her bed. Soldiers who were stationed near Cyrrhus in Syria heard about this and made enquiries; they paid the purchase price and rescued Maria (although not, apparently, the slave). The church historian Theodoret, the local bishop, looked after Maria. Ten months later she heard that her father was alive, and holding high office in the West. Theodoret wrote the letter which is our source for the whole story, asking Eustathius, bishop of the Mediterranean port of Aegeae, to find someone trustworthy to negotiate with mariners, pilots and merchants to arrange a safe passage for her back to the West, in expectation of an abundant reward from her father.[18]

In this case, the resources of the Church were harnessed for the return of one Christian enslaved by barbarians; but frequently the Church negotiated mass releases. Caesarius, bishop of Arles from 502 to 542, and someone who therefore had to negotiate successively with Visigothic, Ostrogothic and Frankish masters, was one of the heroic figures in this kind of enterprise. Once when the Goths had brought back to Arles a large number of captives, Caesarius went to work:

> To those in great need the man of God gave sufficient food and clothing, until he could free them individually with the gift of redemption. He first spent all the silver that his predecessor, the venerable Aeonius, had left for the bishop's table, maintaining that the Lord had dipped bread into an earthen dish and not a silver cup and had advised his disciples not to possess gold or silver. . . . Even today the blows of axes are visible on podiums and railings from which the silver ornaments of the small columns were cut away. For the man of God said that no rational man who had been redeemed by the blood of Christ should, as a punishment for having lost his freedom, become perhaps an Arian or a Jew, or a slave instead of a free man or a slave of man rather than of God.[19]

The last comment reminds one that the real fear of a Christian bishop was not that a Christian slave would suffer physically, but that being enslaved by a pagan, a heretic or a Jew would endanger those slaves' souls, either because they would be forced to follow their owner's religion or would simply be contaminated through proximity.

Stories can be found in numerous saints' lives of the ransoming of captives from the barbarians. St Severinus, for instance, in the Danube province of Noricum, was active in this field. Once he ordered a man whom he had ransomed, with his wife and children, to cross the Danube and to look in the barbarians' slave market for a particular person, whom he described in minute detail.[20] Such was Severinus's authority that King Gibuldus of the Alamanni trembled so much in his presence that he offered to give the saint whatever he wanted; and Severinus asked for the release of all his captives. The king promised to search the province for all prisoners, and to have them all sent to the saint.[21]

Gregory of Tours tells the story of Attalus, who was a nephew of Gregory's mother's grandfather, also called Gregory, who was bishop of Langres.[22] Attalus thus belonged to a powerful and wealthy family. When two of the sons of Clovis – Theuderic and Childebert – decided to end their feuding in around 530 they exchanged hostages. Gregory says that many of the hostages were the sons of senatorial families, including Attalus. And when the brothers started squabbling again, the hostages were either reduced to state labour or slavery. Attalus was assigned by the king to an unnamed Frank who lived near Trier, and was put to work in the stables. Gregory of Langres tried to buy back his nephew, but was not prepared to pay the 10 pounds of gold which the Frank demanded. Gregory's cook Leo offered to help, and arranged for a friend to sell him to the Frank for 12 gold coins (*aurei*).[23] Leo was so successful as a cook that he was eventually given charge of the Frank's whole household. After a year, he had totally won the Frank's trust, and at that point he organized Attalus's escape by night. The Frank chased them, apparently, all the way from Trier to the region of Reims. A priest in Reims, an old friend of Bishop Gregory, hid the two escaped slaves and lied to the Frank when he came round enquiring about them, and they were able to reach Bishop Gregory of Langres. Leo was given his freedom, and a piece of land, in return for his service. Attalus was luckier than the 300 sons of notables in Italian towns taken as hostage by Totila, Ostrogothic king in the last bitter throes of the Roman wars of reconquest of Italy; they were found by Totila's rival Teias, and killed.[24]

Soldiers

Barbarians had for a long time been used in the Roman armies, as auxiliaries, but it seems that the large-scale recruitment of barbarians directly into the Roman army began under Constantine in the early fourth century. The mobile army with which he united the Empire was largely recruited from among barbarians: from prisoners-of-war within the Empire and from willing recruits from outside. It is likely that it was Constantine too who replaced the praetorian guard, the traditional imperial bodyguard, by the *schola*, which, some historians say, was largely run by barbarians.[25]

Three obvious questions arise: Why did the Romans recruit barbarians into the army? How many were there? What effect did this have on Roman politics (and indeed on the fate of the Roman Empire itself)?

The possible reasons for recruiting barbarians (primarily Germanic-speakers) are: that there was a shortage of manpower within the Empire; that the recruitment of barbarians does not take Romans out of crucial labour markets or out of the pool of tax-payers; that barbarians made better soldiers; or that barbarians were extremely dispensable.

Whether there was a shortage of manpower or not (and this is still a matter of dispute, with few historians being as ready as A.E.R. Boak[26] to be dogmatic on this) there is no doubt that the Roman authorities found it difficult to recruit Roman citizens. In both the 360s and the 380s, for instance, imperial authorities were concerned about those who cut off their own fingers in order to avoid military service;[27] there were also concerns expressed about deserters, although a law preserved in the section of the Theodosian Code about armourers shows that measures were taken to identify recruits to prevent desertion: 'Brands, that is, the official state mark, shall be stamped on the arms of armourers, in imitation of the practice of branding army recruits, so that in this manner at least it may be possible to recognize skulkers.'[28] Other laws in the Theodosian Code are more difficult to evaluate, as is often the case in the Code: in particular, how far were imperial responses to local problems applied and enforced across the Empire, and how far were they simply immediate and short-term responses to local crisis? What, for instance, should we make of the response of Valentinian and Valens to the Vicar of the City of Rome in 367, stating that recruits for the army should be at least 5 feet 7 inches tall (which was almost certainly taller than the average Roman male, suggesting a considerable lack of urgency about recruitment)?[29] What do we make of the extreme measure proposed in an edict addressed by Arcadius broadly to 'the provincials' in 406:

> Although we believe that freeborn persons are aroused by love of country, we exhort slaves also, by the authority of this edict, that as soon as possible they shall offer themselves for the labors of war, and if they receive their arms as men fit for military service, they shall obtain the reward of freedom, and they shall also receive two solidi each for travel money.[30]

This was in direct contradiction of an edict issued to the provincials only 26 years earlier, which had forbidden the recruitment of slaves, of disreputable people, of people from disgraceful occupations and also from the class of cooks and breadmakers (recruitment for which was almost as big a problem as recruitment for the army).[31]

The problem with recruiting was partly about the mechanisms for recruitment of provincials. Landowners, divided up into groups called *consortia*, were responsible for this. In practice they operated a press-gang system, which produced unsuitable and reluctant soldiers, or else they commuted this obligation into the payment of a sum of money, which could, of course, be used to recruit barbarians. Landowners were, quite naturally, reluctant to recruit their own tenants.

Many barbarians were volunteers, attracted, as Jones suggested, by good living conditions, attractive salaries and bonuses and the possibility of promotion and real power within the Empire.[32] These soldiers seem not to have served in special regiments, but to have been alongside Roman soldiers: this was presumably a deliberate measure to avoid barbarians forming factions within the army, and to promote barbarian identification with the Roman cause. It was probably a special favour when Valentianian I appointed Fraomar, an Alamannic chief who had been thrown out of his homeland by an anti-Roman faction, to command an Alamannic unit in Britain.[33]

Some barbarians could be forcibly recruited. Prisoners-of-war who had been compulsorily settled within the Empire, and handed over to landowners, would be liable to recruitment; and indeed a panegyric addressed to Constantine between 307 and 311 implies that this is a major reason for settling such people.

> What shall I say, moreover, about those nations from the interior of Francia, now torn away no longer just from those areas which the Romans had invaded in the past, but right from their original homeland and from the farthest shores of the barbarian world, so that, having been settled in the deserted regions of Gaul, they both promote the peace of the Roman Empire by cultivating the soil and Roman arms by swelling the levy?[34]

Some of these prisoners were settled under special conditions: these were the *laeti*. They were prisoners-of-war too (although some may have been Romans returning from barbarian captivity)[35] who were not settled on the land of individual landowners, but on specially defined public land, *terra laetica*. A Roman official looked after groups of these settlements of *laeti*; and the children of *laeti* remained *laeti*, living under the same obligation to provide military service, so that they are still known in Gaul in the sixth century. It is possible that the most famous clause of the first Frankish law-code, the *Pactus Legis Salicae*, in which women were excluded from the inheritance of *terra salica*, is a memory of the military obligations involved with the possession of *terra laetica*.[36] People called *laeti* are in fact known almost exclusively in Gaul, with the exception of one text relating to Italy.[37] It is possible that barbarians settled under similar terms elsewhere in the Empire were called by different names, such as *gentiles*.[38] There is an imperial edict from 409, to confuse matters still further, which seems to refer to a settlement of defeated members of the little-known Germanic-speaking people called the Sciri, and says that those to whom these Sciri have been granted shall give them 'no other title than that of *colonus*' (that is, the Roman tied peasant).[39] These people should work the land ('because of the shortage of farm produce') and should not be made into slaves. Perhaps this was exceptional, and different from the usual arrangements; on the other hand, we know from the historian Sozomen that after the defeat of the Sciri, only some of them were settled on land (he had seen many farming near Mount Olympus), while others were imprisoned, and others sold or given away as slaves. The main concern of the government, says Sozomen, was to split them up geographically as much as possible, in case they conspired together.[40]

There was an old tradition from the early days of the Empire that non-citizens could be recruited directly into the legions, rather than into the usual auxiliaries, when citizens could not be found; and these non-citizens would be given citizen status.[41] Technically the prisoners-of-war who were recruited into the army remained *dediticii*, of slave status and could not serve in regular units, but this too is likely to have been quietly forgotten. Indeed, by the end of the fourth century new prisoners-of-war could go directly into the regular army, and indeed this could be insisted upon as a condition of peace.[42] Barbarians were not only used in the field army (especially in Gaul), but also in the frontier troops, the *limitanei*. The document known as the *Notitia Dignitatum*, which lists the elements of the Roman army (probably around 394 for the East and 420 for the West), gives barbarian names to a large number of regiments, including the frontier forces of the East, which indicated that at least originally these units were recruited from those barbarian groups. There are a number of known barbarian generals (*duces*) in charge of *limitanei* in the East (Vadomarius, *dux Phoenices*; Munderichus, *dux Arabiae*; Cariobaudes, *dux Mesopotamiae*), which has suggested to some that there were a large number of ordinary barbarians on the ground.[43] A much more mundane piece of evidence suggests this too: there is a Greek papyrus document from fourth-century Egypt in which a mother complains that her son has been sent 'among the barbarians', meaning 'into the army'.[44]

Liebeschuetz is surely right to argue for the feebleness of the link between the recruitment of barbarians and a manpower shortage. There was clearly no manpower shortage in the East; there is some evidence for population decline in the West, but if anything population in the East was increasing in the fourth and fifth centuries. Yet eastern emperors needed western barbarian recruits. The Emperor Constantius begged his nephew Julian to send him barbarian auxiliary troops in 360. Julian was very concerned

> that those men should suffer no inconvenience who had left their abodes beyond the Rhine and come to him under promise that they should never be led to regions beyond the Alps; for he declared that it was to be feared that the barbarian volunteer soldiers, who were often accustomed to come over to our side under conditions of this kind, might on having knowledge of this thereafter be kept from so doing.[45]

Julian offered to send him *laeti* and *dediticii*: in other words, barbarians who had not entered willingly into Roman service. He also said that the Gauls themselves would not allow recruits to be sent outside Gaul, as it would leave their provinces open to barbarian invasions; which implies that in Gaul at least there were not major problems in recruiting Roman provincials into the army. Julian was planning a usurpation at the time; but he at least claimed that there were serious recruitment problems in the East, which could in part be resolved with the help of his western barbarians. Within the Eastern Empire only Isauria and Armenia, both with strong warrior cultures, could be relied upon to send recruits.

There were two other mechanisms for recruiting soldiers: as federates and as *bucellarii*. Federates or *foederati* were those who had agreed a treaty or contract (*foedus*) with the Roman authorities by which military service would be supplied by the barbarian group. The barbarians would continue to be led by their own leaders, who may or may not be referred to as kings. It could be very advantageous for the Romans, because federates could be hired for a specific campaign and then dismissed; there was no need for permanent contracts. Sometimes, as in south-west Gaul in 418/9, federates were given land in return for military service; but federates could be hired for money and/or supplies. Sometimes federates were recruited by an individual Roman officer, and acquired a loyalty to him specifically, which gave him the ability to pursue a personal ambition and to hold on to power much longer than he might have done had he no power base. Liebeschuetz suggests that 'this, rather than the command structure of the Western army, is the basic reason why the *magister militum* in the West became the virtual ruler of the Empire'.[46]

Close to the federate soldier in this context is the *bucellarius* or 'dry-bread-eater'.[47] He is a private soldier, hired to belong to the personal retinue of a great Roman magnate. Many *bucellarii* seem to be barbarian, and there are obvious similarities to the personal retinue of a Germanic chief or king, but this does not mean that the institution was Germanic in origin. Nor were some bands of *bucellarii* necessarily purely private armies. Papyrus documents from sixth-century Egypt show that the great landowning family of the Apions were actually offered tax-breaks by the government for hiring *bucellarii*; these *bucellarii* were used for tasks like keeping order in the hippodrome or for tax-collecting, and could be requisitioned by the government in a crisis.[48] In this sense, the bucellariate was an institution that encouraged individuals to recruit armed retainers, and also an additional mode of recruitment for the army. But that it was potentially a destabilizing factor is suggested by the attempts made by the Emperor Leo (in 468 and 472) to make it illegal.[49]

Barbarians of various types played a significant role in the politics of the Empire after the time of Constantine. In the middle of the fourth century they were generally Alamans; in the later fourth century they were usually Franks. As Liebeschuetz points out, 'of the sixteen *magistri militum* who are known to have held command under Theodosius I, nine at least were not Roman by birth'.[50] The 'at least' has to be added because very often we only know about ethnic origins because of the names. A name that is linguistically Germanic can often be spotted, and in this period we do not know of any Romans who took a Germanic-sounding name. However, we do know (and only thanks to Ammianus)[51] that the Roman generals called Bonitus and Silvanus (father and son), with their very Latin-sounding names, were actually both Franks; but we do not know how many other apparent Romans who appear in sources that are less detailed than Ammianus's were in fact barbarians.

It used to be generally agreed that, whatever the numbers in the main army, the imperial household troops – the *scholae palatinae* – were over-whelmingly barbarian. This was accepted and promulgated by the main study of this group, by R.I. Frank. He starts his chapter on 'Recruitment' with the following statement:

> During the fourth century most of the *scholares* were Germans, and this was especially true of the enlisted men. Thus all the extant descriptions and representations of the emperor's guards show them with distinctly Germanic characteristics of dress and appearance, and they are often armed with the Frankish spear (*ango*).[52]

In fact, however, he does not present the evidence for this. Instead, he quotes Synesius as saying, in front of the emperor in Constantinople, that the guards standing nearby were 'these tall youths with curly blond hair', and Ammianus saying that Julian was sending some barbarian *laeti* and *dedicitii* to Constantius II for his *scholae*.[53] He gives no indication of where he finds his depictions of *angones* (the barbed spears which were indeed, judging by both archaeology and the description by Agathias in the sixth century, a largely Frankish weapon). The most famous depiction of imperial guards – the four guardsmen at the edges of the great silver dish or *missorium* depicting Theodosius on his throne – shows spears which are certainly not *angones* (nor is it easy to see, as Hugh Elton can, that these soldiers depicted in silver had 'long blond hair').[54]

Elton is the modern historian who has launched the most systematic assault on the notion that by the later fourth century 'imported soldiers formed the majority' of soldiers in the Roman Empire and that 'before the century was over, barbarian commanders of essentially barbarian armies had gained control of the empire's fate'.[55] He looks at both the question of numbers, and the question of historical significance.

As everyone acknowledges, the problem is recognizing the barbarians, which generally has to be by the names. But Elton rightly questions our definitions of barbarian too. Stilicho, he suggests, master of the Roman world on either side of 400, should not be considered as a barbarian, as he usually is. His Vandal father was a Roman cavalry officer; his mother was Roman; he married the niece of the Emperor Theodosius I. Only two hostile Christian writers (Jerome and Orosius) mention his barbarian origins; and even someone like Rutilius Namatianus 'makes no mention of his origins in a posthumous torrent of invective describing Stilicho as a traitor to the Empire by letting in barbarians'.[56] Fravitta, a contemporary of Stilicho, was a general of Gothic origins, described by Zosimus as 'by birth a barbarian, but otherwise a Greek, not only in habits but also in character and religion'.[57] So even looking at names is uncertain, and Elton copes with this by dividing up our known personnel into five groups: 'Definitely Barbarian', 'Probably Barbarian', 'Definitely Roman', 'Probably Roman' and 'Others'. Elton does not think that the numbers of barbarians who had taken Roman names is enough to skew the results: out of 110 officers he found who had both Roman names *and* a stated ethnic or geographic origin, only eight were of barbarian origin.[58]

Elton's first conclusion was that fewer than one-third of the army officers were actually barbarian in origin.[59] He does admit that there might be problems with these figures: for instance, the number of *magistri militum* of barbarian origin seems higher than the average for the less high-ranking officers: if this is the result of better evidence for higher ranks then perhaps the proportion of barbarians was higher. But Elton's second conclusion was more important: that the proportion of barbarian officers within the army did not increase over his period, that is, from the 350s to the 470s. The gut feeling that many historians have had – that 'things went from worse to worse' – is simply not borne out by the evidence. As for Frank's assertion that the imperial *scholae* were largely barbarian, Elton found that there was little evidence of this. Like the *auxilia palatina* regiments, there were clearly barbarian members, but there were Roman members as well, and when the known names are tabulated, barbarians are in a definite minority.

The problem of numbers boils down to the question of evidence, and how to interpret it. As an example, let us look, with Hoffmann,[60] at the evidence provided by the late Roman cemetery at Concordia. There are inscriptions from the very end of the fourth century, relating to 23 different military units and mentioning 39 men. Ethnicity derived from name alone is problematical, and some of the names cannot be assigned with any certainty: some that Hoffmann considers 'Celtic' may well be 'Germanic'. It is likely that some 14 of the names – very slightly more than one-third – belonged to those of Germanic descent. Correlation with the units in which these soldiers served showed that Germans served alongside Romans, and that if one served in a unit with an 'ethnic' name, like the Batavi or the *Eruli*, one might well be serving alongside Romans or Goths. The use of epigraphic evidence, however, might be very misleading. Across the Empire there are relatively few inscriptions recording the names of barbarians, perhaps because barbarians who were Romanized enough to want a funerary inscription had given themselves Roman names or, even more likely, that barbarians who were not sufficiently Romanized would not have bothered with inscriptions at all. It was perhaps a Roman mason, or Roman brothers-in-arms, who imagined the feelings of a Frankish soldier, dying in Roman service in Pannonia, rather than any Frank:

Francus ego cives Romanus miles in armis
Egregia virtute tuli bello mea dextera semper

– 'I am a Frankish citizen, a Roman soldier under arms/with outstanding valour I have always gone into battle, my weapon in my hand.'[61]

Of course, numbers are not everything. The 'barbarization' of the Roman army might have taken place, as many historians have assumed, even with the smaller numbers suggested by Elton. This might have had little impact on the army's performance at all; indeed, Elton argues plausibly, following Jones, that, however many barbarians were actually in the army, there is only marginal evidence for any barbarian disloyalty to the emperors.[62] It would be very easy to put together quite a long list of disloyal Romans in the army – the number of successful or abortive usurpations in the later Roman Empire is considerable – and therefore the evidence might well suggest that barbarians were more loyal than Romans. But barbarization could take cultural forms, and might be important even without an obvious military or political consequence.

The cultural impact of the barbarians on the Roman army was partly a result of their frequent military clashes; but just as much a result of their long history of alliance and collaboration. It can be seen in vocabulary. There are four inscriptions, from on or near the Danube frontier, which attest to the Latin word for a Latin-speaking bride of a Roman soldier: *brutis*. It is a word found in Germanic languages (for instance, Old English *bryd*, modern English *bride*), and also in modern Greek (*broútis*); it is assumed to be a Latin borrowing from early Germanic,[63] which gives a hint, perhaps, concerning one aspect of relations on the frontier. Most of the borrowings from Germanic into Latin, as one might expect, are to do with military matters. The word found in Ammianus for a 'barricade of waggons', for instance, is *carrago*, which seems to derive from the Latin for waggon (*carrus*) together with the Germanic *hag*, a barricade or fence. (The last part also occurs in the Old English word for a 'shield-wall': *bordhaga*.) Another example is *framea*, which in classical Latin means 'spear', although in Christian Latin it means 'sword': it seems Germanic in origin, although it must have entered Latin early, because it is found in Tacitus.[64] A German addition to Roman military practice seems to have been the *barritus*. Vegetius warns,

> The war-cry, which they call the *barritus* should not be raised until both lines have engaged each other. It is a mark of inexperienced or cowardly men if they cry out from a distance. The enemy is more terrified if the shock of the war-cry is made to coincide with the blows of weapons.[65]

'This shout,' said Ammianus, 'rises from a low murmur and gradually grows louder, like waves dashing against the cliffs.'[66]

Less impressive, perhaps, but rather more ubiquitous, are trousers. These are the subject of two edicts issued by Arcadius and Honorius in 399 and preserved in Book 14 of the Theodosian Code, which concerned the City of Rome: one is addressed to the people of Rome, and the other to the prefect of the City: both specify that no one should wear either boots or trousers in the City (and the words were of barbarian origins: *tzangae* and *bracchae* – breeches). There are four edicts in this part of Book 14, grouped under the heading 'The garb which must be worn within the City'.[67] The first dates from 382, and forbids a senator to wear military dress: 'he shall lay aside the awe-inspiring military cloak and clothe himself with the sober robes of everyday costume and a civilian cloak'. Lesser public officials likewise had to wear civilian cloaks, with their belts of office keeping their clothes together (thus bearing 'witness to the necessities of their ignoble status'); slaves were allowed to wear 'shaggy coats or hoods', but only if their masters were not in the imperial service. The final edict of the four, dating to 416, says that no one should wear very long hair, and not even slaves should wear clothes made of skins sewn together, not just in the City but in the neighbouring districts.

Since similar laws do not appear anywhere else in the Theodosian Code, one can conclude that still, around 400, Rome was seen as a special city. There is a desire to make sure that the correct attire is worn in the correct circumstances. But it is probably wrong to refer to the law about trousers and boots, as the translator Clyde Pharr does, in terms of 'the Emperor's fear of barbarian influences'. Trousers seem to have been in common use in the Roman army since the third century.[68] The prohibition on senators wearing military garb and others wearing boots and trousers in the City may better be seen together: not fear of barbarians, but fear of the breakdown of the traditional barriers between civilian

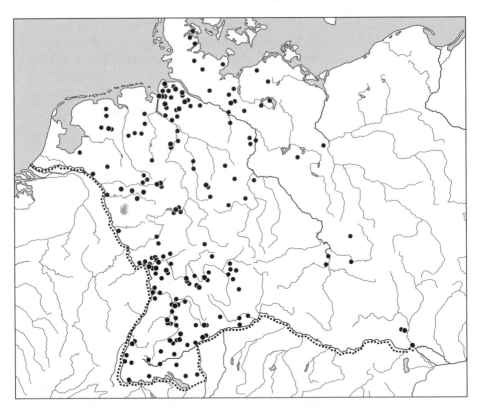

Map 9 The distribution of late Roman military belt fittings in Barbaricum. These are mostly found in graves, possibly the graves of barbarians who had served in the Roman army and returned home. (Map after H.W. Böhme, in Wieczorek, *Die Franken*, 98).

and military, and the desire to avoid any unofficial military takeover of the City.

The adoption of trousers by some Romans might be seen as some kind of endorsement of barbarian habits. Elton suggests that 'some troops were probably encouraged to look "barbarian", for example the members of the imperial bodyguard shown on the Column of Theodosius, the Missorium of Theodosius, and the Ravenna Mosaics of San Vitale, all with long hair and torcs'.[69] That barbarism could become a fashion among Romans, if at a later date, is shown by a fascinating passage in Procopius's so-called *Secret History*. He tells us that at the time of the Emperor Justin, the circus factions (whose rivalry has variously been interpreted as political, or as mere hooliganry) adopted a new hair style:

> For they did not cut it at all as the other Romans did. For they did not touch the moustache or the beard at all, but they wished always to have the hair

of these grow out very long, as the Persians do. But the hair of their heads they cut off in front back to the temples, leaving the part behind to hang down to a very great length in a senseless fashion, just as the Massagetae do. Indeed for this reason they used to call this the 'Hunnic' fashion . . . Also their cloaks and their drawers and especially their shoes, as regards both name and fashion, were called as 'Hunnic'.[70]

Such cultural developments could, of course, have profound political effects. As barbarian ways became more familiar, both inside and outside the army, they could become more acceptable, and the clear dichotomies between 'civilized' and 'barbarous' which ancient writers liked to emphasize, might have come to have little meaning for ordinary Romans. That may have made it more acceptable for Romans in, say, south-west Gaul or Spain to accept the rule of barbarian kings – particularly when those kings themselves had become long accustomed to Roman ways and did their best to imitate the Roman. And, as Liebeschuetz has said, 'patriotic "Roman" behaviour, and support of the imperial army, were not the only defensive options available. The alternative was cooperation with the barbarians'.[71]

What, therefore, was the effect of the recruitment of barbarian soldiers into the Roman army on the fate of the Western Empire? We can say that barbarians remained a minority in the Roman army, and barbarians seem to have been distributed among various units, so that 'only in exceptional cases did units consist entirely of barbarians, or, even worse, entirely of ethnically homogeneous barbarians'.[72] Many of the barbarians who *were* recruited were from peoples who had lived and fought alongside Romans for generations, and had no interest in putting an end to it. If anything, the army was more of an agent of Romanization than a victim of barbarization. Up to 376, concludes Nicasie in his study of the fourth century army up to that date, 'there are virtually no signs of a decline of the Roman army through barbarian influences'.[73]

This may well be true. However, in the decades after 376 the picture changed dramatically. According to Jordanes, the famous Roman victory at Chalons, which halted Attila's invasion of Gaul, was largely carried out by barbarian federates. The king of the Goths commanded one wing on the battlefield, and the Roman general Aetius the other; in the middle were the Alans. But Aetius's force consisted largely of federates Franks, Sarmatians, Liticians, Burgundians, Saxons and Riparians. The Armoricans and the Olibriones, presumably both Romans, were treated as if they were federates themselves: but they were the only actual Romans who seem to be mentioned.[74] Liebeschuetz concludes that by 450 the field army was largely made up of federates.[75] There may still have been Romans in the frontier forces, but these were largely irrelevant in strategic terms.

The years after 376 were also notable for the greatly increased role of barbarians in positions of influence within the Roman Empire. Towards the end of the fourth century there were Merobaudes, Bauto and Arbogast, all Franks; from 395 to 408 there was Stilicho; later in the fifth century there were figures like Ricimer, Gundobad and Odoacer. These people, one could argue, presided over the break-up of the Roman Empire. But one could equally argue that they devoted most of their careers to trying to sustain the Roman Empire, and in fact there is very little in their careers that show them to be acting as 'barbarians' at all. They hold Roman offices, they marry Roman women and, as far as we can tell, have precisely the same career ambitions as Roman generals. 'Late Roman warlords', to use the title of Penny MacGeorge's monograph, look much the same whether they are barbarians or whether they are Romans, like Aetius or the figures whom MacGeorge looks at: Marcellinus, Aegidius, Syagrius and Orestes.[76] It is also notable that a number of these barbarians are of mixed ancestry: either Roman and barbarian, or two different groups of barbarians.

My own conclusion would be that the break-up of the Western Roman Empire occurred because, in the different provinces, local populations began to give their allegiances to local warlords, rather than to the emperor, because those warlords were more effective as protectors and patrons. Not all these warlords were barbarians, but the majority were, because of the domination of barbarians within the Roman army. The Roman warlords were eliminated one by one; and remaining barbarian warlords had little incentive to work for the preservation of the Empire, even though they paid lip-service to its continued existence (for instance, by minting coins with the imperial image on them).

The archaeological evidence for barbarians in the army makes an additional point. It is impossible to say which items of Roman manufacture found, say, in graves in Barbaricum were brought back by barbarians who had retired from the Roman army: they could as well be booty or items of trade. But part of the military belts found east of the Rhine, mostly in the fourth and fifth century, are better evidence of barbarian involvement in the imperial army. These mounts, strap ends and buckles are very easily recognizable, in chip-carved (*Kerbschnitt*) style, and are found widely across western Barbaricum, with particular clusters east of the Middle Rhine, and between the Elbe and the Weser. They are also found, in smaller numbers, within the Roman Empire, particularly along the River Meuse, but also along the north coast of Gaul towards the Seine, and in south-east Britain. Some moulds for their production have been found in Barbaricum itself,[77] but the bulk of the production was probably within the Empire. The clustering relates more to the presence of particular burial customs which preserve these items for us than to the actual distribution of returning soldiers east of the Rhine, but nevertheless it illustrates, in all probability, the fact that employment in the Roman army had a profound effect on the barbarians both inside and outside the Empire. The Roman and barbarian worlds were not isolated from each other; they were symbiotically linked. Even while the Empire was, according to some, being 'barbarized', the barbarian world was going through a profound process of Romanization.

chapter eight

BARBARIANS ON THE MOVE

The Migration Period is, by definition, an age of movement. Maps show it clearly. Imagine, for instance, the way in which the *Times Atlas of World History* maps the process (as described by Walter Goffart).

> The projection is unusual and eye-catching; the lines of tribal movements are broad – ribbons rather than strings; bold arrows are in evidence; and the colors are applied from a rich and carefully assorted palette. Behold the Visigoths: in an almost unbroken run of sinuous green, they branch away from the Ostrogoths at the northern edge of ancient Scythia and flow into Roman territory, coursing to and fro in graceful curves reminiscent of Dark Age inter-lace, until an arrow finally drives them to Toledo.[1]

This is what barbarians (or at least Germanic-speaking barbarians) do: they move. (Though, having used the splendidly beribboned map from Jean Hubert's *Europe in the Dark Ages* for many years in my teaching, I confess that I think of the Visigoths as blue rather than green.)[2]

National background has something to do with the precise way in which one thinks of the barbarians in this period. French historians have tended to think in terms of 'The Great Invasions' or 'The Germanic Invasions'. Germans and Scandinavians often think of it in terms of the translated title of Hans-Joachim Diesner's book – *The Great Migration: The Movement of Peoples across Europe, AD 300–700*.[3] What barbarians did was to invade and to migrate: they are seen as being continually on the move. We are conditioned by the memory of those ribbons on the maps.[4]

This chapter will ask, To what extent are we really dealing with 'the movement of peoples across Europe'? The maps certainly imply that whole peoples – Visigoths, Vandals, Burgundians and so on – moved across Europe. Did this happen? And if not, what did?

Goffart has painstakingly traced these mapping habits back to their origins in early printed atlases.[5] But ultimately we have our written sources to blame for this perception of endlessly mobile barbarians. Strabo, for

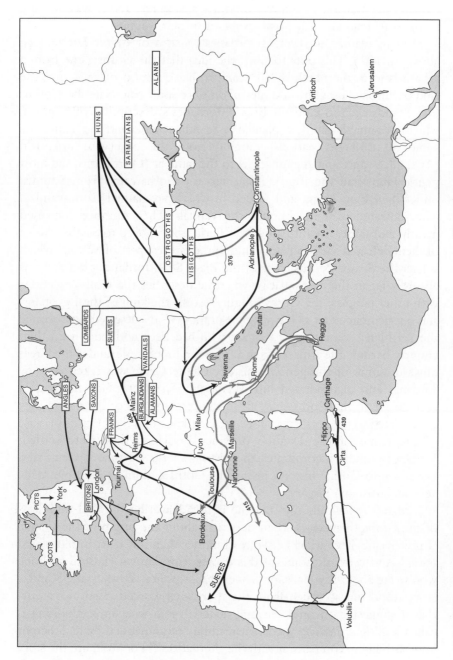

Map 10 A traditional beribboned view of the invasions of the late fourth and fifth centuries. (From Pierre Riché, *Les Invasions Barbares*, map 2).

instance, assures us that the Germans were highly mobile (see above, p. 25): they did not till the soil, but lived off their flocks; they did not have proper houses, but only temporary structures, and it was nothing to them to load all their possessions onto their wagons.[6]

Most to blame, however, is Jordanes's *Getica* or *Gothic History* (see above, p. 107). This puts forward the idea that the Goths came from a great island in the north called Scandza, like a swarm of bees, into the land of Europe (a slightly odd metaphor, since some pages later he explains that Scandza is too cold for bees).[7] Jordanes's description of Scandza, which presumably can be explained as Scandinavia beyond the Baltic, lists some 30 different nations, ranging from the otherwise unknown (Ahelmil, Evagre and Aeragnaricii) to the familiar (Ostrogoths, the most gentle Finns and the Rugi). Long ago the Goths came from Scandza under their king Berig, and settled in what they named Gothiscandza. They defeated their neighbours, the Vandals. Their numbers increased greatly, and under the fifth king after Berig, they moved to Scythia. Some of them defeated the Spali and came to the farthest part of Scythia, which is near the Sea of Pontus (that is, the Black Sea). Jordanes places all this absurdly far in the past, at least when he describes the Goths' relations with other peoples: the Goths fought Vesosis, the king of the Egyptians, and pursued him as far as Egypt; some of these Goths deserted, and became the Parthians; some Gothic women who had been abducted from their country became the Amazons; and from the time of Alexander the Great onwards some of the genuine history of the Getae was taken over by Jordanes and incorporated into this story. The Getae had nothing in common with the Goths apart from the resemblance of the name: they were related to the Scythians, and were later known as the Dacians because of the name of the Danube province in which they were settled. Jordanes grandly incorporates the history of the Scythians, Getae and Dacians into Gothic history, giving the Goths a glorious (and internally very inconsistent) history.

Jordanes specifically says that he is not delivering the oral traditions of the Goths themselves when he writes about the origin of the Goths: 'I prefer to believe what I have read, rather than put trust in old wives' tales.'[8] And certainly some of this comes from known classical authors, who wrote about Scythians, or Getae, or Goths. For Wenskus, the Scandza story stood out so much from the more well-worked classical material that it suggested an origin in oral material: it is what in text editing is called a *lectio difficilior*, 'a correct reading recommended by its inherent improbability in comparison with the alternatives'.[9] For Wolfram, the story allows him to make all kind of assumptions about continuity of traditions: he notes, for instance, that to the Vandals the Goths seem like *trouloi*, 'trolls, as the Scandinavians still call the demons and monsters of the other world', dismissing Olympiodorus of Thebes's explanation, that when the Goths were starving, they bought grain from the Vandals at one *solidus* per spoon (*trulla*) as 'folk etymology'.[10] Pohl likewise regards the Scandza story as an 'unpleasant irruption of archaic-style material', which 'subverts' the 'smooth and well-constructed, if totally fictitious, origin story of the Goths'; it is something which has to be fitted in awkwardly, to satisfy the (Gothic) audience, and therefore it might well be true.[11] In fact, the whole origin story is hardly smooth and well-constructed at all; apart from anything else, it is unbalanced by a long digression on the island of Britain (about which Jordanes knows more than the island of Scandza), and which seems to be there just so that he can display his authority by denying the reports (which he may have made up?) that the Goths came from some island other than Scandza. As Goffart notes, the whole section on Scandza in fact could be seen not as Pohl's 'unpleasant irruption of archaic-style material', but as yet another section in which Jordanes is embroidering his written sources: the idea that the Goths came from the 'snowy region' of the north had been there in Claudian and other Greco-Roman writers.[12] Goffart suggests a plausible reason for the Scandza origin: Jordanes was writing after the fall of Gothic Italy, and was engaged in a project to prove that they were interlopers from a distant barbarian world, 'that they (and their barbarian cousins) belonged outside, not within, the world of Rome in which they had lived and striven to exist enduringly for close to two centuries'.[13] Or, perhaps it comes from Cassiodorus. Christensen notes that when, late in life, Cassiodorus produces a list of useful historical reading for his monks, he does not include his own *History of the Goths*. Christensen speculates that the idea of Scandza had been developed by Cassiodorus out of hints in earlier Latin writers, in order to satisfy a particular political purpose in the days of Theodoric. Once Theodoric was gone, so was the point of the story. He did not recommend the work to his monks: 'he knew they could learn nothing from it, since it has nothing to do with the past'.[14] A third explanation for Scandza (and the passage on Britain which precedes it) is that it deliberately presents a 'combination of the very best and worst of peripheral life', a 'region of intense contradictions', as opposed to the familiar balance and moderation of the Mediterranean world. As Merrills concludes, 'it is the fantastic origin of the Goths that lends the *Getica* its impact and, ultimately, makes the eventual Roman assimilation of the group so meaningful'.[15]

Jordanes was not alone in relating a long migration of Germans from Scandinavia. The *Origo Gentis Langobardorum* (from the later seventh century) notes that the Langobardi came from the 'island of *Scadanan*

...in the regions of the north, where many people dwell'.[16] The Winniles were threatened by the Vandals, and the leaders of the Vandals asked Godan (= Woden) to give them victory. He promised victory to whichever people he saw first at sunrise. The Winniles asked Frea, Godan's wife, to give them victory, and she advised the Winniles to come at sunrise, with all their wives; and their wives were to have their hair down around their faces. Godan said, 'Who are these long-beards?' and Frea responded, 'As you have given them a name, give them also the victory.' And so the Winniles became the Langobards. They moved south and settled there; and then they moved south again into the lands of the Rugians, who had been defeated by King Audoachari (Odoacer); and then they moved south into Pannonia, and stayed there 42 years; and finally they moved south again into Italy.

Paul the Deacon's much more famous account of the *History of the Langobards*, written in the late eighth century, adopts much of this story. He changes the name of the island of origin to *Scadinavia/Scatinavia*, a form found in Pliny's *Natural History*.[17] Paul says that this land was so overcrowded that the peoples who were there organized themselves into three parts and threw lots to see which third should emigrate. The Winnili emigrated; and Paul repeats the story he found in the *Origo* about their change of name, although he says that it is 'a silly story', 'worthy of laughter'.[18] It is because of the men's long beards, not because of what the women of the Winnili did in the presence of Woden, that the Winnili came to be called the Langobards, Paul said. The rest of the trek from the shores of the Baltic to Italy is taken straight from the *Origo*, with a modicum of extra detail.

To some extent the heroic migrations of other peoples, as reconstructed by more recent historians, are borrowed from these accounts.[19] There is, of course, no reason to believe that these accounts are independent of each other. Jordanes wrote in Latin, and his text is known to have been available in Italy. The two Langobard/Lombard accounts probably used Jordanes, and perhaps were inspired by him to produce a Scandinavian origin for the Longobards. In these narratives we also find the Vandals and the Burgundians originating from the shores of the Baltic, and so they too were given a long history of migration.

It is not just within 'the Jordanes tradition' that peoples are said to have migrated long distances from one area to another. Bede, for instance, notes that the Picts came from Scythia. He tells us that the Picts landed first in Ireland, and asked to settle there; the Irish said that there was no room, but advised them to go to the neighbouring island of Britain. The Picts discovered that the Britons had seized the south of the island, so they settled in the north; since they had no women with them, they took Irish women, agreeing in recompense that the Picts would elect their kings from the female rather than the male line: 'and it is well known that the custom has been observed among the Picts to this day'.[20] Bede seems to have found the story among the Irish; since the Picts themselves left no written records, we have no idea whether this was their own origin myth or not.

Migration stories are a common feature of origin legends. John Adams, in a letter to Abigail Adams, described Thomas Jefferson's design for the seal for the newly created United States, which should show

> the children of Israel in the wilderness, led by a cloud by day and a pillar of fire by night, and on the other side, Hengist and Horsa, the Saxon chiefs from whom we claim the honor of being descended, and whose political principles and form of government we have assumed.[21]

Not only was the USA seen as being born from the Bible and from English law, but also, of course, from migration. In a similar way, the Great Trek formed the Afrikaner nation in South Africa, in myth if not fact, and Mao's Long March created Communist China. Sometimes the mythology of migration is purely metaphorical. The appeal of the Exodus story to African Americans in the Civil Rights era and earlier was its power as a story of liberation; and, for some, a new migration to Liberia was seen as a solution. The powerful notion of a 'chosen people' helps explain why Exodus has been evoked so frequently.[22]

Thomas Jefferson's seal refers to the English origin legend. Bede tells how 'they came from three very powerful peoples from Germany, the Saxons, Angles and Jutes', and were led originally by Hengist and Horsa: the sons of Wihtgisl, son of Witta, son of Wecta, son of Woden, 'from whose stock the royal families of many kingdoms claimed their descent'.[23] Hengist and Horsa ('stallion' and 'mare') may be as mythical as Woden; but it does look as if Bede could be relating a genuine English origin legend. The Saxons, he says, came from Old Saxony; the Angles from *Angulus*, which is between Saxony and the land of the Jutes. '*Angulus* is said to have remained deserted from that day to this.'[24]

The Franks too were given their migration stories: again, as with the Picts, we do not know if they had any of their own. For Gregory of Tours, they had come from Pannonia. For Fredegar, who wrote in the mid-seventh century, the Franks were descended from the Trojans. Their first king was Priam. Priam's sons included Aeneas and Frigas. From Aeneas sprang the Romans, as Virgil's *Aeneid* proclaims. Frigas's descendants included the Phrygians, the Macedonians and the Franks, with their king Francio.[25] In short, the Franks had as illustrious an ancestry as the Romans (if not more so); the propaganda point of the legend is obvious. The story is repeated in the eighth-century *Liber Historiae Francorum*, although with one or two interesting changes, which suggest that the source was not Fredegar directly; and it was the Emperor Valentinian who called them 'Franks', from a Greek word meaning 'fierce'.[26]

Now, it is quite clear that some of these origin legends were pure fiction, and not part of genuine 'tribal tradition'. The Trojan origin of the Franks (and, later, of the British too) was designed merely to place the Franks on an equal footing with the Romans, and has no more basis in historical truth than the idea that the Picts came from somewhere near the Danube.

The English origin legend, on the other hand, contains a good deal of truth. The Angles, Saxons and Jutes do indeed seem to have come from Saxony, Angeln and Jutland (even if we cannot tell whether Hengist and Horsa have any basis in reality). J.N.L. Myres argued that cremation urns from Markshall (Norfolk) and Wehden (Lower Saxony) were so similar that they must be the work of the same potter: either the potter himself migrated, or someone else took his toolkit (and found a clientele who was willing to take exactly the same kind of pots).[27] The cremation cemeteries of the homeland match up in many ways with the cremation cemeteries of south-eastern England, although many of the newcomers to England seem to have adopted the inhumation burial custom that they found in Britain. However, the pottery might not be such a clincher as Myres thought. He assumed that fifth-century cremation urns were domestic products, and that the earliest commercially produced pottery in England was the Ipswich ware of the seventh century. But more recent work has shown that as early as the late fifth century pottery was being produced in the Charnwood Forest area (Leicestershire) and distributed widely over the East Midlands, showing that the earliest Anglo-Saxon pottery was by no means outside the exchange system.[28]

The Jutes were the smallest of the named groups to come over, at least judging from the area they colonized: Bede said it was restricted to Kent, the Isle of Wight and the mainland opposite the Isle of Wight (i.e. Hampshire). There are certainly cultural links (pottery types) between Jutland and Kent, and also between Kent and the Isle of Wight. But Chris Arnold has noted that in the Isle of Wight we do not have wholly Kentish-style burials, merely certain Kentish artefacts; the material evidence may not be a result of wholesale settlement, but of links between families who have connections in Kent.[29] *The Anglo-Saxon Chronicle* (compiled first in the 890s) place the arrival of the West Saxons in the fifth century in Hampshire, in precisely the same area as the Jutes are supposed to have been. But, as Barbara Yorke has shown, this is almost certainly a sequence of events concocted in the 890s, precisely to show the descendants of the Jutes that they had no right to be there.[30] It had little effect: the New Forest was still called the Jutish Forest as late as the eleventh century. We know from Bede that the Isle of Wight in particular maintained its independence from the mainland for a long time: perhaps its Anglo-Saxon inhabitants adopted the Jutish ethnicity from Kent deliberately to ensure their distinctiveness and separation from more powerful neighbours on the mainland.

The Angles, Saxons and Jutes, of course, not only brought a material culture, but also their language: the clearest sign of an actual migration. While most of the barbarian peoples who settled within the former Roman Empire seem to have adopted, fairly rapidly, the Latin language of the majority population, the English managed to impose their language extremely successfully on the south-east part of Britain. In the west and south-west of what is now England there are a few signs of a Welsh substratum in the place-names; this is the area which was only conquered by the English in the seventh century or later. But in the south-east corner the place-name picture is almost wholly English.

There have been all kinds of attempts to explain this problem, which Margaret Gelling phrased as 'why aren't we speaking Welsh?'[31] One possibility, obviously, is that the English came over in such numbers, and with such violence, that they simply wiped the Welsh out. Bede used to be quoted frequently, in particular his remark that some of the British accepted perpetual slavery, some fled (to Brittany) and some 'remained in their own land and led a wretched existence, always in fear and dread, among the mountains and woods and precipitous rocks'.[32] (Less often quoted is the beginning of the following chapter, which says that the British emerged from their hiding places and defeated the invaders.) Archaeologists have never been satisfied with genocide as an explanation; they have not found evidence for huge numbers of newcomers, and increasingly have found evidence of the native population. In recent years archaeologists had begun to speak almost as if there was no invasion at all. But could a small number of people impose their language on a much larger group? This problem will be discussed further in the next chapter.

There has been limited speculation about the logistics of the Anglo-Saxon invasions/immigrations. Apart from the crossing of the Straits of Gibraltar by the Vandals, which was clearly a one-off operation directed by the Vandal leadership, there are no other barbarian migrations which involved the crossing of a sea. There is no doubt about the ability of these northern Germans to make the crossing. Late Roman sources seldom mention the 'Saxons' (a catch-all name for all northern Germans) without mentioning their maritime abilities. Most Saxons who appear in the

Roman sources are sea-borne pirates, or at least are assumed to be, as Sidonius Apollinaris jokes with his friend Namatius (who commanded a fleet on behalf of the Visigothic kings in south-west Gaul):

> The curving sloops of the Saxons, who give the impression that every oarsman you see in their crew is a pirate-captain – so universal is it for all of them simultaneously to issue orders and obey orders, to teach brigandage and to learn brigandage. . . . Shipwreck, far from terrifying them, is their training. . . . They gladly endure dangers amid billows and jagged rocks in the hope of achieving a surprise.[33]

Some boats from the period have been discovered, although there is still a lot of debate surrounding them. Are the known boats (mostly clinker built, some 20 m long) typical? Were they able to carry sail, or were they propelled by oars (as Sidonius seems to have thought)? John Haywood imagines a large-scale migration, coming 'in sailing ships with small professional crews who could make several return journeys in a season, building up the settlers' numbers rapidly',[34] although he admits that just because it would have been easier for them to use sails does not prove they did so. Such sailing ships could bring cargoes not only of the new settlers, but their herds and flocks as well. Michael E. Jones imagines not economic migrants, but warriors, sailing in ships that were far from reliable. 'Experiments with replicas of the Nydam and Kvalsund ships have revealed rather alarming features.'[35] For him, the ships would have had to cling to the coast and avoid bad weather: one trip could take anything from two to six months, and most of the space would be needed for the oarsmen and their provisions. Estimates of numbers of the migrants (over a period of perhaps a century and a half, from *c.* 410 to *c.* 550) vary wildly, from a maximum of 200,000 to a minimum (favoured by Jones) of 10,000 to 20,000.[36] Some would now put the population of Roman Britain as a whole at three or four million at its height; even allowing for a large population decline in the Later Roman Period, the Anglo-Saxon migration might have contributed hardly at all numerically to the population of the island.

These discussions between historians, archaeologists and philologists now have to take account of the scientists. In research that was reported in the press in 2002,[37] a team from the Centre for Genetic Anthropology at University College London, led by Mark Thomas, compared genetic samples from men whose paternal grandfathers had lived in seven market towns which had been founded in Anglo-Saxon times with men living in Friesland (Netherlands) and Norway. They looked at the Y-chromosome, which is passed from father to son with very few changes, and they examined particular genetic markers. The English and the Frisians had almost identical genetic make-up (and one can note that the modern Frisian dialect is closer to English than any other continental Germanic dialect today). The English were, however, quite different from the Welsh who were studied. Their conclusion at that time was that the migration of Angles and Saxons was massive, and that the dominance of the English genetic type was the result of ethnic cleansing. However, more recently this same team came to rather different historical conclusions from the same evidence: not 'ethnic cleansing' but 'apartheid'.[38] They estimated that the amount of genetic change indicated would suggest an immigration of over half a million people, which is considerably more than either archaeologists or historians have been accustomed to believe. Computer simulations were used to model the gene pool changes that might have occurred with a relatively small number of immigrants. They concluded that a small military elite could have established themselves as dominant by having more children who lived to adulthood, and by restricting intermarriage between ethnic groups. They point to the evidence from the Continent about bans on intermarriage (but see below p. 194), and to modern work showing that the number of children an individual has correlates significantly with wealth. Their computer model indicated that 'the genetic contribution of an immigrant population can rise from less than 10% to more than 50% in as little as five generations, and certainly less than fifteen generations'.[39]

Another angle to take on this question is investigating the situation in the Anglo-Saxon homeland. Is there evidence that Bede was right in saying that the areas of north Germany from which the migrants came to England were largely depopulated?[40] It has long been argued that there is indeed a real gap in the evidence for settlement in that area between the fifth and the seventh centuries. Some of the *terp/Wurt* settlements (see above, p. 137), such as Feddersen Wierde, seem to have been flooded out, and other coastal settlements also seem to have come to an end at this time. But the same phenomenon is found right across the North Sea world, from the Netherlands up to Denmark and even southern Norway. Those not wishing to say, simply, that this was a result of mass emigration have suggested that this area was depopulated by plague, or by a climatic change producing crisis and famine. However, in the 1980s it became apparent that this gap was more likely to be the result of the difficulty of recognizing sixth- and seventh-century settlements, because of changes in material culture and cultural behaviour. (Similar explanations were being put forward to deny the apparent collapse of the population in parts of northern Gaul in the fifth and sixth centuries.) The old cemeteries come to an end in Bornholm, for instance, because people started placing cremations in small cemeteries or even singly. The sixth- and seventh-century settlements in Vorbasse were discovered once the excavators realized that the settlement shifted around in the landscape. All this encouraged archaeologists to suggest to historians that Bede's account of large-scale migration was 'an origin myth'.[41]

However, work in certain regions would seem to regard this revisionism as misplaced. In Schleswig-Holstein the evidence for depopulation seems irrefutable. There are few signs of activity in the fifth to seventh century; only two of the large cemeteries of the region remain in use after the mid-fifth century, while the rest show clear signs of a dwindling population. Pollen analysis at Kosel, in eastern Schleswig-Holstein, shows a cessation of human activity (the absence of crop pollen for instance) and a recovery of the forest.[42] A very similar pattern is found at Flögeln in Lower Saxony, where cereal production ended and did not resume again until the eighth century. New discoveries might overturn these conclusions, but it looks at the moment as if Bede was indeed right: that portions of the Anglo-Saxon homeland were largely stripped of their inhabitants by the process of migration. Of course, that still does not necessarily mean large numbers: the area of north Germany being considered is a relatively small one, that perhaps never had a large population; a depopulation because of emigration to Britain may still not have contributed more than a hundred thousand to the population of Britain itself.

Numbers

The question of numbers is of course a crucial one, and has been much discussed in relation to other barbarian invasions and/or migrations. The discussion usually starts with our other sea-borne invasion: that of the Vandal invasion of North Africa in 429. Victor of Vita wrote (he says) 60 years after that event, and tells us:

> A large number made the crossing, and in his cunning Geiseric, intending to make the reputation of his people a source of dread, ordered then and there that the entire crowd was to be counted, even those who had come from the womb into the light that very day. Including old men, young men and children, slaves and masters, there was found to be a total of 80,000. News of this has spread widely, until today those ignorant of the matter think that this is the number of their armed men, although now their number is small and feeble.[43]

The first point to be made (and it frequently isn't, by those who cite this information) is that Geiseric supposedly wanted to broadcast a figure which would impress and alarm. People might well be alarmed by 80,000; but, as Victor stressed, this included everyone from the newly born to those on their deathbeds. Procopius makes clear what Victor only implies: that it was a trick perpetrated by Geiseric to make Romans think his forces were stronger than they were. To underline it, he appointed 80 chiliarchs, or leaders, of 1,000 soldiers (even though if 80,000 was the total population, the number of active soldiers would have been less than 10,000).[44] Oddly enough, in the *Secret History* Procopius seems to forget that it had been a lie, and uses the number as the size of the Vandal army in the 530s: 'The Vandals . . . numbered eight myriads, and as for their women and children and slaves, who could guess their number?'[45] As Goffart has pointed out, exactly the same inflation happens between Jerome and Orosius regarding the Burgundians: Jerome's *Chronicle* said that 80,000 Burgundians came up to the Rhine in 370, while Orosius added 'of armed men',[46] Ludwig Schmidt had argued that Geiseric's 80,000 has some validity, because after all Geiseric had to count heads in order to organize the embarkation of all his Vandals for the sea-crossing; and one still sees the figure of 80,000 given as one that might actually be plausible. But it would seem rather to be a standard figure, meaning 'large'. It was common in classical antiquity for certain large numbers to be used rather than others: 30 million sesterces, for instance, was the cost of a decent villa for Pliny, the annual expenditure on the corn dole for Plutarch and the amount spent on poison by Caracalla.[47] It is possible that 80,000 was just such a figure, although precise parallels are not easy to find (King Solomon conscripted 80,000 stonecutters, which is actually one of the largest numbers mentioned in the Bible).[48] Goffart suggests that the 8,000-strong phalanx of the Macedonians, Greeks and Dardanians might be behind this figure.[49]

We have other numbers supplied by our sources. Those barbarians who came across the Alps with Radagaisus in 405 numbered 400,000 according to Zosimus, 200,000 according to Orosius; and Augustine of Hippo said that more than 100,000 were killed.[50] 'It is to be observed,' noted J.B. Bury drily, 'that the lowest of these figures is given (by Augustine) in an argument where a high figure is effective.'[51] Bury himself decided (fairly arbitrarily) that the numbers 'did not exceed 50,000'.[52] Bury dismissed other high figures in equally cavalier fashion (probably quite correctly): thus, 'Jordanes gives the absurd figure of 165,000' for those who fell at Chalons in 451, when Attila invaded Gaul.[53] Bury does not mention, at this point, that Hydatius had given the number of deaths as nearly 300,000.[54] Procopius was capable of similar exaggeration, as when he said that 150,000 Goths besieged Rome in 537, or that the Franks claimed to be able to send half a million men across the Alps in 539.[55] Some sources, however, do give lower numbers, which historians are usually inclined to accept. Ammianus says that the Roman scouts before the battle of Adrianople reported that the Visigothic army numbered around 10,000, which was clearly an underestimate, as it turned out after the Roman defeat, but obviously not so much as to appear implausible to Valens.[56] Jones estimated that the measures of grain given to Wallia in exchange for his hostage Galla Placidia would have kept 15,000 Visigoths fed for a year; and Javier Arce reckons that when Ataulf's Visigoths were in Barcelona (whose population was only just over four figures) they were probably about 12,000 strong.[57] Procopius gave the total number of the warriors of the Herules – a minor but by no means insignificant people – as 4,500; and Bury is surely right to say that the impression that he gives of the numbers of Goths and Romans fighting in Italy in the mid-sixth century suggest armies 'to be counted by tens, not by hundreds of thousands'.[58]

The question of the size of armies in the late Antique and early Medieval Period is closely related to this debate, particularly if we think that many of these 'movements of peoples' are, in effect, much more 'movements of armies' (with their inevitable hangers-on). As Guy Halsall points out pungently, 'no historical writer from this period (and probably no one else either) ever went and counted an army'.[59] We have widely differing estimates even for the troops on the same campaign. A Frankish army fighting on Visigothic territory is nearly wiped out, with 5,000 dead and 2,000 prisoners, says Gregory of Tours; while Isidore of Seville says that the Frankish army was 60,000 strong.[60] Who was right? And who is right in the modern debate between small and large? Halsall is of the opinion that the largest army in the field was unlikely to be more than 5,000, and could be a lot smaller; Bernard Bachrach has argued that there were 100,000 men on the battlefield of Chalons in 451. The problems of provisioning a large army, given the scale of the economy and of markets in the period, would be considerable; and, if provisioning was not well organized, the political damage caused by the inevitable destructiveness of a foraging army in one's own kingdom would be equally considerable. Timothy Reuter suggested that if 20,000 men (four times the population of Paris) really had been put in the field in the ninth century then it would have had an impact on the local economy and society analogous to 'the down-wind ellipse of fall-out from a nuclear weapon'.[61] Logistical problems should be a major factor in our discussion of migrating numbers too. It is very difficult to imagine 80,000 people moving through the countryside, foraging as they went, without bringing untold suffering to the native inhabitants and, more significantly, to themselves, not to mention the loss of any cohesion they might have had as a fighting force.

Scandinavian Origins

As we have seen, origin legends claimed that a number of barbarian peoples came from Scandinavia: which (given that these peoples ended up in the Mediterranean world) immediately builds an element of long-distance migration into their story. Is there archaeological support for the idea of the Scandinavian and Baltic origins of the Goths and other barbarian peoples (the Herules, Gepids and Lombards, for instance)?

At the beginning of the twentieth century the German archaeologists G. Kossinna and E. Blume argued that the appearance of inhumations in the cemeteries of the Lower Vistula in the first century AD was a sign of Gothic emigration from, they suggested, Gotland (the archaeologically rich Swedish island in the western Baltic). Scandinavian specialists, however, argued that south-west Sweden, rather than Gotland, was a more likely origin of these changes in the archaeology of northern Poland. In the 1940s another German archaeologist, R. Schindler, drew up a short list of the new cultural elements appearing south of the Baltic in the first century BC: the appearance of inhumations, the absence of weapons in the tombs and certain types of dress items and pottery which he saw as marking the change from the Oksywie culture to the Wielbark culture, found largely to the east of the Lower Vistula. Another feature is the appearance of tombs with various arrangements of stones: a circular surround, or a mass of stones under a barrow, under which are several tombs, both inhumations and cremations. The Wielbark culture has been taken by many as the first witness of Gothic culture on the Continent.

This has not been a conclusion that all have been willing to accept. To start with, it is notoriously difficult to bring archaeological cultures into direct connection with named ethnic groups. Second, the explanation of the appearance of new cultural features by means of a hypothetical migration is one that has been overused, and brought into some disrepute. In the case of the Wielbark culture, the Polish archaeologist J. Kmiecinski, for instance, has argued that most of the elements can be explained in terms of local developments, without the need for the *dei ex machina* of Scandinavian immigrants. R. Wotagiewicz has examined the sites where these tombs employing stone elements have been found: mostly in Pomerania, to the west of the Vistula, and not in the main Wielbark area: there are analogies in southern Sweden and Norway, and on the islands of Gotland, Öland and Bornholm but, on the other hand, they are found on only 17 sites south of the Baltic. Perhaps, suggested Wotagiewicz, we are looking at the migration of a small (presumably military) elite from Scandinavia, which managed to achieve some kind of dominance south of the Baltic. There is no reason to equate that elite with the Goths alone, since other peoples were closely associated with them, including the Gepids and the Rugians. One of the elements which we find in the Wielbark culture that does seem to repeat elsewhere in the archaeology associated with the Goths is a negative: the absence of iron weapons in graves. There are some Wielbark cemeteries, such as Brulino-Koski, where this absence is underlined, as it were, by the appearance of small replica weapons in bronze, as if recognizing that some taboo about the deposit of iron weapons needed some apology.[62]

Somewhat less controversial than the Wielbark culture as a physical manifestation of the Goths is the culture whose full name ought to be the Sîntana de Mureş/Černjachov culture, but which is frequently known simply as the Černjachov culture.[63] It was recognized early in the twentieth century that the grave-goods found at Černjachov near Kiev in the Ukraine were very similar to those excavated by Romanian archaeologists in Sîntana in Transylvania. The area where these sites are found covers a huge territory, from the Danube to the Don and beyond, and from the Black Sea up to Kiev.[64] The objects from the cemeteries (which provide us with the bulk of our data from this culture) date from the third and fourth centuries, which corresponds to the period during which (according to our written sources) the Goths are dominant in this area. But there is considerable variety within this culture, and it is difficult to know whether it can be ascribed to the Goths, or rather to the whole group of native and incoming peoples whom the Goths may have dominated in this period. What we can say is that we are dealing with a settled agricultural society, living in dispersed villages, keeping a wide variety of livestock, indulging in a variety of crafts and engaged in a good deal of trade with the Empire. It is certain that the Goths must have had some relationship with this archaeological culture; it is much less certain that any people whom we could call 'Goth' had their origins much further north than this region. It is also notable that excavation on a number of sites seems to show continuity from this late Roman Period right the way through into the Middle Ages.

The history of the debate about the origin of the Vandals has followed a similar route.[65] In the early third century Cassius Dio says that they were near the Danube frontier, between the Marcomanni and the Goths: from there they crossed into Gaul in 406, and thence into Spain and beyond to North Africa. There is no doubt about that aspect of their migration, although one might question how many of Geiseric's Vandals could actually trace back their ancestors to the Danube, given that many other groups, notably the Alans, had joined the Vandals by his time. The more basic question is, had the Vandals migrated to the Danube from somewhere else? Jordanes said that the Goths had to fight with the Vandals soon after their arrival from Scandza, which would place them on the Baltic coast. In the first half of the twentieth century, German archaeologists accepted this as fact, identifying the Vandals with the Przeworsk culture of central and southern Poland, and tracing this back to the East Pomeranian culture of an earlier period, and then back still further (with the slender support of a place-name) to the cemetery of Kraghede on Vendsyssel in northern Jutland (Denmark). Pottery from Vendsyssel was regarded as very similar to pottery from Silesia, 'proving' a migration from Jutland towards the south. The discovery that the Przeworsk culture itself expanded south towards the Danube in the second century seemed to show that Cassius Dio's Vandals had arrived on the Danube from the north. Jes Martens, in 1989, showed clearly how theories such as these march hand in hand with contemporary political and cultural assumptions. German archaeologists before the Second World War were keen to promote the idea that Vandals migrated from Denmark down to the Danube, and thence to Africa. After the War, Danish and Polish archaeologists were concerned to present their archaeology in terms of local developments, which did not require migration as an explanatory factor. Archaeological theory in the second half of the twentieth century tended to concentrate on economic and socio-historical processes, and to downplay explanations based on invasion or migration. Martens himself wonders whether it is time to go back to the ideas of a movement of cultures from Denmark down to the Danube; but he also presents all the evidence why this should not be the case. There are similarities between the archaeology of northern Jutland and the Przeworsk culture of Poland; but other explanations for this are possible. On balance, at the moment, it seems safest to begin our history of the Vandal migration not in northern Jutland, but on the Danube.

We have one apparently well-attested case of a long-distance migration, and of connections with Scandinavia – the Herules or *Eruli*. But in this case they were not travelling south into the Roman Empire, but northwards to Scandinavia. They were a group apparently related to the 'Scythians' or Goths;[66] but not much is known about them, and most of that comes from Procopius. He says that they used human sacrifices, and their elderly or sick would climb up onto their funerary pyre and wait for another Herule to kill them with a dagger. A self-respecting widow was expected to commit suicide by hanging herself by the tomb of her husband.[67] (This is all ethnographic embellishment such as is common in Procopius, and does not have to be taken too seriously.) At the time of Anastasius they lost a major battle against the Lombards (who were living near the Danube), and many were killed, including their leader Rodolf. They moved to where the Rugians had lived before they went to Italy with Theodoric: along the Danube upstream from Vienna. Then they went to live near the Gepids, and then – still during the reign of Anastasius (491–518) – they were accepted as federates south of the Danube, and settled in the region of Singidunum (Belgrade).[68] A splinter group of Herules, however, did not want this fate (or perhaps this humiliation?), and crossed all the nations of the Sclavenoi (thus, right across central Europe) as far as the Danes, and then they came to the ocean and went to Thule.[69] Elsewhere Procopius said that the semi-mythical Thule was 10 times the size of Britain; it must be Scandinavia.[70] This was not the end of the story, however: back in Illyricum, the Herules killed their king, "laying against him no other charge than that they wished to be without a king thereafter".[71] But when they reflected on it they decided that they needed a leader after all, and they sent an embassy to those who had gone to Thule, who included many of the royal family, and asked one of them to come south to rule over them.

According to Procopius, there were two main groups of Herules at this time, under the Emperor Justinian, one in Illyricum and one in Thule. But there may have been others: Hydatius says that Herule pirates attacked north-west Spain in 455 and 459;[72] Eugippius talked of Herules attacking Ioviaco on the Danube (see above, p. 74), in the 460s or 470s. They are a people who fragmented, as opposed to groups like the Franks or the Visigoths, who accreted other peoples to them. The Herules disappear from sight in the sixth century 'not because they were exterminated, but because they ceased to call themselves Eruli'.[73] But they do, if we are to trust Procopius, give us an idea of the long-distance movement that was possible in the Migration Period. We see this with individuals as well: Jordanes claims that a Scandinavian king called Roduulf emigrated to Italy to serve under Theodoric;[74] while Agrivulfus, of the Warni (living near the Baltic coast of Germany), served as a general under the Visigothic king Theodorid, who placed him as a ruler of the Suebi in Spain.[75] One might compare this with what one can detect about archaeological connections between Scandinavia and 'Gepidia', largely the Tisza valley of Hungary, in the sixth century: occasional Swedish brooches, and large numbers of beads made of Baltic amber. The great bulk of the amber beads found north of the Danube on either side of 500 are found in the Gepid cemeteries of the Tisza valley, which suggests that somehow the Gepids had managed to monopolize this trade.[76]

Conclusions

The evidence suggests that what migration took place was on a small scale; that barbarians did not move through Barbaricum or the Empire in large numbers; and that some migrations which we read of in our sources never took place at all. Even with small numbers, however, we should not underestimate the amount of devastation that the barbarians might have unleashed on the countryside which they moved through.

The destructiveness of barbarians on the move is best captured in Hydatius's chronicle, which gives a north-west Iberian view of the events of the fifth century. It is a wonderful document for all those who want to believe in the negativity of the barbarians: how they brought disorder, destruction, violence and death into the Roman world. Theodoric II of the Visigoths sent a varied group of barbarians into Asturica in Gallaecia:

> In the city they found crowds of people of every kind whom they imme-diately slaughtered; they broke into the holy churches, tore down and destroyed the altars, and carried off every holy object, both decorative and practical; . . . they set fire to the remaining empty houses of the city and laid waste parts of their fields.[77]

This, repeated again and again, pictures a situation which must have seemed like the end of the world. But, as Richard Burgess has shown, this was exactly what Hydatius intended, for he *knew* that the end of the world was coming. His preface introduced 'all the calamities of this wretched age', and 'the frontiers of the narrowly-confined Roman Empire that are doomed to collapse', and talks of his own Gallaecia, with 'the state of ecclesiastical succession perverted by indiscriminate appointments, the demise of honorable freedom, and the downfall of virtually all religion based on divine instruction', which Hydatius regarded as a result 'of the domination of heretics confounded with the disruption of hostile barbarian tribes'; and all this will be 'brought to completion' by the next generation.[78] Hydatius was convinced not only by the catalogue of disasters he had witnessed, but also by the natural disasters which he recorded (earthquakes, eclipses, comets), and which corresponded to prophecy. As Burgess notes,

> he wrote his chronicle in the full knowledge that he was recording the begin-ning of the end, the end of Gallaecia, the end of the *imperium Romanum*, the end of the world. And in a strange way that he could never have fore-seen, he was right.[79]

Finally, it is worth noting that the barbarians were not the only ones on the move. The arrival of barbarians within the Empire could cause panic and evacuation, particularly by the upper classes, who could not only afford to travel but also probably had estates elsewhere in the Empire to which they could retire. The sack of Rome in 410, the invasion of

Gaul by the Visigoths and the capture of Carthage in 439, all caused refugees to flee elsewhere. The Anglo-Saxon attacks caused a widespread flight of Britons to Armorica, giving it the new name of Brittany. In the sixth century there was a large-scale flight from the Balkans; in the seventh century from the Middle East as a whole, in the face of the rapid advance of the Arabs.[80] Theodore of Tarsus (in southern Asia Minor) may have been one of these refugees; in 668 he found himself, to his surprise (or horror), being appointed Archbishop of Canterbury by the Pope.

Sometimes these evacuations were organized by the authorities. Severinus (see above, p. 73) organized the evacuation of cities that could not be defended, and in the end Odoacer apparently had the whole Roman population of Noricum (including the relics of St Severinus) evacuated to Italy. Some cities in the Balkans seem to have been deliberately evacuated in the sixth and early seventh century. In addition, large numbers of Romans in the Danube provinces fled south, to Thessalonica and to the islands in the Aegean. The bishop of Patras and his flock moved from the Gulf of Corinth right across to Sicily; while the numbers of Greek-speakers in Sicily, southern Italy and Rome increased dramatically. Of the first eight Popes of the eighth century, only one was Italian: the rest were either from the Greek-speaking East or born to parents who were. It is difficult to think of another period before the twentieth century in which migrants, evacuees and refugees played such an important part in the life of Europe.

chapter nine

ASSIMILATION, ACCULTURATION AND ACCOMMODATION

These terms are more familiar to anthropologists and sociologists than to historians, but they may be of use in trying to understand the complex interaction between barbarian societies and Roman societies in the period covered by this book. Assimilation may be defined as an abandonment of ethnic distinctions and the acceptance by an incoming group of the cultural norms of the mainstream culture; acculturation is the bringing together of two cultural groups so that cultural elements may transfer from one to the other; accommodation is a process through which two societies or cultural groups work out a procedure whereby each group retains aspects of their own culture.[1]

In this chapter we shall mostly be looking at these processes in relation to the barbarians who settled in the Roman Empire, basically because our written sources tell us much more about that, and because our archaeological sources for Barbaricum are difficult to interpret. But, as ever, our sources can be very misleading. A barbarian who was totally assimilated into Roman society, for instance, or a Roman assimilated into barbarian society, each adopting the dress, customs and language of the other culture, is invisible to us through either historical or archaeological sources. Usually in our historical sources someone who is a barbarian of some kind, or a Roman, is not signalled as such in the text; their ethnicity is assumed from their name, which is by no means a secure procedure. Nor must we imagine (as historians once did) that there were hard and fast lines between barbarian and Roman, or that all contemporary observers of an individual would agree as to his or her ethnicity, let alone agree with the individual's own estimation of his or her ethnicity or identity. Intermarriage, close social and political relationships and changing ideologies all blurred the distinctions between barbarian and Roman, and enabled assimilation, acculturation and accommodation of different types and at different levels. But the more successful these processes are, the more difficult they are for us to discern and evaluate.

Plate 9 A Latin funerary inscription from Trier, from the end of the 4th century, recording the death of an aristocratic Burgundian in Roman service. It reads: "Hariulf, imperial bodyguard, son of Hanhavaldus, from the royal family of the Burgundians, lived for 20 years and 9 months and 9 days. Reutilo, his uncle, had the stone made".

Impediments to Assimilation

It is worth starting at the most basic domestic level. An imperial law was introduced in the 370s which forbade intermarriage between Roman and barbarian.

> No provincial, of whatever rank or class he may be, shall marry a barbarian wife, nor shall a provincial woman be united with any foreigner. But if there should be any alliances between provincials and foreigners through such marriages and if anything should be disclosed suspect or criminal among them, it shall be expiated by capital punishment.[2]

There are nevertheless a number of known marriages between Romans and barbarians. Soraci lists 15 between men with Roman names and women with German names, and 16 examples of the reverse. Many of these were from the barbarian kingdoms within the former Roman Empire, however; and he omits all those cases of marriage between Roman women and barbarians holding high military office within the Roman army, on the grounds that those barbarians must have acquired Roman citizenship.[3] Blockley's list uses somewhat different criteria (and only overlaps with Soraci's in a few cases), and consists of 32 marriages. If one looks only at the fourth- and fifth-century examples, 17 relate to marriages where Roman women marry barbarians, and 6 where Roman men marry barbarians.[4] But it is really impossible to know how common such marriages were from these lists, which (obviously) only concern those rare couples who happen to be recorded in our literary sources or on an inscription.

As Hagith Sivan notes, this law is an odd one, and probably does not mean what it seems to say. It is the only law like it in the entire corpus of imperial law; and it is addressed to a western *military* official, which suggests a situation of crisis in which civilian administration has been put in military hands. Marriages of this kind are not being punished in themselves; the emphasis of the law is on potential criminality. It uses the word *gentiles*, which can be translated as 'barbarians', but which in legal sources is only otherwise used of the native peoples of North Africa (Berbers) who have received land in return for military service. If this is so, then the most likely historical context is the revolt of Firmus in the 370s: he was a North African chieftain whose revolt seems to have attracted considerable sympathy among Roman provincials and soldiers. It took Theodosius four years to crush this revolt, and one of his main concerns was to seek out evidence of collusion between Romans and 'barbarians'/ Berbers.[5]

The compilers of the Theodosian Code in 438 were instructed to edit out specificities in individual laws to make them appear more universal than had been originally intended. But it is probable that few Romans before 438, and not many afterwards, saw this law as applicable to them. Marriages between Romans and Germans were permitted, and indeed (as in the case of Ataulf and Placidia, above, p. 61) could not only meet with no complaint but could actually be held up as a shining hope for the future. There is in fact no narrative source which says or implies that 'interracial' marriage was morally or politically wrong.

We are still left with the question that perhaps marriages between high-ranking German officers and Roman women met with no opposition because those officers had, by virtue of their rank, achieved Roman citizenship. The question of how barbarians acquired citizenship is a vexed one; of all barbarians, only Stilicho is declared, in one text, to be a citizen (and that may be because of his Roman mother).[6] But, whatever the legalities, at the upper levels of late Roman society, a fascinating picture emerges, literally, in the massive fold-out family tree which Alexander Demandt appended to his article on the 'osmosis of late Roman and Germanic aristocracies'.[7] Almost all the great names of the late Roman world, whether Roman or barbarian, from Constantine on the top left to Clovis in the bottom right, are linked together by marriage bonds. The military and political elite ignored any legal or social pressures against intermarriage, and became one (happy?) family. One might have expected that once the barbarian kingdoms established inside the Empire started issuing laws, the nominal progibition against intermarriage would disappear. On the contrary, the *Breviarium* of Alaric repeats Valentinian's law prohibiting intermarriage, and its commentary (the *interpretatio*) says that it refers to barbarian wives 'of any nation' (a stipulation certainly not found in the original law). Moreover, such marriages are punished by death, not if the marriage should result in anything 'suspect or criminal' as in the original law of the 370s, but simply as a consequence of the marriage. As John Matthews notes, 'it is a startling reflection that these words were written under Gothic overlordship'.[8] Nor does this law seem to have been abrogated among the Visigoths until the time of Leovigild, in the later sixth century.[9] At this point the earlier law was clearly thought to be unjust, or unnecessary:

> The zealous care of the prince is recognized, when, for the sake of future utility, the benefit of the people is provided for; and it should be a source of no little congratulation, if the ancient law, which sought improperly to prevent the marriage of persons equal in dignity and lineage, should be abrogated. For this reason, . . . we decree that if any Goth wishes to marry a Roman woman, or any Roman a Gothic woman, permission being first requested, they shall be permitted to marry.[10]

It is possible that Leovigild's attempt to remove this barrier was inspired by a desire to unify the two main peoples in his realm, Roman and Visigothic, which is also seen in his plan to produce a religious unity by enforcing a modified Arianism. This failed, and the 'unification' was not enacted, in theory at least, until his son Reccared persuaded his Visigoths to convert to Catholicism.

In a number of the barbarian kingdoms, Arianism seems to have served as a way of preventing assimilation. Many historians have noted, how among the Visigoths, Burgundians, Ostrogoths and Lombards, religious difference was preserved for a long time, and have speculated that this might have been done deliberately, in order to preserve the distinction between barbarian and Roman, and in particular in order to prevent the barbarian ruling minority from being totally overwhelmed by the Roman and Catholic culture of the majority. Arianism might thus have been used as a political tool; extrapolating from this, one might see Arianism as a guise for 'nationalism' within each of these peoples. This might be underlined by the continuing use of Ulfila's Gothic Bible in the liturgy of both Visigoths and Ostrogoths. The preservation of their language (which may by the sixth century have been used rarely in everyday life) set them apart from the Romans, as did the misinterpreted law forbidding intermarriage.

On the whole, however, historians have abandoned seeing heresies in these crude terms,[11] and have also modified the idea that all these barbarian peoples were devout Arians. Ian Wood has noted that there is little evidence of staunch Arianism among the Burgundians, apart from in Gundobad's immediate family;[12] while Stephen Fanning has shown that Arianism was not deeply rooted among the Lombards. Most Lombards were still pagan when they came into Italy in 568, and although there were some Arians among them (including some of the kings) the religious history of the Lombards was largely that of a pagan people gradually converting to Catholic Christianity.[13] But there was occasional persecution by Arian kings nevertheless, most notably in the Vandal kingdom of Africa,[14] which does suggest that Arian devotion could be based on religious considerations rather than a determination not to allow their ethnic group be assimilated by the dominant Roman culture.

However, we do actually have an example of a barbarian people taking measures to preserve itself from assimilation; but this people was not afraid of the Romans, but of a more powerful barbarian people, the Goths. The Rugians, who followed Theodoric's Goths into Italy in 489, had been an independent people, wrote Procopius, but had become absorbed into the Gothic people and acted with them in all things. 'But, since they had absolutely no intercourse with women other than their own, each successive generation of children was of unmixed blood, and thus they preserved the name of their nation among themselves.'[15] Such strategies, perhaps, preserved the identities of some barbarian peoples, who disappear from our sources for centuries, only to reappear; in some cases, at least, they had been absorbed or dominated by other barbarian groups (such as the Huns), but then re-emerged to assert their independence.[16]

If barbarians did not preserve a religious distinction to protect themselves from assimilation, what about legal distinctions? It used to be thought that barbarian kings from the later fifth century onwards issued laws for their own peoples, while Romans in their kingdom still continued to use versions of Roman law (abbreviation of the Theodosian Code were fairly widely known in the early Middle Ages).[17] This system of legal personality, whereby one was judged according to the law appropriate for one's ethnicity, was seen to continue into the Carolingian period, and indeed Charlemagne, after his coronation as emperor in 800, issued or reissued law-codes for numerous of the ethnicities within his empire. There were complaints in the ninth century that this produced so many problems in practice that it should be abolished. However, the growing consensus among the legal historians is that 'personality' is a development of the eighth and ninth centuries, and does not reflect attempts by earlier barbarian kings at ethnic separation. Sidonius complained about how the traitor Seronatus wanted 'to trample the laws of Theodosius underfoot and replace them by the laws of Theodoric'.[18] This does not prove that Theodoric II had issued a law-code (rather that Sidonius wanted a play on words between Theodosius and Theodoric); that was probably the achievement of Euric. But it also does not suggest that Theodoric II wanted to set up a separate legal system for the Goths: quite the opposite – it seems that he (and Euric after him) wanted to legislate for both Romans and barbarians. Later on, law-codes issued by the kings of the Burgundians, Franks and West Saxons, to take just three examples, mentioned both barbarians and Romans as operating within the same legal system, and while not specifying that both should always use the same laws did, by offering more favourable legal conditions to barbarians than to Romans, attempt to persuade Romans to assimilate.

The Barbarization of Romans and Vice Versa

Acculturation worked two ways, of course: Romans in the new barbarian kingdoms could adopt barbarian ways just as easily as barbarians could adopt Roman ways. It is likely that there was a class difference here: as Theodoric of Italy said (according to the Anonymus Valesianus), 'a poor Roman plays the Goth, a rich Goth the Roman'.[19] It was the Roman aristocracy which stood to lose the most from the loss of their culture. As Jill Harries notes, Sidonius's letter to his friend Syagrius, who was acquiring far too intimate a knowledge of barbarian culture, disguises insecurity in ridicule.

> You are the great-grandson of a consul . . . You are descended from a poet . . . I am therefore inexpressibly amazed that you have quickly acquired a knowledge of the German tongue with such ease. . . . You have no idea what amusement it gives me, and others too, when I hear that in your presence the barbarian is afraid to perpetrate a barbarism in his own language. A new Solon of the Burgundians in discussing the laws . . . you are much visited, . . . you decide issues and are listened to.[20]

He finished by recommending that Syagrius retain his grasp of Latin, to avoid being laughed at, and keep up his studies of Burgundian so that he might maintain his superiority over the barbarians. Syagrius seems to have been drafting laws for the Burgundians just as Solon did for the early Athenians. What Sidonius feared, suggests Harries, was that 'the new Solon, and many other Roman careerists like him, who chose the service of Germanic kings rather than that of Rome, could "barbarize" the culture Sidonius held dear'.[21]

It seems that Syagrius was acting, in response to popular demand, as an arbitrator; he had removed legal cases from the official courts, and thus subverted the imperial system of law. The extension of informal legal proceedings, as Harries points out, greatly aided the breaking down of legal barriers between Roman and barbarian. Sidonius would like to preserve the sense of difference and superiority that Romans had over barbarians; the Visigothic kings, however, 'took what they wanted from the Romans to help them to rule'.[22] Alaric's *Breviarium* was not an acceptance of Roman ways of doing things: it was his claim to control over Romans and Roman law in his kingdom. Nor was it a simple repetition of Roman law: it was an edited version, which left out much and also repudiated any new laws issued by the emperors in Constantinople, and thus was an assertion of his independence from them. 'Roman law was exploited to emphasize Gothic dominance of the remnants of Rome. The laws of Alaric had supplanted the laws of Theodosius.'[23]

One document for Theodoric II is especially worth looking at: a letter which Sidonius Apollinaris (or his son) placed second in his collection of letters.[24] He says that his friend Agricola has often asked him to describe King Theodoric, and that he is happy to do so, since God and Nature have conspired to 'to endow him with a supreme perfection'. He is impressive to look at, well-shaped, sturdy and taking care in his appearance (and conforming to Roman standards of male propriety by making sure he did not grow a moustache). Before dawn he goes to an Arian church service; he spends the morning dealing with administration. Then he might inspect his treasures or his stables, or perhaps he goes forth hunting: he is a wonderful shot with the bow and arrow. At dinner there is 'Greek elegance, Gallic plenty, Italian briskness, the dignity of state, the attentiveness of a private home, the ordered discipline of royalty'. Then the king has a short nap, perhaps, and plays a board-game, with good humour, but with great competitiveness: this is a good time to ask him a favour, Sidonius adds, from personal experience. Then, around the ninth hour, 'back come the importunate petitioners, back come the marshals to drive them off; everywhere the rivalry of the disputants makes an uproar. This continues until the evening; then the royal supper interrupts and the bustle fades away . . .' There are rarely any low comedians at supper, and there are no hydraulic organs or chorus-singing or the playing of lyre or flute: only the string music that comforts the soul and soothes the ear. Then Theodoric retires to bed, and guards are posted at the royal treasury and at the entrances to the palace.

It is interesting that Sidonius mentions no problems of communication with this king. When Theodoric's successor Euric met with Bishop Epiphanius of Pavia, an ambassador from the emperor in 474/5, Euric spoke in Gothic (or 'I know not what strange tongue') and Epiphanius had to answer through an interpreter.[25] Elsewhere, in other letters, Sidonius expresses some superior contempt when contemplating barbarians (Burgundians stank);[26] and he expresses some disapproval also of his aristocratic friends and colleagues, like Syagrius, who were too friendly with barbarians. But he is prepared to offer this picture of a barbarian king, presented almost as an ideal ruler. It is in a letter addressed to a friend, but we may assume that it was intended to be circulated, and it could thus be seen as an appeal to his aristocratic circle to regard the king controlling their region as someone worth following and supporting – in large part because he was very like them.

Numerous barbarians before Theodoric, of course, had adopted Roman culture, or maintained a judicious medium between Roman and barbarian ways. One can look at and compare individuals from an earlier period, as Chauvot did.[27] He took Arbogast and Modares as examples. Both of them came into conflict with their own compatriots because they had made a decision to join with the Romans. Claudian called Arbogast a *Germanus exsul*; he seems to have been thrown out by his fellow Franks, but in 392 he returned to them at the head of an imperial army, apparently following up old enmities.[28] Modares was a high-status Goth who made the decision to join the Empire in 380; he was Orthodox, and came into conflict with both pagan and Arian Goths, and was responsible for a number of their deaths. Both men had their close links within the Roman Empire: Arbogast to a circle of senatorial pagans, and Modares was a correspondent of Gregory Nazianzus. Some of these prominent barbarians seem to have lived in a dual world. The Frank Mallobaudes, for instance, is called *comes domesticorum et rex Francorum* by Ammianus, around 378.[29] Could he have been both count of the domestics *and* king of the Franks at the same time, or did one follow the other? We must imagine many people having twin loyalties, or even twin identities, like Hariulf, a Burgundian aristocrat from around 400, who was *protector domesticus* and also the son of the *regalis* [petty king] Hanhavald.[30]

We must not, however, underestimate the political difficulties that might ensue from a decision to Romanize. Silvanus was the son of Bonitus: Franks, but both with purely Roman names. Silvanus tried to flee to the Franks after his failed usurpation, but they rejected him (see p. 44). We have already seen (p. 88) how the Ostrogothic regent Amalasuntha wished to bring up her son Athalaric like a Roman prince, and gave him as tutors a Roman teacher and three elderly wise Goths. But the mass of Goths wanted him brought up 'after the barbarian fashion'. They came before Amalasuntha and complained that 'letters are far removed from manliness, and the teaching of old men results for the most part in a cowardly and submissive spirit . . . They added that even Theodoric would never allow any of the Goths to send their children to school; for he used to say to them that, if the fear of the strap once came over them, they would never have the resolution to despise sword or spear'. They told her to let Athalaric have youths his own age as companions, which would give him 'an impulse towards that excellence which is in keeping with the custom of barbarians'.[31]

A Christian Ideology of Assimilation

A fascinating text illuminating the matter of assimilation is provided by Salvian, a priest from Marseille, who fled from the instability produced by the barbarians in northern Gaul to the far south, where he became a monk at the celebrated monastery of Lérins, and wrote (in the 440s) his treatise on *The Governance of God*. David Lambert has recently called this 'perhaps the most substantial literary assessment of ethnic and religious difference to have been written in late antiquity'.[32] It is not a factual source; it is a highly subjective and individual response to the state of affairs in the Western Empire in the 440s – after the takeover of south-west Gaul by the Visigoths and the fall of Carthage to the Vandals.

Salvian's basic premise was that the events of recent decades showed that God was punishing Romans for their sins, through the barbarians. This was nothing new: it is an inevitable conclusion that a Christian would reach after reading the Old Testament, where the Hebrews were constant victims of God's discipline. It was the same conclusion that, a century later, the Welsh monk Gildas reached when he tried to understand the barbarian invasions of Britain, and decided to point out to his contemporary clerics and kings that the correct response was to reform their lives and their morals. Salvian, however, went one step further. Barbarian power was increasing, he said, not just because the barbarians were the instrument of God, but because they were actually morally superior to the Romans. Pagan barbarians were better than the Romans, because although they were lustful, greedy and unjust, like the Romans, they, unlike the Romans, did not know any better. Arian Christian barbarians, on the other hand (and here Salvian must have known he was on shaky ground, praising heretics), also knew no better, because they were reading a version of the Bible which had been so distorted by its Arian editors that it was not really the Bible at all. They could not be blamed; indeed, they should be praised for their greater virtue. 'We love impurity; the Goths abominate it . . . Fornication among them is a crime; with us it is a distinction and an ornament. . . . [The Goths] are now cleansing by chastity those lands which the Romans polluted by fornication.'[33] For Salvian the Vandals are the most chaste of the barbarians: God gave Spain to them not just to punish the Spanish for their impurity, but also to humiliate them by giving them to the weakest of barbarian peoples. And then, with Spain punished, God sent the Vandals into Africa, where the worst of all Romans lived.[34] And the Vandals were not corrupted by this: indeed, they actually set about reforming the morals of the Africans. They acted against homosexuality and prostitution; they restrained adultery and protected the chastity of women. 'What hope can there be for the Roman State when the barbarians are more chaste and more pure than the Romans?'[35]

Most scholars who have looked at Salvian – particularly left-wing scholars – concentrate on his trenchant criticisms of the Roman state, of the exploitation of ordinary Romans by both the state and the property-owning classes and of the appalling burden of taxation upon the poor. 'What towns . . . are there in which there are not as many tyrants as *curiales* [provincial officials and tax-collectors]?'[36] The result of this exploitation is that people flee from it:

> The poor are despoiled, the widows groan, the orphans are tread underfoot, so much so that many of them, and they are not of obscure birth and have received a liberal education, flee to the enemy lest they die from the pain of public persecution. They seek among the barbarians the dignity of the Roman because they cannot bear barbarous indignity among the Romans. . . . They prefer to live as freemen under an outward form of captivity than as captives under an appearance of liberty. . . . Therefore, in the districts taken over by the barbarians, there is one desire among all the Romans, that they should never again find it necessary to pass under Roman jurisdiction.[37]

Of course there is a good deal of rhetoric in Salvian's argument, and a reuse of the classic motif of the noble savage. But it does seem that Salvian genuinely believed that it was the barbarians 'who represented the main active force for the propagation of a truly Christian way of life in his time'.[38]

Britain as a Case Apart?

In Britain the absence of assimilation and cultural contact is quite surprising, and does suggest that the process by which much of lowland Roman Britain became Anglo-Saxon England was very different from what is found in most of continental Europe. There seem to be only around 30 words in Old English which are derived from Brittonic (early Welsh).[39] The English did not apparently allow the British to convert them, but waited for Italian missionaries to arrive, well over a century after the migration to Britain. Although there are some Welsh names in the Anglo-Saxon royal genealogies (the earliest known 'West Saxon' king is called Cerdic, a good Welsh name), no attempt was made at a later date to forge ideas of common identity or ancestry. We have already seen (above p. 183) how the genetic evidence suggests that the two communities lived largely in social isolation from each other, but the historic evidence suggests the same. As Bryan Ward-Perkins has noted, the celebrated Victorian medievalist and fervent Anglo-Saxon nationalist Edward Freeman had commented on different patterns of assimilation: on the Continent the barbarians rapidly went native, but in Britain they either killed the Britons, drove them into exile or enslaved them. He summarized his ideas 'with chilling clarity' in a book for children:

> The British women of course would be made slaves, or they would some-times be married to their masters. Thus there may doubtless be some little British or Roman blood in us . . . Now you will perhaps say that our fore-fathers were cruel and wicked men. . . . But it has turned out much better in the end that our forefathers did thus kill or drive out nearly all the people whom they found in the land . . . [since otherwise] I cannot think that we should ever have been so great and free a people as we have been for many ages.[40]

Few historians these days believe that large numbers of Britons were massacred by the Saxon invaders. Enslavement, or forced labour of some kind, was more likely. And as for 'some little British or Roman blood in us', it is worth remembering the Irish historian Edward Thompson's remark: 'Genteel English historians speak of "intermarriage" and "co-existence" at this stage between Britons and Saxons: it is not respectable to mention rape.'[41]

Bryan Ward-Perkins has not only produced an explanation for the whole-sale Anglo-Saxonization of Britain which sounds very plausible, but has also produced medieval parallels on the Continent which show that England was not such a unique case as it first appeared. In the late ninth century, for instance, the Magyars conquered what had been the Roman province of Pannonia. Probably most of the conquered people were by then Slavic-speakers, but in due course the population of Hungary became Magyar-speakers. Likewise, in the ninth century or thereabout, Pictish-speakers disappear from Scotland, and the language of the Irish migrants to Scotland became dominant in the west and north of Scotland: what became modern Gaelic. And in the period covered by this book, the language of the British migrants to north-west Gaul totally swamp the native speakers of Latin or, possibly, Gallic, to give us modern Breton.

There were, as Ward-Perkins points out, a number of differences in the British situation. To start with, the British actually resisted the barbarian advance much better than did the provincials of the continental Empire; this helped create a wall between 'Welsh' and 'English' that preserved two separate cultures, but also perhaps made it much more difficult for the British living under Anglo-Saxon rule to preserve their own culture. Even east of the Pennines the British kingdom of Elmet preserved its independence until the seventh century; what is now western England survived even longer. It was only in 1282 that the English, under Edward I, conquered the north Welsh kingdom of Gwynedd. 'Indeed, a strong case can be made for Gwynedd as the very last part of the entire Roman Empire, east and west, to fall to the barbarians' (remembering that even Constantinople fell, temporarily, to the 'Franks' in 1204).[42] The second factor was that Britain seems to have de-Romanized before it was Anglo-Saxonized. The strong Roman institutions which helped preserve *Romanitas* under Frankish rule in Gaul were simply not there. When invaders discover a strong native culture, they borrow heavily from it; where they find one they perceive to be inferior, they impose their own. The case, Ward-Perkins suggests, may be like that later in the Middle Ages when Germans moved eastwards into Slav lands east of the Elbe. Large numbers of Slavs adopted German culture, and in the process donated very few words of Slavic to German. Many Welsh may have adopted Englishness willingly, or under pressure. The laws of King Ine of Wessex, from the later seventh century, show that the West Saxons discriminated legally against the Welsh in Wessex (some of whom were clearly of high social status), which must have been an incentive for many to declare a shift of identity.[43]

Mechanisms of Settlement

The integration or assimilation of barbarians into the Roman Empire may relate to the mechanisms by which they were settled in the Empire. Some barbarians, like Saxons or Vandals, conquered. But most barbarian peoples seem to have come to some kind of agreement with the Empire. There are two words which appear in our Latin sources in particular: *deditio* and *foedus*. Those barbarians who had undergone the two processes were *dediticii* ('captives') and *foederati* ('federates'). As far as the Roman state was concerned in its early centuries, *deditio* was 'the surrender of a state, including the destruction of its political, religious, and national existence'.[44] Since each war was a breach of contract, and thus a kind of religious sacrilege, the victor of the war (Rome) was carrying out the punishment of the gods or God. Dedition could also be entered into voluntarily, to ensure survival in the face of attack by another barbarian people, for instance. Dedition arrangements were common in the late Roman period, and varied. Some *dediticii* were settled within the Empire as *coloni* or farmers, and were liable to be called up into the army; other *dediticii* remained within their peoples, either inside or outside the Empire, under the terms of the negotiated arrangements. It is likely that those negotiations favoured the growth of monarchical power within the peoples defined by *deditio*: it was easier for Romans to negotiate with individuals. It is possible that the amalgamation of smaller groups into larger ones (the federations of Alamans, Franks and Goths) occurred also as a result of the demands of negotiation.

Historians used to regard *dediticii*, surrendered peoples, and *foederati*, those who had freely entered into a *foedus* or treaty, as quite separate groups of people. But a *foedus* is precisely what is negotiated after a *deditio*, whether freely entered into or not; and really all depends on what the conditions laid down by the treaty actually were. Procopius and Jordanes (both writing in the sixth century) regard *foederati* as barbarians acting as paid soldiers for the Empire; they treat these arrangements as made almost as between equals. But Ammianus uses the word *foedus* of almost any kind of agreement made by a capitulating barbarian people.[45] The details of the agreement differed. Sometimes barbarians might be required to supply men for the army; Suomarius, an Alamannic king defeated by Julian, had to provide food for the Roman army; another Alaman, Hortarius, had to provide carts and timber to help repair the damage caused by his attack.[46] There was no uniformity, not even in the way the treaty was drawn up. Presumably in most cases it was drawn up following Roman protocols, but Ammianus tells us that in 354 Constantius drew up his treaty with the Alamanni 'in accordance with the rites of the Alamanni', while in 357 Julian made peace with three Alamannic kings who 'took oaths in words formally drawn up after the native manner that they would not disturb the peace'.[47] As Heather notes, the surprising thing is that these agreements, made after formal submission to the Empire, often seem to have included the payment of rich gifts to the barbarians on a regular basis. In 365 the Alamanni took up arms in response to Valentinian's decision to reduce the size of their annual gifts.[48] In effect, the Romans paid tribute to defeated barbarians on many occasions, as a very practical way of keeping the peace on the frontiers: the 'iron fist of imperialism . . . in a practical, well-informed velvet glove'.[49] It was a way in which barbarians might be drawn into the Roman system; it was a very obvious precedent for the different types of federate agreements that one finds from the early fifth century onwards.

The problem of the mechanisms of assimilation was given a new twist back in 1980 by Walter Goffart in his book *Barbarians and Romans*.[50] Goffart looked in detail at the mechanisms by which certain barbarian peoples – Visigoths, Burgundians, Ostrogoths and Lombards – were settled on Roman soil, and suggested the process was not only a peaceful one, which caused the minimum of resentment within the Roman population, but also allowed for the rapid acceptance of barbarians within Roman society. What is in question is the terms of the treaty (*foedus*) by which these peoples were settled within the Roman Empire, in 418/19 for the Visigoths, 443 for the Burgundians, 476 for Odoacer's barbarians and *c.* 584 for the Lombards. Sources in Gaul (but not in Italy) use the term *hospitalitas* for the process. It is a word which is sometimes used (though not exclusively) of the system of billeting soldiers on the civilian population. One expression of this was an imperial edict of 398, which specified precisely how a house in which a soldier was going to be billeted should be divided up.[51] There are laws which protect hosts from having their resources exploited (only those of the very highest rank could demand hot baths, for instance); literary sources suggest that the women in the household had the most to fear.[52] But, as Goffart pointed out pungently, all this has nothing to do with rules for dividing up landed property.[53]

Before Goffart, it had been assumed that the settlement of barbarians on Roman soil involved the expropriation of between one- and two-thirds of Roman properties in the area of settlement; in Italy, indeed, it was thought to have applied to all Roman landowners, depriving them of one-third of their properties. One of the main problems with this hypothesis is that there is no proof that Romans *were* deprived of their property on this scale, and no evidence of any opposition to this arrangement or resentment at the outcome. Ennodius, bishop of Pavia, wrote to Liberius, the bureaucrat responsible for arranging the settlement in Italy, saying 'You have enriched the countless hordes of Goths with generous grants of lands, and yet the Romans have hardly felt it. The victors desire nothing more, and the conquered have felt nothing.'[54] Cassiodorus, writing in the name of King Theodoric to the Roman Senate in praise of the same Liberius, took a comparable tone:

> It is my delight to mention how, in the assignment of one-third shares, he united both the estates and the hearts of Goths and Romans. For although neighbourhood usually causes men to quarrel, for them the sharing of property seems to have inspired harmony. . . . Behold, a new and admirable achievement: division of the soil joined its masters in good will; losses increased the friendship of the two peoples, and a share of the land purchased a defender, so that property might be preserved secure and intact.[55]

It is, as Goffart said, difficult to see how Cassiodorus's Roman audience could have shared in Theodoric's delight at this 'admirable achievement' if they had just been deprived of one-third of their property.

Somehow or other barbarians had been allotted *tertia* or thirds, and the words used by people like Ennodius and Cassiodorus are *terra*, *ager*, *possessiones*, which all refer to land. This is a serious difficulty for Goffart, who wanted to prove that what was given to barbarians was not land, but tax assessments. He admitted that 'there is no doubt' that the Goths were awarded 'land';[56] the problem is to understand what 'land' actually means in this context. The *illatio tertiarum*, a tax discussed in two of Cassiodorus's letters, may help explain it. Traditionally it had been understood as a tax amounting to one-third of a landowner's revenues, paid in lieu of actually ceding estates to Ostrogoths. In Goffart's view the evidence suggested that the *illatio tertiarum* was not a new tax, but was simply one-third of the normal tax levy, paid into a separate account. Another piece of Italian evidence supporting that was the use of the word *millenarii* of the Goths. This had been interpreted as a leader of a thousand troops (analogous to *centenarius*); but a *millena* was in fact a unit of tax assessment, first documented in Italy in 440. In one of Cassiodorus's official letters, we see King Theodoric ordering that one *millena* be assigned to the public baths in Spoleto: Goffart interprets this as meaning that an official would locate within the tax register an estate which would provide this value of tax, and transfer it to the *millenarius*, who would collect at source the value of his tax.[57] For Goffart, the references to Gothic *millenarii* must be linked to this institution; and a letter which implied that most Goths had their *sortes* or allotments, suggested that the transfer of tax assessments may have been on a large scale.[58] In Goffart's reconstruction, Goths did not pay tax on these *sortes*; but they did pay tax on land which they acquired by purchase or other means. As Goffart pointed out, if his theory is correct, acquisition of 'thirds' did not make the Goths landowners: their income came from tax proceeds, and thus 'their private interests were intimately associated, not just with something so elementary as private property, but with the state-instituted system of privilege on which their annual salaries depended'.[59]

It is tempting (and possibly rash) to read back from the relative detail afforded by Cassiodorus's letters to the much less well documented settlements in Gaul. We know something of how people in Spain and Gaul remembered the settlements, two or more generations later. The best evidence of all comes from law 54 of the Burgundian Code, issued by King Gundobad in the early sixth century (and thus a half-century from the original arrangements).[60] The words used here seem to argue against Goffart: the talk is all of slaves, lands, woods, houses and gardens. The houses and gardens which are shared between Roman and Burgundian, are, at least, one of the few signs in the evidence that some kind of billeting arrangements were made; but Goffart still reckons that the basic settlement involved a transfer of tax revenues. The more complex system described in law 54, he suggested, might be the result of a second donation by the king to his men, which turned the Burgundians into landowners.

Goffart failed to convince most of his fellow historians at the time.[61] Barnish, for instance, picked on the passage quoted above, in praise of Liberius, and emphasized that Cassiodorus-Theodoric had talked of the *losses* which increased the friendship between the two peoples: something that makes no sense if Liberius had been implementing a system in which *no one* lost, as Goffart argued.[62] Barnish was not convinced of other aspects of Goffart's interpretation either: on the non-military meaning of *millenarius*, for instance. The other early criticism of the Goffart position came from Ian Wood, who, like Barnish, concluded that barbarians must have received land, not tax proceeds.[63] Goffart received support from Jean Durliat, who in various studies of the late Roman taxation system and its survival argued that the procedures of tax collection were such that the transfer of tax-collecting rights to the barbarians could have been achieved relatively painlessly.[64] But the 'Goffart-Durliat theory' was itself criticized, most notably and cogently by Wolf Liebeschuetz, who admitted that Goffart's solution was 'a painless and administratively simple solution to the seemingly fiendishly difficult problem of accommodating the barbarians',[65] but nevertheless argued that it did not fit the surviving evidence. However, at the moment, I think that Noble is right to suggest that a majority of scholars accept the broad outlines of 'the accommodationist thesis although they vigorously argue about details'.[66] And this does have a profound effect on the way in which we regard the question of assimilation, at least in those provinces where agreements of this kind were reached. Barbarians were incorporated into the Roman structure as tax-collectors and soldiers. They may have been no more popular than Roman tax-collectors and soldiers among the general population, but they had a secure role, and one which gave them every incentive to preserve as much of the Roman system as they could for as long as possible.

It is often difficult to know how ancient authors are using particular Latin words. This can be seen in what survives as evidence of the Lombard settlement: two sentences in the *History of the Lombards* by Paul the Deacon. After 574, he says, 'many of the noble Roman nobles were killed from greed; the rest (*reliqui*) were apportioned among "guests" (*hospites*) and made tributaries (*tributarii*), that they should pay the third part of their products' to the Lombards.[67] Ten years later, 'the dukes gave up half of their possessions to royal uses . . . The "oppressed people" (*populi adgravati*), however, were parcelled out among their Lombard "guests" '.[68] First of all, of course, we have to assume that Paul – writing two centuries later – knew what he was talking about. But then we have to ask who the *reliqui* were: the whole Roman population, the landowners or a group of the landowners?[69] Was the third that they had to pay a third of the produce, of their income, of their tax or what? Who were the *populi adgravati*? What is a *tributarius*? He is clearly someone who pays tribute: but *tributum* in sixth-century sources can mean several things: the taxes paid by cities or individuals; the sum paid to a foreign ruler; or the rent, particularly perhaps that paid in respect of royal property held by someone else. Pohl has found various parallels between this text and the description given by Gregory of Tours of the arrival of King Childebert's tax inspectors in Tours in 589,[70] which suggests that what Paul the Deacon was talking about was, basically, the workings of the tax system. The *populi adgravati* were those who felt themselves to be unjustly assessed: that term is found in Gregory's account. There was certainly a good deal of violence and disruption involved in the settlement of the Lombards – more so than in other settlements in the former Western Empire – but ultimately the result was the same: the insertion by the Lombards of themselves at the head of the regime of exploitation that was the Roman Empire, and very little change of status for their Roman partners.

Archaeology and Assimilation

To what extent can we detect assimilation in the archaeological material? Again we have to look primarily at the cemetery evidence, and the first thing we have to do is question a number of common assumptions that have been (and are still being) made about burials in this period: that 'furnished graves' (that is, graves with items of dress and other grave-goods) are those of barbarians; that it is possible to determine the ethnicity of the person buried by the grave-goods placed in the grave; and that the custom of furnished burial is something to do with pagan ideas of the afterlife, and disappears with the conversion to Christianity (see above, p. 112).

At the level of basic generalization, a furnished burial in the centuries from *c.* 300 to *c.* 600 is much more likely to be the grave of a barbarian than that of a Roman. A typical cemetery of, say, southern France, with a disordered and closely packed array of stone-lined graves, with no grave-goods except the occasional pottery vessel, and with evidence of reuse of the graves and the cutting of one grave into earlier graves, is likely to belong to a community of Gallo-Romans. A cemetery in northern France, where the graves are aligned in fairly regular rows, where there is little overlap of burials and where the dead are buried fully dressed (with the survivals of metal items of dress-fasteners or adornments to prove it) and often with other items (spears, swords, vessels and so on), is, it has usually been argued, likely to belong to a community of barbarians. These 'row-grave cemeteries' (*Reihengräberfelder*), with more or less local variation in the particulars, can be found in the sixth and seventh centuries in a swathe of northern Europe from eastern Britain across northern France, the Low Countries and most of Germany, with outliers in Spain, northern Italy and central Europe. It was very natural to interpret these cemeteries as those of barbarian immigrants: the burial type was very different from that known earlier among Roman inhabitants of the Empire. Sometimes (as in eastern England and parts of northeastern Gaul) there were cemeteries of cremations, where the ashes were often placed in pottery vessels which were again very different from those of Roman manufacture. Not only had cremation to all intents and purposes died out in the Roman Empire two centuries or more earlier, but the burials bore close resemblance to those found in northern Germany, far from the Roman frontiers.

Using the cemetery evidence, maps of the Roman provinces could be drawn which showed where barbarians had settled. Some parts of the Empire, however, where barbarians are known to have settled from historical sources, proved to be blank on the distribution map of row-grave cemeteries. The tens of thousands of Visigoths who supposedly lived in south-west Gaul between 418/9 and 507 left not a trace of their presence on the archaeological record.[71] This could be explained by arguing that the Visigoths (who had been present in the Empire for several decades by 418/9) had taken on Roman burial customs – and, indeed, Roman dress-customs as well; or perhaps they were settled largely in the towns, and were buried in Roman urban cemeteries following Roman habits, and did not establish new rural cemeteries (as they seem to have done in the regions where row-grave cemeteries are found).

More sophistication in mapping was possible if one looked at smaller areas, where cemeteries of Romans and of barbarians could both be identified, and thus (assuming that one could identify the Roman cemeteries, which were often largely deprived of artefacts) gain some idea of how the Germanic newcomers fitted into the settlement pattern of an area. Focusing down still further, it was possible to find 'mixed cemeteries', where some graves exhibited 'Roman' styles and others 'barbarian' ones – though again there was sometimes the quick assumption that an unfurnished grave was that of a Roman rather than, say, that of a poor barbarian or of someone buried towards or beyond the end of the custom of furnished burial (which was the early eighth century in most of western Europe). One of the flaws in this argument was that the custom of fully furnished burial was rare in Barbaricum before the migrations; and the fully fledged row-grave cemetery was unknown. The new burial rite in fact developed within the Roman world.

For a long time archaeologists have clung to the idea that even though it developed within the Empire, the origins of the 'row-grave civilization', to use Joachim Werner's phrase, were nevertheless barbarian.[72] Werner argued that the prototype for the characteristic sixth-century row-grave cemetery was to be found in northern Gaul in the later fourth century. There were cemeteries to the west of the Rhine which contained burials of men with weapons and other artefacts, and women with quite elaborate jewellery. Some of these cemeteries were associated with Roman forts, but others with Roman towns and villas, while others were in the open countryside. But some must indeed have belonged to communities of soldiers, such as the cemetery of Furfooz, close by a fortified spur of the Ardennes, where 70 per cent of the male graves had weapons, and there were very few women. Werner interpreted all these furnished graves as those of barbarian *laeti*: that is, of barbarian captives settled forcibly on Roman soil in return for military service. The very rich military grave found outside the Roman fortifications of Vermand he interpreted as that of a *praefectus laetorum*: the Roman official (perhaps of barbarian origins) appointed to command these troops. In 1963 Kurt Böhner argued that these cemeteries belonged not to *laeti* – former captives – but to *foederati*, barbarian allies of Rome who had a higher social status than *laeti*. Horst-Wolfgang Böhme, in what remains the most detailed study of these 'Germanic grave-finds',[73] supported the *foederati* interpretation, and noted that the female jewellery was best paralleled in the cemeteries on the north German coast, which might suggest an origin for the barbarians in question. When I came to write about these graves myself, in 1988, I concluded:

> The presence of Germanic, perhaps largely Frankish, communities within northern Gaul already by the fourth century is an important fact, particularly when we consider that archaeologically, in terms of burial customs and material culture, they prefigure the Merovingian culture which was to emerge in northern Gaul around AD 500, neither German nor Roman but a mixed culture: in Böhme's phrase, a 'gallisch-germanische Mischzivilisation'.[74]

I even rashly said that 'surely' these graves were those of free soldiers who had come into Roman Gaul from Barbaricum: this despite the fact

that elsewhere I had been sceptical about the ready tendency of archaeologists to assign ethnicity to graves.[75]

Now I would prefer to yield to the arguments of Guy Halsall, who
has cast doubt on the barbarian or 'Germanic' origins of these cemeteries altogether.[76] He noted that there were numerous points of similarity between these inhumations and late Roman burials, including the
positioning of the vessels (which were of Roman type in these *foederati*
graves, and the placing of a coin in the dead person's mouth (a long-
standing Roman tradition). In these graves were found military belt-fittings
which were almost certainly of Roman manufacture; and the women's
jewellery may be as well. 'Had we no documentary evidence to confuse
the issue, it is highly unlikely that anyone nowadays would link the appearance of this rite to a migration of people.'[77] Halsall concluded in 1992
that the appearance of these graves in northern Gaul should be seen as
a product of social stress and competition for community leadership. The
assertion by civilians of the right to bear arms in self-defence in an increasingly unstable society was part of that competition for leadership. These
graves coincide, very roughly, with the revolts of the Bacaudae (see above,
p. 35) in northern Gaul. As Halsall stresses, these graves should be seen
as high-status burials (with a military emphasis): those people in those
weapon graves might be 'Roman or German, civilian or military'.[78]

These ideas were duly taken to task by some, and ignored by others,
but more recently Halsall has defended and developed his position.[79] One
problem is that of the female graves in north Gaul, in which are found
the *tutulus*-brooches which can be paralleled in Saxony. Brooches as dress-
fasteners are not found in the Gallo-Roman population, but are well known
in Barbaricum; on the other hand, these 'federate women' in Gaul were
buried with earrings, hairpins, necklaces and bracelets, which were common among Romans in Gaul and not among women in Barbaricum. It
is not particularly logical to imagine that the wearing of the brooches
alone is something to be explained ethnically (as Hines: above p. 105),
while the wearing of all the other items of dress is 'merely fashion'. Halsall
also looked at the weapons found in these graves, which include what
is generally regarded as the typical Frankish weapon, the throwing-axe,
which Isidore of Seville called the *francisca* (see above, p. 92). Most of
the weapons are in fact Roman in manufacture, and Halsall suggests that
even the throwing-axe may have developed within northern Gaul in the
Roman Period: there are none found in the Frankish homelands east of
the Lower Rhine. The clinching argument for many is that Roman soldiers would not have had their weapons placed in the grave with them:
not only was this not a Roman custom, but military-issue weapons did
not belong to the individual, but to the Roman state. But it is of course

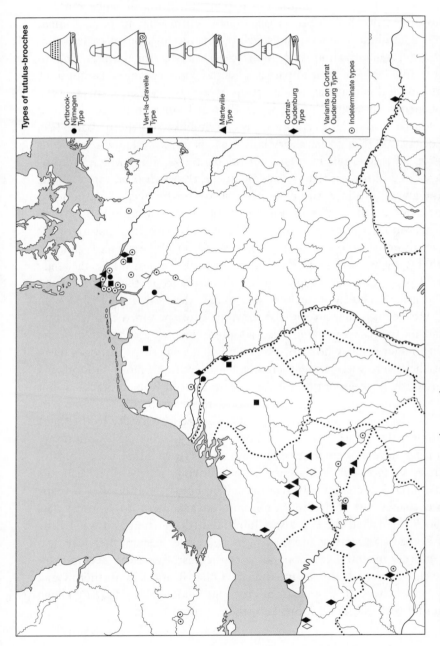

Map 11 The distribution of the 4th and 5th century women's brooches known as *tutulus*-brooches, which may be a map of burial-customs as much as of the areas where a particular brooch was worn. (From H.-W. Böhme's map in *Die Franken*, 94).

very dangerous to assume that the laws established at the centre reflect social realities on the periphery, and moreover we have to remember that weapon-burial was not common in Barbaricum either. Its appearance as a custom in northern Gaul in the fourth century has to be explained, and it could be explained just as well by changes in Roman society – an increasing militarization at a local level – as by the immigration of barbarians. Perhaps what in part lies behind some common assumptions of this period is that the militarization of society – which seems to have happened right across the European Roman Empire in the period from the fourth to the sixth centuries – is closely linked to the barbarization of society. There is no necessary link at all: as far as we know the warrior society that emerged in western Britain at this time, which is com-memorated in the earliest Welsh epic poem, the *Gododdin*, was a wholly home-grown product, the result, of course, of the need to respond to barbarians, but nevertheless not the result of barbarization as such.[80]

This should lead us to be sceptical about the 'barbarian' nature of the great efflorescence of row-grave cemeteries from the early sixth century, both inside and outside the former Roman Empire. If your family buried you with your weapons in northern France in the sixth century, it did not necessarily mean that you were a descendant of Franks who had moved into that area in the previous century. On the other hand, it did mean that your family had adopted customs associated with the ruling military elite, who were ethnically Frank, so perhaps that does mean that they were identifying themselves with ethnic Franks. Adopting a consciously new burial rite, different from the old Roman practices, but different from former Frankish customs too, was perhaps a conscious way of adopting the new ethnicity, characterized by loyalty to the kings of the Franks. As we have seen (above, p. 125), in Frankish Gaul nearly all military leaders seem to have Frankish names (even if they were Romans, such as Gregory of Tours's great-uncle), while nearly all bureaucrats and church-leaders have Roman ones. The Frankish army offered many more chances of social and economic advancement to a lower-class Gallo-Roman than the Frankish Church did (dominated as it was by the old Roman aristocracy); and the lower-class Gallo-Roman, therefore, was given every incentive to adopt some of the customs of the new military elite, as well as of its dominant ethnicity. Other Romans in northern Gaul, if we may believe the passage from Procopius quoted above (p. 81), joined together with the Franks, but kept their own customs.

chapter ten

FROM PAGANISMS TO CHRISTIANITIES

The most important part of assimilation into Roman ways concerns the adoption by the barbarians of the dominant belief-system of the late Roman Empire, Christianity. It was a slow process; it was not until the thirteenth century that the last European people was converted.[1] Conversion was not a simple process of changing from one set of beliefs to another. There were numerous types of paganism, which can only be partially reconstructed from archaeology and from much later literary accounts; there were also various types of Christianity. This chapter will look at what we can know about the religious beliefs which the barbarians were abandoning, at the process of conversion itself and will also examine the implications of the barbarians' adoption, in most cases, of Arianism, a heretical form of Christianity.

Greco-Roman writers told us a little about the religion of Celtic- and Germanic-speaking barbarians, and we can piece together more about the continuing paganism of Gauls within the Roman Empire from archaeology. But much of what we know about pre-Christian barbarian religion comes from Christian writers. Our most detailed account of 'Germanic paganism' is to be found in the *Prose Edda*, written by Snorri Sturlason in Iceland around 1220, 220 years after the decision of the Icelandic 'parliament' (the Althing) to convert. Snorri's account can be supplemented by the poems that make up the *Poetic Edda*: some of these may go back to pagan times, but they were actually written down (also in Iceland) even later than Snorri's time.[2] Is the story of Ragnarok, the last battle between good and evil which ends the world, a genuine story from Scandinavian paganism, or is it modelled on the Christian story of the Apocalypse? More significantly from our point of view, is the Odin of Nordic tradition 'the same' as the Woden of the West Germans (in England or in Germany) seven centuries earlier? After all, Romans considered that Woden was 'the same' as Mercury, and that Thor was 'the same' as Jupiter. The two former gods were associated with wisdom, and the two latter with thunder; but that is really where the similarities end.

Our problems are similar with 'Celtic paganism': the stories of the Irish gods are likewise preserved in manuscripts of around 1,200 or later. Some scholars (the 'nativists') think that these traditions were accurately handed down over the six or seven centuries since the conversion; but 'revisionists' suggest that much of Irish mythology was created in later centuries in imitation of Greco-Roman tradition, pointing, for instance, to parallels between the classic Irish epic the *Táin Bá Cúailnge* ('The Cattle Raid of Cooley') and the *Iliad*. Criticism of the probably twelfth-century Welsh text *The Mabinogion* has followed a similar pattern.

Historians sometimes treat paganism as if it was a religion, like Christianity or Islam. But 'paganism' as such does not exist; it is a word used by Christians to describe all religions that do not acknowledge the Jewish Bible as the word of God. Paganism comes in many shapes and forms, even though one common feature is that pagans are usually prepared to admit that many gods exist, and that one can choose the god or gods one prays to. Many pagans in the barbarian world may well have begun to worship the Christian god as an experimental addition to their pantheon. The paradigm here is Helgi the Lean, one of the earliest settlers of Iceland, living most of his life at a place he called Kristnes, which would seem to indicate his religion. But 'he was very mixed in his beliefs: he believed in Christ, and yet made vows to Thor for sea-voyages and in tight corners, and for everything which struck him as of real importance'.[3] Centuries earlier, in the 620s, King Rædwald of the East Angles, 'seemed to be serving both Christ and the gods whom he had previously served; in the same temple he had one altar for the Christian sacrifice and another small altar on which to offer victims to devils [i.e. pagan gods]'.[4] Many pagans did not give up their old gods when they accepted baptism, however furiously the Church disapproved of this. As far as the Church was concerned, the crucial step was not persuading someone to be baptized – after all, in the pagan Roman world it was possible to be initiated into several mystery religions, sometimes in rituals resembling baptism – but persuading them to abandon all their previous gods.

Given that barbarian pagans have no ability to speak for themselves – our written sources all come from Christians – it is important not to put the wrong words in their mouths. For a long time, for instance, both historians and archaeologists simply assumed that when objects – weapons, items of clothing, vessels – were placed in the grave that these were intended for use in the afterlife. There was no contemporary evidence for this belief; but the Egyptians apparently did it, so why not barbarians? The custom became widespread over western Europe at the end of the fifth century, and lasted until the eighth. In England it was thus possible to argue that it was a pagan custom and that it died out a few generations after the conversion, when the Anglo-Saxons had been Christianized enough to recognize that it was a custom that was inappropriate and unnecessary for Christians. But in Francia it was a custom that only became widespread *after* the conversion of the Franks, and some of the most spectacularly rich burials of this kind were made under churches and cathedrals. Contemporary churchmen could not have seen it as a pagan custom; and there is no evidence that they did. Nowadays archaeologists would normally explain it as a way of displaying status in public: 'burial with grave-goods represents a society where local power is open to competition, and thus somewhat unstable'.[5]

It is in fact only with care that we can use archaeology to determine religious change. We cannot assume that objects of symbols that we recognize as having a Christian or a pagan meaning had the same meaning to the person in whose tomb they are found, or to the relatives who placed that object in the tomb. Only when we have clearly religious buildings (and churches are not infallibly identified by archaeologists) can we start talking about religious meaning. And on the whole, Christian meaning can be detected more reliably than pagan meaning.

For a long time, the only certain pagan survivals from Anglo-Saxon England were place-names, studied first in a classic article by Sir Frank Stenton.[6] There are place-names incorporating *hearh* (idol or temple), a number of which are associated with hill-tops, such as Harrow (Middlesex) and Harrowdown (Essex); *weoh* (Weedon in Buckinghamshire, Weoley in Worcestershire) likewise seems to refer to a holy site of some kind.[7] There are also appearances of the names of gods such as Thor/Thunor and Woden: although placenames like Woden's Dyke (Wansdyke) may come from Christian times, as equivalents of Devil's Dyke. Many of these place-names show us the gods in association with the landscape: Thor's pool, Woden's field and so on. People have often thought that pagan worship was involved therefore in sacred natural sites. But we know from Bede that there were temples, and Aldhelm describes them as places where the images of a snake and a stag 'were worshipped with coarse stupidity', and where now are 'dwellings for students' (i.e. monasteries).[8] John Blair has suggested that if we want to find evidence for Anglo-Saxon shrines, we would be better employed to look not for (non-existent) prototypes on the Germanic continent, but at pre-Roman and Roman-Period prototypes in Britain.[9] There are a number of different sites which might be seen as Anglo-Saxon cult-sites. At Slonk Hill at Shoreham (Sussex) there is a square fenced enclosure built exactly over the ring-ditch of a Bronze Age barrow; it is very like the squared enclosure associated with a ring-ditch at Yeavering, the well-known British and Anglo-Saxon palace site in Northumbria. It is possible that an intriguing site at Blacklow Hill in Warwickshire is also an Anglo-Saxon cult-site; it has two large enclosures, one circular and one rectangular, with 270 small pits cut into the bedrock within those enclosures. There are two graves, aligned on a point a few metres away: possibly suggesting that there was a 'ritual' post, as is found on a number of these sites (including Yeavering). Although this remains totally conjectural, one wonders whether there is any connection between these cultic posts and the later Anglo-Saxon tradition of erecting standing crosses in the open air (some of which have graves aligned on them).

If these speculations are found, through later survey and excavation, to illustrate a real phenomenon, then it tells us something very interesting not just about Anglo-Saxon paganism, but about the Anglo-Saxon settlement as a whole. The Anglo-Saxons did not, apparently, bring all their traditions with them from northern Germany, but adopted the type of cult-site that had been used for a long time in Britain; in addition, they were using prehistoric features in the landscape as foci for cult and burial. Perhaps they felt they needed to fit into their landscape rather than impose new features upon it; perhaps their religion was itself changing as they moved from the cult sites which they had known for generations in north Germany.

Given the contacts which the barbarian world had with the Empire, barbarians must have known about Christianity long before they actually met missionaries. The words for 'church' may provide support for this. There are basically three words for 'church' current in the Roman Empire which are preserved in modern European languages: *ekklesia*, *kyriakón* and *basilike*. The first was adopted from Greek into Latin in the third century, and comes through as *église* in French or *eglwys* in Welsh. In Romanian 'church' is *biserica* (from *basilike*). But in the Germanic languages it is the Greek *kyriakón* which is dominant: 'church' in English (Old English *cirice*), *Kirche* in German, 'kirk' in Scottish and so on. The problem is how and when *kyriakón* reached the Germanic dialects. Dennis Green has rejected the hypothesis it came through Gothic, and suggests that it reached the Franks in the fourth century – before the word had fallen out of use in the Empire – but also before there is any record of Franks converting.[10] The 'official' conversion of the Franks does not begin, possibly, until the early sixth century;[11] but this may have been preceded by many 'unofficial' conversions through informal contacts.

Occasionally we get to hear about these informal contacts. A story in the *Life of St Ambrose of Milan* by Paulinus, one of Ambrose's clerics, is placed towards the end of his account of the bishop (who died around

397). Fritigil, queen of the Marcomanni, had heard of Ambrose's reputation from 'a Christian who happened to come to her from Italy': perhaps a merchant. She became a believer herself, and asked for instructions: he wrote her a catechism (which does not survive), and urged her to stay at peace with the Empire. She came to visit him in Milan, but arrived after his death. There is no confirmation of the truth of this story in any other source.[12]

Such informal contacts are presumably often not recorded and are impossible to quantify, which is why histories of the conversion of barbarian Europe are predominantly missionary histories. Missionaries very occasionally provide us with direct information (the writings of St Patrick and St Boniface, for instance). But missionary histories generally underestimate the background context: the personnel and information that passed backwards and forwards across the frontiers, and the great cultural dominance that the Roman Empire wielded, far beyond its borders. After the adoption of Christianity by Constantine (312–37), Christianity (ironically, no doubt, given its humble origins) must have come to be seen as the religion of power, wealth and success. As Bishop Daniel of Winchester wrote to the Anglo-Saxon cleric Boniface in Germany in the 720s, if the gods reward those who worship them, why do Christians 'possess lands rich in oil and wine and abounding in other resources' while pagans have 'lands stiff with cold'?[13]

God had willed the Roman Empire into existence in the generation before the birth of Christ (said the historian Eusebius) in order to facilitate the rapid expansion of Christianity.[14] The structure of the Church mirrored that of the Empire. Each of the four great cities of the Empire – Rome, Constantinople, Antioch and Alexandria – was controlled ecclesiastically by a patriarch (Jerusalem was made an honorary patriarchate in 451 because of its previous history). The metropolis or chief city of each province of the Empire had a metropolitan bishop at its head, who had some authority over the bishops within his province (later on the metropolitan bishop would take the title 'archbishop'). Within the province would be a number of city-territories, the basic administrative units of the Empire. At the heart of these territories were the cities themselves, in all of which (by 400) a bishop would sit on his throne (*cathedra*), in his main church (the cathedral). Most baptisms took place in the cathedral; and most preaching took place there too, as it was not until the sixth century that some churchmen, at least, thought that the important task of preaching should be allowed to be carried out by ordinary priests. The Church, in other words, was a thoroughly urban institution, and had become a thoroughly Roman one. Indeed, some seem to have thought that this was part of God's plan for the future; if God intended to bring

Christianity to the barbarians, then He would bring the barbarians into the Christian Roman Empire.

Few people, as far as we can tell, had thought about how Christianity might be extended into rural barbarian societies. The general pattern seems to have been that bishops appointed to non-urban societies would become bishops of peoples: thus under Constantine a bishop was appointed for the Iberians of the Caucasus; in the sixth century we find a 'bishop of the Homarenes', who are probably the Himyarites of the Yemen.[15] The Council of Constantinople in 381 legislated for churches established among barbarian peoples: but all it really said was that these churches were anomalies, both within and beyond the jurisdiction of the imperial Church.[16]

It is interesting that only occasionally do we get the idea that converting barbarians would pacify them, and would therefore serve as a useful arm of imperial diplomacy. At the very beginning of the fifth century Paulinus of Nola wrote a poem congratulating his friend Niceta of Remesiana on converting some Goths in Dacia, who would now live at peace with the Romans.[17] In a letter, Paulinus also implied that Victricius of Rouen had brought peace to the Channel coast of Gaul by converting and hence pacifying barbarians (probably Saxons) and brigands.[18] Orosius too regarded a barbarian people who had been converted as more peaceful; he instances how the Burgundians, now they were Christian, lived 'mild, gentle, and harmless lives'.[19] But the authorities did not draw the obvious conclusion: that a mass missionary effort might help to preserve the Roman Empire.

Arian Christianity

Early missions tended to be sent outside the Empire not in order to convert the barbarians, but to minister to communities of Christians who were already established there. The first great apostle to the barbarians himself came from such a community: Ulfila (also 'Ulfilas' and 'Wulfila') was descended from Romans who had been captured in the 260s by Goths raiding in Cappadocia. The Arian writer Philostorgius, an excerpt of whose work is preserved in a much later text, tells us that Ulfila was on a mission to Constantine, sent by the king of the Goths, and he was chosen (in around 341) by a number of bishops to be 'bishop of the Christians in the Getic land'.[20] He may not have been the first – Theophilos, bishop of Gothia, was called Ulfila's teacher – but he is certainly the most important.[21] However, seven years later Ulfila was forced out of Gothia, and Emperor Constantius II, who regarded him as the 'Moses of our times' according to Philostorgius, settled him and his followers in the province of Moesia.[22] Jordanes claimed that these Moesian Goths, taught to write by Ulfila, were still there in his day: 'numerous, but poor and unwarlike, rich in nothing save flocks of various kids and pasture-lands for cattle and forests for wood . . . Most of them drink milk'.[23]

The Goths resisted Christianization on at least two occasions, both of them probably inspired by anti-Roman feelings. The first time was when Ulfila was thrown out, in around 347, and the second was following a peace treaty in around 370, which apparently gave the Goths more freedom of action. The spread of Christianity, as the Goths must have realized, went hand in hand with the extension of imperial influence over them. The persecution of the Christians in the early 370s was led by the Gothic ruler Athanaric, and we know about it partly from a remarkable document written by the Christian community in Gothia to the churches in Cappadocia and elsewhere: the *Passion of St Saba*.[24] It told of the refusal of a Goth called Saba to participate in the eating of meat consecrated to the pagan gods: a test that was imposed on the Goths in order to identify the Christians. All the other Christians were prepared to eat the meat, to save themselves; but Saba denounced them. Eventually he was captured again, and tortured to death, on 12 April 372. He was not only devout, celibate and abstinent, he was also orthodox, said the *Passion*.

The text emphasized Saba's orthodoxy because Ulfila himself was a heretic; or, rather, when he was appointed bishop in 340 he was of the same religious persuasion as the emperor, and therefore perhaps could be seen as orthodox. He followed a belief condemned by the Council of Nicaea in 325, which, by the later fourth century, was generally agreed to be a heresy. His heresy was Arianism: that is, he subscribed to beliefs first put forward by Arius, that God the Son and God the Holy Ghost were created by God the Father and were not equal to him.[25] The disputes that raged through the fourth century often moved far from Arius's own position, and it is now generally agreed that the word 'Arian' groups together people who actually had quite different opinions.[26] But a crucial fact is that debates about the nature of the Trinity were important to many people at his time, in the way that political ideologies are today; and in the fifth century the disputes about the nature of Christ reached just the same fever pitch of interest, and not just among theologians. Gregory of Nyssa was in Constantinople at the time of the Council called by Theodosius I to settle the matter: 'If you ask the price of a loaf, the answer is "the Father is greater and the Son inferior"; if you ask "Is my bath ready?" the attendant declares that the Son is of nothing.'[27]

Ulfila took an active part in these debates after his exile from Gothia, and some idea of his views can be gathered from a letter written about him quoted in a piece by Maximinus, a fifth-century Arian bishop.[28] But all this would be irrelevant in this book were it not for one rather puzzling fact: most barbarian peoples in the fifth and sixth centuries – Visigoths, Ostrogoths, Vandals, Burgundians, Lombards and others – adhered to Arianism, a creed which had been successfully marginalized within the Roman Empire itself: marginalized, that is, until barbarian kingdoms were established within the former Roman Empire which were directed by Arian elites.

How was it that a relatively short-lived mission by Ulfila among one group of Goths should have spread out among so many barbarian peoples? It seems quite likely that the great bulk of those Goths who crossed the Danube in 376 were pagan, and not converted until after 376. As E.A. Thompson pointed out,[29] the conversion of the Visigoths was more likely to have been carried out by Arian Goths, 'the Gothic Bible in their hands', than by Roman Arians. He instances an Arian commentary on Matthew's Gospel, which remarks that 'the barbarian nations are in the habit of giving their sons names which recall the havoc caused by wild beasts or scavenging birds: they think it glorious to have such names, suitable for war and raging for blood', and castigated priests who wasted their time trying to bring the word of God to 'unlearned, undisciplined, and barbarian peoples, who neither seek nor hear it with judgement and who have the name of Christians by the manners of pagans'. There were some churchmen, however, who tried to win the Goths over to Catholic (or Nicene) Christianity. John Chrysostom ('Golden Mouth'), for instance, created a church in Constantinople which was staffed by clergy who could speak both Greek and Gothic. He used to preach there himself, using an interpreter, and persuaded other preachers to do the same. One of the sermons that he preached there survives: he told his Goths that Abraham, Moses and the Three Wise Men were all barbarians too. Chrysostom's ecumenical project may have had no ultimate success: a good part of his audience was probably wiped out in the massacre of Goths in Constantinople in 400 (see above, p. 54).[30]

Most barbarian peoples seem, like the Goths, to have been pagan or very largely pagan when they entered the Empire.[31] Some Romans who joined the Vandals at the time of their invasion turned from Christianity to paganism, which fits with the idea that the Vandals were pagan and probably did not convert until they were in Spain. The Sueves who settled in Spain were still ruled by a pagan king in the 440s, but his successor was a Catholic (later on the Suevian kings were Arian). The Burgundians may have become Arians around 430. The *Gallic Chronicle of 452* ends with a general statement about the world in 451:

At this time the pitiable condition of the state was quite evident, for there was no province without a barbarian settler, and the unspeakable heresy of the Arians, which had permeated the barbarian nations, spread over the whole world and laid claim to the name Catholic.[32]

Outside the Roman Empire the conversion to Arianism was probably later than this: those peoples who were under the domination of the Huns – Ostrogoths, Gepids and Rugians – probably did not become Arian Christians until after the collapse of the Hunnic Empire in the 450s. The Franks, notably, did not convert until after 500, and they converted directly from paganism to Catholic Christianity, without going through a phase of Arianism. At least, this is what Gregory of Tours maintained in the late sixth century; but the Catholic convert King Clovis's sister was Arian, and in a letter Avitus of Vienne congratulates the king for having uncovered the lies of the heretics, so perhaps a conversion to Arianism had been a real possibility.[33] And, finally, the Lombards, when they came into the Roman Empire, were probably still largely pagan although some might have converted to Catholicism while in Pannonia; but in Italy Arianism developed among them to some extent, fostered by a number of their kings.[34]

The usual explanation of the great triumph of Arianism among the barbarians is the activity of Gothic missionaries. There is certainly little evidence of the activity of Roman Arian missionaries; but, then, there is precious little evidence for Gothic or other Germanic missionaries either. One of the few individuals who might be seen as an Arian missionary was Ajax, mentioned by the chronicler Hydatius under 465–6:

> Ajax, a Greek apostate and leading Arian, arose among the Sueves, with the help of the king, as an enemy of the orthodox faith and the divine Trinity. This noxious venom emanating from this hateful man was conveyed from the Gallic home of the Goths.[35]

Ajax seems to have converted the Sueves, from Catholicism and/or paganism to Arianism. He was a *senior Arrianus*, possibly a 'leading Arian', but possibly also an 'Arian senior'. There is no evidence for Arian bishops in the kingdom of Toulouse: only for priests, and perhaps Ajax was one of them.[36] We are maybe wrong to think in terms of formal missions. The Goths acquired their Christianity initially from an Arian missionary. But perhaps later conversions were much more informal affairs, driven rather more by political pragmatism than by religious conviction. We must imagine that barbarian incomers realized that their power over the Roman majority was dependent on the preservation of their own separate identity. By adhering to Arianism, they may well have been doing what they could to stop their culture and identity from being swamped by Romans. Arianism was an expression of their identity; but it was also an assertion of their independence. If they converted to Catholicism they would be under the authority of Catholic bishops and, depending on circumstances, of the Catholic emperor. But we do also have evidence of the knowledge of Biblical texts among Arian laymen, and we do have to reckon with the possibility that Arians adhered to their beliefs because they thought they were *right*.

Catholic clerics were, of course, concerned to convert Arians to the true religion; but were also worried about the level of fraternization between Catholics and Arians, which sometimes resulted in conversion in the 'wrong' direction. The Gallic church, at least, did not make it easy for lapsed Catholics to rejoin the church: they had to do penance for two years, fasting every third day, and regularly attending church. However, it was made easy for Arians, clergy and lay, to renounce their Arianism; and despite Gregory there is actually some evidence that contacts between the churches were relatively easy. Arians were welcome to attend Nicene services; Sidonius Apollinaris (after his consecration as bishop of Clermont) admits to attending Arian services.

Most of those barbarian peoples who had converted to Arianism accepted Catholicism in the course of the sixth century – or else were given no alternative. The Ostrogoths were effectively wiped out by imperial forces; the Vandals likewise surrendered to the Empire, and their Arian brand of Christianity died with them; Gundobad of the Burgundians alleged that he was convinced of the truth of Catholicism but did not dare suggest conversion to his people,[37] although soon after he died they did in fact convert. The most public conversion was that of the Visigothic king Reccared. He had himself baptized in secret, but then called together three meetings (according to Gregory of Tours, a contemporary, but not necessarily reliable witness, and one whose hostility to Arianism was implacable).[38] First he met with his Arian bishops. Then he convened a meeting of both Arian and Catholic bishops, in order to debate their faith: the king's contribution was noting that Arian bishops did not seem able to work miracles of healing. After this he met with the Catholic bishops. The conversion itself was proclaimed in the Third Council of Toledo of 589, two years after the king's initial conversion. In that period there was a conspiracy against him led by the Arian bishop of Mérida, another conspiracy led by the (Arian) widow of his father Leovigild, and an Arian revolt in the Gallic part of his kingdom. Even though all these were crushed easily, it suggests that some Arians were far from lukewarm in their faith. Reccared's anti-Arian measures are similarly suggestive: he burned Arian books, banned Arians from public employment and suppressed the Arian church organization.[39]

It is interesting to speculate on what this meant for Gothic Arians. We have to speculate, as it happens: Reccared's burning of Arian books (together with the vicissitudes of manuscript survival through the Islamic conquest of Spain and the Christian Reconquest) was very successful, and our information about Gothic Arians is extremely limited. We may note that in the reign of Reccared's father Leovigild Arianism seems still to have been able to attract Catholics. At an Arian council in Toledo in 580 Leovigild had said that 'Those coming from the Roman religion to our Catholic faith ought not to be baptized, but ought to be cleansed only by means of the imposition of hands and the receiving of communion.' The chronicler John of Biclar commented that many of 'our own' inclined to Arianism out of self-interest rather than conviction.[40] Note that Leovigild had referred to 'our Catholic faith': heretics, needless to say, always think of themselves as being Catholic or orthodox. But he opposed 'Roman' to this, which means that Thompson perhaps was right when he argued that 'our' meant not 'Arian' but 'Gothic'.[41] For him the victory of Catholicism was in a sense a defeat for the Visigothic element of the population, or at least might be regarded so by some Visigoths. But there was relatively little trouble in 589; and if we look at 580 more closely, we can see that what Leovigild was probably worrying about was the way in which Goths (including his own son Hermenegild) were abandoning their Arianism for Catholicism. John of Biclar thought Leovigild was trying to attract Romans to Arianism; but he might well have been trying to stem the flow of Goths away from Arianism.

Ireland and Britain

Prosper of Aquitaine's *Chronicle* has two interesting and possibly related entries. Under the year 429, he said that Pope Celestine was advised by the deacon Palladius to send Bishop Germanus of Auxerre to guide the Britons to the Catholic faith, and this was duly done.[42] Under 431 Prosper says that Palladius, presumably the same Palladius, 'having been ordained by Pope Celestine, was the first bishop sent to the Scots believing in Christ'.[43] It is likely that Palladius was Germanus's deacon, sent to Rome to secure papal approval for an intervention in Britain. Just three years later, Prosper writes, in a different work, of Celestine: 'while he labours to keep the Roman island Catholic, he has also made the barbarian island Christian'. As Thomas Charles-Edwards notes, this not only suggests that Palladius arrived and had great success (not something alluded to in any Irish source) but also that Celestine had actually envisaged 'not just pastoral care for a few Irish Catholics or for British slaves living in

Ireland, but a full-scale mission to the entire island'.[44] If so, this may have been the first ever papally inspired mission to convert people outside the former Roman Empire. One wonders if, at first at least, it was spurred on by a fear that British Pelagians would infect Ireland with their heresy. Pelagianism stemmed from the theological teaching of Pelagius, a British monk, who believed that Christians could achieve salvation by their own efforts; St Augustine of Hippo, his most distinguished opponent, argued that humans, oppressed by original sin, could only ever hope to achieve salvation through God's freely given grace. Pelagius's ideas were certainly easier to understand than Augustine's, and for monks and nuns who were trying to win salvation, they must have seemed attractive.

Palladius's mission to Ireland was almost totally eliminated from Irish tradition. Early medieval Irish churchmen had read their Prosper, and they knew that Palladius had been sent to be the first bishop of the Irish. But they retained no tradition that he had had any successes; he had either been martyred, or else immediately and ignominiously expelled. Irish annals inserted the arrival of the true 'apostle of Ireland' as soon after Palladius's mission as they dared: in 432. That apostle, of course, is Patrick, who remains the only missionary to the barbarians in our period to have left autobiographical information: his *Confessio* and his *Letter to the Soldiers of Coroticus*. As is well-known, Patrick was a Romano-Briton, the son of a deacon and grandson of a priest, from somewhere in the west of Britain. The location is assumed by the fact that Irish raiders captured him on a raid (though the Irish could have sailed into the Channel, for instance), and brought him back to Ireland. He languished in slavery, along with thousands of others; he might, indeed, have been one of the Christians in Ireland to whom Palladius had been sent. He did not, however, regard himself as a good Christian; he discovered his vocation after he had escaped and returned to Britain. At that point, God (not a bishop or any cleric) told him to return to Ireland to preach to the Irish. The following declaration, placed at the head of his *Letter*, may well reflect his knowledge that he had no official sanction; perhaps he had even had no official consecration as bishop.

> I, Patrick, a sinner, yes, and unlearned, established in Ireland, put on record that I am a bishop. I am strongly convinced that what I am I have received from God. And so I live among barbarian peoples, a stranger and an exile for the love of God.[45]

He wrote this letter to the soldiers of Coroticus, a Christian British king, to complain about their capture and killing of newly baptized Irishmen, and comparing their behaviour unfavourably with that of the barbarian Franks, who allow baptized captives to be ransomed by the Church, 'whereas you kill them or sell them to a foreign people which does not know God': he is possibly referring to the Picts, whom he has already described as among Coroticus's allies.[46]

His most famous work, however, is the *Confessio*, which he wrote after accusations had been made against him in Britain. These relate to a grave sin of some kind that he had committed when he was 15; but also to the suspicion that he had gone to Ireland for financial gain. Patrick was, on his own confession, so to speak, not the kind of cleric who never handled money. Indeed, he showed himself fully conversant with the habit of almost every barbarian society: that social relations were oiled by the continual offering of gifts. He gave gifts to kings, to the sons of kings and to judges, and yet he maintained that he did not accept gifts himself. Those conversant with the large body of early Irish legal material suggest that this shows that Patrick was actually claiming an exalted position in early Irish society.[47] He travelled around with the sons of kings in his retinue, something only done by those of the highest status. He gave gifts without receiving counter-gifts: something which over-kings did with regard to their under-kings. Although Patrick's position in Ireland appears always to have been insecure, he seems to have had considerable successes. He not only baptized many, but managed to persuade the sons and daughters of kings to become monks and nuns. The introduction of monastic customs, notably celibacy, was high on Patrick's to-do list, and, as Charles-Edwards suggests, the lack of any clear distinction in Patrick's mind between the monastic life proper and the life of any good Christian might explain the strange lack of clarity about such things in the Irish church which emerged from the first decades of the conversion.[48]

There are all kinds of problems with our understanding of the early years of the conversion of Ireland. But they are as nothing compared to the problems connected with the story of the conversion of the barbarians in what is now Scotland. There was even heated discussion on this issue in 1997, when two rival 'apostles of Scotland' were remembered: St Columba, whose death was in 597, and St Nynia, whose modern supporters maintained that he had arrived in Scotland in 397. They are indeed mentioned together in the same passage in Bede's *Ecclesiastical History*,[49] where he says that Columba preached to the northern Picts and Nynia to the southern Picts, 'on this side of the mountains'. Nynia's base was at Whithorn, in southern Galloway, in the midst of territories controlled by the Britons (whom the English called 'Welsh'), a long way from the Picts; and he had built a stone church there, called Candida Casa: a style of building which was 'unusual among the Britons'. Bede has two sentences about Nynia; that is all that is known about him. Much more is known about Columba, thanks to the life of this first abbot of Iona written by the ninth abbot, Adomnán. Iona, a small island off the west coast of the Isle of Mull, played an important part in the conversion of the Anglo-Saxons, as I shall mention below. But its precise role in converting the northern Picts is more problematic. Adomnán describes Columba in several encounters with Pictish 'wizards' (presumably pagan priests), but these tales have the feel of folk tale rather than of history. Iona certainly founded a number of daughter-houses up the west coast of Scotland, towards northern Pictland, and it may have been clerics from those monasteries, in the generations after Columba, who actually had an impact on the Picts. Conversion was not without its enemies: in 617 the *Annals of Ulster* report the burning of Donnán of Eigg along with 150 martyrs: presumably monks on Eigg, an island some 60 km north of Iona. Another important missionary was Maelrubai, who travelled far north not from Iona, but direct from Ireland; another not connected with Iona was Kentigern, who was British, and worked in the British kingdom of Strathclyde (in the region of Glasgow).

Patrick and Kentigern were two British missionaries who worked among the Celtic-speaking peoples of Britain. But Bede complained bitterly that no British cleric had tried preaching to the Anglo-Saxons in Britain. This crime, Bede thought, ought to be added to all the other unspeakable crimes of the British.[50]

Bede, an Anglian, may have had the natural prejudice of an Englishman of his day, who not only saw the British as schismatics (because the customs of the church did not fit in with those of the rest of the Church), but regarded them as the natural enemies of the English. The fact that the Old English word *wealh* meant both 'Welshman' and 'slave' tells us volumes. But in part Bede inherited his low opinion of the British (Welsh) from the British monk Gildas, who blamed the sins of the British for the barbarian invasions of Roman Britain. He took from Gildas the idea that the British were so weak-minded that they latched on to any heresy that was around, and took any opportunity to sin that was presented to them. It was providential that these dreadful people did not preach Christianity to the pagan English, and that Christianity should instead come to the English from the most sacred place in western Christendom, from Rome itself.

Some historians have seen the conversion of England as part of a papal missionary strategy. And there is some evidence that Gregory the Great (Pope Gregory I, 590–604) was planning something. In September 595, for instance, he asked his agent in Gaul to buy some Anglian slaves and place them in monasteries. We hear elsewhere of this as a strategy: it is a good way of providing oneself with reliable interpreters. On the other hand, the initiative for the mission to England – or to the most power-ful and closest of the English kingdoms, Kent – was not, it seems, a mat-ter of papal initiative. King Æthelberht of Kent, who had married a Christian Frank, Bertha, and who had been living at court with Bertha's bishop, Liudhard, apparently decided that he wanted to convert. Rome heard about it; and the earliest letter in the Gregory's register of letters which relates to the mission is a letter of 596 to the two Frankish kings, announcing this fact, and asking them to protect Augustine on his way north. Gregory says that the English had been asking for priests from nearby without success: from the Franks, or from the Welsh?

Gregory's response was not that of a man with a missionary strategy. He sent a group of monks, with their prior, Augustine. Only later did he make Augustine their abbot, and then a bishop. If the series of ques-tions that Augustine wrote to Gregory about how to carry out his mission are actually genuine, and by Augustine, then he was just as ill-prepared for it as Gregory was.[51] Augustine arrived in Kent in 597, and Æthelberht gave him land in Canterbury, the largest former Roman town in his kingdom – probably little more than a pile of Roman rubble at this stage – and Augustine established his cathedral there. In June 601, Gregory sent reinforcements, under Abbot Mellitus, with letters to Augustine and to Æthelberht. He told Augustine that he should found metropolitan sees in London and York, and that each metropoli-tan should have 12 bishops in his province (Augustine was clearly expected to move his base from Canterbury to London). Augustine should have all the bishops of Britain under his jurisdiction; through his ignorance of the political circumstances Gregory was laying down the foundations for centuries of dispute within the churches in Britain.

Up to this point Gregory had perhaps spent a couple of mornings dealing with England: specifically, almost all his previous letters on the subject were dated 23 July 596 or 22 June 601. Now Gregory appar-ently sat down to think a little about what he was doing; and on 18 July 601 he wrote a letter to Abbot Mellitus, who was by this time well on his way to the Alps, and sent it off by messenger. It contained his famous instructions on how to convert barbarians. Tell Augustine, he wrote,

> that the idol temples of that race should by no means be destroyed, but only the idols in them. Take holy water and sprinkle it in these shrines, build altars and place relics in them . . . When this people see that their shrines are not destroyed they will be able to banish error from their hearts and be more ready to come to the places they are familiar with, but now recognising and wor-shipping the true God. . . . It is doubtless impossible to cut out everything at once from their stubborn minds: just as the man who is attempting to climb to the highest place, rises by steps and degrees and not by leaps.[52]

Various archaeological finds have been interpreted by Anglo-Saxon archaeologists as the physical result of this letter, that is, a temple turned into a church (though none of the evidence is conclusive).

Æthelberht himself accepted baptism, after initial reluctance: perhaps he wanted to sound out the views of his followers before abandoning their traditional practices. Augustine created 2 of the 12 bishoprics in the south that Gregory had asked for: Rochester in Kent, and London in the kingdom of the East Saxons. But Augustine was only able to found the see of London because the East Saxons were subordinate to Æthelberht at the time. The fragility of all this became apparent on the death of Æthelberht in around 616. The East Saxons expelled their bishop from London and abandoned Christianity; Rædwald of the East Angles, who had accepted Christianity while Æthelberht was his overlord, also reverted to paganism, as did Æthelberht's own son. Augustine's successor Laurence almost decided to abandon the mission altogether: a vision of St Peter convinced him to stay, says Bede, and convinced Æthelberht's son to ask for baptism.[53] Æthelberht's son-in-law Edwin of Northumbria was baptized, by the last of Gregory's missionaries, Paulinus. But when Edwin was killed in battle in 633, Bishop Paulinus fled back south to Kent. Thirty-six years after Augustine arrived in Kent, all that had been achieved by the Roman mission was the conversion of a handful of kingdoms in the south-east of England.

Gregory's missionary policy was probably ill-conceived. Founding cathedrals in Canterbury, London and York – all of which were probably, in the early seventh century, little more than piles of rubble – was a somewhat unimaginative attempt to recreate the town-centred church of the former Empire in a totally barbarian land. The conversion of England was completed not by the Romans, but by the Irish. Edwin's ultimate successor in Northumbria was Oswald, who had been in exile in Ireland; and he brought Aidan from Iona to be his bishop. Aidan set up his base at Lindisfarne, on Holy Island, off the eastern coast of Northumbria. The Irish, with no towns, had learned rather better than the Romans how to adapt the Church to a rural society. Bishops needed clergy to help them: on the Continent clerics could be found in the town, but in a rural society the sensible thing was to place the bishop within a monastic community. Monks needed to learn enough Latin to follow the liturgy and perhaps to read the Bible: on the Continent, in the former Roman Empire, the daily vernacular was a language not far removed from Latin, and this was relatively easy, but in areas where Latin was not the spoken language, in England or in Ireland, monasteries had to become educational institutions, where a foreign language could be studied.

Bede had one or two worries about the way the Irish did things – particularly the old-fashioned method of calculating Easter that some of them held on to into his day – but he is also largely responsible for first espousing the idea, still preserved, of early Ireland being a land of 'saints and scholars'. When he wanted to look for an ideal bishop in the past whom he could select to serve as a role model for his contemporaries he chose the Irish monk-bishop Aidan, whose 'life was in great contrast to our modern slothfulness.' He was a model, literally, of abstinence, self-control, humility, enthusiasm and bravery: 'neither respect nor fear made him keep silent about the sins of the rich'.[54] He travelled every-where on foot, not on horseback: on foot he was approachable, and able to talk to anyone, regardless of status; men on horseback were men in a hurry, and men of the elite.

An astonishing proportion of the first bishops of English dioceses were men trained in Lindisfarne. Such clerics (including those who were English by birth) introduced the ideas of the Irish throughout the English church. St Wilfrid of York, one of the most prominent Lindisfarne alumni, was responsible for the conversion of the last pagan Anglo-Saxon kingdom, that of the South Saxons (Sussex), and was also the first Englishman to try his hand at converting pagan German-speakers on the Continent. Englishmen at this time thought of the Saxons and Frisians and others as their cousins, and after Wilfred's time there was a stream of English-men who went abroad to serve as missionaries – or, if one prefers, to act as stooges for the Frankish princes who wanted to extend their power eastwards, hiding in the shadow of Anglo-Saxon clergy.

Christianizing the Barbarians

Conversion and Christianization are two very different processes. Conversion is signalled by the public acceptance of Christianity through baptism; Christianization involves changing the practices of a pagan soci-ety in order to conform to Christian ideas and setting up mechanisms to teach people about Christianity. Bede, and other narrators of conversion stories, frequently write as if conversion was the end of the story; indeed, they write as if the conversion of a king was the end of the story, as if the king was able to make his country Christian overnight.

That the process of Christianization was a slow one can be seen by looking at the three earliest English law-codes that we have, which are all from kings of Kent: Æthelberht (d. 616); Hlothhere (673–85) and Eadric (d. 686); and Wihtred (690–725). These law-codes are all found only in the Textus Roffensis, a much later manuscript, and it is possible that changes had been made by scribes long after composition. But as we have them, the lawcode of Æthelberht, the first Christian king in England, has only one reference to Christianity, in clause 1, which lays down the penalties for stealing from different grades of cleric, from bishop down to grades of cleric below deacon. (This particular clause is mentioned by Bede.)[55] The laws of Hlothhere and Eadric do not mention Christianity at all. A good half of the laws of Wihtred, however, dating from as much as a century after the arrival of Augustine in Kent, are devoted to the business of fitting the Church into the legal structure of traditional society, and to putting the weight of the law behind some of the teachings of the Church. The Church is given immunity from taxation, and provided with the same level of legal protection as the king. Both a bishop and a king can clear themselves of an accusation of crime by a simple statement; lesser people have to swear a formal oath and persuade other people (oath-helpers) to swear to their innocence as well. The king puts his weight behind the new concept of 'illicit unions'; that is, the Church's teaching about prohibited degrees of relationship which redefined incest for the Anglo-Saxons, and made many of their traditional marriages (such as the marriage of a man to his brother's widow) illicit. Working on Sundays, sacrificing to devils and eating meat during a fast (such as during Lent) were all prohibited.

A similar delay of many decades between the conversion and the arrival of ecclesiastically inspired legislation can be found in the Frankish law (although there are serious problems relating to manuscript survival here, too). The earliest stratum of Frankish law (the so-called *Pactum Legis Salicae*) seems to have been issued under Clovis (d. 511). There is no mention of Christianity here; indeed, the only mention of religion at all, however allusive, relates to the penalty for stealing a sacrificial pig. The influence of Christianity only arrives in the surviving legal material with the Decree of Childebert II (575–95), Clovis's great-grandson. This document mentions taking sanctuary in a church; it also says that those who indulge in marriages which the Church regards as incestuous shall be excommunicated by the Church, and, if no remedy is made, all the person's property will be confiscated.[56]

From the sixth century onwards on the Continent, the parish system was slowly developed, by which each individual Christian was brought in close proximity to a Christian priest, within a mechanism of control that, in theory at least, ought to bring Christianization in depth. But, of course, much rested on the ability and determination of the parish priest, and his willingness to impose policies given to him from on high – policies which sometimes paid little attention to the practicalities of enforcement or to entrenched public opinion. Parish priests tended not to be as zealous as missionaries.

For some missionaries a key element was the elimination of references to the pagan gods in daily speech.

> Let us even disdain to utter with our lips those exceedingly despicable names, and let us never say the day of Mars, or the day of Mercury, or the day of Jupiter. Let us rather call them the first or second or third day.[57]

A glance at English shows the extent of their failure at least in this instance. English has taken over the pagan Roman planetary week in its entirety, although with some Roman gods being replaced by their normal Germanic equivalences. We start the week with the *dies solis*, go back to work on *dies lunae*, and then have days dedicated to the god of war (Tiw replaced Mars, although he is still there in the French *Mardi*), the god of wisdom (Woden replaces Mercury), the god of thunder (Thor fills in for Jupiter/Jove) and the goddess of fertility (Freyja, Venus). English is actually an extreme version; most European languages at least nod to the arguments of the missionaries. Thus, Saturday in German (*Samstag*) or in French (*samedi*), as in most modern European languages, is derived from *sabbatum*, the Sabbath; while most also use 'the Lord's Day' for Sunday (*dimanche*, *domenico* and so on). The pagan Roman *Saturni dies* comes through into Germanic dialects only in England (as 'Saturday'), Holland and Westphalia.[58] There were models which could be adopted which neutralized the days of the week: the ancient Greeks and Hebrews used numbers. But in Europe only Portuguese and the Slavonic dialects opted for this.[59]

In our written sources of this period references to the pagan practices which missionaries were trying to stamp out relate very largely to Roman paganism and not to the beliefs of the barbarians. And we do have to be wary of assuming that just because there are practices deemed to be pagan by missionaries the people carrying them out like-wise thought of them as non-Christian. Even when we have healing-charms from late Anglo-Saxon England which invoke the name of Woden, we do not have to imagine they continued covert existence of Woden-worshippers. Of one such charm Karen Louise Jolly commented,

> I do not think it is pagan in a religious sense so much as it is a type of highly conservative folklore. This kind of memorized and performed remedy lived a long life, gradually absorbing, as this one had begun to, the new religious overtones.[60]

There is indeed remarkably little about surviving paganism among the barbarians who had entered the Empire, though we do see an interest-ing twist in terminology in Gregory of Tours's *History*. He talks about a particular man observing the flight of birds as an augury, *ut mos barbarorum est,* 'as is the custom of barbarians'. But the name of the man who did this was Claudius, and thus clearly a Roman.[61] It looks as if the word *barbarian* was making a shift from 'non-Roman' to 'someone who ignores the customs of Christian Romans'. The new distinction in Gregory's world-view was not between Roman and non-Roman, but between Christian and pagan.

chapter eleven

KINGDOMS, KINGSHIP AND LAW

Historians often used to pick out certain features of barbarian society from our (later) written sources and label them as 'primitive' – because they 'looked' primitive – and assume that they therefore give us some idea of early barbarian customs. A classic case of this is in relation to 'sacral kingship'.[1] Alcuin of York, scholar and adviser to kings, wrote to King Æthelred of the Northumbrians in the 790s, that 'a good king means a prosperous nation, victorious in war, temperate in climate, rich in its soil, blessed with sons and a healthy people'. This, says William Chaney, is the perfect statement of what is desired of the 'divinely descended, sacrificial priest-king of Germanic heathenism'; it shows the level of continuity there was between the 'sacral kingship' of pagan times and the new Christian kingship.[2] But Chaney left out the opening words of that quotation: 'We read that . . .'[3] Alcuin is referring to Samuel's words to the Israelites, or maybe to one of the Psalms. It is a primitive idea, perhaps; but it is not specifically 'Germanic'. Even some cautious modern historians fall into the Chaney trap, as when Heather commented on Theodoric's generosity in the following terms: 'The distribution by their lord of due reward to the brave is straight out of heroic poetry, and Cassiodorus's Latin rhetoric surely hides a thoroughly Germanic event designed to preserve ties of lord and follower.'[4] Patrick Amory comments, somewhat brutally,

> The above quotation appears in a scholarly journal published in 1995, but it could just as well have appeared in 1895. The techniques are Victorian: 'seeing through' a written text to the rude oral reality, ignoring late antique social models in favour of subsequent medieval social models, and appealing to common sense ('surely') of European nationalist notions, based in the Victorian era on race, in the modern era on ethnicity.[5]

It is a useful rigorous reminder of the dangers of an approach based on assumption about what is 'Germanic' or 'primitive'.[6]

Kingship, whether 'sacral' or not, certainly appears ubiquitous in the barbarian world, but the type of kingship that appears in our Greco-Roman sources relates mostly to the kingship of the Migration Period, which might be very different from the kingship of Tacitus's day.[7] Our Latin sources show us peoples ruled by monarchs described as *reges* (singular, *rex*) or by some diminutive (*regulus, subregulus*); these may be designated in the vernacular by a related word (*rí* in Irish; *reiks* in Gothic). The Old English word for king is from a different root: *cyning* means 'a man from the kin'. It gives us the modern 'king', and is related to modern German *König*; but an Old English *cyning* ruled a *rice* (pronounced 'ree-cha', and equivalent to German *Reich*), which is from the same Indo-Germanic root as *rex*. The English also had the word *theoden*, though this was generally used of Christ. Ulfila's Gothic Bible uses *thiudans* of Christ and the Roman emperor, while *reiks* is used not just of a king, but also to translate the Greek word *archon*, meaning a governor or military commander. The Old English poem *Beowulf* on more than one occasion combines the two English words, and calls its hero *thiod-cyning*.[8]

One of the very few apparent exceptions to the rule of ubiquity were the Saxons on the Continent; Bede says that they have no king, but *satrapas plurimos*, 'many satraps'.[9] When war comes, he adds, they cast lots, and follow the one on whom the lot falls, and when the war ends all the satraps become equal again. It is an odd word for Bede to choose: he would have found it in his Latin Bible, referring to the governor of a Persian province. Wallace-Hadrill suggests that it should be translated 'chieftain', rather than the 'viceroy' found in the standard translation of Bede, but he also notes that perhaps it was a word which Bede took from whoever told him about the martyrdom of the two Hewalds, Anglo-Saxon missionaries in Saxony. Anglo-Saxons writing in Latin generally used other words to mean 'rulers of lesser rank', such as *principes, subreguli* or *duces regii*.[10] It is likely that the Saxon satraps were rulers of small subgroups of the Saxon people, whom we may call 'tribes'; and whether one gives a tribal ruler a royal title (a *rex*- or *cyning*- related word) probably depends on one's own social and political context.

Bede's own social and political context makes him a misleading commentator upon kingship among the English, as well as among the Saxons.[11] For Bede, the word *rex* is reserved for the rulers of the large kingdoms that emerged in England in the early seventh century: the so-called Heptarchy – the kings of the Northumbrians, the Mercians, the East Angles, the West Saxons, the East Saxons, the South Saxons and the Men of Kent (the *Cantuari*). These kings are all rulers of groups that Bede thinks of as *peoples*. Sometimes one of those kings holds overlordship over most of the others: Bede calls such a power *imperium*, or empire, and lists seven who held it in his lifetime (although he omitted any of the Mercian kings who almost certainly held that power, probably because of his Northumbrian prejudice against the Mercians). *The Anglo-Saxon Chronicles* call such a king, in Old English, a *Bretwalda* or *Brytenwalda*, meaning 'Wide Ruler' or 'Ruler of Britain'.[12] But some at least of those seven kingdoms of the Heptarchy had been relatively recently assembled from smaller kingdoms, and some at least of those smaller kingdoms retained their kings. The kings of Lindsey, in Lincolnshire, survived into the late eighth century, and they even minted coins, although Bede does not mention them and gives us the impression that Lindsey has been submerged into the larger kingdoms of, first, Northumbria and, later, Mercia.

The association between king and people was a strong one in the early Middle Ages, and certainly well established by the Carolingian Period. Back in 1989, I confidently stated that 'royal titles are almost invariably ethnic or national titles rather than territorial ones'; and I think I was doing no more than stating orthodoxy.[13] It fitted in with the fixed idea that *we* had in the twentieth century that ethnicity was important, and ought therefore to have been an all-important category in late antiquity. But Andrew Gillett has shown that the key word in titulature was *rex* or *dominus*, and not the ethnic descriptor (*rex Francorum, rex Gothorum* and so on).[14] We certainly find the *rex . . . orum* formula in narrative sources, poetry, hagiography and other literature genres; but if we look in sources which we might regard as 'official' (legal material, inscriptions, coin legends, letters to and from rulers) the ethnic marker is rarely found. Gillett reckons that out of some 1,500 examples, only about 100 use the marker; he concludes that the standard title was *rex* or *dominus*, which expressed a rulership over all the people of his kingdom (which in many cases was ethnically diverse). It is only at a secondary stage, after the settlement within the Empire, that the ethnic marker is added – and it need not be a 'barbarian self-definition; it is at least as likely to be an internalization by the . . . monarchy of a defining term imposed upon it "from below", by the Roman populace which dominated the civil administration, Church, and other institutions of their polity'.[15]

We are faced, however, with a chicken-and-egg problem. Did a king create a people, or a people create a king? The corollary is: what constitutes a king, or a people? A fascinating text survives, possibly from the mid-seventh century, called the *Tribal Hidage*. It lists the hides (taxable units) belonging to each of the 34 Anglo-Saxon peoples listed. Some of these are the peoples we are familiar with from Bede – the West Saxons, the East Angles and so on – but others are known only from the *Tribal*

Hidage: the East and West Wixna, the Noxgaga, the Ohtgaga. Some of them can be located, as the Wihtgara (the men of the Isle of Wight), the Cilternsæten (the Chiltern-sitters), the Pecsæten (the Peak-sitters, of the Peak District) and the Hwicce of Worcestershire. For the latter area we have charters, confirmed by the Mercian king, but also by the

Elmedsætna

Heath feld land

PECSÆTNA

LINDES FARONA

MYRCENES LANDES

(Bilmiga)

WOCEN SÆTNA

?Widerigga

(Wigesta)

North gyrwa

South gyrwa

Sweordora

West Wixna   East Wixna   EAST ENGLE

Arosætna

HEREFINNA

(Spalda)

(West   East)

?WESTERNA

HWINCA

(West   East)

(Willa)

Gifla

Hicca

?Færpinga

CHILTERN SÆTNA

EAST SAXENA

(UNECUNG-GA)

(NOXGAGA)

?HENDRICA

(OHTGAGA)

CANTWARENA

WEST SEXENA

SOUTH SEXENA

Wihtgara

(Possible identification)
Probably identification

0   50 miles
0   100 km

Map 12 The location of the various Southumbrian 'tribes' listed in the Tribal Hidage. (After John Blair, in Lapidge *et al.*, ed. *The Blackwell Encyclopaedia of Anglo–Saxon England*, 1999, 456).

subregulus of the Hwicce: so, like the people of Lindsey, the Hwicce still had their ruler despite being incorporated into Mercia. And although the king of the Mercians might call the ruler of the Hwicce a *subregulus* (a 'little under-king'), the *subregulus* himself probably called himself a *cyning*. One wonders how many of the 30 'tribes' within Mercia had their own rulers, and one inevitably thinks of the battle in 655, in which Penda of Mercia and most of the 30 *duces regii* who had come with him were killed. Are the *duces regii* of Bede's text the *subreguli* of the charters: the rulers of the tribes of the *Tribal Hidage*?

In England, therefore, there are grades of king, and, likewise (and the two things go together) grades of people. One may compare this structure with what we see in Ireland. There the basic kingdom is called the *túath*, often translated as 'tribe'; its king is the *rí*, or *rí túaithe*. A more important king was one who was over-king of three or more 'tribal kings': the *rí buiden*. He in turn would have his own overlord: the provincial over-king, or 'king of great kings', the *rí ruirech*. There are five provinces (*cóiceda*, or fifths): Ulaid, Connachta, Mumu, Laigin and Mide (Ulster, Connaught, Munster, Leinster and Meath). Kings at times aspired to be *ardrí*, high-king of Ireland: the Irish equivalent of *Bretwalda*.

Various reasons have been put forward for why Ireland preserved this system of multiple kingship for so long, right into the later Middle Ages, when other parts of Europe had created national kingships. One possibility is that it derived from the way in which kings, or overrkings, could be selected from major and minor branches of the dynasty. Heads of subordinate branches of dynasties might be kings as well, and ambitious kings depended on the support of other kings; 'the pressure was thus to multiply minor kingships in order to maintain internal dynastic support for the major kings'.[16] There was not a simple correspondance between people and kingdom. The people called the Fothairt had one small kingdom in the far south-east of Leinster, another in the centre and yet other (but possibly not royal) branches of the people in the far north-west of Leinster, in the area of Kildare, the cult-site of their saint, Brigid.

The cases of England and Ireland may give us a hint as to the nature of kingship in those parts of Barbaricum outside the former Roman Empire, such as Scandinavia from which no written material survives until very much later. Archaeology can also suggest developments. Bjørn Myhre, for instance, has argued that a population growth and the appearance of a more complex social and political organization can be observed in southern Norway between the fourth and sixth centuries. Much more richly furnished graves appear from around AD 300 (and disappear again in the sixth century); these are equipped with items in precious metals, tools, weapons and various Roman imports, including glasses. These graves appear in clusters along the south Norwegian coastline, which may indicate where the centres of power are, and if one associates these centres with the hill forts in this area it is possible to hypothesize nine chiefdoms, stretching from Grenland in the south to Nordfjord in the north. Myhre describes a model territory in this way:

> At the mouth of a large river valley or a fiord is found the political centre with the richest grave finds, surrounded by the rich densely populated farm area and the defense area with hill forts. Resources from the varied ecological zones of the territory were transferred from the outer districts to the centre from where they were redistributed, or converted into chieftain's prestige and authority by gift exchange or administered trade.[17]

The hypothesis that these political units were a reality (and perhaps at the time the leaders called themselves 'kings') is strengthened by the fact that the borders suggested by the archaeological survey roughly equate with the borders of the counties of the later Middle Ages, and that the richest grave-finds came from near sites that were royal estates or administrative centres in the Middle Ages. Indeed, there may be considerable continuity over a whole millennium and more from the fourth century onwards, since the distribution of Viking sites corresponds to what is found from the Migration Period. Whether one should link the later county names (such as Grenland, Agder, Rogaland and Hordaland) with some of the 30 tribal names (*Grannii, Augandzi, Rugi, Arochi*) mentioned by Jordanes, writing 2,500 km away in Constantinople, is another matter.

For Sweden we have a different type of evidence: a number of apparently royal sites, the three most important of which lie on the same river system, the Fyrisbå, that flows from Lake Vendel south (through Uppsala) to Lake Mälaren (at the east end of which Stockholm stands). A few kilometres from the present town of Uppsala is Gamla Uppsala, which in the Viking Period was the main centre of the kings of the Svear, the people of central eastern Sweden (Uppland.) The best-known monuments are three large mounds, the 'Royal Mounds', which excavations in the mid-nineteenth century showed to contain Migration Period burials; but these monuments were in the midst of a burial ground containing hundreds, if not thousands, of smaller mounds (most of which have been ploughed away). It was not just a cemetery: according to Adam of Bremen, writing in the eleventh century, there was a large temple here; and other evidence suggests that there was a *thing* or assembly too. The place-name *Uppsala* itself means 'high dwellings', which suggests the presence of a royal palace. Although the evidence relates to the post-Viking Period, the archaeology shows that it was an important site in the fifth century and earlier, and may indeed have already been the royal centre.

Plate 10   The three so-called royal mounds at Gamla Uppsala, the most prominent features of this large royal complex in Uppland, Sweden.

The Valsgärde cemetery, discovered in 1928, is 3 km north of Gamla Uppsala; 25 km north of that is Vendel, another cemetery, excavated 1881–91, which has given its name to the whole period in Sweden from *c.* 550 to the onset of the Viking Period in the eighth century. Vendel and Valsgärde are characterized above all by their boat-burials: burial within a ship, accompanied by rich grave-goods, including weapons, helmets, horse-bits and traces of saddles and imported items such as Frankish glassware. Vendel was only partially excavated, but Valsgärde was fully explored, which enabled a number of observations to be made. The objects buried with the dead were frequently magnificent, but often worn, mended or incomplete, which suggests that they came from the family's store, rather than representing what the individual actually used. Unlike most furnished graves of the period, there were no personal items like rings or buckles: all the items like helmets, swords, shields and so on were placed beside the body. The helmets were perhaps the most astonishing items found in these graves, partly because finding more than one helmet in a cemetery is very unusual (there are only four known from Anglo-Saxon England altogether). The Valsgärde helmets were often decorated with cast bronze plaques depicting armed and helmeted warriors, either standing and holding spears, or else seated on a horse. There were horses and other animals (including dogs) buried with the dead; the horses had an ice-nail in each hoof, for gaining grip on wintery roads.

The rich graves of Vendel and Valsgärde were once regarded as 'royal graves', though this sat oddly with the view that Gamla Uppsala itself was the royal centre of the kingdom. More recently these graves have been called those of 'peasant landowners' or 'peasant chieftains', whatever those terms mean precisely, or of 'royal agents'. In Uppland, at least, the boat-burials were not in the most obvious place: near the sea. Indeed, they are as far away as they could be: in the far west or north of the main area of settlement around Lake Mälaren, which led Björn Ambrosiani to suggest that the occupants of these graves were patrons of trade and industry rather than military or political leaders; they lack the distinctive items which might be regarded as 'regalia'.[18] But, as Peter Sawyer has pointed out, a contemporary boat-burial at Tuna in Badelunda is that of a woman, and Vendel grave 12 is that of a boy, with a boy-sized sword and helmet, both suggesting a hereditary system, 'and, further, that the people buried . . . are more likely to have been rulers than agents'.[19] The helmets from Valsgärde are another clue: they are based not on the conical helmets common among the western barbarian peoples such as the Franks, but on the crestless, hemispherical helmets of late Roman type found at such sites as Deurne (Netherlands) and Aquincum (Budapest), and also seen on the heads of emperors on coins of Constantinople or later Byzantine mosaics.[20] Even this far from the Mediterranean, rulers are, it could be argued, finding their visual propaganda in the Roman Empire.

There are various kinds of boat-burials in the northern world. The most typical consists of a boat placed in a trench, covered by a timber roof and then covered over with soil (which eventually falls through the decomposed roof). The boat might be quite small: 3.5 to 5.5 m in length, with larger ones the exception. The corpse is generally in the stern, richly dressed and surrounded by high-status objects, ranging from musical instruments to the corpses of bridled horses and leashed dogs. There is also a type of ship-burial in which the corpse and the ship have been cremated, and all that survives of the ship are the remains of rivets and other iron fittings. And finally there is the type of ship-burial which survives in literary contexts – the funeral of Scyld Scefing in the opening lines of *Beowulf*, and the funeral of Balder, son of Odin, in Norse mythology – but which does not, for obvious reasons, survive archaeologically: the corpse is laid out in a ship that is then pushed out to sea. Contemporary with the actual boat-burials are larger numbers of 'ship-settings': burials placed in a ship-shaped double-arc of stones standing above the ground.[21] There has been a lot of debate on the meaning of the boat-burial in Scandinavian tradition. The boats may have been convenient coffins; they may have been symbols of secular power, with the ship-settings thus being

Plate 11 The Sutton Hoo ship in the late stages of excavation, in 1939. None of the wood survived; only the rivets and an image in the sand.

imitations by those of lower social status of the elaborate graves of the powerful; they may have been seen as a ferry taking the man or woman to Valhalla (though there is no evidence for this and, from what we know of Valhalla, no place there for the many women found in boat-burials); or they may be an offering to the gods, perhaps specifically the god and/or goddess of fertility. That is the explanation offered by Ole Crumlin-Pedersen in his study of the boat-burials at Slusegård on Bornholm (where there were 45 boat-burials in a cemetery, and 467 inhumation graves, dating from the Migration Period and earlier); but we may confidently predict that this is not the end of the debate.[22]

Vendel-type kingship may have left its traces a long way outside Sweden. The Swedish connections of the royal cemetery of the East Angles, at Sutton Hoo, were noted soon after its discovery and excavation in 1938 and 1939. The helmet, which was decorated all over with tinned-bronze plaques, depicting, among other things, spear-carrying 'dancing warriors' and a horsed warrior riding down another, who is in the act of killing the horse with his sword. This was almost certainly manufactured in Sweden, for it has very close parallels with the helmets found in the Valsgärde graves. The shield, decorated with plaques depicting a dragon and a bird of prey, was almost certainly from Sweden. Now, this by itself is not indicative of any origin for the king or his dynasty: after all, the grave also contained items manufactured in the British world, in Francia and in Byzantium, as well as local Anglo-Saxon artefacts. But the habit of burial in a ship was not something that is at all common in the western barbarian world, whereas it was a feature of burial in Scandinavia, and specifically in Sweden, at this period. It is easy to pick up helmets; not so easy to acquire burial customs. It is possible therefore that the East Anglian dynasty, the Wuffingas, had connections with Sweden, or indeed were descended from Swedes who came, along with many other northern barbarians, into Britain and helped to create new peoples and new polities. Martin Carver's popular book, written during his exhaustive re-evaluation of the site (1983–2005), puts a question mark after the phrase 'burial ground of kings',[23] which displays admirable caution. Carver summarizes the evidence for Sutton Hoo in this way:

> It could be termed 'royal' in so far as that word can be given precision in seventh-century England: it is the cemetery of an aristocracy (implied by its wealth), which was dynastic (implied by the suite of cremations in bronze bowls), which claimed a regional supremacy (implied by the symbolic apparatus in Mound 1), and international recognition (implied by the exotic objects).[24]

In practice many historians have been content to ascribe it to King Rædwald of the East Angles (d. c. 625), who on balance is the most likely candidate.

Symbolically he is appropriate, too, for with his policy of having both a Christian and a pagan altar[25] he seems to stand at the exact watershed between pagan and Christian kingship.

What the archaeology cannot do is give a clear idea of the sources of this man's wealth. The Byzantine silverware, which included two silver spoons with the Greek words SAULOS and PAULOS inscribed on them, might well have been part of diplomatic gifts that had come from Byzantium, perhaps by way of some continental monarch. The gold coins were an interesting item, in that they were clearly taken from some larger treasure: each coin that had been placed in the purse came from a different mint-site, which could never have happened if a random handful of coins had been taken out of a bag.[26] The distribution of the mint-sites of the coins is interesting, too: the two main groupings consist of coins from southern Gaul (though not the port of Marseille, the most prolific mint-site in this period) and coins from mint-sites on the main river-systems in Francia opposite to the river-systems of East Anglia. Two generations after Rædwald, the new port of Ipswich, less than 15 km from Sutton Hoo, became a significant entrepot, importing luxury goods for the court and, no doubt, earning the king a good profit in customs dues. In Rædwald's time, however, it would seem that trade – to which the coins might be witness – was a less well-organized operation. Rædwald's income must have come predominantly from the produce of what royal estates he owned; from food-rents; and from tribute of various kinds.

Most barbarian kingdoms would have started, at least, with very considerable estates acquired either directly by conquest or else, it would seem, acquired by laying claim to the extensive portfolio of estates that had once been part of the imperial fisc. It is highly unlikely that kings had a clear idea of what their total estates were, but the counts, who ran the king's affairs for him in each *civitas*, would probably have had a clearer idea. The total portfolio must have been constantly changing, as kings gave out estates to churches and monasteries in perpetuity, or gave estates to followers or officials for a set period of time, and acquired new lands by conquest or by confiscation from rebels or criminals. The Merovingian dynasty of the Franks, who were the longest lasting of all early medieval dynasties, lost power eventually, as is well known, because they had given away or otherwise lost almost all the royal estates; but this was a process that took two and a half centuries, and for the sixth and much of the seventh century the Frankish royal family seems to have been immensely wealthy. Chilperic might complain in the 580s that his treasury was always empty and all wealth – and hence power and respect – was falling into the hands of the Church, but is seems likely that he was exaggerating, and that his problems were merely temporary.[27]

In addition to the royal estates, kings could acquire income by military power: not just newly conquered territories, but by demanding tribute from lesser powers. The Saxons paid an annual tribute of 500 cows to the Franks in the second half of the sixth century.[28] The 50,000 gold *solidi* paid by the Byzantine Empire for the promise of military help from the Franks (which was only fulfilled several years later),[29] makes the Saxon tribute (500 *solidi*?) seem small change. In the early 630s the Visigoths paid over 200,000 *solidi* to King Dagobert of the Franks in lieu of a piece of their national treasure that their King Sisenand had promised Dagobert in return for his military help in gaining his Spanish throne.[30] Military campaigning could be very profitable too, as the Franks discovered in both Italy and Spain. The profits did not all go to the king, of course, and on occasion (according to Gregory of Tours) Frankish soldiers forced their king to go to war for the sake of the booty. In one case, Chlothar I was forced to attack the Saxons against his better judgement, with dire consequences;[31] in another Theuderic I did not want to support his brothers in an attack on the Burgundians, but, facing a revolt by his men, agreed to let them attack Auvergne, a rebellious part of his own kingdom: 'You will be able to lay your hands on so much gold and silver that even your lust for loot will be satisfied.' He urged them to steal anything they wished, and (apparently) to enslave as many of the population as they wanted.[32] We must always make allowance for Gregory's tendency to exaggerate the brutality of Frankish rule; but we must also remember that his Auvergnat parents and relatives lived through this attack, and bitter memories clearly remained for many years.

There was one other source of wealth which kings could exploit: and again we are better informed for the Franks than for, say, the Visigoths or the Lombards. The barbarians in the former Roman Empire were able to salvage something of what survived of the Roman taxation system, and of the bureaucracy who knew how to operate it.

Gregory of Tours is very good at telling us about the failures of the Frankish kings to collect tax, but in the process tells us a fair amount about a process that often did still work. Our picture is fragmentary, however, and, as Goffart has pointed out, there is no point in trying to fill in the gaps from our knowledge of the late Roman systems of the fourth century: Roman taxation had changed by the sixth century anyway, and what the Franks had inherited from the different parts of their conquests was no doubt in several different states of disarray.[33] There is no record of a number of major taxes from the Roman Period, and the curials, the city councillors, who were in the late Roman Period responsible for collecting taxes from the *civitates* (and whose shortcomings were recorded in such detail in the Theodosian Code) seem no longer to exist by the sixth century. Gregory's tax-collectors (*exactores*) seem to be, not locals from the *civitas*, but outsiders and agents of central government.

When Gregory talks about taxation in Tours, he is almost invariably concerned with proving to all concerned that Tours had been exempt from taxation for many years. Other nearby towns such as Limoges or Poitiers were not so lucky. Thus, he tells us that in around 579, King Chilperic decreed new and extremely harsh taxes in his kingdom. A landowner had to pay one *amphora* of wine (five or six gallons) for every *aripennis* of land (120 square feet) possessed; and there was a tax on the number of employees. Some people fled their cities (that is, presumably, the cities where they had their land) and went into exile. The people of Limoges, however, decided to kill the tax-collector and burn his tax-books. The bishop saved the life of Mark, the tax-collector, but failed to preserve the books: Chilperic punished the town severely, even torturing abbots and priests for allegedly having incited the people to revolt.[34] In the following year, however, Chilperic fell ill, as did his two sons. The king recovered, but the boys did not. Chilperic's wife Fredegund decided that this was God's punishment for over-taxation.

> 'It is the tears of paupers which are the cause of their death, the sighs of orphans, the widows' lament. Yet we still keep on amassing wealth . . . We still lay up treasures, we who have no one to whom we can leave them . . . Were our treasure-houses not already full enough with gold, silver, precious stones, necklaces and every regal adornment one could dream of?' So she took the tax-demands which this same tax-collector Mark had brought back from her own cities (the cities whose income had been given to her in her marriage-agreement) and tossed them on the fire; and then Chilperic did the same with his tax-demands, and gave orders that 'no such assessments should ever be made again'.[35]

We may imagine, if we wish, that Gregory was told by one of the royal couple what happened in their private chambers (and the image of the king and queen keeping all their own tax-records in their chambers is a nice one); but we are probably more sensible to imagine that this is all pure fantasy on Gregory's part. It is what he wanted to have happened.

We are on much surer ground with a story he reported from 589. Bishop Maroveus of Poitiers asked King Childebert II to send tax-inspectors to Poitiers. They were very senior officials: the mayor of the queen's palace and the count of the king's palace. The problem was that the tax-assessments had not been updated for some years; apparently since the time of his father Sigibert (who had been assassinated in 575). Many of those on the lists were dead, and widows, orphans and the sick were being expected to pay their bills. The inspectors basically updated the lists, gave relief to those unable to pay and discovered who should in justice be paying tax even though they had perhaps avoided it for some years.[36] As Ian Wood has pointed out, this story shows us that taxation was normal, relatively well-organized and relatively fair.[37] It also indicates that tax-records were kept on individuals, and that beneath this tax effort was a considerable bureaucratic underpinning.

The Franks themselves, in the sense of the Germanic-speaking new-comers and their descendants, did not feel that they should pay these taxes at all: these were Roman taxes. Frankish resentment ended in 548, on the death of King Theudebert, with the stoning to death of his tax-collector Parthenius (a Roman bureaucrat trained in Provence),[38] and Gregory specifies that it was *Franks* who killed him, and in Trier, a part of Francia where there had been heavy Frankish settlement. After the death of Chilperic (584), Franks attacked Audo, taking all his property and forcing him to take sanctuary in Notre-Dame in Paris with Queen Fredegund, because under King Childebert I (d. 548) he had 'exacted taxes from many Franks who had been free men'.[39] Gregory seems inclined to present these cases as summary justice. From the point view of the king and his officials, it may well have been not a question of denying that free Franks should be free of taxes, but rather, as the *Lex Romana Burgundionum* said, 'all should acknowledge that they cannot buy fields unless, immediately on taking possession, they under-take to pay their tax liability'.[40] However, it is clear that Franks did not want to pay, and in the seventh century Fredegar alleged that the Burgundians were invited in to the Empire so Romans could avoid taxes.[41]

Law and Society

Law-codes and law-tracts are a valuable guide to social life and attitudes in the early Middle Ages. We need to be very careful to avoid the trap of searching for the 'primitive', and assuming that this was how the law operated in the years before settlement in the Empire; but with caution we can learn something. The most 'primitive' of the barbarian law-codes – the ones which are visibly least influenced by either Christianity or Roman legal ideas – are the laws of the Franks, written down at the time of Clovis, *c.* 500 (the *Pactus Legis Salicae*) and the laws of Æthelberht of Kent, *c.* 600. Both these kings were the first of their people to convert to Christianity, and both of them probably saw producing a written law-code as being a token of their membership of the essentially Roman club of Christendom. Both codes would seem to be not royal decrees but the writing down of the hitherto unwritten law of their people, and neither demonstrate much of an attempt to be systematic or thorough. Æthelberht's has one clause which mentions Christianity; Clovis's has none. Both codes do, however, suggest roughly similar societies (which is not necessarily proof of anything about ubiquitous 'Germanic' institutions, given the strong influence which the Franks seem to have had on their neighbours in Kent).

Both societies are, to start with, distinctly hierarchical. Kings and those who are close to them are given special protection; in Frankish law Romans are given less legal protection than Franks, but those Romans who are 'dining companions' of the king are given higher protection. Beneath these people of higher status (perhaps we can call them 'aristocrats') are ordinary freemen. Beneath them are the half-free – læt in Old English and letus in Latin; Æthelberht divides the half-free into three classes. And finally there are the slaves. Æthelberht divides the female slaves into three classes too: those who belong to the king, grinding slaves and third-class slaves. The distinction between the free and the slave is a clear one. In the Frankish law, if a free man is killed, then 200 *solidi* compensation has to be paid to the free man's family, unless he is in the king's retinue, in which case the price is 600 *solidi*. Slaves, on the other hand, have a price: 'a swineherd, vine dresser, metalworker, miller, carpenter or groom', for instance, or 'an overseer, steward, butler, horsekeeper, . . . gold-worker . . . or domestic servant' is each worth 25 *solidi*.[42] Their theft, or the theft of a stallion or a mare, results in a fine of 35 *solidi*, plus the price, plus a compensation for the loss of use.[43]

The essence of the legal system is the application of monetary penalties: both lawcodes are essentially lists of penalties. Nearly 40 of Æthelberht's 90 clauses are devoted to enumerating the parts of the body, with the penalties associated with their injury or loss: so we know, for instance, the relative value that Kentishmen placed on each digit of the hand (the cutting off of a toe costs half the amount for the equivalent finger). There are 20 clauses in *Pactus Legis Salicae* laying down the penalties for the theft of different kinds of pig (including a sacrifical boar). The penalties are monetary: laid down in *solidi* and *denarii* for *Pactus Legis Salicae* (40 *denarii* to the *solidus*) and in sceattas and shillings for Æthelberht (20 sceattas to the shilling). How this worked in practice is not clear: as far as we know no coins of the denomination of a *denarius* were in circulation under Clovis (the third of a *solidus*, the *triens* or *tremissis* was the basic coin), and the Anglo-Saxons did not mint coins at all in Æthelberht's day (though they might have used Frankish ones). Presumably these represent a scale of values rather than actual amounts of coin.

The largest fine in the *Pactus Legis Salicae* is 600 *solidi*, for the murder of a high-status man, or a pregnant woman of free status, or a free boy under 12 years of age (over 12 and it is assumed he can defend himself). In monetary terms, that is 1,800 gold coins (*trientes*), a sum of money which could buy a herd of 300 oxen, or 600 cows, or 200 mares, or an armoury of 300 spear-and-shield sets.[44] This fact has led some people to suggest that the 'free' in Frankish society were not the majority, but actually a small elite; others believe that the sum mentioned is simply a starting point for a process of negotiation and haggling.

The king may have been the ultimate enforcer of payment; but the most effective enforcer may have been the injured party and his kin or other associates. For a long time, in both Frankish and Anglo-Saxon society, it was accepted that feud could be prosecuted by injured parties; that is, that the alternative to the payment of compensation in the case of murder was death at the hands of the kin group. Narrative texts told horror stories about what happened when attempts at mediation or judgement failed, and death was repaid by death again and again; but, as Tacitus implies in *Germania*, in most cases there is 'resolution, for by a fixed number of cattle and sheep they can make amends even for manslaughter' and resolution is to 'public advantage, since feuds waged freely are more fraught with danger'.[45] It is fairly clear that Tacitus described a very similar legal system to that which is described in sketchy fashion in both these lawcodes from over half a millennium later.

The legal system described in the codes looks 'primitive'; and it corresponds loosely to what Tacitus depicted. Does it therefore give us a clear idea of early barbarian custom? Well, yes and no; and we have to look carefully at each aspect. As an example, let us take questions of innocence and guilt. An accused person could take an oath that he was innocent; this could be taken with an appropriate number of neighbours or friends (oath-helpers), who were willing to swear to his innocence (I say 'he' advisedly, because women had to be represented by men in barbarian lawcourts). This oath might be taken in a church, in front of relics; Gregory of Tours records various warning stories about the awful things that happen to perjurers in churches. Another common method of proof when an accused person had not been caught red-handed was the ordeal. This is not known before the sixth century; but thereafter it is common in western Europe down to the twelfth century. The ordeal takes various forms,[46] but the most common one at an early period (mentioned in *Pactus Legis Salicae*) was by cauldron. The accused person plunged his arm into a cauldron of boiling water and plucked out some small object. If the person's wound healed quickly, he was innocent. The ordeal rests on the same belief as the oath: that God will reveal the guilty party. One might also note that the belief-system behind the ordeal and the oath might flush out a guilty party before the ritual was undertaken, unless he had unusual reserves of confidence: in other words, it seems 'primitive'; but it might have been fairly effective. The ordeal has often been seen as an intrusion of barbarian thinking into the more 'rational' Roman world. But we might well doubt that: it might be the arrival of Christianity rather than the arrival of barbarians into the Empire which caused both the oath and the ordeal to become so widespread. It is significant that the earliest actual ordeal by cauldron took place, probably in southern Gaul, in the fifth or early sixth century (that is, around the time of the *Pactus*), in a situation where both parties were Romans and priests.[47]

An aspect of the 'Germanic' laws which have attracted attention in recent decades in particular has been what they show us about the treatment of women. Women are, to start with, unable to represent themselves in the law-courts: they have to have a male protector and spokesman, who may be the father, brother or husband. This is why those without obvious protectors, such as widows and orphans, receive specific attention in the laws. The inability of a woman to speak for herself obviously denotes a patriarchal society; but we might relate it specifically to the fact that barbarian society was a patriarchal and *arm-bearing* society. The enforcement of legal decisions ultimately depended on the threat of physical force; and there are barbarian laws that punish women who carry arms as if they were men, a clear violation of the accepted view of the world's norms.

One aspect of marriage which has puzzled some commentators is 'marriage by abduction'.[48] Æthelberht's law said that 'if a man forcibly carries off a maiden, he shall pay 50 shillings to the person who pos-sesses right of guardianship over her and afterwards buy his consent [to the union]'.[49] The two following clauses mention extra compensation if she had already been betrothed, and again if she was returned after abduction. But there is nothing about requiring her return, and the penalty is not high; the result (and it is possible to compare this with various other barbarian law-codes) seems often to be marriage. In some cases (since the consent of the woman is mentioned) it is clear that 'abduction' is a matter of a woman gaining freedom from marriage arrangements that her family has made on her behalf. In later legal texts (from the tenth and eleventh century) it is stated that 'no widow or maiden is ever to be forced to marry a man she dislikes',[50] but, Rebecca Colman suggests, it is probable that this idea went further back, and was not necessarily an innovation introduced by the Church, which was 'obliged, like everyone else, to come to terms with stubborn maidens'.[51]

'Celts' and 'Germans'

If we cannot easily see how 'German' barbarians operated before they came under the influence of *Romanitas* and Christianity, we might have more chance with 'Celts'. In fact, the law-tracts of the seventh and eighth century from Ireland bring together more legal material than we have for the rest of barbarian Europe together. Although written down within a Christian society, some of them at least show little trace of Christianity, and even less trace of Roman influence. Whether or not this is 'a window on the Iron Age', as Kenneth Jackson described the earliest Irish literary traditions,[52] it is at least a window that sheds more light onto an early medieval barbarian people than any other.

All the surviving legal material from early Ireland has been collected into a six-volume edition by Daniel Binchy.[53] Very few of these texts have been translated, and the Old Irish they were written in can be read by relatively few scholars today (and probably could not be well understood by those who wrote the late medieval or early modern manuscripts in which the texts survive). As a consequence in what follows I rely on Fergus Kelly's excellent guide to the laws.[54]

It is worth first of all dwelling on the similarities with what we have found for the Franks and the Kentishmen. Irish society is, first, as hierarchical as Frankish or Kentish society, if not more so. There are various grades of king (see above, p. 239). There are also a number of grades of lord. At the bottom is the basic 'lord of vassalry', who has an honour-price (what the codes from Germanic-speaking barbarians call *wergild*) of ten *sets*, a retinue of six persons, five horses including a saddle horse with silver bridle, a house a certain number of metres in diameter with eight bed-cubicles, and ten clients.[55] As can be seen from those details, the law-tracts can be very prescriptive and schematic. One hardly needs to believe the prescriptions; but the impression it gives of a hierarchy of legal and social status is inescapable. Below the lord are two grades of client: the base client and the free client. These people, however, are still freemen; below them is the *fuidir*, a 'half-freeman', who cannot make any legal commitments without his lord's permission and has to do what his lord commands; one law-text distinguishes 10 different types of *fuidir*, the lowest of whom is the criminal who has been unable to pay his fine and has been ransomed by the lord. Finally there are slaves: those who have been captured in warfare, bought from slave-traders, or those who fell into debt. These are used for agricultural and domestic use, and their importance may be indicated by the fact that the word *cumal* (female slave) is the most common measure of value.

As in the 'Germanic' lawcodes, 'payment can atone for almost any crime'.[56] If payment is not forthcoming, then the guilty party might be put to death, or else taken into slavery: this might well have been true in the case of our 'Germanic' societies too, although it is not so clearly specified. The amounts are not given in monetary terms, although they have borrowed words for weight from Latin, such as the words for scruple and ounce (*screpul* and *ungae*) (there are 24 scruples to the ounce). Occasionally payments are couched in terms of ounces of silver, although one also finds 'the value of half an ounce of silver in pigs'; more commonly, payments are made by the *cumal*, cattle (particularly 'a milch-cow and calf') and the *sét*, which seems to be a large sum of vague amount (the word means 'treasure').[57]

In terms of legal proof, oaths are very important, and although they are frequently given a Christian context (such as swearing on the Gospels) there is an early text that says that a Christian must do penance if he swears before a druid in the pagan manner. As in Anglo-Saxon society, the higher one's status, the more one's oath is worth (and the fewer oath-helpers one needs). The most common form of the ordeal is 'the proof of the cauldron', as elsewhere in western Europe, and here, of course, there is a strong possibility that it was introduced along with Christianity. As in the 'Germanic' codes, the kin play a role in the legal procedures, and the feud is an accepted procedure. In certain circumstances in relation to homicide, the kin of the victim are obliged to hunt the man down, and if the victim was a lord, his clients have the same obligation. Given that an obvious thing for a guilty person to do was to flee into a neighbouring kingdom (a neighbouring kingdom is never far away in Ireland), there was a provision made in one law-tract for pursuing the guilty party into another kingdom, providing there was a treaty between the two kingdoms.

What we can surmise of property law – on which there is some detailed evidence from Ireland, much less from Francia, and none at all from Æthelberht's Kent – is that the 'Celtic' and 'Germanic' experience may not have been so different either. In Ireland most farmland is *fintiu* or 'kin-land', which is shared with one's fellow-heirs and which cannot be sold without the permission of the others. The kin even have some rights over what an individual acquires in addition to what he acquired by inheritance. All the sons inherit an individual's land (the division is made by the youngest, but the eldest gets first choice); a daughter only inherits if she has no brother. When she dies, the property all reverts to her own kin, and none of it goes to her husband or sons. All of this is very similar to the situation in early Frankish society, although the situation as we see it in the *Pactus* was rapidly changing. The *Pactus* lays down precisely what happens when the individual holder dies: it is divided among the children; if there are no children, then it goes to the parents; if there are no parents, then to the brothers and sisters; and so on. There was clearly some debate later in the sixth century about whether 'children' (*filios*) really meant 'children' rather than 'sons', and this was complicated by another ambiguous clause that stated that daughters could not inherit *terra salica*. In the late Middle Ages this clause was invoked to stop the kingdom of France being inherited by the king of England. In the seventh century, in another surviving Frankish lawcode (the *Lex Ribvaria*), it was clarified as 'ancestral land': women could inherit land that had been acquired in the parent's lifetime, but not the land which 'belonged' to the kin, *unless* there were no male heirs: in other words, this was very similar to the Irish position.[58]

The situation was changing in Francia in the sixth century (and in England and Ireland at a slightly later date) because of the influence of Roman law, but specifically because of the influence of the Church. If an individual had no right to bequeath ancestral land to whoever he wished, then the pious act of donating land in one's will (to the Church, for instance) was an impossibility. The last will and testament was a Roman idea, but it was one adopted by newly converted peoples such as the Franks. To a traditionally minded Frank, of course, the last will and testament was an underhand means by which the legal heirs were disinherited of their rightful property. Gregory of Tours complained that King Chilperic (d. 584) would make a habit of tearing up wills in which people had left property to the Church;[59] for Gregory it merely proved his wickedness, but the Franks who were about to lose 'their' property to the Church no doubt celebrated the king as a great preserver of their rights. In England, and perhaps elsewhere, there grew up two types of land: ancestral land (folkland), which could not be alienated from the kin, and land that had been freed from these restrictions by will of the king, and could be alienated by means of a land-deed or 'charter': in Old English a written document was a *boc*, and so this land was 'bookland'.

This comparison between some 'Germanic' and 'Celtic' areas suggests that there is much less difference between the two than has often been argued. Barbarian societies may have operated in very similar ways; and Roman and Christian ideas may have likewise had a comparable impact. Of course, the absence of evidence prevents us from making any firm assumptions about the situation in those parts of the barbarian world which were still, in the seventh century, in a prehistoric condition – that is, without written documents. However much surviving evidence from the sixth or seventh centuries reminds us of what Tacitus told us about Germans in the first century, we should be cautious about assuming that barbarian society was either uniform or changeless.

chapter twelve

CONCLUSIONS

There is no single thesis to this book, and therefore no single or simple conclusion. The intention has been to present the interested reader with basic information, not only about the barbarians themselves, but also about the academic debates surrounding almost every aspect of their existence. Many of these debates have so far been inconclusive, and perhaps will remain so. I frequently encounter history students who find it disconcerting that there is so much uncertainty about our knowledge of the late antique or early medieval world; sometimes they retreat to the apparent security of nineteenth- or twentieth-century history, where historians are so overwhelmed by the quantity of their evidence that (it seems to me) they seldom worry enough about its quality, or sufficiently acknowledge the uncertainty that exists everywhere in the historical project. Those of us working in late antiquity or the early Middle Ages are perhaps more used to thinking of our task as asking questions, just as much as finding answers.

One theme running through this book is the way in which the history of the barbarians has been misinterpreted and manipulated in the interests of modern nationalism. We Europeans still live in the shadow of nationalist myths which were, for the most part, forged only in the nineteenth century. As Patrick Geary said, in *The Myth of Nations*, these received traditions have 'summoned millions of people into the streets and sent millions more to their graves in the twentieth century'.[1] Modern nationalists have imagined that nations, and the medieval peoples that preceded them, are far more distinct and unchanging than they really are.

A second theme is that of barbarism and civilization. To a large extent these are myths too. 'Barbarians' were invented in order to reassure some people of their superiority or, as some Roman writers would have admitted, in order to assure others that living under a civilized despot was better than living in barbarian freedom. 'Barbarism' and 'civilization' are grand words which enable one to simplify the world: to forget, for instance, that in terms of some things that are still with us – like torture and 'ethnic cleansing' – the Romans were even more 'barbaric' than the barbarians. Civilization is not, perhaps, the ability to produce books (which our barbarians did not have) so much as to find the right things to put in them.

If this book is partly designed to puncture myths, then it is also intended to show that simplifying the world is itself a myth. The barbarians did not assassinate the Roman Empire, as André Piganiol asserted (not long after living through the fall of France in 1940).[2] The Roman Empire did not 'decline and fall' of its own volition, either. The role of the barbarians in the collapse of the Western Empire is one that is not addressed openly in the course of this book, although it is implicit throughout; and that role was complex, varied across both time and space and ultimately unquantifiable.

Another issue that is not addressed in this book is the question of 'the origins of the Middle Ages'. Historians have even tried to date when 'ancient' became 'medieval'; some have suggested 476, as the year of the end of the Western Roman Empire (but see p. 76), and many have at least placed it somewhere in the period covered by this book. More recently, historians have suggested a quite new periodization: the ancient world followed by late antiquity, and only then allowing the Middle Ages to begin, in the seventh or eighth century.[3] This at least avoids what is certainly not a helpful debate, too often seen in terms inherited from the Italian Renaissance, in which the barbarians introduced the Middle Ages by destroying Roman civilization and setting back progress for a thousand years. As far as I am concerned, periodization itself tends to set back progress: that is, it creates artificial memes which distort and limit historical debate and the historical imagination.

A final theme of this book needs to be mentioned at the very end. Every period sees barbarians in its own light; every generation recreates them for its own purposes. We can see several trends at the moment. The Late Antiquity project, which has attracted many American scholars in particular, on the whole concentrates on the Greek East, and on spirituality, and has tended to marginalize the role of barbarians in the late Roman world. The Transformation of the Roman World project in the 1990s, funded by the European Science Foundation, tended to look at the barbarians in terms of their relatively peaceful assimilation into the Roman world; after all, it hardly befits the ethos of the European Union to remember ethnic conflict or destructive wars. But undoubtedly the growth of the European Union, in the wake of the disappearance of the Iron Curtain, has brought new horizons to the study of the barbarians which are going to bring great changes. There is ever-increasing collaboration between scholars right across Europe, and the work of scholars in central and eastern Europe is becoming much better known in the West, and vice versa. Narrow nationalistic approaches to Europe's barbarians never did make sense. We need to see late antique Europe from the Atlantic to the Urals as one entity, and that is becoming ever more possible.

We tend to laugh or sneer at the simplicities or distortions of past views of the barbarians; sooner or later, this will be the fate of this book too. I welcome the day; we will have made another small step towards a proper understanding of the past.

NOTES

Acknowledgements

1. Lucien Musset, *The Germanic Invasions: The Making of Europe AD 400–600*, trans. Edward James and Columba James. London: Elek, 1975.
2. A former colleague at Reading is sympathetic: see Heinrich Härke, 'The German experience', in *Archaeology, Ideology and Society*, ed. Härke, 2000, 12–32.
3. Guy Halsall, *Barbarian Migrations and the Roman West, 376–568*. Cambridge: Cambridge University Press, 2007.

Chapter one

1. Arno Borst, *Barbaren, Ketzer und Artisten: Welten des Mittelalters*. Munich and Zurich: Piper, 1988, 19.
2. Though for the way French and Italian imperialism influenced classical archaeology in North Africa, see David J. Mattingly, 'From one colonialism to another: imperialism and the Maghreb', in *Roman Imperialism*, eds Webster and Cooper, 1996, 49–69. My thanks to Antony Keen for this reference.
3. Léon Poliakov, *The Aryan Myth: A History of Racist and Nationalist Ideas in Europe*. London: Chatto Heinemann, 1974, Chapters 1 and 2.
4. See Chapter 5, 'The disappearance of comfort', in Bryan Ward-Perkins, *The Fall of Rome and the End of Civilization*. Oxford: Oxford University Press, 2005, 87–122.
5. Guy Halsall, 'Movers and Shakers: the barbarians and the Fall of Rome', *Early Medieval Europe* 8 (1999), 145.
6. For this, see Glanville Price, ed., *Encyclopedia of the Languages of Europe*. Oxford: Blackwell, 1998.
7. Although see the relatively restrained words in Edward James, *Britain in the First Millennium*. London: Edward Arnold, 2001, 164–70.
8. Hans-Werner Goetz, 'Introduction', in *Regna and Gentes*, eds Goetz, Jarnut and Pohl, 2003, 7.
9. Claude Rawson, *God, Gulliver, and Genocide: Barbarism and the European Imagination, 1492–1945*. Oxford: Oxford University Press, 2001, viii.
10. For Greek views of barbarians see Paul Cartledge, *The Greeks: A Portrait of Self and Others*. Oxford: Oxford University Press, 1993, 36–62.
11. Edith Hall, *Inventing the Barbarian: Greek Self-Definition through Tragedy*. Oxford: Clarendon, 1989, 222–3.
12. Hall, *Inventing the Barbarian*, ix.
13. Michel de Montaigne, 'On cannibals', in J.M. Cohen, trans., *Montaigne: Essays*. Harmondsworth: Penguin, 1958, 110. Gonzalo in *The Tempest*, Act

II Scene 1, would likewise in his Commonwealth have no magistrates, no letters, no riches, no poverty and so on.

14. For the European reaction to the 'new barbarians' see Roger Schlesinger, *In the Wake of Columbus. The Impact of the New World on Europe, 1492–1650*, 2nd ed. Wheeling, IL: Harlan Davidson, 2007, 61–91.

15. Strabo 7.3.7; Jones 3, 198–9.

16. Strabo 4.5.4; Jones 2, 258–61.

17. St Jerome said that when he had been a young man he saw 'a British tribe' called Attacotti, who not only ate human flesh, but also carved their meat from living animals: see Jerome, *Against Jovinian* 2.9 (*PL* 23, col. 296) and J.N.D. Kelly, *Jerome: His Life, Writings and Controversies*. London: Duckworth, 1975, 26.

18. W. Arens, *The Man-Eating Myth: Anthropology and Anthropophagy*. Oxford and New York: Oxford University Press, 1979, 13, who made the comment about Strabo's postscript.

19. Y.A. Dauge, *Le Barbare: recherches sur la conception romaine du barbare et de la civilisation*. Brussels: Latomus, 1981, 621–2.

20. See Frank M. Snowden, *Before Color Prejudice: The Ancient View of Blacks*. Cambridge, MA: Harvard University Press, 1983, among others; although Snowden's conclusions have been challenged.

21. Dauge, *Le Barbare*, 19–20: my translation.

22. Dauge, *Le Barbare*, 170: my translation.

23. Themistius, Oration 10, trans. Heather and Matthews, 38–9. This passage is discussed in Peter Heather, 'Literacy and power in the migration period', in *Literacy and Power in the Ancient World*, eds Alan K. Bowman and Greg Woolf, Cambridge: Cambridge University Press, 1994, 177 and John Vanderspoel, *Themistius and the Imperial Court: Oratory, Civic Duty, and Paideia from Constantius to Theodosius*. Ann Arbor: University of Michigan Press, 1995, 173–6.

24. Dauge, *Le Barbare*, 122, 243, 735.

25. Dauge, *Le Barbare*, 325–7.

26. The words of Dauge, *Le Barbare*, 263, summarizing Tacitus's view.

27. A story told in Plutarch's *Life of Crassus*, 33; Perrin 3, 421.

28. Peter Heather, 'The late Roman art of client management: imperial defence in the fourth century West', in *The Transformation of Frontiers*, ed. Pohl, Wood and Reimitz, 2001, 51.

29. John F. Drinkwater, 'The "Germanic threat on the Rhine frontier": a Romano-Gallic artefact?' in *Shifting Frontiers*, eds Mathisen and Sivan, 1996, 27–8.

30. Patrick Amory, *People and Identity in Ostrogothic Italy, 489–554*. Cambridge: Cambridge University Press, 1997, 25.

31. A.K. Bowman, *Life and Letters on the Roman Frontier: Vindolanda and its People*. London: British Museum, 1994, 36.

32. http://www.dmgh.de/ is free; http://pld.chadwyck.com is not.

33. Brian Hope-Taylor's excavations at Yeavering, begun in 1953, were published in 1977; the ship-burial at Sutton Hoo, excavated in 1938–9, was published between 1975 and 1983.

Chapter Two

1. For a brief but useful introduction, see Benjamin Isaac, *The Invention of Racism in Classical Antiquity*. Princeton, NJ: Princeton University Press, 2004, 60–9.
2. Isaac, *Invention of Racism*, 68.
3. Edward W. Said, *Orientalism*. New York: Pantheon, 1978.
4. Livy, *History of Rome* 5.47, Foster 3, 156–9.
5. Strabo 4.4.5; Jones 2, 246–7.
6. See, e.g., Jane Webster, 'Ethnographic barbarity: colonial discourse and "Celtic warrior societies"', in *Roman Imperialism*, ed. Webster and Cooper, 1996, 111–23.
7. *Gallic War* 2.4; Edwards 92–3.
8. *Gallic War* 1.1; Edwards 2–3.
9. *Gallic War* 2.15; Edwards 110–11.
10. Strabo 4.3.4; Jones 2, 231.
11. Stephen Oppenheimer, *The Origins of the British: A Genetic Detective Story*. London: Constable, 2006.
12. *Gallic War* 6.21–2; Edwards 344–7.
13. *Gallic War* 6.24; Edwards 348–9.
14. See W. Schluter and R. Wiegels, eds, *Rom, Germanien und die Ausgrabungen in Kalkriese*, Osnabrück: Universitätsverlag Rasch, 1999.
15. Sebastian Brather, 'Acculturation and ethnogenesis along the frontier: Rome and the ancient Germans in an archaeological perspective', in *Borders, Barriers*, ed. Curta, 2005, 143.
16. I have taken this from Hugh Elton, *Frontiers of the Roman Empire*. London: Batsford, 1996, 38.
17. Strabo 7.2.4.
18. Katherine Clarke, *Between Geography and History: Hellenistic Constructions of the Roman World*. Oxford: Oxford University Press, 1999, 215; see also Eran Almagor, 'Who is a barbarian? The barbarians in the ethnological and cultural taxonomies of Strabo', in *Strabo's Cultural Geography. The Making of a Kolossourgia*, ed. Daniela Dueck *et al.* Cambridge: Cambridge University Press, 2005, 42–55.
19. Strabo 3.4.16; Jones 2, 108–9.
20. Strabo 4.4.2; Jones 2, 238–9.
21. Strabo 4.4.5; Jones 2, 246–7.
22. Strabo 4.5.4; Jones 2, 258–61. See my comment above, p. 00.
23. Strabo 7.1.2; Jones 3, 152–3.
24. Strabo 7.1.3; Jones 3, 156–9.
25. Pliny the Elder, 16.2–4; Rackham 4, 386–9. The discussion is at the beginning of his book on trees, to illustrate the nature of peoples who live without them. I am following the excellent analysis of Trevor Murphy, *Pliny the Elder's Natural History: The Empire in the Encyclopedia*. Oxford: Oxford University Press, 2004, 166–74.
26. Tacitus, *Agricola* 11; Hutton, 46–7.
27. Tacitus, *Agricola* 13; Hutton, 50–1.
28. Tacitus, *Agricola* 21; Hutton, 66–7.

29. Tacitus, *Agricola* 24; Hutton, 70–1.

30. Tacitus, *Germania* 4.1; Rives, 78.

31. Tacitus, *Germania* 1.1; Rives, 77.

32. Tacitus, *Germania* 46.2; Rives, 96.

33. Tacitus, *Germania* 19.1; Rives, 85.

34. These comments are found in these chapters of the *Germania*: gold 5; dress 6, 17; adultery 19; children 20; hospitality 21; no entertainers 24; position of freedmen 25; usury 26, funerals 27.

35. Tacitus, *Germania* 33; Rives, 90 and, for commentary, 259–60.

36. Tacitus, *Germania* 38; Rives, 92. See John Hines, 'Culture groups and ethnic groups in northern Germany in and around the Migration Period', *Studien zur Sachsenforschung* 13 (1999), 225.

37. Tacitus, *Germania* 45.6; Rives, 96.

38. Patrick Geary, *Before France and Germany: The Creation and Transformation of the Merovingian World*. New York: Oxford University Press, 1988, vi.

39. On all this see André Chastagnol, 'La signification géographique et ethnique des mots *Germani* et *Germania* dans les sources latines', *Ktèma* 9 (1984), 97–101.

40. *Scriptores Historiae Augustae*, at Firmus, 13.3; Magie 3, 408–9.

41. Claudian, *On Stilicho's Consulship* 2.243; Platnauer 2, 20–1.

42. Jerome, *Vita S. Hilarionis* 2; *PL* 23.39.

43. *Barbaria* was the usual word before the fourth century; and *finis* was more common than *limes*: see Hugh Elton, 'Defining Romans, Barbarians, and the Roman Frontier', in *Shifting Frontiers*, ed. Mathisen and Sivan, 1996, 126.

44. Here I am following the excellent study by Lynn F. Pitts, 'Relations between Rome and the German "kings" on the Middle Danube in the first to the fourth century AD', *Journal of Roman Studies* 79 (1989), 45–58.

45. Tacitus, *Annals* 2.62; Jackson, 478–9.

46. Pitts, 'Relations between Rome', 49.

47. And of Sarmatia, according to the *Scriptores Historiae Augustae*, Marcus 24.6; Magie 1, 192–3.

48. I follow here the convenient narrative of the early years of the war in Chapters 7 and 8 of Anthony Birley, *Marcus Aurelius: A Biography*, 2nd ed. London: Batsford, 1987.

49. On the early development of these three federations, see Pat Southern, *The Roman Empire from Severus to Constantine*. London and New York: Routledge, 2001, 207–26.

50. Southern, *The Roman Empire*, 208.

51. See David S. Potter, *The Roman Empire at Bay, AD 180–395*. London and New York: Routledge, 2004, 245.

52. Potter, *Empire at Bay*, 245 and n.122.

53. Géza Alföldy, 'The crisis of the third century as seen by contemporaries', *Greek, Roman and Byzantine Studies* 15 (1974), 95–7.

54. R.P. Duncan-Jones, 'Economic change and the transition to Late Antiquity', in *Approaching Late Antiquity*, eds Simon Swain and Mark Edwards, Oxford: Oxford University Press, 2004, 20–52.

55. For translation and commentary, see Peter Heather and John Matthews, *The Goths in the Fourth Century*. Liverpool: Liverpool University Press, 1991, 1–11.

56. Heather and Matthews, *Goths*, 9.

57. The inscription is translated in Potter, *Empire at Bay*, 256.

58. Lawrence Okamura, 'Roman withdrawals from three transfluvial frontiers', in *Shifting Frontiers*, ed. Mathisen and Sivan, 1996, 11–19.

59. Alaric Watson, *Aurelian and the Third Century*. London and New York: Routledge, 1999, 104–5.

60. Zosimus 1.68; Ridley, 21.

61. VIII. Panegyric of Constantius (297?), 18.3; Nixon and Rodgers, 139.

62. E.A. Thompson, 'Peasant revolts in late Roman Gaul and Spain', *Past and Present* 2 (1952), 11–23.

63. S.J.B. Barnish, 'Old Kaspars: Attila's invasion of Gaul in the literary sources', in *Fifth-Century Gaul*, eds Drinkwater and Elton, 1992, 38–48.

64. John F. Drinkwater, 'Peasants and Bagaudae in Roman Gaul', *Echoes du Monde Classique* ns 3 (1984), 368.

65. A.N. Sherwin-White, *The Roman Citizenship*, 2nd ed. Oxford: Clarendon Press, 1973, 454.

66. VI. Panegyric of Constantine (310), 12.3; Nixon and Rodgers, 235.

67. Synesius, *On Kingship*; Fitzgerald, 108–47.

68. On the later history of this policy, see Peter Charanis, 'The transfer of population as a policy in the Byzantine Empire', *Comparative Studies in Society and History* 3 (1961), 140–54.

69. See Mark Shchukin, 'Forgotten Bastarnae', in *International Connections*, ed. Istvánovits and Kulcsár, 2001, 57–64.

70. On Constantine, see Michael Kulikowski, 'Constantine and the northern barbarians', in *The Cambridge Companion to the Age of Constantine*, ed. Noel Lenski. New York: Cambridge University Press, 2006, 347–76.

71. Reported by Philostorgius, *Church History*, 2.5; for translation and commentary see Heather and Matthews, *Goths*, 143–5.

72. Taken from the *Laterculus Veronensis*, ed. Seeck, pp. 251–2. I have normalized the spelling.

73. Arnaldo Momigliano, 'The lonely historian Ammianus Marcellinus', in *Essays in Ancient and Modern Historiography*, Oxford: Blackwell, 1977, 128.

74. John F. Drinkwater, 'Julian and the Franks and Valentinian I and the Alamanni: Ammianus on Romano-German relations', *Francia* 27/1 (1997), 1.

75. In what follows I make much use of John F. Matthews, *The Roman Empire of Ammianus*. London: Duckworth, 1988, especially Chapter 14, 'Barbarians and bandits', 304–82.

76. Okamura, 'Roman withdrawals', 15.

77. Ammianus 16.2.12; Rolfe 1, 208–9.

78. Symmachus, Oration 2.16; see Matthews, *Roman Empire*, 285.

79. Ammianus 17.1.7; Rolfe 1, 306–7.

80. Matthews, *Roman Empire*, 310.

81. Ammianus 27.10.7ff; see Joachim Werner, 'Zu den alamannischen Burgen des 4. und 5. Jahrhunderts', in *Speculum Historiale: Festschrift für Johannes Spörl*, 1965, 439–53.

82. Ammianus 30.3.4–5; Rolfe 3, 317.

83. Ammianus 16.12.24; Rolfe 1, 295.

84. Ammianus 16.12.60; Rolfe 1, 297.
85. Ammianus 16.12.25; Rolfe 1, 277.
86. Ammianus 18.2.17; Rolfe 1, 415.
87. Ammianus 21.3.4–5; Rolfe 2, 102–5.
88. See *PLRE* 1, 928.
89. Ammianus 29.4.7: stationed in Britain; 18.2.2: Hariobaudes; 21.10.3: Lentienses.
90. Ammianus 28.5.9, 11; Rolfe 3, 165, 167.
91. Orosius 7.32.11; Raymond, 371; see Matthews, *Roman Empire*, 310 and n. 11, 524.
92. Ammianus 28.5.14; Rolfe 3, 169.
93. See Matthews, *Roman Empire*, 525 n.15.
94. Ammianus 15.5.11; Rolfe 1, 141.
95. *PLRE* 1, 598–9.
96. *PLRE* 2, 756–8. For translation, see below, p. 000.
97. On whom see the subtle analysis of David Hunt, 'The outsider inside: Ammianus on the rebellion of Silvanus', in *The Late Roman World*, eds Drijvers and Hunt, 1999, 51–63.
98. Ammianus 15.5.16; Rolfe 1, 143.
99. Ammianus 22.7.8.
100. Ammianus 26.4.5.
101. Ammianus 27.5.6; Rolfe 3, 33.
102. Ammianus 31.22.11; Rolfe 3, 381–7.
103. Ammianus 31.2.17–25.
104. Brent D. Shaw, ' "Eaters of flesh and drinkers of milk": the ancient Mediterranean ideology of the pastoral nomad', *Ancient Society* 13/14 (1982–3), 5–31.
105. See T.E.J. Wiedemann, 'Between men and beasts: barbarians in Ammianus Marcellinus', in *Past Perspectives*, eds I.S. Moxon *et al.*, Cambridge: Cambridge University Press, 1984, 198–201.
106. Sandwiched between the descriptions of the Huns and the Alans, at 31.2.15.
107. Although doubts have been cast on the idea that those relatively few deformed skulls we find in cemeteries always represent Huns: see Eric Crubézy, 'Merovingian skull deformations in the south-west of France', in *From the Baltic to the Black Sea: Studies in Medieval Archaeology*, eds David Austin and Leslie Alcock, London: Unwin Hyman, 1990, 189–208.
108. Ammianus 20.1.1; Rolfe 2, 2–3.
109. Herodian 3.14.7; Whittaker 1, 358–9.
110. See above, p. 00.
111. Ammianus 27.8.1; Rolfe 3, 50–1.
112. As I argue in James, *Britain*, 92.
113. Ammianus 28.3.9; Rolfe 3, 137.
114. See S. Ireland, *Roman Britain: A Sourcebook*, 2nd ed. London: Routledge, 1996, 151–2 and, in the context of a full translation, *Claudian's Panegyric*, Barr, 33.
115. As argued for northern Britain by B.R. Hartley and R. Leon Fitts, *The Brigantes*. Gloucester: Sutton, 1988, 109.

Chapter Three

1. See in particular Peter Heather, 'The Huns and the end of the Roman Empire in Western Europe', *English Historical Review* 110 (1995), 4–41.
2. Ammianus 31.4.11; Eunapius, fr. 42; Blockley, 60–1; Zosimus 4.20.6; Ridley, 79.
3. Noel Lenski, *Failure of Empire; Valens and the Roman State in the Fourth Century AD*. Berkeley, CA: University of California Press, 2002, 331.
4. T.S. Burns, *Barbarians within the Gates of Rome. A Study of Roman Military Policy and the Barbarians, ca 375–425 AD*. Bloomington, IN: Indiana University Press, 1994, 1.
5. Noel Lenski, '*Initium mali Romano imperio*: contemporary reactions to the battle of Adrianople', *Transactions of the American Philological Association* 127 (1997), 162–3.
6. Peter Heather, *The Fall of the Roman Empire: A New History*. London: Macmillan, 2005, 185.
7. Ammianus 31.16.8; Rolfe 3, 503–5.
8. Themistius, Oration 16; Heather and Moncur, 280; discussed in context in John Vanderspoel, *Themistius and the Imperial Court: Oratory, Civic Duty and Paideia from Constantius to Theodosius*. Ann Arbor: University of Michigan Press, 1995, 205–8.
9. Orosius 7.35.19; Raymond, 380.
10. Peter Heather, 'The Anti-Scythian tirade of Synesius' *De Regno*', *Phoenix* 42 (1988), 152–72; and, coming to the same conclusion, Alan Cameron, Jacqueline Long and Lee Sherry, *Barbarians and Politics at the Court of Arcadius*. Berkeley: University of California Press, 1993, 109–21.
11. Translation from Cameron, Long and Sherry, *Barbarians and Politics*, 103–6.
12. Cameron, Long and Sherry, *Barbarians and Politics*, 120.
13. Gibbon, *Decline and Fall*, Chapter 30; Bury 3, 269. See Michael Kulikowski, 'Barbarians in Gaul, usurpers in Britain', *Britannia* 31 (2000), 326.
14. Zosimus 6.3; Ridley, 128. On the British reaction see John F. Drinkwater, 'The usurpers Constantine III (407–411) and Jovinus (411–413)', *Britannia* 29 (1998), 269–98 and Kulikowski, 'Barbarians in Gaul', 325–45.
15. Zosimus 5.35.
16. Zosimus 5.40; Ridley, 121.
17. Zosimus 5.41; Ridley, 121.
18. Zosimus 5.50; Ridley, 125.
19. Zosimus 5.50; Ridley, 125.
20. Sozomen, *Ecclesiastical History* 9.9; Hartranft, 424.
21. Zosimus 5.51; Ridley, 125.
22. Procopius, *Wars* 3.2.25; Dewing 2, 16–17.
23. Jerome, Letter 127, to Principia; Wright, 462–3.
24. Augustine, *City of God* 1.16 and 1.12; Bettenson, 21, 26.
25. Orosius 7.39; Raymond, 387.
26. Sozomen 9.10.

27. Orosius 7.39; Raymond, 388. On this, see Hagith Sivan, '*Alaricus Rex*: Legitimising a Gothic king', in *The Construction of Communities*, eds Corradini, Diesenberger and Reimitz, 2003, 109–21.
28. Orosius 7.39; Raymond, 390. See Pierre Courcelle, *Histoire littéraire des grandes invasions germaniques*, 3rd ed. Paris: Études Augustiniennes, 1964, 54–5.
29. Procopius, *Wars* 3.2.24; Dewing 2, 16–17.
30. *Liber Pontificalis*, 46; Davis, 37.
31. Quoted Courcelle, *Histoire littéraire*. 58; *Ad Ursacium*, PG 12, 583–6.
32. Quoted Courcelle, *Histoire littéraire*. 59; Preface to Book III of *In Ezechiel*; PL 25, 75.
33. Augustine, *The City of God* 1.32.31.
34. Procopius, *Wars* 3.2.11–13; Dewing 2, 12–13.
35. Rutilius Namatianus, *De Reditu Suo/A Voyage Home to Gaul*, 37–40; Duff and Duff, 767.
36. *Gallic Chronicle of 452*; Murray, 80.
37. Rutilius, *De Reditu Suo/A Voyage Home to Gaul*, 210–15; Duff and Duff, 783.
38. Ammianus 30.6.3–6.
39. For the latest account of these invasions, see Walter Goffart, *Barbarian Tides: The Migration Age and the later Roman Empire*. Philadelphia: University of Pennsylvania Press, 2006, 73–118.
40. *Commonitorium* 2.184: see Michael Roberts, 'Barbarians in Gaul: the response of the poets', in *Fifth-Century Gaul*, eds Drinkwater and Elton, 1992, 97–106.
41. Hydatius AD 410; Burgess, 82–3.
42. Hydatius AD 411; Burgess, 82–3.
43. A story told in a recently discovered letter from Consentius to Augustine of Hippo: for commentary, see Javier Arce, 'The enigmatic fifth century in Hispania: some historical problems', in *Regna and Gentes*, eds Goetz, Jarnut and Pohl, 2003, 135–59.
44. Zosimus 6.5; Ridley, 128–9.
45. *Gallic Chronicle of 452*; Murray, 80, 84.
46. Olympiodorus, fragment 24; Blockley, 187–9.
47. Orosius 7.43.4; Raymond, 396. See J.F. Matthews, *Western Aristocracies and Imperial Court, AD 364–425*. Oxford: Oxford University Press, 1975, 317.
48. For some recent commentary, see John F. Matthews, 'Roman laws and barbarian identity in the late Roman west', in *Ethnicity and Culture*, eds Mitchell and Greatrex, 2000, 31–3. It was the starting point for J.M. Wallace-Hadrill, 'Gothia and Romania', *Bulletin of the John Rylands Library* (1961), 213–37.
49. Hydatius AD 417; Burgess, 84–5.
50. Paulinus, *Eucharisticus* 306–7; White 2, 328–9.
51. Following the arguments of Andreas Schwarcz, 'The Visigothic settlement in Aquitania: chronology and archaeology', in *Society and Culture*, eds Mathisen and Shanzer, 2001, 15–25.

52. For the history of this kingdom, see Ralph W. Mathisen and Hagith Sivan, 'Forging a new identity: the kingdom of Toulouse and the frontiers of Visigothic Aquitania (418–507)', in *The Visigoths*, ed. Ferreiro, 1999, 1–62.

53. Walter Goffart, *Barbarians and Romans, A.D. 418–584: The Techniques of Accommodation*. Princeton, NJ: Princeton University Press, 1980, 35.

54. Goffart, *Barbarian Tides*, 192.

55. Hydatius AD 428; Burgess, 89.

56. For discussion of the numbers, see below p. 184.

57. See *PLRE* 2, 21–9.

58. Strictly speaking, Procopius called both Aetius and his rival Bonifatius by this epithet: *Wars* 3.3.15; Dewing 2, 26–7.

59. Sidonius, *Poem* 7.230–1; Anderson 1, 138–9.

60. Gildas 20; Winterbottom, 23–4.

61. Hydatius AD 431; Burgess, 91.

62. Merobaudes, Panegyric 2; Clover, 14–16.

63. J.R. Moss, 'The effects of the politics of Aetius on the history of Western Europe', *Historia* 22 (1973), 716.

64. Malalas 14.10; Jeffreys, Jeffreys and Scott 195–6.

65. On all this, see Sidonius, Poem 7; and *PLRE* 2, 1070–1.

66. Quodvultdeus, *In Barbarian Times*, 2.5; quoted in translation in Heather, *Fall*, 289.

67. Matthias Hardt, 'The nomad's greed for gold: from the fall of the Burgundians to the Avar treasure', in *The Construction of Communities*, eds Corradini, Diesenberger and Reimitz, 2003, 97.

68. For what little we do know about this episode, see Andrew Gillett, *Envoys and Political Communication in the Late Antique West, 411–533*. Cambridge: Cambridge University Press, 2003, 114–15.

69. Priscus, fragment 22.3; Blockley, 315.

70. Malalas, *Chronicle*, 14.10; Jeffreys, Jeffreys and Scott 195–6. See now Michael A. Babcock, *The Stories of Attila the Hun's Death: Narrative, Myth, and Meaning*. Lewiston, NY, Queenston, Ontario, Lampeter: Edwin Mellen, 2001.

71. Priscus, fragment 11; Blockley, 254–7.

72. Priscus, fragment 11; Blockley, 272–73.

73. Priscus, fragment 11; Blockley, 273–5.

74. Bede, *Ecclesiastical History* 1.21; Colgrave and Mynors, 66–7.

75. See *PLRE* 2, 168.

76. See Brian Croke, 'Dynasty and ethnicity: Emperor Leo I and the eclipse of Aspar', *Chiron* 34 (2005), 147–203.

77. It was Tarasicodissa, or Codisseus, or Aricmeseus, or perhaps Trascalissaeus: see *PLRE* 2, 1200.

78. For a discussion of this and of Aspar, see Philip Rousseau, 'Inheriting the fifth century: who bequeathed what?' in *The Sixth Century*, eds. Allen and Jeffreys, 1996, 1–19.

79. For a map, see *RGA* 11, 121; and see István Bóna, *The Dawn of the Dark Ages: The Gepids and the Lombards in the Carpathian Basin*. Budapest: Corvina, 1976.

80. For example, Edward James, *The Origins of France: From Clovis to the Capetians, 500–100*. London and Basingstoke: Macmillan, 1982, 16–18.

81. Andrew Gillett, 'The accession of Euric', *Francia* 26/1 (1999), 33.

82. Sidonius, *Letters* 1.7; Anderson 1, 366–79. See H.C. Teitler, 'Un-Roman activities in late antique Gaul: the cases of Arvandus and Seronatus', in *Fifth-Century Gaul*, eds Drinkwater and Elton, 1992, 309–17.

83. Sidonius, *Letters* 2.2; Anderson 1, 412–17.

84. Sidonius, *Letters* 5.13; Anderson 2, 212–15.

85. Sidonius, *Letters* 7.7; Anderson 2, 324–31.

86. C.E. Stevens, *Sidonius Apollinaris and His Age*. Oxford: Clarendon Press, 1933, 160.

87. See Jill Harries, 'Sidonius Apollinaris, Rome and the barbarians: a climate of treason?' in *Fifth-Century Gaul*, eds Drinkwater and Elton, 1992, 298–308.

88. As argued by Patrick Wormald, 'The decline of the Western Empire and the survival of its aristocracy', *Journal of Roman Studies* 66 (1976), 224.

89. E.A. Thompson, *Romans and Barbarians: The Decline of the Western Empire*. Madison, WI: University of Wisconsin Press, 1982, 133: 'unsavory', because he only owned one cloak, which he never ever removed, night or day (Eugippius, *Life of Severinus*, 39.2). See Andreas Schwarcz, 'Severinus of Noricum between fact and fiction', in *Eugippius und Severin*, eds Pohl and Diesenberger, 2001, 25–31.

90. Eugippius, *Life of Severinus* 1; Bieler, 57.

91. Eugippius, *Life* 44.5; Bieler, 98.

92. Géza Alföldy, *Noricum*. London and Boston Routledge and Kegan Paul, 1974, 226.

93. Eugippius, *Life* 24.3; Bieler, 81.

94. Eugippius, *Life* 22.2; Bieler, 79.

95. For the textual references for all these activities, see Bieler's introduction, 19–26.

96. Walter Goffart, 'Does the *Vita Severini* have an underside?' in *Eugippius und Severin*, eds Pohl and Diesenberger, 2001, 38.

97. These questions are asked by Neil Christie, 'Towns, land and power: German-Roman survivals and interactions in fifth- and sixth-century Pannonia', in *Towns and their Territories*, eds Brogiolo, Gauthier and Christie, 2000, 275–97.

Chapter Four

1. See Brian Croke, 'AD 476: the manufacture of a turning point', *Chiron* 13 (1983), 81–119.

2. See Brian Croke, *Count Marcellinus and his Chronicle*. Oxford: Oxford University Press, 2001.

3. Marcellinus Comes, *Chronicle*, at AD 476; Croke, 27.

4. Gregory, *History* 2.34; Thorpe, 149.

5. Sidonius, *Letters* 5.5.3; Anderson 2, 82–3.

6. Sidonius, *Letters* 8.3.3; Anderson 2, 410–11.
7. Sidonius, *Letters* 3.9; Anderson 2, 34–7.
8. See 'The Arthurian gap' in James, *Britain*, 99–101.
9. On the date, see Guy Halsall, 'Childeric's grave, Clovis's succession, and the origins of the Merovingian kingdom', in *Society and Culture*, eds Mathisen and Shanzer, 2001, 116–33.
10. See, e.g., Michel Kazanski and Patrick Périn, 'Le mobilier funéraire de la tombe de Childéric Ier; état de la question et perspectives', *Revue archéologique de Picardie* (1988), 13–38 and Raymond Brulet, 'La sépulture du roi Childéric à Tournai et le site funéraire', in *La Noblesse romaine*, eds Vallet and Kazanski, 1995, 309–26.
11. Gregory, *History* 2.12; Thorpe, 128.
12. Gregory, *History* 2.38; Thorpe 154. For the many problems in this passage, see Michael McCormick, 'Clovis at Tours, Byzantine public ritual and the origins of medieval ruler symbolism', in *Das Reich und die Barbaren*, eds Chrysos and Schwarcz, 1989, 155–80.
13. Procopius, History 5.12.13–19; Dewing 3, 120–3.
14. Ian N. Wood, 'Kings, kingdoms and consent', in *Early Medieval Kingship*, eds Sawyer and Wood, 1977, 6–29.
15. See above all John Moorhead, *Theodoric in Italy*. Oxford: Clarendon, 1992 and Peter Heather, *The Goths*. Oxford: Blackwell, 1996.
16. Anonymus Valesianus 12.60; Rolfe, 545.
17. Heather, *Goths*, 222.
18. Translation from Heather, *Goths*, 221.
19. Heather, *Goths*, 225.
20. *CIL* 10.6850–2; Moorhead, *Theodoric in Italy*, 47–8.
21. Translated by Heather, *Goths*, 229.
22. Cassiodorus, *Variae* 1.46; Barnish, 24. See the comments of Danuta Shanzer, 'Two clocks and a wedding: Theodoric's diplomatic relations with the Burgundians', *Romanobarbarica* 14 (1998), 225–58.
23. Regarded as two separate individuals by *PLRE* 2, 767–8. I am following the reconstruction of Brian Croke, 'Mundo the Gepid: from freebooter to Roman general', *Chiron* 12 (1982), 125–35.
24. Procopius, History 3.8.12; Dewing 2, 76–7.
25. Cassiodorus, *Variae* 3.1–4; Barnish, 45–9.
26. Procopius, History 5.12.47; Dewing 3, 130–1.
27. E.A. Thompson, *The Goths in Spain*. Oxford: Clarendon Press, 1969, 11.
28. See Heather, *Goths*, 245 and Moorhead, *Theodoric in Italy*, 94–7.
29. See Procopius 5.13.4–8; Dewing 3, 134–5 and Thompson, *Goths in Spain*, 10–11.
30. See John Moorhead, 'Italian loyalties during Justinian's Gothic war', *Byzantion* 53 (1983), 575–96.
31. Procopius 5.10.24–9 and 6.21.39; Dewing 3, 98–101 and 4, 54–5.
32. Procopius 2.22.12; Dewing 1, 468–9.
33. For a discussion and references see Jo N. Hays in the recent excellent book, Lester K. Little, ed., *Plague and the End of Antiquity: The Pandemic of 541–750*, Cambridge: Cambridge University Press, 2007.

34. For a brief discussion of the debate, see J.H.W.G. Liebeschuetz, *The Decline and Fall of the Roman City*. Oxford: Oxford University Press, 2001, 53–4.

35. Joel D. Gunn, ed., *The Years without Summer: Tracing AD 536 and its Aftermath*, Oxford: BAR, 2000.

36. Cassiodorus *Variae* 12.25, Barnish, 179–81; Procopius, 4.14.5–6, Dewing 2, 328–9. Bailey Young's contribution to Gunn, ed., *Years without Summer*, 35–42 is very useful, although his reference to Procopius is wrong.

37. Procopius 4.14.6; Dewing 2, 328–9.

38. On all this, see 'Appendix; The Byzantine Province' in Thompson, *Goths in Spain*, 320–34.

39. See Walter Goffart, 'Byzantine policy in the West under Tiberius II and Maurice: the pretenders Hermenegild and Gundovald (579–585)', *Traditio* 13 (1963), 73–118.

40. Procopius, *Wars* 8.33.2; Dewing 5, 388–9.

41. Gregory, *History* 3.31.

42. Gregory, *History* 3.32; Thorpe 189.

43. Procopius 6.25.4; Dewing 4, 84–5. Isidore, *Etymologies* 18.6.6; Barney *et al.*, 362. See Walter Pohl, 'Telling the difference: signs of ethnic identity', in *Strategies of Distinction*, ed. Pohl, 1998, 31–7.

44. Agathias 2.5.5–8; Frendo, 37.

45. Marcellinus, *Chronicle* at 539; Croke, 48.

46. Procopius 6.25.9–10; Dewing 4, 86–7.

47. See Procopius 7.33; 8.24.

48. Procopius 8.33.5; Dewing 5, 390–1.

49. Gregory, *History* 3.32; Agathias 2.10.1; Frendo, 42.

50. Neil Christie, *The Lombards: The Ancient Longobards*. Oxford: Blackwell, 1995, 73.

51. Paul the Deacon, *History of the Lombards*, 2.7; Foulke, 62–5, where there is a discussion of the date. Some people prefer 569.

52. Gregory, *History* 4.41–4.

53. On which see, though with caution, B.S. Bachrach, *The Anatomy of a Little War: A Diplomatic and Military History of the Gundovald Affair (568–586)*. Boulder, CO: Westview Press, 1994.

54. Gregory, *History* 4.44; Thorpe, 241.

55. I summarize here from Florin Curta, *The Making of the Slavs: History and Archaeology of the Lower Danube Region, c.500–700*. Cambridge: Cambridge University Press, 2001, 74.

56. See P.M. Barford, *The Early Slavs: Culture and Society in Early Medieval Eastern Europe*. London: British Museum, 2001, 40–1.

57. Florin Curta, 'From Kossinna to Bromley: ethnogenesis in Slavic archaeology', in *On Barbarian Identity*, ed. Gillett, 2002, 218.

58. Procopius 7.40.5–6; Dewing 5, 38–9.

59. Although some suggest that the Antes were closely related to Iranian peoples such as the Sarmatians: see John V.A. Fine, *The Early Medieval Balkans: A Critical Survey from the Sixth to the Late Twelfth Century*. Ann Arbor: University of Michigan Press, 1983, 26.

60. Procopius 7.14.22–30; Dewing 4, 268–73.

61. Florin Curta, 'Frontier ethnogenesis in late antiquity: the Danube, the Tervingi, and the Slavs', in *Borders, Barriers*, ed. Curta, 2005, 184.

62. Maurice, *Strategikon* 11.4; Dennis, 123, 120.

63. Procopius 7.14.4–6; Dewing 4, 264–5.

64. Procopius, *Secret History* 11.8–11; Dewing 6, 132–3

65. Procopius, *Wars* 7.13.26; 7.14.1–36.

66. Procopius 7.14.11; Dewing 4, 264–5.

67. Procopius 7.38.19–23; Dewing 5, 24–7.

68. Procopius 7.40.33; Dewing 5, 48–9.

69. Procopius 7.40.31–45.

70. Curta, 'Frontier ethnogenesis', 186.

71. Menander, fragment 12; Blockley, 128–33.

72. Florin Curta, *Southeastern Europe in the Middle Ages, 500–1250*. Cambridge: Cambridge University Press, 2006, 63.

73. See Hardt, 'Nomad's greed for gold', 99.

74. See Hardt, 'Nomad's greed for gold', 101.

75. *Russian Primary Chronicle*, 12; Cross and Sherbowitz-Wetzor, 56.

76. *Ecclesiastical History* 6.24 and 2.30; see Rachael Pallas-Brown, 'East Roman perceptions of the Avars in the mid- and late-sixth century', in *Ethnicity and Culture*, eds Mitchell and Greatrex, 2000, 315.

77. Pallas-Brown, 'Perceptions of the Avars', 316–17.

78. Corippus, *In Praise of Justin II*, 3.240–62; Cameron, 107.

79. Maurice, *Strategikon* 11.2; Dennis, 116.

80. Maurice, *Strategikon* 8.2.4; Dennis, 83. See above, p. 00.

81. Florin Curta, 'Before Cyril and Methodius: Christianity and barbarians beyond the sixth- and seventh-century Danube frontier', in *East Central and Eastern Europe*, ed. Curta, 2005, 189.

82. Quoted in Barford, *Early Slavs*, 63.

83. Curta, *Making of the Slavs*, 112, 118.

84. *Chronicle of 754*, 7; Wolf, 113.

85. P. Lemerle, *Les plus anciens recueils des miracles de Saint Démétrius et la pénétration des Slaves dans les Balkans. 2. Le commentaire*. Paris: Centre Nationale de la Recherche Scientifique, 1981.

86. Fine, *Early Medieval Balkans*, 36.

Chapter Five

1. And for the eighteenth-century background to the political use of 'British', see Linda Colley, *Britons: Forging the Nation, 1707–1837*. New Haven, CT and London: Yale University Press, 1992.

2. Quoted in Poliakov, *Aryan Myth*, 1974, 269.

3. Quoted in Poliakov, *Aryan Myth*, 270.

4. Quoted in Ivan Hannaford, *Race: The History of an Idea in the West*. Washington, DC and Baltimore, MD: Woodrow Wilson Center Press and Johns Hopkins University Press, 1996, 358.

5. Jordanes, 25; Mierow, 57. 'A womb of nations' (or even 'a mother of nations') is the usual somewhat mealy-mouthed translation of *vagina gentium*.

6. For Scotland, see Hugh Trevor-Roper in Eric Hobsbawm and Terence Ranger, eds, *The Invention of Tradition*, Cambridge: Cambridge University Press, 1983, 15–42; and see Barbro Klein and Mats Widbom, eds, *Swedish Folk Art: All Tradition is Change*, New York: Abrams, 1994, 26–7 and 81.

7. See Hubert Fehr, '*Volkstum* as paradigm: Germanic people and Gallo-Romans in early medieval archaeology since the 1930s', in *On Barbarian Identity*, ed. Gillett, 2002, 187–98 and Bonnie Effros, 'Dressing conservatively: women's brooches as markers of ethnic identity?' in *Gender in the Early Medieval World*, eds Leslie Brubaker and Julia M.H. Smith, Cambridge: Cambridge University Press, 2004, 165–84.

8. Hines, 'Culture groups', 227.

9. Jordanes, 50; for the translation and commentary on this passage, see Pohl, 'Telling the difference', 27–8.

10. Claudian, *Panegyric on the Third Consulship of Honorius*, 27; quoted by Pohl, as in previous note.

11. Eugen Ewig, 'Volkstum und Volksbewußtsein im Frankenreich des 7. Jahrhunderts', *Settimane di Studio* . . . 5 (1958), 587–648.

12. Reinhard Wenskus, *Stammesbildung und Verfassung: Das Werden der frühmittelalterlichen Gentes.* Cologne: Graz, 1961. The English translation of the title is from Thomas F.X. Noble, ed., *From Roman Provinces to Medieval Kingdoms*, London and New York: Routledge, 2006, 10.

13. Noble, ed., *From Roman Provinces*, 10.

14. Suspicions that Wenskus's 600-plus pages of dense academic German has been little read outside the German-speaking world have been voiced by a number of my colleagues.

15. For a useful analysis, putting his work in the general context of German historical scholarship, see Alexander Callander Murray, 'Reinhard Wenskus on 'Ethnogenesis', ethnicity and the origin of the Franks', in *On Barbarian Identity*, ed. Gillett, 2002, 39–68; but see the criticisms of Walter Pohl, 'Ethnicity, theory, and tradition: a response', in *On Barbarian Identity*, ed. Gillett, 2002, 222–5.

16. Herwig Wolfram, '*Origo et religio*: ethnic traditions and literature in early medieval texts', *Early Medieval Europe* 3 (1994), 28.

17. Ian N. Wood, 'The barbarian invasions and the first settlements', in *The Cambridge Ancient History XIII*, eds Cameron and Garnsey, Cambridge: Cambridge University Press, 1998, 21.

18. Wood, 'Barbarian invasions', 28.

19. Charles E. Bowlus, 'Ethnogenesis: the tyranny of a concept', in *On Barbarian Identity*, ed. Gillett, 2002, 242.

20. Jordanes, *Gothic History* 315; Mierow, 142.

21. Jordanes, *Gothic History* 316; Mierow, 142.

22. Jordanes, *Gothic History* 1; Mierow, 51.

23. Jordanes, *Gothic History* 2–3; Mierow, 51. Some argue that the word *relegere* implies that he was merely rereading a book which he had read earlier at greater leisure; others would translate *relegere* as 'read', not 'reread'. See Walter Goffart, *The Narrators of Barbarian History (A.D. 550–800):*

Jordanes, Gregory of Tours, Bede, and Paul the Deacon. Princeton, NJ: Princeton University Press, 1988, 60–1.

24. A point made by Amory, *People and Identity,* 306, in relation to the theories of Johann Weissensteiner.

25. Walter Goffart, 'Does the distant past impinge on the Invasion Age Germans?' in *On Barbarian Identity,* ed. Gillett, 2002, 34, citing Herwig Wolfram, *History of the Goths.* Berkeley: University of California Press, 1988, 324.

26. As pointed out by Goffart, 'Does the distant past . . .?', 32.

27. Cassiodorus, *Variae* 9.4–6; Barnish, 128.

28. Goffart, *Narrators,* 62.

29. Goffart, *Narrators,* 68.

30. Goffart, *Narrators,* 67.

31. Goffart, 'Does the distant past . . . ?', 21.

32. 'Why Goffart is so hostile to historical tradition is not entirely clear' is the plaintive cry in a book which discusses the considerable evidence for oral tradition among the barbarians, Hermann Moisl, *Lordship and Tradition in Barbarian Europe.* Lewiston: Edwin Mellon, 1999, 36.

33. Ammianus 31.7.11; Rolfe 3, 430–3.

34. Goffart, 'Does the distant past . . . ?', 24.

35. Arne Søby Christensen, *Cassiodorus, Jordanes and the History of the Goths: Studies in a Migration Myth.* Copenhagen: Museum Tusculanum/University of Copenhagen, 2002, 223–5.

36. Peter Heather, *Goths and Romans, 332–489.* Oxford: Clarendon Press, 1991, 24–6.

37. Patrick Geary, 'Ethnic identity as a situational construct in the early Middle Ages', *Mitteilungen der anthropologischen Gesellschaft in Wien* 113 (1985), 18.

38. Geary, 'Ethnic identity', 26.

39. V. Gordon Childe, 'Changing methods and aims in prehistory. Presidential address for 1935', *Proceedings of the Prehistoric Society* 1 (1935), 1–15, quoted in Siân Jones, *The Archaeology of Ethnicity: Constructing Identities in the Past and Present.* London and New York: Routledge, 1997, 17.

40. Jones, *Archaeology of Ethnicity,* 28.

41. Cited in Ulrich Veit, 'Gustaf Kossinna and his concept of a national archaeology', in *Archaeology, Ideology and Society,* ed. Härke, 2002, 41.

42. Heinrich Härke, 'All quiet on the western front? Paradigms, methods and approaches in West German archaeology', in *Archaeological Theory in Europe: The Last Three Decades,* ed. Ian Hodder, London: Routledge, 1991, 188–9.

43. On whom see Henning Haßmann, 'Archaeology in the "Third Reich"', in *Archaeology, Ideology and Society,* ed. Härke, 2002, 83–8.

44. See Fig. 1 of E.T. Leeds, 'Visigoth or Vandal?' *Archaeologia* 94 (1951), 197.

45. See, e.g., Sebastian Brather, *Ethnische Interpretationen in der frühgeschichtlichen Archäologie: Geschichte, Grundlagen und Alternativen.* Berlin: Walter De Gruyter, 2004, 266.

46. Gisela Ripoll López, 'The arrival of the Visigoths in Hispania: population problems and the process of acculturation', in *Strategies of Distinction*, eds Pohl and Reimitz, 1998, 178.

47. Schwarcz, 'Visigothic settlement'.

48. Ernst Gamillscheg, *Romania Germanica: Sprach- und Siedlungsgeschichte der Germanen auf dem Boden des alten Römerreiches*, 2nd ed., vol. 1. Berlin: De Gruyter, 1970, 83.

49. Gregory, *History*, 10.9. To put this into context with Gregory's ideas about difference and dress, see Bonnie Effros, 'Appearance and ideology: creating distinctions between clerics and laypersons in early medieval Gaul', in *Encountering Medieval Textiles and Dress; Objects, Texts, Images*, eds Désirée Koslin and Janet E. Snyder, New York: Palgrave Macmillan, 2002, 7–24.

50. E.g., Patrick Périn, *La Datation des tombes mérovingiennes: Historique – Méthodes – Applications*. Geneva: Droz, 1980 or Lars Jørgensen, ed., *Chronological Studies of Anglo-Saxon England, Lombard Italy and Vendel Period Sweden*, Copenhagen: University of Copenhagen, 1992.

51. See Edward James, 'The militarization of Roman society, AD 400–700', in *Military Aspects of Scandinavian Society in a European Perspective, AD 1–1300*, eds A.M. Jørgensen and B.L. Clausen, Copenhagen: The National Museum, 1997, 19–24.

52. Guy Halsall, *Early Medieval Cemeteries: An Introduction to Burial Archaeology in the Post-Roman West*. Skelmorlie: Cruithne Press, 1995, 67.

53. Edward James, 'Cemeteries and the problem of Frankish settlement in Gaul', in *Names, Words and Graves: Early Medieval Settlement*, ed. P.H. Sawyer, Leeds: School of History, University of Leeds, 1979, 85. For a study of the development of ideas about the archaeology of ethnicity in the Frankish kingdoms, see Fehr, '*Volkstum* as paradigm'.

54. Sebastian Brather, 'Ethnic images as constructions of archaeology: the case of the *Alamanni*', in *On Barbarian Identity*, ed. Gillett, 2002, 149–75.

55. Brather, 'Ethnic images', 159.

56. Brather, 'Ethnic images', 172.

57. Brather, *Ethnische Interpretationen*; for the reaction, see Florin Curta, 'Some remarks on ethnicity in early medieval archaeology', *Early Medieval Europe* 15 (2007), 159–85.

58. Heinrich Härke, '"Warrior graves"? The background of the Anglo-Saxon burial rite', *Past and Present* 126 (1990), 33.

59. Härke, '"Warrior graves"?', 40.

60. On this and what follows, see Christensen, *Cassiodorus, Jordanes*, 216–29.

61. Amory, *People and Identity*, 452–4.

62. Ed. K.A. Eckhardt, *Die Gesetze des Karolingerreiches, 714–911. III. Sachsen, Thüringer, Chamaven un Friesen* (Germanenrechte 2) (Weimar: Böhlau, 1934).

63. *Vita Maximini Treverensis*, 10: *Acta Sanctorum* May VII, 23.

64. *MGH, SSRM*, 7, 773. There is a somewhat more extended discussion in James, *Origins of France*, 31–2; see also James, 'Gregory of Tours and the Franks', in *After Rome's Fall*, ed. Murray, 1998, 51–66.

65. See Matthias Hardt, 'The Bavarians', in *Regna and Gentes*, eds Goetz, Jarnut and Pohl, 2003, 429–61.
66. Eddius Stephanus, *Life of Wilfrid* 30; Colgrave, 60–1 (although Colgrave unhelpfully translates *Saxonia* as 'England').
67. Patrick Wormald, 'Bede, the *Bretwaldas* and the origins of the *Gens Anglorum*', in *Ideal and Reality in Frankish and Anglo-Saxon Society*, ed. Wormald *et al.*, Oxford: Blackwell, 1983, 99–129.
68. Bede, *Ecclesiastical History* 2.1; Colgrave and Mynors, 132–5.
69. Bede, *Ecclesiastical History* 5.9. See Susan Reynolds, 'What do we mean by "Anglo-Saxon" and "Anglo-Saxons"?' *Journal of British Studies* 24 (1985), 395–414; and several articles by Patrick Wormald, including 'Bede, the *Bretwaldas*'.
70. Here I am following Hines, 'Culture groups', 230–1.
71. Ian N. Wood, 'Ethnicity and the ethnogenesis of the Burgundians', in *Typen der Ethnogenese*, eds Wolfram and Pohl, 1990, 53.
72. Patrick Amory, 'The meaning and purpose of ethnic terminology in the Burgundian laws', *Early Medieval Europe* 2 (1993), 9.
73. Patrick Amory, 'Names, ethnic identity, and community in fifth- and sixth-century Burgundy', *Viator* 25 (1994), 1.
74. *Constitutiones extravagentes* 21.11, quoted by Amory, 'Names', 27.
75. Gregory, *History* 6.11.
76. As noted in Walter Pohl and Helmut Reimitz, eds, *Strategies of Distinction*, 1998, 10.
77. Amory, 'Names', 30.
78. Gregory, *History* 7.3, 8.18 and 10.22. See James, 'Gregory of Tours and the Franks'.
79. Here I am following Geoffrey Greatrex, 'Roman identity in the sixth century', in *Ethnicity and Culture*, eds Mitchell and Greatrex, 2000, 267–92.
80. Procopius, *Wars* 7.12.12; Dewing 4, 212–13.
81. Procopius, *Wars* 2.6.23; Dewing 1, 312–13.
82. Procopius, *Wars* 3.19.5.
83. Greatrex, 'Roman identity', 274.
84. Greatrex, 'Roman identity', 278; *CIL* 13.2402.

Chapter Six

1. Brather, 'Acculturation and ethnogenesis', 145.
2. Hines, 'Culture groups', 225.
3. Brather, 'Acculturation and ethnogenesis', 147.
4. On the cremation graves, see Malcolm Todd, *The Early Germans*, 2nd ed. Oxford: Blackwell, 2004, 80–1.
5. Alfried Wieczorek and Patrick Périn, eds, *Das Gold der Barbarenfürsten: Schätze aus Prunkgräbern des 5. Jahrhunderts n. Chr. zwischen Kaukasus und Gallien*, Stuttgart: Theiss, 2001.
6. Wieczorek and Périn, eds, *Barbarenfürsten*, 156–60.
7. See K. Horedt and D. Protase, 'Das zweite Fürstengrab von Apahida', *Germania* 50 (1972), 174–220 and Wieczorek and Périn, eds, *Barbarenfürsten*, 147–55.

8. Agathias 3.15.2; Frendo, 84–5.

9. Michael Schmauder, 'Imperial representation or barbaric imitation? The imperial brooches (Kaiserfibeln)', in *Strategies of Distinction*, eds Pohl and Reimitz, 1998, 281–96.

10. But see Guy Halsall, 'The origins of the *Reihengräberzivilisation*: forty years on', in *Fifth-Century Gaul*, eds Drinkwater and Elton, 1992, 197–207.

11. See P.O. Nielsen, K. Randsborg and H. Thrane, *The Archaeology of Gudme and Lundeborg. Papers presented at a Conference at Svendborg, October 1991*. Copenhagen: Akademisk Forlag, 1994 and the convenient discussion in Lotte Hedeager, '*Asgard* reconstructed: Gudme, a "central place" in the north', in *Topographies of Power*, eds De Jong and Theuws, 2001, 467–507.

12. See Karl Hauck, 'Gudme in der Sicht der Brakteatenforschung', *Frühmittelalterliche Studien* 21 (1987), 147–81 and Karl Hauck, 'Gudme als Kultort und seine Rolle beim Austausch von Bildformulären der Goldbrakteaten', in *The Archaeology of Gudme*, eds Nielsen, Randsborg and Thrane, 1994, 78–88.

13. Hedeager, '*Asgard* reconstructed', 480.

14. Hedeager, '*Asgard* reconstructed', 502.

15. Birgitta Hårdh, 'Uppåkra – a centre in south Sweden in the first millennium AD', *Antiquity* 74 (2000), 640–8; Birgitta Hårdh and Lars Larsson, eds, *Central Places in the Migration and Merovingian Periods: Papers from the 52nd Sachsensymposium, Lund, August 2001 (Uppåkrastudier 6)*. Stockholm: Almqvist & Wiksell International, 2002, and Lars Larsson and Birgitte Hårdh, *Centrality – Regionality: The Social Structure of Sweden During the Iron Age (Uppåkrastudier 7)*. Stockholm: Almqvist & Wiksell International, 2003.

16. For a map of the find-spots, see *RGA* 33, 38.

17. Quoted in Edel Bhreathnach and Conor Newman, *Tara*. Dublin: Stationery Office, 1995, 7. Grey-bearded ollamhs were and are the learned men: my current university title of Professor of Medieval History translates as Ollamh le Stair na Meánaoise (although my beard is white).

18. See Charles Doherty, 'Kingship in early Ireland', in *The Kingship and Landscape of Tara*, ed. Edel Bhreathnach. Dublin: Four Courts Press/The Discovery Programme, 2005, 3–31.

19. Wonderfully described in Mairéad Carew, *Tara and the Ark of the Covenant: A Search for the Ark of the Covenant by British Israelites on the Hill of Tara (1899–1902)*. Dublin: The Discovery Programme/Royal Irish Academy, 2003.

20. See Howard Williams, 'Ancient landscapes and the dead: the reuse of prehistoric and Roman monuments as early Anglo-Saxon burial sites', *Medieval Archaeology* 41 (1997), 1–31.

21. Howard Williams, 'Cemeteries as central places – place and identity in migration period eastern England', in *Central Places*, eds Hårdh and Larsson, 2002, 359.

22. Helena Hamerow, *Early Medieval Settlements: The Archaeology of Rural Communities in Northwest Europe, 400–900*. Oxford: Oxford University Press, 2002, 5.

23. *RGA* 34, 351.

24. For Ezinge and Feddersen Wierde, see *RGA* 8, 60–76 and 249–66.

25. Quoted in Hamerow, *Settlements*, 7.

26. Pliny, *Natural History*, 19.2.9; trans. Rackham 5, 424–5. For various reconstructions of SFBs in south-west Germany, see Folke Damminger, 'Dwellings, settlements and settlement patterns in Merovingian south-west Germany and adjacent areas', in *Franks and Alamanni*, ed. Wood, 1998.

27. Tacitus, *Germania* 16.3; Rives, 84.

28. Dominic Powlesland, *25 Years of Archaeological Research on the Sands and Gravels of Heslerton*. Yedingham, North Yorks: Landscape Research Centre, 2003, 37–8.

29. Curta, *Making of the Slavs*. 277–85 and Sebastian Brather, *Archäologie der westlichen Slawen. Siedlung, Wirtschaft und Gesellschaft im früh- und hochmittelalterlichen Ostmitteleuropa*. Berlin: Walter De Gruyter, 2001, 98–106.

30. Paul van Ossel, *Établissments ruraux de l'Antiquité tardive dans le nord de la Gaule*. Paris: CNRS, 1992, 183. He raises the doubts in 'L'insécurité et militarisation en Gaul du nord au Bas-empire. L'exemple des campagnes', *Revue du Nord 77* (1995), 28.

31. Powlesland, *25 Years*, 33–4.

32. Hamerow, *Settlements*, 54.

33. See the map in Hamerow, *Settlements*, 55.

34. Harold Mytum, *The Origins of Early Christian Ireland*. London: Routledge, 1992, 131.

35. Nancy Edwards, *The Archaeology of Early Medieval Ireland*. London: Batsford, 1990, 27.

36. E.g., Figs 54–66, E.R. Norman and J.K.S. St Joseph, *The Early Development of Irish Society: The Evidence of Aerial Photography*. Cambridge: Cambridge University Press, 1969.

37. I am following Ulf Näsman, 'Strategies and tactics in Migration Period defence: on the art of defence on the basis of the settlement forts of Öland', in *Military Aspects of Scandinavian Society*, eds Jørgensen and Clausen, 1997, 146–56.

38. Näsman, 'Strategies and Tactics', 149.

39. Näsman, 'Strategies and Tactics', 150 and Ulf Näsman, 'The gates of Eketorp II: to the question of Roman prototypes of the Öland ringforts', in *The Birth of Europe: Archaeology and Social Development in the First Millennium AD*, ed. Klaus Randsborg. Rome: L'Erma di Bretscheider, 1989, 129–39.

40. Kurt Weber in Kaj Borg, Ulf Näsman and Erik Wegraeus, *Eketorp: Fortification and Settlement on Öland/Sweden. The Monument*. Stockholm: Almqvist and Wiksell, 1976, 98.

41. Näsman, 'Strategies and Tactics', 151.

42. In what follows I am relying on Brather, 'Acculturation and ethnogenesis', 155–9.

43. See *RGA* 34, 398–417.

44. Heiko Steuer, 'Handwerk auf spätantiken Höhensiedlungen des 4./5. Jahrhunderts in Südwestdeutschland', in *The Archaeology of Gudme* eds Nielsen, Randsborg and Thrane, 1994, 128–44.

45. Pliny, *Natural History*, 10.54; for this, amber and soap, see Dennis H. Green, *Language and History in the Early Germanic World*. Cambridge: Cambridge University Press, 1998, 186–8.

46. Green, *Language and History*, 228.

47. Barford, *Early Slavs*, 167.

48. Tacitus, *Germania* 17.1; Rives, 84.

49. Though a surprising amount about textiles can be learnt from the imprints they make on metal objects which they were in contact with: see in Lisa Bender Jørgensen, *North European Textiles until AD 1000*. Aarhus: Aarhus University Press, 1992.

50. Tacitus, *Germania* 45.4; Rives, 96.

51. For this trade, see P. Wielowiejski, 'Bernstein in der Przeworsk-Kultur', *Bericht der Römisch-Germanische Kommission* 77 (1996), 215–347; but see Florin Curta, 'The amber trail in early medieval Eastern Europe', in *Paradigms and Methods in Early Medieval Studies*, eds Felice Lifschitz and Celia Chazelle, New York: Palgrave Macmillan, 2007, 61–79.

52. T. Kolník, 'Q. Atilius Primus – interprex, centurio und negotiator. Eine bedeutende Grabinschrit aus dem 1. Jh. u. Z. im Quadischen Limes-Vorland', *Acta Archaeologica Academiae Scientiarum Hungaricae* 30 (1978), 61–75. Translated in Elton, *Frontiers*. 80.

53. Tacitus, *Annals* 2.62; Jackson, 478–9.

54. Michael Erdrich, *Rom und die Barbaren. Das Verhältnis zwischen dem Imperium Romanum und den germanischen Stämmen vor seiner Nord-westgrenze von der späten römischen Republik bis zum Gallischen Sonderreich*. Mainz: Von Zabern, 2001.

55. C.R. Whittaker, *Frontiers of the Roman Empire: A Social and Economic Study*. Baltimore and London: Johns Hopkins University Press, 1994.

56. C.R. Whittaker, *Rome and its Frontiers: The Dynamics of Empire*. London: Routledge, 2004, 16. For a translation, see Elton, *Frontiers*, 68–9.

57. Whittaker, *Frontiers*, 114, 117.

58. Though note that Michael Fulford, 'Roman and barbarian: the economy of Roman frontier systems', in *Barbarians and Romans*, eds Barrett, Fitzpatrick and Macinnes, 1989, 81–95 casts doubt on this permeability.

59. Sigrid Dušek, *Römische Handwerker im germanischen Thüringen: Ergebnisse der Ausgrabungen in Haarhausen, Kreis Arnstadt*. Stuttgart: Theiss, 1992.

60. Heather and Matthews, *Goths*, 77.

61. Eugen S. Teodor, 'The shadow of a frontier: the Wallachian Plain during the Justinianic Age', in *Borders, Barriers*, ed. Curta, 2005, 205–46.

62. Curta, 'Frontier ethnogenesis', 192–3.

63. For a list of trade prohibitions in the Theodosian and Justinianic legislation, see Hugh Elton, *Warfare in Roman Europe, AD 350–425*. Oxford: Clarendon Press, 1996, 187 n.31.

64. Thompson, *Romans and Barbarians*, 10–12.

65. Ulla Lund Hansen, *Römischer Import im Norden: Warenaustausch zwischen dem Römischen Reich und dem freien Germanien während der Kaiserzeit unter besonderer Berücksichtigung Nordeuropas*. Copenhagen: Det Kongelige Nordiske Oldskriftselskab, 1987, 225; and *RGA* 15, 346–54.

66. *Theodosian Code* 9.40.24; Pharr, 258. For comment, see Fergus Millar, *A Greek Roman Empire: Power and Belief under Theodosius II (408–450)*. Berkeley, CA: University of California Press, 2006, 11 and 77.

67. Ulf Näsman, 'The Justinianic era of South Scandinavia: an archaeological view', in *The Sixth Century*, eds Hodges and Bowden, 1998, 264–9.

68. Todd, *The Early Germans*, 92.

69. Philip Grierson, 'Commerce in the Dark Ages: a critique of the evidence', *Transactions of the Royal Historical Society* 5th series 9 (1959), 123–40.

70. On silver dishes distributed by emperors and consuls on special occasions, see Ruth E. Leader-Newby, *Silver and Society in Late Antiquity: Functions and Meanings of Silver Plate in the Fourth to Seventh Centuries*. Aldershot: Ashgate, 2004.

71. B.A. Raev, *Roman Imports in the Lower Don Basin*. Oxford: BAR, 1986.

72. Todd, *The Early Germans*, 94.

73. Aleksander Bursche, 'Roman gold medallions as power symbols of the Germanic élite', in *Roman Gold*, ed. Magnus, 2001, 83–102.

74. Chilperic proudly showed them to Gregory of Tours himself: *History* 6.2.

75. See in particular M. Axboe, K. Düwel, K. Hauck and L. Von Padberg, eds, *Die Goldbrakteaten der Völkerwanderungszeit*, 3 vols. Munich: Fink, 1985–89. A bibliography of his 64+ studies collectively called 'Zur Iconologie der Goldbrakteaten' can be found at http://www.uni-muenster.de/Fruehmittelalter/Projekte/Brakteaten. The most accessible study is his entry in *RGA* 3, at 'Brakteatenikonologie'.

76. I am here following Morten Axboe, 'Amulet pendants and a darkened sun: on the function of the gold bracteates and a possible motivation for the large gold hoards', in *Roman Gold*, ed. Magnus, 2001, 119–36.

77. Axboe, 'Amulet pendants', 125.

78. Märit Gaimster, 'Gold bracteates and necklaces: political ideals in the sixth century', in *Roman Gold*, ed. Magnus, 2001, 143–56.

79. Axboe, 'Amulet pendants', 126.

80. See O. Seeck, in *Paulys Real-Encyclopädie der Classischen Altertumswissenschaft*, 4 (Stuttgart, 1896), cols 2856–7.

81. Birgit Arrhenius, *Merovingian Garnet Jewellery: Emergence and Social Implications*. Stockholm: Kungl. Vitterhets Historie och Antikvitets Akademien, 1985, 196.

82. Bernhard Salin, *Die altgermanische Thierornamentik: Typologische Studie über germanische Metallgegenstände aus dem IV. bis IX. Jahrhundrt, nebst einer Studie über irische Ornamentik*, 2nd ed. Stockholm: Wahlström & Widstrand, 1935.

83. As noted by Heather, 'Literacy and power', 178.

84. Heather, 'Literacy and power', 181.

85. Caesar, *Gallic War* 6.13.10.

86. T.M. Charles-Edwards, *Early Christian Ireland*. Cambridge: Cambridge University Press, 2004, 190.

87. Charles-Edwards, *Early Christian Ireland*, 128.

88. *Uraicecht na Ríar*, BN II, 1; Breatnach, 30.

89. Einhard, *Life of Charlemagne*, 29; Thorpe, 82.
90. Venantius Fortunatus, Poem 7.8; George, 64.
91. R.L.S. and M. Bruce-Mitford, 'The Sutton Hoo lyre, Beowulf, and the origins of the frame harp', *Antiquity* 44 (1970), 7–13.
92. Bede, *Ecclesiastical History* 4.23.
93. And here I am following Moisl, *Lordship*, 62–83; see also Moisl, 'Anglo-Saxon royal genealogies and Germanic oral tradition', *Journal of Medieval History* 7 (1981), 215–48.
94. For translations see Bradley, *Anglo-Saxon Poetry*, 336, 362 and 408.
95. *Beowulf*, lines 866–73; Heaney, 23.
96. Moisl, *Lordship*, 75.
97. Moisl, *Lordship*, 76.

Chapter Seven

1. A.H.M. Jones, *The Later Roman Empire, 284–602: A Social, Economic and Administrative Survey*, 3 vols. Oxford: Blackwell, 1964, 851.
2. Sulpicius Severus, *Life of St Martin* 2; Hoare, 13.
3. Libanius, Oration 31; Norman, 73.
4. Procopius, *Wars* 8.3.21; Dewing 5, 80–1.
5. Themistius, Oration 10.136; Heather and Matthews, 44.
6. Jones, *Later Roman Empire*, 853.
7. Symmachus 2.46; Callu 1, 184–5. For the context, see Cristiana Sogno, *Q. Aurelius Symmachus: A Political Biography*. Ann Arbor: University of Michigan Press, 2006, 78.
8. *De Regno* 15; Fitzgerald, 136.
9. Ammianus 22.7.8; Rolfe 2, 210–11.
10. Zosimus 2.42.1; Ridley, 42.
11. Eugippius, *Life of Severin* 5.3; Bieler, 63; see Thompson, *Romans and Barbarians*, 124–5.
12. *Theodosian Code* 3.4.1; Pharr, 65.
13. *Theodosian Code* 13.4.4; Pharr, 391.
14. St Patrick, *Confessio*, 10: Hood, 43.
15. Gildas, *The Ruin of Britain*, 25: Winterbottom, 27.
16. *Theodosian Code* 5.7.1 at AD 366; Pharr, 108.
17. *Theodosian Code* 5.7.2 at AD 408; Pharr, 108.
18. Theodoret, *Letters* 70: Jackson, 270.
19. *Life of St Caesarius* 32; Klingshirn, 25. See William E. Klingshirn, *Caesarius of Arles: The Making of a Christian Community in Late Antique Gaul*. Cambridge: Cambridge University Press, 1994 and William E. Klingshirn, 'Charity and power: Caesarius of Arles and the ransoming of captives in Sub-Roman Gaul', *Journal of Roman Studies* 75 (1985), 183–203.
20. Eugippius, *Life of St Severinus* 9.1; Bieler, 67.
21. Eugippius, *Life* 10; Bieler, 77–8.

22. Gregory, *History* 3.15; Thorpe, 175–9.
23. The Council of Mâcon, 581–3, canon 16, offered Jews 12 *solidi* each for the Christian slaves which they had to surrender: see *Carons*, trans. Gaudemet and Basdevant, 436–7.
24. Procopius 8.34.8; Dewing 5, 400–1.
25. Following R.I. Frank, *Scholae Palatinae: The Palace Guards of the later Roman Empire*. Rome: American Academy, 1969.
26. A.E.R. Boak, *Manpower Shortage and the Fall of the Roman Empire in the West*. Ann Arbor: University of Michigan Press, 1955.
27. *Theodosian Code* 7.13.4 and 5; Pharr, 170; and 7.13.10; Pharr, 172.
28. *Theodosian Code* 10.22.4; Pharr, 289; on deserters see 7.13; Pharr, 170–3. That soldiers may have been tattooed rather than branded, see Vegetius 1.8; Milner, 9; on which see C.P. Jones, 'Stigma: tattooing and branding in Graeco-Roman Antiquity', *Journal of Roman Studies* 87 (1987), 139–55.
29. *Theodosian Code* 7.13.3; Pharr, 170. Vegetius 1.5 Milner, 6 specified between 5 foot 10 and 6 foot (which is between 1.72 m and 1.77 m in modern measurement).
30. *Theodosian Code* 7.13.16; Pharr, 172–3.
31. *Theodosian Code* 7.13.8.
32. Jones, *Later Roman Empire*, 619.
33. Jones, *Later Roman Empire*, 621. See Ammianus, 29.4.7.
34. Panegyrics 6.6.2; Nixon and Rodgers, 225.
35. Reference from J.H.W.G. Liebeschuetz, *Barbarians and Bishops: Army, Church, and State in the Age of Arcadius and Chrysostom*. Oxford: Clarendon Press, 1990, 12.
36. See T. Anderson, 'Roman military colonists in Gaul, Salian ethnogenesis and the forgotten meaning of *Pactus Legis Salicae* 59.5', *Early Medieval Europe* 4 (1995), 129–44.
37. *Theodosian Code* 7.20.10.
38. See Liebeschuetz, *Barbarians and Bishops*, 12.
39. *Theodosian Code* 5.6.3; Pharr, 108.
40. Sozomen 9.5; Hartranft, 422.
41. J.C. Mann, *Legionary Recruitment and Veteran Settlement during the Principate*. London: Institute of Archaeology, University of London, 1983, 51–2.
42. For examples, see Liebeschuetz, *Barbarians and Bishops*, 14.
43. Liebeschuetz, *Barbarians and Bishops*, 15.
44. *Abinnaeus Archive*, Letter 34, 86–7.
45. Ammianus 20.4.4; Rolfe 2, 18–19.
46. Liebeschuetz, *Barbarians and Bishops*, 43.
47. Olympiodorus, Frag. 12; Blockley, 170–1.
48. Liebeschuetz, *Barbarians and Bishops*, 45–6.
49. Liebeschuetz, *Barbarians and Bishops*, 47.
50. Liebeschuetz, *Barbarians and Bishops*, 10.
51. Ammianus 15.5.33; Rolfe 1, 152–3.
52. Frank, *Scholae Palatinae*, 59.
53. Synesius, *De Regno* 12; Ammianus 20.8.13.
54. Elton, *Warfare*, 151.

55. Ramsey MacMullen, *Corruption and the Decline of Rome*. New Haven, CT: Yale University Press, 1988, 176–7.
56. Elton, *Warfare*, 141–2.
57. Zosimus 5.20; Ridley, 109.
58. Elton, *Warfare*, 146.
59. Elton, *Warfare*, 147.
60. D. Hoffmann, *Das spätrömische Bewegungsheer und die Notitia Dignitatum*, 2 vols. Düsseldorf: Rheinland Verlag, 1969, 61–116, and Martijn Nicasie, *Twilight of Empire. The Roman Army from the Reign of Diocletian until the Battle of Adrianople*. Amsterdam: Thesis Publishers, 1998, 105–6.
61. *CIL* III.3576. Discussed in Georg Scheibelreiter, *Die barbarische Gesellschaft. Mentalitätsgeschichte der europäischen Achsenzeit 5.–8. Jahrhundert*. Darmstadt: Wissenchaftliche Buchgesellschaft, 1999, 15.
62. Jones, *Later Roman Empire*, 621; Elton, *Warfare*, 138.
63. Green, *Language and History*, 184.
64. Green, *Language and History*, 185–6.
65. Vegetius 3.18; Milner, 101.
66. Ammianus 16.12.43; Rolfe 1, 286–9. It is mentioned again at 26.7.17 and 31.7.11.
67. *Theodosian Code* 14.10.1–4; all translated Pharr, 415.
68. Elton, *Warfare*, 145.
69. Elton, *Warfare*, 145.
70. Procopius, *Anecdota*, 7.1–7: Dewing 6, 78–9.
71. J.H.W.G. Liebeschuetz, 'The end of the Roman army in the western empire', in *War and Society in the Roman World*, eds John Rich and Graham Shipley, London and New York: Routledge 1993, 274.
72. Nicasie, *Twilight*, 112.
73. Nicasie, *Twilight*, 115.
74. Jordanes 36; Mierow, 104–5.
75. Liebeschuetz, 'The end of the Roman army', 273.
76. Penny MacGeorge, *Late Roman Warlords*. Oxford: Oxford University Press, 2002.
77. Steuer, 'Handwerk auf spätantiken Höhensiedlungen', 133–5.

Chapter Eight

1. Walter Goffart, 'The maps of the barbarian invasions: a preliminary report', *Nottingham Medieval Studies* 32 (1988), 49.
2. Jean Hubert, Jean Porcher and W.F. Volbach, *Europe in the Dark Ages*. London: Thames and Hudson, 1969, Fig. 355.
3. London: Orbis, 1982.
4. See Walter Goffart, 'What's wrong with the map of the barbarian invasions?' in *Minorities and Barbarians*, eds Ridyard and Benson, 1996, 159–73. He discusses the obsession in Goffart, 'Does the distant past . . . ?' 26–8.
5. See note above, and Walter Goffart, 'The maps of the barbarian invasions: a longer look', in *The Culture of Christendom: Essays in Medieval History in Memory of Denis L.T. Bethell*, ed. Marc A. Meyer. London and Rio Grande: Hambledon, 1993, 1–27.

6. Strabo 7.1.3; Jones 3, 156–9.
7. Jordanes 9 and 19; Mierow, 53 and 55.
8. Jordanes 38; Mierow, 60.
9. Wenskus, *Stammesbildung*, 464. Here I am following Goffart, *Barbarian Tides*, 62.
10. Noted on p. 1 of Andrew Gillett, ed., *On Barbarian Identity. Critical Approaches to Ethnicity in the Early Middle Ages*, Turnhout: Brepols, 2002. See Wolfram, *History of the Goths*, 26–7 and 389; and Olympiodorus, fragment 29.1; Blockley, 192–3; and for a full discussion, see Gillett, *On Barbarian Identity*, 2.
11. Pohl, 'Ethnicity, theory, and tradition: a response', 228–9.
12. Goffart, *Barbarian Tides*, 62.
13. Goffart, *Barbarian Tides*, 70.
14. Christensen, *Cassiodorus, Jordanes*, 317.
15. A.H. Merrills, *History and Geography in Late Antiquity*. Cambridge: Cambridge University Press, 2005, 154–5, citing Gilbert Dagron, 'Discours utopique et récit des origines: I. Une lecture de Cassiodore-Jordanes: les Goths de Scandza à Ravenne', *Annales: Économies, Sociétés, Civilisations* 26 (1971), 298.
16. Translated in Foulke's translation of Paul the Deacon, *History*, 315–21.
17. Pliny, *Natural History* 4.13.96; Rackham *et al.* 2, 192–3.
18. Paul the Deacon, *History* 1.8; Foulke, 16–17.
19. For an excellent introduction to medieval origin myths, see Susan Reynolds, 'Medieval *Origines Gentium* and the community of the realm', *History* 68 (1983), 375–90.
20. Bede, *Ecclesiastical History* 1.1; Colgrave and Mynors, 8–19.
21. Quoted by Nicholas Howe, *Migration and Mythmaking in Anglo-Saxon England*. New Haven, CT: Yale University Press, 1989, 1.
22. See Anthony D. Smith, *Chosen Peoples*. Oxford: Oxford University Press, 2003.
23. Bede, *Ecclesiastical History* 1.15. I have not followed Colgrave and Mynors' translation (50–1), which talks of 'three very powerful Germanic tribes', rather than Bede's 'three powerful peoples from Germany'. Both 'Germanic' and 'tribe' are loaded words. Later in the same paragraph, Colgrave and Mynors used the even more unfortunate phrase 'the Northumbrian race'.
24. Bede, *Ecclesiastical History* 1.15; Colgrave and Mynors, 50–1.
25. Fredegar 2.4–6; Murray, 592.
26. *Liber Historiae Francorum* 2; Bachrach, 24.
27. J.N.L. Myres and B. Green, *The Anglo-Saxon Cemeteries on Caistor-by-Norwich and Markshall, Norfolk*. London: Thames and Hudson, 1973, 237–8.
28. For references, see Hines, 'Culture groups', 221.
29. Chris Arnold, 'The Anglo-Saxon cemeteries of the Isle of Wight: an appraisal of nineteenth-century excavation data', in *Anglo-Saxon Cemeteries: A Reappraisal*, ed. Edmund Southworth, Stroud: Sutton, 1990, 170. See the comments of John Moreland, 'Ethnicity, power and the English', in *Social Identity in Early Medieval Britain*, eds William O. Frazer and Andrew Tyrell, London and New York: Leicester University Press, 2000, 43–4.

30. Barbara Yorke, 'The Jutes of Hampshire and Wight and the origins of Wessex', in *Origins*, ed. Bassett, 1989, 84–96.

31. Margaret Gelling, 'Why aren't we speaking Welsh?' *Anglo-Saxon Studies in Archaeology and History* 6 (1993), 51–6.

32. Bede, *Ecclesiastical History* I.15; Colgrave and Mynors, 52–3.

33. Sidonius, *Letters* 8.6; Anderson 2, 428–31.

34. John Haywood, *Dark Age Naval Power. A Reassessment of Frankish and Anglo-Saxon Seafaring Activity*. London and New York: Routledge, 1991, 73–4.

35. Michael E. Jones, *The End of Roman Britain*. Ithaca, NY: Cornell University Press, 1996, 81.

36. Jones, *End of Roman Britain*, 27.

37. http://news.bbc.co.uk/1/hi/wales/2076470.stm, 30 June 2002, accessed July 2006.

38. http://news.bbc.co.uk/1/hi/sci/tech/5192634.stm, 18 July 2006, accessed July 2006.

39. Mark G. Thomas, Michael P.H. Stumpf and Heinrich Härke, 'Evidence for an apartheid-like social structure in early Anglo-Saxon England', *Proceedings of the Royal Society, B* (2006), doi: 10.1098/rspb.2006.3627.

40. On all this see the very useful discussion in Hamerow, *Settlements*, 106–12.

41. Noted in Hamerow, *Settlements*, 109.

42. Hamerow, *Settlements*, 110–11.

43. Victor of Vita, *History of the Vandal Persecution*, 2; Moorhead, 3.

44. Procopius, *Wars* 3.5.18; Dewing 2, 52–3.

45. Procopius, *Anecdota* 18.6; Dewing 6, 212–13.

46. Goffart, *Barbarians and Romans*, 233–4.

47. Walter Scheidel, 'Finances, figures and fiction', *Classical Quarterly* 46 (1996), 222–38. My thanks to Walter Goffart for this reference.

48. See 1 Kings 5:15 and 2 Chronicles 2:2 and 2:18. The only precise figure in the Bible that is larger is the 87,000 who fought against the clans of Issachar: 1 Chronicles 7:5.

49. Vegetius, *Epitome* 2.2; Milner, 30; Goffart, *Barbarians and Romans*, 233.

50. Zosimus, *History* 5.25; Orosius, *History*, 7.37; Raymond, 384; Augustine, *City of God* 5.23 (Bettenson, 218).

51. J.B. Bury, *History of the Later Roman Empire from the Death of Theodosius I to the Death of Justinian*. London: Macmillan, 1923, 104.

52. Bury, *Later Roman Empire*, 167.

53. Bury, *Later Roman Empire*, 293.

54. Hydatius AD 451; Burgess, 101.

55. Procopius, *Wars* 5.24.3, which is a figure apparently given by Belisarius in a letter to Justinian; and *Wars* 6.28.10.

56. Ammianus 31.12.3; Rolfe 3, 462–5.

57. The grain measures are mentioned by Olympiodorus, Fragment 3 (Blockley, 194–5) and discussed in Javier Arce, *Bárbaros y romanos en Hispania, 400–507 A.D.* Madrid: Marcial Pons, 2005, 80–1.

58. Procopius *Wars* 7.34.42; Bury, *later Roman Empire*, 105.

59. Guy Halsall, *Warfare and Society in the Barbarian West, 450–900*. London: Routledge, 2003, 121.

60. Gregory *History* 9.31; Isidore, *History of the Goths*, 54. See Halsall, *loc. cit.*

61. Timothy Reuter, 'The recruitment of armies in the Early Middle Ages: what can we know?' in *Military Aspects of Scandinavian Society*, ed. Jørgensen and Claussen, 1997, 36, cited by Halsall, *Warfare and Society*, 129.

62. For the above I am following Michel Kazanski, *Les Goths (Ier-VIIe siècle après J.-C.)*. Paris: Errance, 1991, 9–28.

63. For a useful summary, see Heather and Matthews, *Goths*, 51–101.

64. See the map at Heather, *Goths and Romans*, 51–2.

65. Here I follow Jes Martens, 'The Vandals: myths and facts about a Germanic tribe of the first half of the first millennium AD', in *Archaeological Approaches to Cultural Identity*, ed. Stephan Shennan. London: Routledge, 1989, 57–65.

66. *Scriptores Historiae Augustae*, at Claudius, 6.2; Magie 3, 162–3. In what follows I am largely relying on Alvar Ellegård, 'Who were the Eruli?' *Scandia: Tidskrift för historisk forskning* 53 (1987), 5–34.

67. Procopius 6.14.1–7; Dewing 3, 402–05.

68. Procopius 7.33.13.

69. Procopius 6.15.1ff.

70. Procopius 6.15.4; Dewing 3, 414–15.

71. Procopius 6.14.38; Dewing 3, 412–13.

72. Hydatius AD 455 and 459; Burgess 106–7 and 110–11.

73. Ellegård, 'Who were the Eruli?', 30.

74. Jordanes 24; Mierow, 57.

75. Jordanes 233; Mierow, 116.

76. Curta, *Making of the Slavs*, 195–6.

77. Hydatius AD 457; Burgess, 108–11.

78. R.W. Burgess, 'Hydatius and the final frontier: the fall of the Roman Empire and the end of the world', in *Shifting Frontiers*, eds Mathisen and Sivan, 1996, 324.

79. Burgess, 'Hydatius', 332.

80. For a discussion of the whole phenomenon, see J.H.W.G. Liebeschuetz, 'The refugees and evacuees in the Age of Migrations', in *The Construction of Communities*, eds Corradini, Diesenberger and Reimitz, 2003, 65–79.

Chapter Nine

1. For these definitions I am relying heavily on the three relevant sections in volume 1 (A-B) of George Ritzer, ed. *The Blackwell Encyclopedia of Sociology*, Malden, MA and Oxford: Blackwell, 2007.

2. *Theodosian Code* 3.14.1; Pharr, 76. For commentary, see Hagith Sivan, 'Why not marry a barbarian? Marital frontiers in late antiquity (the example of CTh 3.14.1)', in *Shifting Frontiers*, eds Mathisen and Sivan, 1996, 136 and see also Hagith Sivan, 'The appropriation of Roman law in barbarian hands: "Roman-barbarian" marriage in Visigothic Gaul and Spain', in *Strategies of Distinction*, eds Pohl and Reimitz, 1998, 189–203.

3. See Rosario Soraci, *Ricerche sui conubia tra Romani e germani nei secoli IV-VI*, 2nd ed. Catania: Muglia, 1974.

4. R.C. Blockley, 'Roman-barbarian marriages in the late Empire', *Florilegium* 4 (1982), 63–79. See further Alain Chauvot, *Opinions romaines face aux barbares au IVe siècle ap. J.-C.* Paris: De Boccard, 1998, 132–4.
5. On this see Sivan, 'Why not marry a barbarian?'.
6. Claudian, *On Stilicho's Consulship* 3.180–1, Platnauer 2, 54–5. For a full discussion of this issue, see Ralph W. Mathisen, '*Peregrini, barbari,* and *cives Romani*: concepts of citizenship and the legal identity of barbarians in the later Roman Empire', *American Historical Review* 111 (2006), 1011–40.
7. Alexander Demandt, 'The osmosis of late Roman and Germanic aristocracies', in *Das Reich und die Barbaren*, eds Chrysos and Schwarcz, 1989, 75–87.
8. Matthews, 'Roman laws and barbarian identity in the late Roman west', 37.
9. P.D. King, *Law and Society in the Visigothic Kingdom*. Cambridge: Cambridge University Press, 1972, 13–14.
10. *Visigothic Code* 3.1.2.
11. Particularly since A.H.M. Jones, 'Were ancient heresies national or social movements in disguise?' *Journal of Theological Studies* n.s. 10 (1959), 280–98.
12. Wood, in *Avitus of Vienne* (see bibliography of primary sources), 19–20.
13. Steven C. Fanning, 'Lombard Arianism reconsidered', *Speculum* 56 (1981), 241–58.
14. For which the main source is Victor of Vita; but see Andrew Cain, 'Miracles, martyrs, and Arians: Gregory of Tours' sources for his account of the Vandal kindom', *Vigiliae Christianae* 59 (2005), 412–37.
15. Procopius 7.2.1–3; Dewing 4, 166–7.
16. See Peter Heather, 'Disappearing and reappearing tribes', in *Strategies of Distinction*, eds Pohl and Reimitz, 1998, 95–112.
17. Roger Collins, 'Law and ethnic identity in the western kingdoms in the fifth and sixth centuries', in *Medieval Europeans: Studies in Ethnic Identity and National Perspectives in Medieval Europe*, ed. Alfred P. Smyth, Basingstoke: Macmillan, 1998, 1–23; Ian N. Wood, 'The Code in Merovingian Gaul', in *The Theodosian Code: Studies in the Imperial Law of Late Antiquity*, eds Jill Harries and Ian Wood, London: Duckworth, 1993, 161–77.
18. Sidonius, *Letters* 2.1.3; Anderson 1, 416–17.
19. Anonymus Valesianus 12.61; Rolfe 3, 546–7.
20. Sidonius, *Letters* 5.5; Anderson 2, 180–3.
21. Jill Harries, 'Legal culture and identity in the fifth-century West', in *Ethnicity and Culture*, eds Mitchell and Greatrex, 2000, 51; see also Matthews, 'Roman laws and barbarian identity'.
22. Harries, 'Legal culture', 54.
23. Harries, 'Legal culture', 55.
24. Sidonius, *Letters* 1.2; Anderson 1, 335–45.
25. Ennodius, *Life of St Epiphanius* 89; Cook, 323–5.
26. Because of the rancid butter they put on their hair: Sidonius, Poem 12; Anderson 1, 212–13.
27. Alain Chauvot, 'Représentations du Barbaricum chez les barbares au service de l'Empire au IVe siècle après J.-C.' *Ktèma* 9 (1984), 145–57.

28. Gregory of Tours, *History* 2.9.
29. Ammianus Marcellinus 31.10.6; Rolfe 3, 448–9.
30. *CIL* 13.3682.
31. Procopius 5.2.6–19; Dewing 3, 16–19.
32. David Lambert, 'The barbarians in Salvian's *De Gubernatione Dei*', in *Ethnicity and Culture*, eds Mitchell and Greatrex, 2000, 103.
33. Salvian 7.6; O'Sullivan, 193–4.
34. Salvian 7.15; O'Sullivan, 207.
35. Salvian 7.23; O'Sullivan, 222.
36. Salvian 5.4; O'Sullivan, 134.
37. Salvian 5.5–8; O'Sullivan, 135–41.
38. Lambert, 'The barbarians in Salvian's *De Gubernatione Dei*', 113.
39. Bryan Ward-Perkins, 'Why did the Anglo-Saxons not become more British?' *English Historical Review* 115 (2000), 514.
40. Ward-Perkins, 'Why did the Anglo-Saxons . . . ?' 518, quoting E.A. Freeman, *Old English History for Children*. London: Macmillan 1869, 17–19.
41. Thompson, *Romans and Barbarians*, 214.
42. Ward-Perkins, 'Why did the Anglo-Saxons . . . ?', 527.
43. The debate continues in Nick Higham, ed., *Britons in Anglo-Saxon England*, Woodbridge: Boydell, 2007.
44. Gerhard Wirth, 'Rome and its Germanic partners in the fourth century', in *Kingdoms of the Empire*, ed. Walter Pohl, 1997, 16.
45. On all this, see Peter Heather, '*Foedera* and *foederati* of the fourth century', in *Kingdoms of the Empire*, ed. Walter Pohl, 1997, 57–74.
46. Ammianus 17.10.3–4 and 17.10.6–9; 18.2.13.
47. Ammianus 14.10.16; Rolfe 1, 88–9 and 17.1.12–13; Rolfe 1, 310–311. See Heather, '*Foedera* and *foederati*', 69.
48. Ammianus 27.1.1.
49. Heather, '*Foedera* and *foederati*', 71.
50. Goffart, *Barbarians and Romans, A.D. 418–584: The Techniques of Accommodation*. Princeton, NJ: Princeton University Press, 1980.
51. *Theodosian Code* 7.8.5; Pharr, 166.
52. Goffart, *Barbarians and Romans*, 45.
53. *Burgundian Code*, 54.1; Drew, 62.
54. Ennodius, Letters 9.23; translated in Jones, *later Roman Empire*, 251.
55. Cassiodorus, *Variae* 2.16; Barnish, 29.
56. Goffart, *Barbarians and Romans*, 73.
57. Cassiodorus, *Variae* 2.37; Goffart, *Barbarians and Romans*, 81–2.
58. Cassiodorus, *Variae* 8.26; Goffart, *Barbarians and Romans*, 83.
59. Goffart, *Barbarians and Romans*, 102.
60. Burgundian Code 54, Drew, 62–3, and in Goffart, *Barbarians and Romans*, 127–9.
61. S.J.B. Barnish, 'Taxation, land and barbarian settlement in the Western Empire', *Papers of the British School at Rome* 54 (1986), 170 notes only one favourable review: by Edward James in *Speculum* 57 (1982), 885–7.
62. Barnish, 'Taxation', 181.
63. Wood, 'Ethnicity and the ethnogenesis of the Burgundians'.

64. See, e.g., Jean Durliat, 'Cité, impôt et intégration des barbares', in *Kingdoms of the Empire*, ed. Pohl, 1997, 153–83.

65. J.H.W.G. Liebeschuetz, 'Cities, taxes, and the accommodation of the barbarians', in *Kingdoms of the Empire*, ed. Pohl, 1997, 142. This chapter is reprinted in Noble, ed., *From Roman Provinces*, 309–23.

66. Noble, ed., *From Roman Provinces*, 20.

67. Paul the Deacon, *History* 2.32; Foulke 88–91.

68. Paul, *History* 3.16; Foulke, 114.

69. Here I am following the discussion in Walter Pohl, 'The Empire and the Lombards: treaties and negotiations in the sixth century', in *Kingdoms of the Empire*, ed. Pohl, 1997, 113ff.

70. Pohl, 'Empire and the Lombards', 120; Gregory of Tours, *History*, 9.30.

71. As argued in Edward James, *The Merovingian Archaeology of South-West Gaul*, 2 vols. Oxford: BAR, 1977.

72. Joachim Werner, 'Zur Entstehung der Reihengräberzvilisation', *Archaeologia Geographica* 1 (1950), 23–32.

73. H.W. Böhme, *Germanische Grabfünde des vierten bis fünften Jahrhunderts zwischen unteren Elbe und Loire*. Munich: 1974.

74. Edward James, *The Franks*. Oxford: Blackwell, 1988, 51.

75. James, 'Cemeteries and the problem of Frankish settlement in Gaul'.

76. First in Halsall, 'Origins'.

77. Halsall, 'Origins', 201.

78. Halsall, 'Origins', 207.

79. Guy Halsall, 'Archaeology and the late Roman frontier in northern Gaul: the so-called Föderatengräber reconsidered', in *Grenze und Differenz im Frühmittelalter*, eds Walter Pohl and Helmut Reimitz, Vienna: Verlag der Österreichischen Akademie der Wissenschaften, 2000, 167–80.

80. For some more thoughts on this, see James, 'The militarization of Roman society, AD 400–700'.

Chapter Ten

1. For the complete story, see Richard Fletcher, *The Conversion of Europe: From Paganism to Christianity, 371–1386 AD*. London: HarperCollins, 1997.

2. Convenient translations are to be found in *Snorri Sturlason: Edda*, by Andrew Faulkes. London: Everyman/Dent, 1987; and *The Poetic Edda*, by Lee M. Hollander, 2nd edition. Austin University of Texas Press, 1994.

3. *The Book of the Settlements* (*Landnámabók*), trans. by G. Jones, *The Norse Atlantic Saga*. London: Oxford University Press, 1964, p. 125.

4. Bede, *Ecclesiastical History*, 2.15; Colgrave and Mynors, 190–1.

5. Halsall, *Early Medieval Cemeteries*, 67.

6. F.M. Stenton, 'The historical bearing of place-name studies: Anglo-Saxon heathenism', *Transactions of the Royal Historical Society*, 4th series, 23 (1941), 1–24.

7. But see now Sarah Semple, 'Defining the OE *hearg*: a preliminary archaeological and topographic examination of *hearg* placenames and their hinterlands', *Early Medieval Europe* 15 (2007), 364–85.

8. Bede, *Ecclesiastical History* 1.30; 2.13; 2.15; 3.30; Aldhelm, Letter 5; Lapidge and Herren, 160–1.

9. On what follows, see John Blair, 'Anglo-Saxon pagan shrines and their prototypes', *Anglo-Saxon Studies in Archaeology and History* 8 (1995), 1–28.

10. Green, *Language and History*, 296–301.

11. Recent scholarship seems inclined to favour 507 or 508 for the baptism of Clovis, not the traditional 496: see Danuta Shanzer, 'Dating the baptism of Clovis: the bishop of Vienne vs the bishop of Tours', *Early Medieval Europe* 7 (1998), 29–57.

12. Paulinus, *Life of St Ambrose* 26: Hoare, 176.

13. Letter translated by Emerton, 48–50.

14. Eusebius, *Tricennial Oration: On Christ's Sepulchre*, 16.4–6; Drake, 120.

15. Ralph W. Mathisen, 'Barbarian bishops and the churches 'in barbaricis gentibus' in late Antiquity', *Speculum* 72 (1997), 667.

16. *Decrees of the Ecumenical Councils*, trans. Tanner, 31.

17. Paulinus of Nola, Poem 17; Walsh, 111–12.

18. Paulinus of Nola, Letter 18; Walsh 1, 170. See E.A. Thompson, 'Christianity and the Northern Barbarians', in *The Conflict between Paganism and Christianity in the Fourth Century*, ed. A.D. Momigliano, Oxford: Clarendon Press, 1963, 65–6.

19. Orosius 7.32; Raymond, 372.

20. Heather and Matthews, *Goths*, 144.

21. On Theophilos, see Schwarcz in Peter Heather, ed., *The Visigoths from the Migration Period to the Seventh Century: An Ethnographic Perspective*, Woodbridge: Boydell, 1999, 451. But Theophilos may have been bishop to the Crimean Goths: see Mathisen, 'Barbarian bishops', 670–1.

22. Heather and Matthews, *Goths*, 145.

23. Jordanes 267; Mierow, 128.

24. For translation and commentary, see Heather and Matthews, *Goths*, 109–17.

25. For a brief modern summary, see David Rankin, 'Arianism', in *The Early Christian World*, ed. Philip F. Esler, London and New York: Routledge, 2000, 975–1001.

26. 'Arianism' should be relegated 'to inverted commas, and preferably to oblivion' wrote Rowan Williams in a review of Hanson, *The Search for the Christian Doctrine of God*, in *Scottish Journal of Theology*, 45 (1992), 102.

27. Quoted in the context of a classic discussion of the possible meanings of these feelings (and answering his own question 'No'): Jones, 'Were ancient heresies national or social movements in disguise?' 297.

28. Translated in Heather and Matthews, *Goths*, 146–53.

29. Thompson, 'Christianity and the Northern barbarians', 69.

30. Mathisen, 'Barbarian bishops', 674–5.

31. Here I follow Thompson, 'Christianity and the Northern Barbarians', as most scholars have on this issue.

32. *Gallic Chronicle of 452*; Murray, 85.

33. Avitus, Letter to Clovis; Shanzer and Wood, 369.

34. On this see Fanning, 'Lombard Arianism reconsidered'.

35. Hydatius AD 465–6; Burgess, 119.
36. Mathisen, 'Barbarian bishops', 683–4.
37. Gregory, *History* 2.34; see above p. 00.
38. Gregory, *History* 9.15.
39. See Thompson, *Goths in Spain*, 101–4.
40. John of Biclar 58: Wolf, 68.
41. Thompson, *Goths in Spain*, 105.
42. As we see from Constantius's *From Rome to Merovingian Gaul, Life of St Germanus* (trans. Hoare).
43. Prosper; Murray, 68.
44. Charles-Edwards, *Early Christian Ireland*, 212.
45. Patrick, *Letter*, 1; Hood, 35, 55.
46. Patrick, *Letter*, 14; Hood, 37, 57.
47. Charles-Edwards, *Early Christian Ireland*, 221.
48. Charles-Edwards, *Early Christian Ireland*, 225.
48. Bede, *Ecclesiastical History* 3.4; see James, *Britain*, 84.
50. Bede, *Ecclesiastical History* 1.22.
51. See Bede, *Ecclesiastical History* 1.27.
52. Bede, *Ecclesiastical History* 1.30; Colgrave and Mynors, 106–9.
53. Bede, *Ecclesiastical History* 2.6.
54. Both quotations from Bede, *Ecclesiastical History* 3.5; Colgrave and Mynors, 226–7.
55. Bede, *Ecclesiastical History* 2.5. The Old English text of the laws, with translation, is conveniently edited by F.L. Attenborough in *The Laws of the Earliest English Kings*.
56. Decree of Childebert, 1 and 2; Drew, *Laws of the Salian Franks*, 156–7.
57. From a sermon preached c. 500 on the Kalends of January (a day which Christians frequently celebrated with rituals inherited from pagans); Mueller, 34.
58. Green, *Language and History*, 214.
59. On all this see Chapter 13 of Green, *Language and History*; and see Philip Shaw, 'The origins of the theophoric week in the Germanic languages', *Early Medieval Europe* 15 (2007), 386–401.
60. Karen Louise Jolly, *Popular Religion in Late Saxon England: Elf Charms in Context*. Chapel Hill: University of North Carolina Press, 1996, 128.
61. Gregory of Tours, *History* 7.29.

Chapter Eleven

1. An example I have used before: see James, *Britain*, 122.
2. William A. Chaney, *The Cult of Kingship in Anglo-Saxon England: The Transition from Paganism to Christianity*. Manchester: Manchester University Press, 1970, 65.
3. Letter 13 in Allott, 22.
4. Peter Heather, 'Theodoric King of the Goths', *Early Medieval Europe* 4 (1995), 161–2.
5. Amory, *People and Identity*, 326.

6. On the problems of distinguishing 'primitive' *Irish* ideas of sacral kingship from later Christian accretions, see the discussion in Kim McCone, *Pagan Past and Christian Present in Early Irish Literature*, Maynooth: An Sagart, 1990, 138–60.

7. Edward James, 'The origins of barbarian kingdoms: the continental evidence', in *Origins*, ed. Bassett, 1989, 40–52.

8. See James, 'Origins of barbarian kingdoms'. Tolkien was of course alluding to this when in *The Lord of the Rings* he gave a character the name of 'Théoden King'.

9. Bede, *Ecclesiastical History* 5.10.

10. J.M. Wallace-Hadrill, *Bede's Ecclesiastical History of the English People: A Historical Commentary*. Oxford: Clarendon, 1988, 183.

11. See James Campbell, *Bede's Reges and Principes*. Jarrow: St Paul's Church, 1979.

12. Bede, *Ecclesiastical History* 2.5; *Anglo-Saxon Chronicles* at 827: Swanton, 61.

13. James, 'Origins of barbarian kingdoms', 47.

14. Andrew Gillett, 'Was ethnicity politicized in the earliest medieval kingdoms?' in *On Barbarian Identity*, ed. Gillett, 2002, 85–121.

15. Gillett, 'Was ethnicity politicized . . . ?' 121.

16. Charles-Edwards, *Early Christian Ireland*, 14.

17. Bjørn Myhre, 'Chieftain's graves and chiefdom territories in South Norway in the Migration Period', *Studien zur Sachsenforschung* 6 (1987), 185.

18. Ambrosiani in J.P. Lamm and H.-Å. Nordström, eds, *Vendel Period Studies. Transactions of the Boat-Grave Symposium in Stockholm, February 2–3, 1981*, Stockholm: Statens Historiska Museum, 1983, 21–2 and 28–9.

19. Peter Sawyer in Lamm and Nordström, eds, *Vendel Period Studies*, 122.

20. Bertil Almgren in Lamm and Nordström, eds, *Vendel Period Studies*, 11–13.

21. See Bengt Schönbäck in Lamm and Nordström, eds, *Vendel Period Studies*, 124–6.

22. See Ole Crumlin-Pedersen, 'Boat-burials at Slusegaard and the interpretation of the boat-grave custom', in *The Ship as Symbol in Prehistoric and Medieval Scandinavia*, eds Ole Crumlin-Pedersen and Birgitte Munch Thye, Copenhagen: National Museum, 1995, 87–99 and the contribution of Michael Müller-Wille to the same volume, pp.101–9.

23. See, as an interim report, Martin Carver, *Sutton Hoo: Burial Ground of Kings?* London: British Museum, 1998.

24. Carver, *Sutton Hoo*, 136.

25. Bede, *Ecclesiastical History* 2.15.

26. But see Alan M. Stahl, 'The nature of the Sutton Hoo coin parcel', in *Voyage to the Other World: The Legacy of Sutton Hoo*, eds Calvin B. Kendall and Peter S. Wells, Minneapolis: University of Minnesota Press, 1992, 3–14.

27. Gregory of Tours, *History* 6.46.

28. Fredegar 4.74; Wallace-Hadrill, 63.

29. Gregory of Tours, *History* 6.42.

30. Fredegar 4.73.

31. Gregory of Tours, *History* 4.14.

32. Gregory of Tours, *History* 3.11; Thorpe, 171.

NOTES

33. See Walter Goffart, 'Old and new in Merovingian taxation', *Past and Present* 96 (1982), 3–21.
34. Gregory of Tours, *History* 5.28; Thorpe, 291–2.
35. Gregory of Tours, *History* 5.34; Thorpe, 287–98.
36. Gregory of Tours, *History* 9.30.
37. Ian N. Wood, *The Merovingian Kingdoms, 450–751.* London: Longman, 1994, 63.
38. Gregory of Tours, *History*, 3.36; for his long administrative career, see *PLRE* 2, 833–4.
39. Gregory of Tours, *History* 7.15; Thorpe, 399.
40. *Lex Romana Burgundionum* 40; quoted in the context of a discussion of these cases in Goffart, 'Old and new', 14.
41. Goffart, 'Old and new', 14 and 16.
42. *Pactus Legis Salicae* 10.6–7; Drew, *Laws of the Salian Franks*, 75.
43. *Pactus Legis Salicae* 10.1; Drew, *Laws of the Salian Franks*, 74.
44. See the scale laid down in the early seventh-century Frankish *Lex Ribvaria*, 40.11: *MGH* Leges, Sectio 1, 3.2, 94.
45. Tacitus, *Germania* 21.1; Rives, 86.
46. See Robert Bartlett, *Trial by Fire and Water: The Medieval Judicial Ordeal.* Oxford: Clarendon, 1986.
47. Gregory of Tours, *Glory of the Martyrs* 80; Van Dam, 104–5.
48. See Rebecca V. Colman, 'The abduction of women in barbaric law', *Florilegium* 5 (1983), 62–75.
49. Æthelbert 82; Attenborough, *Laws of the Earliest English Kings*, 14–15.
50. II Cnut 74; Robertson, *Laws of the Kings of England*, 212–13.
51. Colman, 'Abduction', 71.
52. Kenneth H. Jackson, *The Oldest Irish Tradition: A Window on the Iron Age.* Cambridge: Cambridge University Press, 1964.
53. Binchy, Daniel A. *Corpus iuris hibernici.* Dublin: Dublin Institute for Advanced Studies, 1978. On which, see now Liam Breatnach, *A Companion to the Corpus Iuris Hibernici.* Dublin: Dublin Institute for Advanced Studies, 2005.
54. Fergus Kelly, *A Guide to Early Irish Law.* Dublin: Dublin Institute for Advanced Studies, 1988.
55. Kelly, *Guide*, 28.
56. Kelly, *Guide*, 214.
57. Kelly, *Guide*, 112–16.
58. There is a discussion of this in James, *Origins of France*, 84–6.
59. Gregory, *History* 6.46.

Chapter Twelve

1. Patrick Geary, *The Myth of Nations: The Medieval Origins of Europe.* Princeton, NJ: Princeton University Press, 2002, 13.
2. On the last page of André Piganiol, *L'Empire chrétien, 325–395.* Paris: Presses Universitaires de France, 1947.
3. On this see Edward James, 'The rise and function of the concept "late antiquity"', *Journal of Late Antiquity* 1, 2008, 20–30.

BIBLIOGRAPHY

Primary Sources

The Abinnaeus Archive: Papers of a Roman Officer in the Reign of Constantius II, eds H.I. Bell, V. Martin, E.G. Turner, D. Van Berchem. Oxford: Clarendon Press, 1962.

Agathias: *The Histories of Agathias*, trans. Joseph D. Frendo. Berlin and New York: Walter De Gruyter, 1975.

Alcuin of York, trans. Stephen Allott. York: Sessions, 1974.

Aldhelm: The Prose Works, trans. Michael Lapidge and Michael Herren. Ipswich and Cambridge: D.S. Brewer, 1979.

Ammianus Marcellinus: History, trans. John C. Rolfe, 3 vols, revised ed. Loeb Classical Library. London: William Heinemann, 1950–2.

The Anglo-Saxon Chronicles, trans. Michael Swanton, 2nd ed. London: Phoenix, 2000.

Anglo-Saxon Poetry, trans. S.A.J. Bradley. Everyman's Library. London: Dent, 1982.

Anonymus Valesianus (or *Excerpta Valesiana*): in *Ammianus Marcellinus: History*, vol. 3, trans. John C. Rolfe, revised ed. Loeb Classical Library. London: William Heinemann, 1952, 506–69.

Augustine: Concerning the City of God against the Pagans, trans. Henry Bettenson. Harmondsworth: Penguin, 1972.

Ausonius, trans. Hugh G. Evelyn White, 2 vols. Loeb Classical Library. London: William Heinemann, 1919, 1921.

Avitus of Vienne: Letters and Selected Prose, trans. Danuta Shanzer and Ian Wood. TTH 38. Liverpool: Liverpool University Press, 2002.

Bede's Ecclesiastical History of the English People, trans. Bertram Colgrave and R.A.B. Mynors. Oxford: Clarendon Press, 1969.

Beowulf: A Verse Translation, trans. Seamus Heaney, ed. Daniel Donoghue. Norton Critical Edition. New York: Norton, 2002.

Boniface: *The Letters of Saint Boniface*, trans. Ephraim Emerton. New York: Columbia University Press, 1940.

The Burgundian Code, trans. Katherine Fischer Drew. Philadelphia: University of Pennsylvania Press, 1949.

Caesar: The Gallic War, trans. H.J. Edwards. Loeb Classical Library. London: William Heinemann, 1917.

Caesarius of Arles: Life, Testament, Letters, trans. William E. Klingshirn. TTH 19. Liverpool: Liverpool University Press, 1994.

Saint Caesarius of Arles, Sermons III (187–238), trans. M.M. Mueller. Washington, DC: Catholic University of America Press, 1973.

Les Canons des Conciles Mérovingiens (VIe–VIIe Siècles), trans. Jean Gaudemet and Brigitte Basdevant. Sources Chrétiennes, 354. Paris: Éditions du Cerf, 1989.

Cassiodorus: *The Variae of Magnus Aurelius Cassiodorus Senator*, trans. S.J.B. Barnish. TTH 12. Liverpool: Liverpool University Press, 1992.

Chronicle of 754, in *Conquerors and Chroniclers of Early Medieval Spain*, trans. Kenneth Baxter Wolf, 2nd ed. TTH 9. Liverpool: Liverpool University Press, 1999, 111–60.

Claudian, trans. Maurice Platnauer, 2 vols. Loeb Classical Library. London: William Heinemann, 1956.

Claudian's Panegyric on the Fourth Consulate of Honorius: Introduction, Text, Translation and Commentary, trans. William Barr. Liverpool: Francis Cairns, 1981.

Constantius, *The Life of St Germanus*, in *The Western Fathers*, trans. F.R. Hoare. London and New York: Sheed and Ward, 1954, 283–320; reprinted in *Soldiers of Christ*, 75–106.

Corippus, *In Praise of Justin II*; *Flavius Cresconius Corippus: In Laudem Iustini Augusti Minoris Libri IV*, trans. Averil Cameron. London: Athlone Press, 1976.

Decrees of the Ecumenical Councils, Volume One, Nicaea I to Lateran V, ed. Norman P. Tanner. London: Sheed and Ward, and Washington, DC: Georgetown University Press, 1990.

Eddius: *The Life of Bishop Wilfrid by Eddius Stephanus*, trans. Bertram Colgrave. Cambridge: Cambridge University Press, 1927.

Einhard, *Life of Charlemagne*, in *Einhard and Notker the Stammerer: Two Lives of Charlemagne*, trans. Lewis Thorpe. Penguin Classics. Harmondsworth: Penguin, 1969.

Ennodius, *Life of St Epiphanius*, trans. Genevieve Mary Cook, in R.K. Deferrari, ed., *Early Christian Biographies*. Fathers of the Church 15. New York: Fathers of the Church Inc., 1952.

Eugippius: The Life of Saint Severin, trans. Ludwig Bieler, with Ludmilla Brestan. Fathers of the Church, 55. Washington, DC: Catholic University of America Press, 1965.

Eunapius: *History*: trans. in R.C. Blockley, *The Fragmentary Classicising Historians of the later Roman Empire: Eunapius, Olympiodorus, Priscus and Malchus*, vol. 2. ARCA Classical and Medieval Texts, Papers and Monographs 10. Liverpool: Francis Cairns, 1983, 1–150.

Eusebius, *Tricennial Orations*, trans. H.A. Drake, *In Praise of Constantine: A Historical Study and New Translation of Eusebius' Tricennial Orations*. Los Angeles: University of California Press, 1975.

Fredegar, *Chronicle*, extracts from Books 1–3, trans. in *From Roman to Merovingian Gaul*, 591–4 and 597–621.

Fredegar: *The Fourth Book of the Chronicle of Fredegar*, trans. J.M. Wallace-Hadrill. Nelson's Medieval Texts. London and New York: Nelson, 1960.

From Roman to Merovingian Gaul, trans. Alexander Callander Murray, Peterborough, ON: Broadview, 2000.

Gallic Chronicle of 452, trans. in *From Roman to Merovingian Gaul*, 76–85.

Gallic Chronicle of 511, trans. in *From Roman to Merovingian Gaul*, 98–108.

Genovefa, Life of. In Sainted Women of the Dark Ages, trans. Jo Ann McNamara and John E. Halborg, with E. Gordan Whatley. Durham, NC and London: Duke University Press, 1992, 17–37.

Gildas: The Ruin of Britain and Other Documents, trans. Michael Winterbottom. Arthurian Period Sources 7. London and Chichester: Phillimore, 1978.

Gregory Thaumaturgus: *Canonical Letter*, trans. in Peter Heather and John Matthews, eds, *The Goths in the Fourth Century*. TTH 11. Liverpool: Liverpool University Press, 1991, 5–11.

Gregory of Tours: Glory of the Martyrs, trans. Raymond Van Dam. TTH 3. Liverpool: Liverpool University Press, 1988.

Gregory of Tours: History of the Franks, trans. Lewis Thorpe. Penguin Classics. Harmondsworth: Penguin, 1974.

Herodian's History. Herodian in Two Volumes, trans. C.R. Whittaker. Loeb Classical Library. London: Heinemann, 1969–70.

Hydatius: *The* Chronicle *of Hydatius and the* Consularia Constantinopolitana: *Two Contemporary Accounts of the Final Years of the Roman Empire*, ed. and trans. R.W. Burgess, Oxford: Clarendon Press, 1993.

Ireland, S. *Roman Britain; A Sourcebook*, 2nd ed. London: Routledge 1986.

Isidore: *The* Etymologies *of Isidore of Seville*, trans. Stephen A. Barney, W.J. Lewis, J.A. Beach and Oliver Berghof. Cambridge: Cambridge University Press, 2006.

Isidore of Seville's History of the Kings of the Goths, Vandals and Sueves, trans. Guido Donini and Gordon B. Ford, Jr. Leiden: Brill, 1966.

Jerome: Select Letters, trans. F.A. Wright. Loeb Classical Library. Cambridge, MA: Harvard University Press, 1933.

John of Biclaro, *Chronicle*; in *Conquerors and Chroniclers of Early Medieval Spain*, trans. Kenneth Baxter Wolf, 2nd ed. TTH 9. Liverpool: Liverpool University Press, 57–77.

Jordanes: *The Gothic History of Jordanes*, trans. Charles Christopher Mierow. 2nd ed. Princeton, NJ: Princeton University Press, 1915.

Laterculus Veronensis, ed. Otto Seeck, in *Notitia Dignitatum accedunt Notitia Urbis Constantinopolitanae et Laterculi Prouinciarum*. Berlin: Weidmann, 1876, 251–2.

Laws of the Earliest English Kings, The, trans. F.L. Attenborough. Cambridge: Cambridge University Press, 1922.

Laws of the Kings of England from Edmund to Henry I: Part I. Edmund to Canute, trans. A.J. Robertson. Cambridge: Cambridge University Press, 1925.

The Laws of the Salian Franks, trans. Katherine Fischer Drew. Philadelphia: University of Pennsylvania Press, 1991.

Libanius: *Antioch as a Centre of Hellenic Culture as Observed by Libanius*, trans. A.F. Norman. TTH 34. Liverpool: Liverpool University Press, 2000.

Liber Historiae Francorum, trans. Bernard S. Bachrach. Lawrence, KS: Coronado, 1973.

Liber Pontificalis: *The Book of Pontiffs (Liber Pontificalis): The Ancient Biographies of the First Ninety Roman Bishops to AD 715*, trans. Raymond Davis, revised ed. TTH 6. Liverpool: Liverpool University Press, 2000.

Livy, trans. B.O. Foster, 5 vols. Loeb Classical Library. London: William Heinemann, 1919–29.

Malalas: *The Chronicle of John Malalas*, trans. Elizabeth Jeffreys, Michael Jeffreys and Roger Scott. Byzantina Australiensia 4. Melbourne: Australian Association for Byzantine Studies, 1986.

Marcellinus Comes: *The Chronicle of Marcellinus*, trans. Brian Croke. Byzantina Australiensia 7. Sydney: Australian Association for Byzantine Studies, 1995.

Maurice's Strategikon: Handbook of Byzantine Military Strategy, trans. George T. Dennis. Philadephia: University of Pennsylvania Press, 1984.

Menander: *The History of Menander the Guardsman*, trans. R.C. Blockley. ARCA Classical and Medieval Texts, Papers and Monographs 17. Liverpool: Francis Cairns, 1985.

Merobaudes: trans. F.M. Clover, 'Flavius Merobaudes: a translation and historical commentary', *Transactions of the American Philosophical Society*, New Series 61 (1971), 1–78.

Montaigne, Michel de: 'On Cannibals' in *Montaigne: Essays*, trans. J.M. Cohen. Harmondsworth: Penguin, 1958.

Olympiodorus: as 'Eunapius' above, 151–220.

Orosius: *Seven Books of History Against the Pagans: The Apology of Paulus Orosius*, trans. Irving Woodworth Raymond. New York: Columbia University Press, 1936.

Panegyrics: *In Praise of Later Roman Emperors: The Panegyrici Latini*, trans. C.E.V. Nixon and Barbara Saylor Rogers. Transformation of the Classical Heritage, 21. Berkeley: University of California Press, 1994.

Patrick: *St Patrick: His Writings and Muirchu's Life*, trans. A.B.E. Hood. Arthurian Period Sources 9. London and Chichester: Phillimore, 1978.

Paul the Deacon: History of the Lombards, trans. William Dudley Foulke. Philadelphia: University of Pennsylvania Press, 1907.

Paulinus, *Life of St Ambrose*, in *The Western Fathers*, trans. F.R. Hoare. London and New York: Sheed and Ward, 1954, 147–88.

Paulinus of Nola: *Letters of St Paulinus of Nola*, trans. P.G. Walsh, 2 vols. Ancient Christian Writers 35 and 36. Westminster, MD: Newman Press, 1967.

Paulinus of Nola: *The Poems of St Paulinus of Nola*, trans. P.G. Walsh. Ancient Christian Writers 40. New York: Newman Press, 1975.

Paulinus of Pella, *Eucharisticus*, trans. Hugh G. Evelyn White, see *Ausonius*, above, 2, 295–351.

Pliny: Natural History, trans. H. Rackham, W.H.S. Jones and D.E. Eichholz, 10 vols. Loeb Classical Library. London: William Heinemann, 1938–62.

Plutarch, *Life of Crassus*, in *Plutarch's Lives*, trans. Bernadotte Perrin, vol. 3. Loeb Classical Library. London: William Heinemann, 1916, 314–423.

Priscus: as 'Eunapius' above, 221–400.

Procopius: The Anecdota or Secret History, trans. H.B. Dewing, as vol. 6 of the 7-volume Loeb Classical Library edition of Procopius. London: William Heinemann, 1935.

Procopius: History of the Wars, trans. H.B. Dewing, 5 vols. Loeb Classical Library. London: William Heinemann, 1914–28.

Procopius: On Buildings, trans. H.B. Dewing, as vol. 7 of the 7-volume Loeb Classical Library edition of Procopius. London: William Heinemann, 1940.

Prosper of Aquitaine, *Chronicle*, trans. in *From Roman to Merovingian Gaul*, 62–76.

The Russian Primary Chronicle: Laurentian Text, trans. Samuel Hazzard Cross and Olgerd P. Sherbowitz-Wetzor. Cambridge, MA: Medieval Academy of America, 1953.

Rutilius Namatianus, *A Voyage Home to Gaul* [*De Reditu Suo*], trans. in J.W. Duff and A.M. Duff, eds, *Minor Latin Poets*. Loeb Classical Library. London: William Heinemann, 1934, 764–829.

Salvian: *The Writings of Salvian the Presbyter*, trans. Jeremiah O'Sullivan. Fathers of the Church 3. New York: Cima, 1947.

The Scriptores Historiae Augustae, trans. David Magie, 3 vols. Loeb Classical Library. London: William Heinemann, 1921–32.

Sidonius Apollinaris: *Sidonius: Poems and Letters*, trans. W.B. Anderson, 2 vols. Loeb Classical Library. London: William Heinemann, 1935, 1965.

Soldiers of Christ: Saints and Saints' Lives from Late Antiquity and the Early Middle Ages, eds Thomas F.X. Noble and Thomas Head. London: Sheed and Ward, and University Park: Pennsylvania State University Press, 1995.

Sozomen: *The Ecclesiastical History of Sozomen*, trans. Charles D. Hartranft, in *A Select Library of Nicene and Post-Nicene Fathers of the Christian Church*, 2nd series, vol. 2, reprinted. Grand Rapids, MI: Eerdmans, 1969, 237–427.

Strabo: *The Geography of Strabo*, trans. H.L. Jones, 8 vols. Loeb Classical Library. London: William Heinemann, 1917–32.

Sulpicius Severus, *The Life of St Martin*, in *The Western Fathers*, trans. F.R. Hoare. London and New York: Sheed and Ward, 1954, 1–44; reprinted in *Soldiers of Christ*, 1–30.

Symmachus: *Symmaque: Letters, Livres I–II*, ed. and trans. Jean-Pierre Callu. Paris: Les Belles Lettres, 1972.

Synesius of Cyrene: *The Essays and Hymns of Synesius of Cyrene*, trans. Augustine Fitzgerald, 2 vols. London: Oxford University Press, 1930.

Tacitus: Agricola, trans. M. Hutton, revised by R.M. Ogilvie, in *Tacitus: Agricola, Germania, Dialogus*. Loeb Classical Library. William Heinemann, 1970.

Tacitus: Annals, trans. John Jackson, in *Tacitus, Histories, Books IV–V; Annals, Books I–III*. Loeb Classical Library. London: William Heinemann, 1930.

Tacitus: Germania, trans. J.R. Rives. Oxford: Clarendon, 1999.

Themistius: Orations 8 and 10, trans. David Moncur, in Peter Heather and John Matthews, *The Goths in the Fourth Century*. TTH 11. Liverpool: Liverpool University Press, 1991, 26–50.

Themistius: *Politics, Philosophy, and the Empire in the Fourth Century: Select Orations of Themistius*, trans. Peter Heather and David Moncur. TTH 36. Liverpool: Liverpool University Press, 2001.

Theodoret: Church History, Dialogues, and Letters, trans. Blomfield Jackson, in *A Select Library of Nicene and Post-Nicene Fathers of the Christian Church*, 2nd series, vol. 3, reprinted. Grand Rapids, MI: Eerdmans, 1969, 33–159.

The Theodosian Code and Novels and the Sirmondian Constitutions, trans. Clyde Pharr. Princeton, NJ: Princeton University Press, 1952.

Tribal Hidage, see in Wendy Davies and Hayo Vierck, 'The contents of the Tribal Hidage: Social aggregates and settlement patterns', *Frühmittelatterliche Studien* 8 (1974), 223–93.

Uraicecht na Ríar: The Poetic Grades in Early Irish Law, trans. Liam Breatnach. Dublin: Dublin Institute for Advanced Studies, 1987.

Vegetius: Epitome of Military Science, trans. N.P. Milner, 2nd ed. TTH 16. Liverpool: Liverpool University Press, 1996.

Venantius Fortunatus; Personal and Political Poems, trans. Judith George. TTH 23. Liverpool: Liverpool University Press, 1995.

Victor of Vita: History of the Vandal Persecution, trans. John Moorhead. TTH 10. Liverpool: Liverpool University Press, 1992.

The Visigothic Code, trans. S.P. Scott. Boston: Boston Book Co., 1910; available at http://libro.uca.edu/vcode/visigoths.htm, accessed 27.10.08.

Zosimus: New History, trans. Ronald T. Ridley. Byzantina Australiensis 2. Sydney: Australian Association for Byzantine Studies, 1982.

Secondary Sources

Ahrens, Claus, ed. *Sachsen und Angelsachsen*, Veröffentlichungn des Helms-Museums, 32. Hamburg: Helms-Museum, 1978.

Alföldy, Géza. *Noricum*, The Provinces of the Roman Empire. London and Boston: Routledge and Kegan Paul, 1974.

———. 'The crisis of the third century as seen by contemporaries', *Greek, Roman and Byzantine Studies* 15 (1974), 89–111.

Allen, Pauline and Jeffreys, Elizabeth, eds. *The Sixth Century: End or Beginning?*, Byzantina Australiensia 10. Brisbane: Australian Association for Byzantine Studies, 1996.

Almagor, Eran. 'Who is a barbarian? The barbarians in the ethnological and cultural taxonomies of Strabo', in *Strabo's Cultural Geography. The Making of a Kolossourgia*, edited by Daniela Dueck, Hugh Lindsay and Sarah Pothecary. Cambridge: Cambridge University Press, 2005, 42–55.

Ament, Hermann. 'Der Rhein und die Ethnogenese der Germanen', *Prähistorische Zeitschrift* 59 (1984), 37–51.

Amory, Patrick. 'The meaning and purpose of ethnic terminology in the Burgundian laws', *Early Medieval Europe* 2 (1993), 1–28.

———. 'Ethnographic rhetoric, aristocratic attitudes and political allegiance in post-Roman Gaul', *Klio* 76 (1994), 438–53.

———. 'Names, ethnic identity, and community in fifth- and sixth-century Burgundy', *Viator* 25 (1994), 1–30.

———. *People and Identity in Ostrogothic Italy, 489–554*. Cambridge: Cambridge University Press, 1997.

Anderson, Benedict. *Imagined Communities: Reflections on the Origin and Spread of Nationalism*. London: Verso, 1983.

Anderson, T. 'Roman military colonists in Gaul, Salian ethnogenesis and the forgotten meaning of *Pactus Legis Salicae* 59.5', *Early Medieval Europe* 4 (1995), 129–44.

Anton, Hans Hubert. 'Origo gentis–Volksgeschichte: Zur Auseinandersetzung mit Walter Goffarts Werk "The Narrators of Barbarian History"', in *Historiographie im frühen Mittelalter*, edited by Anton Scharer and Georg Scheibelreiter. Vienna and Munich: R. Oldenbourg, 1994, 262–307.

Arce, Javier. 'The enigmatic fifth century in Hispania: some historical problems', in *Regna and Gentes*, edited by Goetz, Jarnut and Pohl, 2003, 135–59.

———. *Bárbaros y romanos en Hispania, 400–507 A.D.* Madrid: Marcial Pons, 2005.

Arens, W. *The Man-Eating Myth: Anthropology and Anthropophagy.* Oxford and New York: Oxford University Press, 1979.

Arnold, Chris. 'The Anglo-Saxon cemeteries of the Isle of Wight: an appraisal of nineteenth-century excavation data', in *Anglo-Saxon Cemeteries: A Reappraisal*, edited by Edmund Southworth. Stroud: Sutton, 1990, 163–75.

Arrhenius, Birgit. *Merovingian Garnet Jewellery: Emergence and Social Implications.* Stockholm: Kungl. Vitterhets Historie och Antikvitets Akademien, 1985.

Axboe, Morten. 'Amulet pendants and a darkened sun: on the function of the gold bracteates and a possible motivation for the large gold hoards', in *Roman Gold*, edited by Magnus, 2001, 119–36.

———. *Die Goldbrakteaten der Völkerwanderungszeit – Herstellungsprobleme und Chronologie*, Ergänzungsbände zum Reallexikon der Germanischen Altertumskunde 38. Berlin: Walter De Gruyter, 2004.

———, Düwel, K., Hauck, K. and Von Padberg, L., eds. *Die Goldbrakteaten der Völkerwanderungszeit.* 3 vols. Munich: Fink, 1985–9.

Babcock, Michael A. *The Stories of Attila the Hun's Death: Narrative, Myth, and Meaning.* Lewiston, Queenston, Lampeter: Edwin Mellen, 2001.

Bachrach, B.S. 'The Alans in Gaul', *Traditio* 23 (1967), 476–89.

———. 'Another look at the barbarian settlement in southern Gaul', *Traditio* 25 (1969), 354–8.

———. 'Procopius, Agathias and the Frankish military', *Speculum* 45 (1970), 435–41.

———. 'Procopius and the chronology of Clovis's reign', *Viator* 1 (1970), 21–31.

———. *A History of the Alans in the West.* Minneapolis: University of Minnesota Press, 1973.

———. *The Anatomy of a Little War: A Diplomatic and Military History of the Gundovald Affair (568–586).* Boulder, CO: Westview Press, 1994.

———. 'The Hun army at the battle of Chalons (451): an essay in military demography', in *Ethnogenese und Überlieferung*, edited by Brunner and Merta, 1994, 59–67.

Baldwin, B. 'The purpose of the Getica', *Hermes* 107 (1979), 489–92.

———. 'Priscus of Panium', *Byzantion* 50 (1980), 18–61.

———. 'Sources for the *Getica* of Jordanes', *Revue Belge de Philologie et d'Histoire* 59 (1981), 141–5.

Balsdon, J.P.V.D. *Romans and Aliens.* London: Duckworth, 1979.

Barford, P.M. *The Early Slavs: Culture and Society in Early Medieval Eastern Europe*. London: British Museum, 2001.

Barnes, Timothy D. *Ammianus Marcellinus and the Representation of Historical Reality*. Ithaca, NY: Cornell University Press, 1998.

Barnish, S.J.B. 'The Anonymus Valesianus as a source for the last years of Theodoric', *Latomus* 42 (1983), 572–96.

———. 'The genesis and completion of Cassiodorus's Gothic History', *Latomus* 43 (1984), 336–61.

———. 'Taxation, land and barbarian settlement in the Western Empire', *Papers of the British School at Rome* 54 (1986), 170–95.

———. 'Old Kaspars: Attila's invasion of Gaul in the literary sources', in *Fifth-Century Gaul*, edited by Drinkwater and Elton, 1992, 38–48.

——— and Marazzi, Federico, eds. *The Ostrogoths from the Migration Period to the Sixth Century: An Ethnographic Perspective*, Studies in Historical Archaeoethnology, 7. Woodbridge: Boydell and Brewer, 2007.

Barnwell, P.S. *Emperors, Prefects and Kings: The Roman West 395–565*. London: Duckworth, 1992.

———. *Kings, Courtiers and Imperium: The Barbarian West, 565–725*. London: Duckworth, 1997.

Barrett, John C., Fitzpatrick, Andrew P. and Macinnes, Lesley, eds. *Barbarians and Romans in North-West Europe: from the Later Republic to Late Antiquity*, British Archaeological Reports International Series 471. Oxford: BAR, 1989.

Bartlett, Robert. *Trial by Fire and Water: The Medieval Judicial Ordeal*. Oxford: Clarendon, 1986.

———. 'Symbolic meanings of hair in the Middle Ages', *Transactions of the Royal Historical Society*, 6th series 4 1994, 43–60.

Bassett, Steven, ed. *The Origins of Anglo-Saxon Kingdoms*. Leicester: Leicester University Press, 1989.

Beck, Heinrich, ed. *Germanenprobleme in heutiger Sicht*, Ergänzungsbände zum Reallexikon der Germanischen Altertumskunde 1. Berlin and New York: Walter De Gruyter, 1986.

Beck, Heinrich, Ellmers, Detlev and Schier, Kurt, eds. *Germanische Religionsgeschichte: Quellen und Quellenprobleme*, Ergänzungsbände zum Reallexikon der Germanischen Altertumskunde 5. Berlin: Walter De Gruyter, 1992.

Bhreathnach, Edel and Newman, Conor. *Tara*. Dublin: Stationery Office, 1995.

Bierbrauer, Volker. 'Archäologie und Geschichte der Goten vom 1.–7. Jahrhundert. Versuch einer Bilanz', *Frühmittelalterliche Studien* 28 (1994), 51–171.

Bintliff, John, ed. *European Social Evolution: Archaeological Perspectives*. Bradford: University of Bradford, 1984.

——— and Hamerow, Helena, eds. *Europe between Late Antiquity and the Middle Ages: Recent Archaeological and Historical Research in Western and Southern Europe*, British Archaeological Reports International Series 617. Oxford: BAR, 1995.

Birley, Anthony. 'The third-century crisis in the Roman Empire', *Bulletin of the John Rylands Library* 58 (1976), 253–81.

———. *Marcus Aurelius: A Biography.* 2nd ed. London: Batsford, 1987.

Blair, John. 'Anglo-Saxon pagan shrines and their prototypes', *Anglo-Saxon Studies in Archaeology and History* 8 (1995), 1–28.

Blockley, R.C. 'Roman-barbarian marriages in the late Empire', *Florilegium* 4 (1982), 63–79.

Boak, A.E.R. *Manpower Shortage and the Fall of the Roman Empire in the West.* Ann Arbor: University of Michigan Press, 1955.

Böhme, H.W. *Germanische Grabfünde des vierten bis fünften Jahrhunderts zwischen unteren Elbe und Loire.* Munich, 1974.

———. 'Das Ende der Römerherrschaft in Britannien und der angelsächsischen Besiedlung Englands in 5. Jahrhundert', *Jahrbuch der Römisch-Germanische Zentralmuseum, Mainz* 33 (1986), 466–574.

Bóna, István. *The Dawn of the Dark Ages: The Gepids and the Lombards in the Carpathian Basin.* Budapest: Corvina, 1976.

———. *Les Huns: Le grand empire barbare d'Europe, IVe-Ve siècles.* Translated by Katalin Escher. Paris: Errance, 2002.

Borg, Kaj, Näsman, Ulf and Wegraeus, Erik. *Eketorp: Fortification and Settlement on Öland/Sweden. The Monument.* Stockholm: Almqvist and Wiksell, 1976.

Borst, Arno. *Barbaren, Ketzer und Artisten: Welten des Mittelalters.* Munich and Zurich: Piper, 1988.

Bowersock, G.W., Brown, Peter and Grabar, Oleg. *Late Antiquity: A Guide to the Postclassical World.* Cambridge, MA: Belknap Press of Harvard University Press, 1999.

Bowlus, Charles E. 'Ethnogenesis: the tyranny of a concept', in *On Barbarian Identity*, edited by Gillett, 2002, 242–56.

Bowman, A.K. *Life and Letters on the Roman Frontier: Vindolanda and its People.* London: British Museum, 1994.

Brather, Sebastian. *Archäologie der westlichen Slawen. Siedlung, Wirtschaft und Gesellschaft im früh- und hochmittelalterlichen Ostmitteleuropa*, Ergänzungsbände zum Reallexicon der Germanischen Altertumskunde 30. Berlin: Walter De Gruyter, 2001.

———. 'Ethnic images as constructions of archaeology: the case of the *Alamanni*', in *On Barbarian Identity*, edited by Gillett, 2002, 149–75.

———. *Ethnische Interpretationen in der frühgeschichtlichen Archäologie: Geschichte, Grundlagen und Alternativen*, Ergänzungsbände zum Reallexikon der Germanischen Altertumskunde 42. Berlin: Walter De Gruyter, 2004.

———. 'Acculturation and ethnogenesis along the frontier: Rome and the ancient Germans in an archaeological perspective', in *Borders, Barriers*, edited by Curta, 2005, 139–72.

Braund, David. *Rome and the Friendly King: The Character of the Client Kingship.* London and Canberra: Croom Helm, 1984.

———. 'Ideology, subsidies and trade: the king on the northern frontier revisited', in *Barbarians and Romans*, edited by Barrett, Fitzpatrick and Macinnes, 1989, 14–23.

Breatnach, Liam. *A Companion to the Corpus Iuris Hibernici*, Early Irish Law 5. Dublin: Dublin Institute for Advanced Studies, 2005.

Brogiolo, Gian Pietro and Ward-Perkins, Bryan, eds. *The Idea and Ideal of the Town between Late Antiquity and the Early Middle Ages*, The Transformation of the Roman World 4. Leiden: Brill, 1999.

Brogiolo, Gian Pietro, Gauthier, Nancy and Christie, Neil, eds. *Towns and their Territories between Late Antiquity and the Early Middle Ages*, The Transformation of the Roman World 9. Leiden: Brill, 2000.

Bruce-Mitford, R.L.S. and Bruce-Mitford, M. 'The Sutton Hoo lyre, Beowulf, and the origins of the frame harp', *Antiquity* 44 (1970), 7–13.

Bruce-Mitford, R.L.S., ed. *The Sutton Hoo Ship-Burial*, 3 vols. London: British Museum Press, 1975–83.

Brulet, Raymond. 'La sépulture du roi Childéric à Tournai et le site funéraire', in *La Noblesse romaine*, edited by Vallet and Kazanski, 1995, 309–26.

Brun, Patrice, Leeuw, Sander van der, and Whittaker, Charles R., eds. *Frontières d'Empire. Nature et signification des frontières romaines*, Mémoires du Musée de Préhistoire d'Ile-de-France 5. Nemours: Association pour la Promotion de la Recherche Archéologique en Ile-de-France, 1993.

Brunner, Karl and Brigitte, Merta, eds. *Ethnogenese und Überlieferung: Angewandte Methoden der Frühmittelalterforschung.* Vienna and Munich: Oldenbourg, 1994.

Bullough, D.A. 'Burial, community and belief in the early medieval West', in *Ideal and Reality*, edited by Wormald, Bullough and Collins, 1983, 177–201.

Burgess, R.W. 'Hydatius and the final frontier: the fall of the Roman Empire and the end of the world', in *Shifting Frontiers*, edited by Mathisen and Sivan, 1996, 321–32.

———. 'The Gallic Chronicle of 452: a new critical edition with a brief introduction', in *Society and Culture*, edited by Mathisen and Shanzer, 2001, 52–84.

———. 'The Gallic Chronicle of 511: a new critical edition with a brief introduction', in *Society and Culture*, edited by Mathisen and Shanzer, 2001, 85–100.

Burns, T.S. *The Ostrogoths: Kingship and Society*, Historia Einzelschriften 36. Wiesbaden: Steiner, 1980.

———. *A History of the Ostrogoths.* Bloomington: Indiana University Press, 1984.

———. 'The settlement of 418', in *Fifth-Century Gaul*, edited by Drinkwater and Elton, 1992, 53–63.

———. *Barbarians within the Gates of Rome. A Study of Roman Military Policy and the Barbarians, ca 375–425 AD.* Bloomington: Indiana University Press, 1994.

———. *Rome and the Barbarians, 100 B.C.–A.D. 400.* Bloomington: Indiana University Press, 2003.

Bursche, Aleksander. 'Roman gold medallions as power symbols of the Germanic élite', in *Roman Gold*, edited by Magnus, 2001, 83–102.

Bury, J.B. *History of the Later Roman Empire from the Death of Theodosius I to the Death of Justinian.* London: Macmillan, 1923.

Cain, Andrew. 'Miracles, martyrs, and Arians: Gregory of Tours' sources for his account of the Vandal kingdom', *Vigiliae Christianae* 59 (2005), 412–37.

Cameron, Alan. *Claudian: Poetry and Propaganda at the Court of Honorius*. Oxford: Clarendon, 1970.

Cameron, Alan, Long, Jacqueline and Sherry, Lee. *Barbarians and Politics at the Court of Arcadius*, The Transformation of the Classical Heritage 19. Berkeley: University of California Press, 1993.

Cameron, Averil. 'Agathias on the Early Merovingians', *Annali della Scuola Normale Superiore de Pisa* 2nd series 37 (1968), 95–140.

———. *Procopius and the Sixth Century*. London: Duckworth, 1985.

———. *Christianity and the Rhetoric of Empire*. Berkeley: University of California Press, 1991.

———. *The Later Roman Empire, AD 284–430*. London: Fontana, 1993.

———. *The Mediterranean World in Late Antiquity, AD 395–600*. London: Routledge, 1993.

——— and Garnsey, Peter, eds. *The Cambridge Ancient History, XIII. The Late Empire, A.D. 337–425*. Cambridge: Cambridge University Press, 1998.

———, Ward-Perkins, Bryan and Whitby, Michael, eds. *The Cambridge Ancient History, XIV. Late Antiquity. Empire and Successors, AD 425–600*. Cambridge: Cambridge University Press, 2000.

Campbell, James. *Bede's Reges and Principes*, Jarrow Lecture. Jarrow: St Paul's Church, 1979.

Carew, Mairéad. *Tara and the Ark of the Covenant: A Search for the Ark of the Covenant by British Israelites on the Hill of Tara (1899–1902)*. Dublin: The Discovery Programme/Royal Irish Academy, 2003.

Carnap-Bornheim, Claus von. 'The social position of the Germanic goldsmith AD 0–500', in *Roman Gold*, edited by Magnus, 2001, 263–78.

Cartledge, Paul. *The Greeks: A Portrait of Self and Others*. Oxford: Oxford University Press, 1993.

Carver, Martin. *Sutton Hoo: Burial Ground of Kings?* London: British Museum, 1998.

Chaney, William A. *The Cult of Kingship in Anglo-Saxon England: The Transition from Paganism to Christianity*. Manchester: Manchester University Press, 1970.

Charanis, Peter. 'The transfer of population as a policy in the Byzantine Empire', *Comparative Studies in Society and History* 3 (1961), 140–54.

Charles-Edwards, T.M. 'Early medieval kingships in the British Isles', in *Origins*, edited by Bassett, 1989, 28–39.

———. *Early Christian Ireland*. Cambridge: Cambridge University Press, 2004.

Chastagnol, André. 'La signification géographique et ethnique des mots *Germani* et *Germania* dans les sources latines', *Ktèma: Civilisations de l'Orient, de la Grèce et de Rome antique* 9 (1984), 97–101.

Chauvot, Alain. 'Représentations du Barbaricum chez les barbares au service de l'Empire au IVe siècle après J.-C.' *Ktèma. Civilisations de l'Orient, de la Grèce et de Rome antique* 9 (1984), 145–57.

————. *Opinions romaines face aux barbares au IVe siècle ap. J.-C.* Paris: De Boccard, 1998.

Christensen, Arne Søby. *Cassiodorus, Jordanes and the History of the Goths: Studies in a Migration Myth.* Copenhagen: Museum Tusculanum/University of Copenhagen, 2002.

Christie, Neil. *The Lombards: The Ancient Longobards,* The Peoples of Europe. Oxford: Blackwell, 1995.

————. 'Towns and peoples on the Middle Danube in late Antiquity and the early Middle Ages', in *Towns in Transition,* edited by Christie and Loseby, 1996, 71–98.

————. 'Towns, land and power: German-Roman survivals and interactions in fifth- and sixth-century Pannonia', in *Towns and their Territories,* edited by Brogiolo, Gauthier and Christie, 2000, 275–97.

———— and Loseby, S.T., eds. *Towns in Transition: Urban Evolution in Late Antiquity and the Early Middle Ages.* Aldershot: Scolar, 1996.

Christlein, Rainer. *Die Alamannen: Archäologie eines lebendigen Volkes.* 2nd ed. Stuttgart: Theiss, 1979.

Chrysos, Evangelos. 'Legal concepts and patterns for the barbarians' settlement on Roman soil', in *Das Reich und die Barbaren,* edited by Chrysos and Schwarcz, 1989, 13–23.

———— and Schwarcz, Andreas, eds. *Das Reich und die Barbaren,* Veröffentlichungen des Instituts für österreichische Geschichtsforschung 29. Vienna: Böhlau, 1989.

Clarke, G.W., ed. *Identities in the Eastern Mediterranean in Antiquity,* Mediterranean Archaeology 11. Sydney: Meditarch, 1998.

Clarke, Katherine. *Between Geography and History: Hellenistic Constructions of the Roman World.* Oxford: Oxford University Press, 1999.

Claude, Dietrich. *Geschichte der Westgoten.* Stuttgart: Kohlhammer, 1970.

————. 'Zur Ansiedlung barbarischer Föderaten in der ersten Hälfte des 5. Jahrhunderts', in *Anerkennung und Integration,* edited by Wolfram and Schwarcz. Vienna, 1988, 13–16.

————. 'Zur Begründung familiärer Beziehungen zwischen dem Kaiser und barbarischenm Herrschen', in *Das Reich und die Barbaren,* edited by Chrysos and Schwarcz, 1988, 25–56.

Clover, Frank M. 'Geiseric and Attila', *Historia* 22 (1973), 104–17.

————. 'The symbiosis of Romans and Vandals in Africa', in *Das Reich und die Barbaren,* edited by Chrysos and Schwarcz, 1989, 57–73.

————. *The Late Roman West and the Vandals,* Collected Studies 401. Aldershot: Variorum, 1994.

Colley, Linda. *Britons: Forging the Nation, 1707–1837.* New Haven, CT and London: Yale University Press, 1992.

Collins, Roger. *The Basques,* The Peoples of Europe. Oxford: Blackwell, 1986.

————. *Law, Culture and Regionalism in Early Medieval Spain,* Collected Studies 356. Aldershot: Variorum, 1992.

————. 'Law and ethnic identity in the western kingdoms in the fifth and sixth centuries', in *Medieval Europeans: Studies in Ethnic Identity and National*

Perspectives in Medieval Europe, edited by Alfred P. Smyth. Basingstoke: Macmillan, 1998, 1–23.

Colman, Rebecca V. 'The abduction of women in barbaric law', *Florilegium* 5 (1983), 62–75.

Corradini, Richard, Diesenberger, Max and Reimitz, Helmut, eds. *The Construction of Communities in the Early Middle Ages: Texts, Resources and Artefacts*, The Transformation of the Roman World 12. Leiden: Brill, 2003.

Corradini, Richard, Meens, Rob, Pössel, Christina and Shaw, Philip, eds. *Texts and Identities in the Early Middle Ages*, Forschungen zur Geschichte des Mittelalters 12. Vienna: Verlag der Österreichischen Akademie der Wissenschaften, 2006.

Courcelle, Pierre. *Histoire littéraire des grandes invasions germaniques*. 3rd ed. Paris: Études Augustiniennes, 1964.

Courtois, Christian. *Les Vandales et l'Afrique*. Paris: Arts et Métiers Graphiques, 1955.

Croke, Brian. 'Mundo the Gepid: from freebooter to Roman general', *Chiron* 12 (1982), 125–35.

———. 'AD 476: the manufacture of a turning point', *Chiron* 13 (1983), 81–119.

———. *Christian Chronicles and Byzantine History, 5th–6th centuries*, Collected Studies 386. Aldershot: Variorum, 1992.

———. *Count Marcellinus and his Chronicle*. Oxford: Oxford University Press, 2001.

———. 'Dynasty and ethnicity: Emperor Leo I and the eclipse of Aspar', *Chiron* 34 (2005), 147–203.

Crubézy, Eric. 'Merovingian skull deformations in the south-west of France', in *From the Baltic to the Black Sea: Studies in Medieval Archaeology*, edited by David Austin and Leslie Alcock. London: Unwin Hyman, 1990, 189–208.

Crumlin-Pedersen, Ole. 'Boat-burials at Slusegaard and the interpretation of the boat-grave custom', in *The Ship as Symbol in Prehistoric and Medieval Scandinavia*, edited by Ole Crumlin-Pedersen and Birgitte Munch Thye. Copenhagen: National Museum, 1995, 87–99.

Curta, Florin. 'Slavs in Fredegar and Paul the Deacon: medieval *gens* or "scourge of God"?' *Early Medieval Europe* 6 (1997), 141–67.

———. 'Hiding behind a piece of tapestry: Jordanes and the Slavic Venethi', *Jahrbücher für Geschichte Osteuropas* 47 (1999), 1–18.

———. 'Pots, Slavs and "imagined communities": Slavic archaeologies and the history of the early Slavs', *European Journal of Archaeology* 4 (2001), 367–84.

———. *The Making of the Slavs: History and Archaeology of the Lower Danube Region, c.500–700*. Cambridge: Cambridge University Press, 2001.

———. 'From Kossinna to Bromley: ethnogenesis in Slavic archaeology', in *On Barbarian Identity*, edited by Gillett, 2002, 201–18.

———. 'Before Cyril and Methodius: Christianity and barbarians beyond the sixth- and seventh-century Danube frontier', in *East Central and Eastern Europe*, edited by Curta, 2005, 181–219.

———. 'Frontier ethnogenesis in late antiquity: the Danube, the Tervingi, and the Slavs', in *Borders, Barriers*, edited by Curta, 2005, 173–204.

———. *Southeastern Europe in the Middle Ages, 500–1250*, Cambridge Medieval Textbooks. Cambridge: Cambridge University Press, 2006.

———. 'Some remarks on ethnicity in early medieval archaeology', *Early Medieval Europe* 15 (2007), 159–85.

———. 'The amber trail in early medieval Eastern Europe', in *Paradigms and Methods in Early Medieval Studies*, edited by Felice Lifschitz and Celia Chazelle. New York: Palgrave Macmillan, 2007, 61–79.

———, ed. *Borders, Barriers, and Ethnogenesis: Frontiers in Late Antiquity and the Middle Ages*, Studies in the Early Middle Ages 12. Turnhout: Brepols, 2005.

———, ed. *East Central and Eastern Europe in the Early Middle Ages*. Ann Arbor: University of Michigan Press, 2005.

Dagron, Gilbert. 'Discours utopique et récit des origines: I. Une lecture de Cassiodore-Jordanes: les Goths de Scandza à Ravenne', *Annales: Économies, Sociétés, Civilisations* 26 (1971), 290–305.

Dahmlos, U. 'Francisca, bipennis, securis. Bemerkungen zu archäologischem Befund und schriftlicher Überlieferung (+ Römische, byzantinische und fränkische Quellen)', *Germania* 55 (1977), 141–65.

Daim, Falko. *Awarenforschungen*, Archaeologia Austriaca. Monographien 1. Vienna: Institut für Ur- und Frühgeschichte der Universität Wien, 1992.

———. 'Archaeology, ethnicity and the structures of identification: the example of the Avars, Carantanians and Moravians in the eighth century', in *Strategies of Distinction*, edited by Pohl and Reimitz, 1998, 71–94.

———. 'Avars and Avar archaeology: an introduction', in *Regna and Gentes*, edited by Goetz, Jarnut and Pohl, 2003, 463–570.

Daly, L.J. 'The mandarin and the barbarian: the response of Themistius to the Gothic challenge', *Historia* 21 (1972), 351–79.

Daly, W.M. 'Clovis: how barbaric, how pagan?' *Speculum* 69 (1994), 619–64.

Damminger, Folke. 'Dwellings, settlements and settlement patterns in Merovingian south-west Germany and adjacent areas', in *Franks and Alamanni*, edited by Wood, 1998, 33–106.

Dannheimer, Hermann and Dopsch, Heinz, eds. *Die Bajuwaren: Von Severin bis Tassilo 488–788*. Munich: Prähistorische Staatssammlung, 1988.

Dark, K.R. *Civitas to Kingdom: British Political Continuity 300–800*. London and New York: Leicester University Press, 1994.

———. *Britain and the End of the Roman Empire*. Stroud: Tempus, 2000.

Dauge, Y.A. *Le Barbare: recherches sur la conception romaine du barbare et de la civilisation*, Collection Latomus 176. Brussels: Latomus, 1981.

Demandt, Alexander. 'Der spätrömische Militäradel', *Chiron* 10 (1980), 609–36.

———. *Der Fall Roms: die Auflösung des römischen Reiches im Urteil der Nachwelt*. Munich: Beck, 1984.

———. 'The osmosis of late Roman and Germanic aristocracies', in *Das Reich und die Barbaren*, edited by Chrysos and Schwarcz, 1989, 75–87.

Demougeot, Émilienne. *De l'unité à la division de l'empire romain, 395–410.* Paris: Aclrien-Maison-Neuve, 1951.

———. 'Bedeutet das Jahre 476 das Ende des römischen Reiches in Okzident?' *Klio* 60 (1978), 371–81.

———. *La formation de l'Europe et les invasions barbares.* Paris: Aubier, 1979.

———. 'Le conubium dans les lois barbares du VIe siècle', *Recueil de mémoires et travaux publié par la Société d'Histoire de Droit et des Institutions des Anciens Pays de Droit Ecrit* 12 (1983), 69–82.

———. 'L'image officielle du barbare dans l'empire romain d'Auguste à Théodose', *Ktèma. Civilisations de l'Orient, de la Grèce et de Rome antiques* 9 (1984), 123–43.

———. *L'Empire romain et les barbares d'occident (IVe-VIIIe siècles). Scripta Varia.* Paris: Publications de la Sorbonne, 1988.

Diesner, Hans-Joachim. *Das Vandalenreich: Aufstieg und Untergang.* Stuttgart: Kohlhammer, 1966.

———. *The Great Migration: The Movement of Peoples across Europe, AD 300–700.* Leipzig: Edition Leipzig, 1978.

Doherty, Charles. 'Kingship in early Ireland', in *The Kingship and Landscape of Tara*, edited by Edel Bhreathnach. Dublin: Four Courts Press/The Discovery Programme, 2005, 3–31.

Dolukhanov, Pavel M. *The Early Slavs. Eastern Europe from the Initial Settlement to the Kievan Rus.* London and New York: Longman, 1996.

Drijvers, Jan Willem and Hunt, David, eds. *The Late Roman World and its Historian: Interpreting Ammianus Marcellinus.* London: Routledge, 1999.

Drinkwater, John F. 'Peasants and Bagaudae in Roman Gaul', *Echoes du Monde Classique/Classical Views* ns 3 (1984), 349–71.

———. 'The Bacaudae of fifth-century Gaul', in *Fifth-Century Gaul*, edited by Drinkwater and Elton, 1992, 208–17.

———. 'The "Germanic threat on the Rhine frontier": a Romano-Gallic artefact?' in *Shifting Frontiers*, edited by Mathisen and Sivan, 1996, 20–30.

———. 'Julian and the Franks and Valentinian I and the Alamanni: Ammianus on Romano-German relations', *Francia* 27/1 (1997), 1–15.

———. 'The Usurpers Constantine III (407–411) and Jovinus (411–413)', *Britannia* 29 (1998), 269–98.

———. 'Ammianus, Valentinian and the Rhine Germans', in *The Late Roman World*, edited by Drijvers and Hunt, 1999, 127–37.

——— and Elton, Hugh, eds. *Fifth-Century Gaul: A Crisis of Identity?* Cambridge: Cambridge University Press, 1992.

Duncan-Jones, R.P. 'Economic change and the transition to Late Antiquity', in *Approaching Late Antiquity: The Transformation from Early to Late Empire*, edited by Swain and Edwards. Oxford: Oxford University Press, 2004, 20–52.

Durliat, Jean. 'Cité, impôt et intégration des barbares', in *Kingdoms of the Empire*, edited by Pohl, 1997, 153–83.

Dušek, Sigrid. *Römische Handwerker im germanischen Thüringen: Ergebnisse der Ausgrabungen in Haarhausen, Kreis Arnstadt*, Weimarer Monographien zur Ur- und Frühgeschichte 27. Stuttgart: Theiss, 1992.

Edwards, Nancy. *The Archaeology of Early Medieval Ireland*. London: Batsford, 1990.

Effros, Bonnie. 'Appearance and ideology: creating distinctions between clerics and laypersons in early medieval Gaul', in *Encountering Medieval Textiles and Dress; Objects, Texts, Images*, edited by Désirée Koslin and Janet E. Snyder. New York: Palgrave Macmillan, 2002, 7–24.

———. *Body and Soul: Burial and the Afterlife in the Merovingian World*. University Park: Pennsylvania State Press, 2002.

———. *Creating Community with Food and Drink in Merovingian Gaul*. New York and Basingtoke: Palgrave Macmillan, 2002.

———. *Merovingian Mortuary Archaeology and the Making of the Early Middle Ages*, The Transformation of the Classical Heritage 35. Berkeley: University of California Press, 2003.

———. 'Dressing conservatively: women's brooches as markers of ethnic identity?' in *Gender in the Early Medieval World*, edited by Leslie Brubaker and Julia M.H. Smith. Cambridge: Cambridge University Press, 2004, 165–84.

Ellegård, Alvar. 'Who were the Eruli?', *Scandia: Tidskrift för historisk forskning* 53 (1987), 5–34.

Elton, Hugh. 'Defining Romans, Barbarians, and the Roman frontier', in *Shifting Frontiers*, edited by Mathisen and Sivan, 1996, 126–35.

———. *Frontiers of the Roman Empire*. London: Batsford, 1996.

———. *Warfare in Roman Europe, AD 350–425*. Oxford: Clarendon Press, 1996.

———. 'The nature of the sixth-century Isaurians', in *Ethnicity and Culture*, edited by Mitchell and Greatrex, 2000, 293–308.

Erdkamp, Paul, ed. *A Companion to the Roman Army*. Oxford: Blackwell, 2007.

Erdrich, Michael. *Rom und die Barbaren. Das Verhältnis zwischen dem Imperium Romanum und den germanischen Stämmen vor seiner Nordwestgrenze von der späten römischen Republik bis zum Gallischen Sonderreich*, Römisch-Germanische Forschungen 58. Mainz: Von Zabern, 2001.

Ewig, Eugen. 'Volkstum und Volksbewußtsein im Frankenreich des 7. Jahrhunderts', *Settimane di Studio del Cenlro Italiano di Studi sull'Alto Medioevo* 5 (1958), 587–648.

Fanning, Steven C. 'Lombard Arianism reconsidered', *Speculum* 56 (1981), 241–58.

Fehr, Hubert. '*Volkstum* as paradigm: Germanic people and Gallo-Romans in early medieval archaeology since the 1930s', in *On Barbarian Identity*, edited by Gillett, 2002, 177–200.

Ferreiro, Alberto, ed. *The Visigoths: Studies in Culture and Society*. Leiden: Brill, 1999.

Fine, John V.A. *The Early Medieval Balkans: A Critical Survey from the Sixth to the Late Twelfth Century*. Ann Arbor: University of Michigan Press, 1983.

Fletcher, Richard. *The Conversion of Europe: From Paganism to Christianity, 371–1386 AD*. London: HarperCollins, 1997.

Foster, Sally. *Picts, Gaels and Scots: Early Historic Scotland*. London: Batsford, 1996.

Frank, R.I. *Scholae Palatinae: The Palace Guards of the later Roman Empire*, American Academy in Rome Papers and Monographs 23. Rome: American Academy, 1969.

Frassetto, Michael, ed. *Encyclopedia of Barbarian Europe: Society in Transformation*. Santa Barbara, CA: ABC-Clio, 2003.

Fulford, Michael. 'Roman and barbarian: the economy of Roman frontier systems', in *Barbarians and Romans*, edited by Barrett, Fitzpatrick and Macinnes, 1989, 81–95.

Gaimster, Märit. *Vendel Period Bracteates on Gotland: On the Significance of Germanic Art*, Acta Archaeologica Lundensia, Series in 8o, 27. Stockholm: Almqvist and Wiksell International, 1998.

———. 'Gold bracteates and necklaces: political ideals in the sixth century', in *Roman Gold*, edited by Magnus, 2001, 143–56.

Gamillscheg, Ernst. *Romania Germanica: Sprach- und Siedlungsgeschichte der Germanen auf dem Boden des alten Römerreiches*. 2nd ed. Vol. 1. Berlin: De Gruyter, 1970.

García Moreno, Luis. 'Gothic survivals in the Visigothic kingdoms of Toulouse and Toledo', *Francia* 21/1 (1994), 1–15.

Geary, Patrick. 'Ethnic identity as a situational construct in the early Middle Ages', *Mitteilungen der anthropologischen Gesellschaft in Wien* 113 (1985), 15–26.

———. *Before France and Germany: The Creation and Transformation of the Merovingian World*. New York: Oxford University Press, 1988.

———. *The Myth of Nations: The Medieval Origins of Europe*. Princeton, NJ: Princeton University Press, 2002.

Gelling, Margaret. 'Why aren't we speaking Welsh?' *Anglo-Saxon Studies in Archaeology and History* 6 (1993), 51–6.

Geuenich, Dieter, ed. *Die Franken und die Alamannen bis zur 'Schlacht bei Zülpich' (496–97)*, Ergänzungsbände zum Reallexikon der Germanischen Altertumskunde, 19. Berlin: Walter De Gruyter, 1998.

Gibbon, Edward. *The History of the Declint and Fall of the Roman Empire*, ed. J.B. Bury, 7 vols. London: Methuen, 1896–1900.

Gillett, Andrew. 'The purpose of Cassiodorus' *Variae*', in *After Rome's Fall*, ed. Murray, 1998, 37–50.

———. 'The accession of Euric', *Francia* 26/1 (1999), 1–40.

———. 'Introduction: ethnogenesis, history and methodology', in *On Barbarian Identity*, edited by Gillett, 2002, 1–18.

———. 'Was ethnicity politicized in the earliest medieval kingdoms?' in *On Barbarian Identity*, edited by Gillett, 2002, 85–121.

———. *Envoys and Political Communication in the Late Antique West, 411–533*. Cambridge: Cambridge University Press, 2003.

———, ed. *On Barbarian Identity. Critical Approaches to Ethnicity in the Early Middle Ages*, Studies in the Early Middle Ages 4. Turnhout: Brepols, 2002.

Gimbutas, Marija. *The Balts*, Ancient Peoples and Places. London: Thames and Hudson, 1963.

——. *The Slavs*, Ancient Peoples and Places. London: Thames and Hudson, 1971.

Goetz, Hans-Werner. '*Gens*. Terminology and perception of the "Germanic" peoples from Late Antiquity to the Early Middle Ages', in *The Construction of Communities*, edited by Corradini, Diesenberger and Reimitz, 2003, 351–96.

——. 'Introduction', in *Regna and Gentes*, edited by Goetz, Jarnut and Pohl, 2003, 1–11.

——. '*Gens*, kings and kingdoms: the Franks', in *Regna and Gentes*, edited by Goetz, Jarnut and Pohl, 2003, 307–44.

——, Jarnut, Jörg and Pohl, Walter, eds. *Regna and Gentes: The Relationship between Late Antique and Early Medieval Peoples and Kingdoms in the Transformation of the Roman World*, The Transformation of the Roman World 13. Leiden: Brill, 2003.

Goffart, Walter. 'Byzantine policy in the West under Tiberius II and Maurice: the pretenders Hermenegild and Gundovald (579–585)', *Traditio* 13 (1963), 73–118.

——. *Barbarians and Romans, A.D. 418–584: The Techniques of Accommodation*. Princeton: Princeton University Press, 1980.

——. 'Rome, Constantinople and the barbarians', *American Historical Review* 86 (1981), 275–306.

——. 'Old and new in Merovingian taxation', *Past and Present* 96 (1982), 3–21.

——. 'The maps of the barbarian invasions: a preliminary report', *Nottingham Medieval Studies* 32 (1988), 49–64.

——. *The Narrators of Barbarian History (A.D. 550–800): Jordanes, Gregory of Tours, Bede, and Paul the Deacon*. Princeton: Princeton University Press, 1988.

——. *Rome's Fall and After*. London: Hambledon, 1989.

——. 'The maps of the barbarian invasions: a longer look', in *The Culture of Christendom: Essays in Medieval History in Memory of Denis L.T. Bethell*, edited by Marc A. Meyer. London and Rio Grande: Hambledon, 1993, 1–27.

——. 'What's wrong with the map of the barbarian invasions?' in *Minorities and Barbarians*, edited by Ridyard and Benson, 1996, 159–73.

——. 'Does the *Vita Severini* have an underside?' in *Eugippius und Severin*, edited by Pohl and Diesenberger, 2001, 33–9.

——. 'Conspicuously absent: martial heroism in the *Histories* of Gregory of Tours', in *The World of Gregory of Tours*, edited by Mitchell and Wood, 2002, 365–94.

——. 'Does the distant past impinge on the Invasion Age Germans?' in *On Barbarian Identity*, edited by Gillett, 2002, 21–37.

——. *Barbarian Tides: The Migration Age and the later Roman Empire*. Philadelphia: University of Pennsylvania Press, 2006.

Gojda, Martin. *The Ancient Slavs: Settlement and Society*. Edinburgh: Edinburgh University Press, 1991.

Greatrex, Geoffrey. 'Roman identity in the sixth century', in *Ethnicity and Culture*, edited by Mitchell and Greatrex, 2000, 267–92.

Green, Dennis H. *Language and History in the Early Germanic World*. Cambridge: Cambridge University Press, 1998.

———— and Siegmund, Frank, eds. *The Continental Saxons from the Migration Period to the Tenth Century: An Ethnographic Perspective*, Studies in Historical Archaeoethnology 6. Woodbridge: Boydell Press, 2003.

Grierson, Philip. 'Commerce in the Dark Ages: a critique of the evidence', *Transactions of the Royal Historical Society*, 5th series 9 (1959), 123–40.

Groenman-Van Waateringe, W. 'Food for soldiers, food for thought', in *Roman and Barbarian*, edited by Barrett, Fitzpatrick and Macinnes, 1989, 96–107.

Gunn, Joel D., ed. *The Years without Summer: Tracing AD 536 and its Aftermath*, British Archaeological Reports International. Series 872. Oxford: BAR, 2000.

Hachmann, Rolf. *Die Goten und Skandinavien*. Berlin: De Gruyter, 1970.

Hall, Edith. *Inventing the Barbarian: Greek Self-Definition through Tragedy*. Oxford: Clarendon, 1989.

Halsall, Guy. 'The origins of the *Reihengräberzivilisation*: forty years on', in *Fifth-Century Gaul*, edited by Drinkwater and Elton, 1992, 197–207.

————. *Early Medieval Cemeteries: An Introduction to Burial Archaeology in the Post-Roman West*, New Light on the Dark Ages 1. Skelmorlie: Cruithne Press, 1995.

————. *Settlement and Social Organisation: The Merovingian Region of Metz*. Cambridge: Cambridge University Press, 1995.

————. 'Movers and Shakers: the barbarians and the Fall of Rome', *Early Medieval Europe* 8 (1999), 131–45.

————. 'Archaeology and the late Roman frontier in northern Gaul: the so-called Föderatengräber reconsidered', in *Grenze und Differenz im Frühmittelalter*, edited by Walter Pohl and Helmut Reimitz. Vienna: Verlag der Österreichischen Akademie der Wissenschaften, 2000, 167–80.

————. 'Childeric's grave, Clovis's succession, and the origins of the Merovingian kingdom', in *Society and Culture*, edited by Mathisen and Shanzer, 2001, 116–33.

————. *Warfare and Society in the Barbarian West, 450–900*, Warfare and History. London: Routledge, 2003.

————. *Barbarian Migrations and the Roman West, 376–568*. Cambridge: Cambridge University Press, 2007.

Hamerow, Helena. 'The archaeology of rural settlement in early medieval Europe', *Early Medieval Europe* 3 (1994), 167–79.

————. *Early Medieval Settlements: The Archaeology of Rural Communities in Northwest Europe, 400–900*. Oxford: Oxford University Press, 2002.

Hannaford, Ivan. *Race: The History of an Idea in the West*. Washington, DC and Baltimore, MD: Woodrow Wilson Center Press and Johns Hopkins University Press, 1996.

Hansen, Ulla Lund. *Römischer Import im Norden: Warenaustausch zwischen dem Römischen Reich und dem freien Germanien während der Kaiserzeit unter besonderer Berücksichtigung Nordeuropas*, Nordiske Fortidsminder Ser. B 10. Copenhagen: Det Kongelige Nordiske Oldskriftselskab, 1987.

———. 'Origins of glass during the Late Roman Period', in *International Contacts*, edited by Istvánovits and Kulcsár, 2001, 325–40.

Hårdh, Birgitta. 'Uppåkra – a centre in south Sweden in the first millennium AD', *Antiquity* 74 (2000), 640–8.

——— and Larsson, Lars, eds. *Central Places in the Migration and Merovingian Periods: Papers from the 52nd Sachsensymposium, Lund, August 2001 (Uppåkrastudier 6)*, Acta Archaeologica Lundensia Series in Octavo 39. Stockholm: Almqvist & Wiksell International, 2002.

Hardt, Matthias. 'The Bavarians', in *Regna and Gentes*, edited by Goetz, Jarnut and Pohl, 2003, 429–61.

———. 'The nomad's greed for gold: from the fall of the Burgundians to the Avar treasure', in *The Construction of Communities*, edited by Corradini, Diesenberger and Reimitz, 2003, 95–107.

Harhoiu, R. *The Treasure from Pietroasa, Romania*, British Archaeological Reports International Series 24. Oxford: BAR, 1977.

Härke, Heinrich. ' "Warrior graves"? The background of the Anglo-Saxon burial rite', *Past and Present* 126 (1990), 22–43.

———. 'All quiet on the western front? Paradigms, methods and approaches in West German archaeology', in *Archaeological Theory in Europe: The Last Three Decades*, edited by Ian Hodder. London: Routledge, 1991, 187–222.

———. 'The German experience', in *Archaeology, Ideology and Society*, edited by Härke, 2000, 12–39.

———. 'The circulation of weapons in Anglo-Saxon society', in *Rituals of Power*, edited by Theuws and Nelson, 2000, 377–99.

———, ed. *Archaeology, Ideology and Society: The German Experience*, Gesellschaften und Staaten im Epochenwandel 7. Frankfurt-am-Main: Peter Lang, 2002.

Harries, Jill. 'Sidonius Apollinaris, Rome and the barbarians: a climate of treason?' in *Fifth-Century Gaul*, edited by Drinkwater and Elton, 1992, 298–308.

———. *Sidonius Apollinaris and the Fall of Rome*. Oxford: Oxford University Press, 1994.

———. *Law and Empire in Late Antiquity*. Cambridge: Cambridge University press, 1998.

———. 'Legal culture and identity in the fifth-century West', in *Ethnicity and Culture*, edited by Mitchell and Greatrex, 2000, 45–58.

———. 'Not the Theodosian Code: Euric's law and late fifth-century Gaul', in *Society and Culture*, edited by Mathisen and Shanzer, 2001, 39–51.

Hartley, B.R. and Fitts, R. Leon. *The Brigantes*. Gloucester: Sutton, 1988.

Haßmann, Henning. 'Archaeology in the "Third Reich" ', in *Archaeology, Ideology and Society*, edited by Härke, 2002, 67–142.

Hauck, Karl. 'Gudme in der Sicht der Brakteatenforschung', *Frühmittelalter-liche Studien* 21 (1987), 147–81.

———. 'Der religions- und sozialgeschichtliche Quellenwert der völkerwan-derungszeitlichen Goldbrakteaten (Zur Ikonologie der Goldbrakteaten, XLVII)', in *Germanische Religionsgeschichte*, edited by Beck, Ellmers and Schier, 1992, 229–69.

———. 'Gudme als Kultort und seine Rolle beim Austausch von Bildformulären der Goldbrakteaten', in *The Archaeology of Gudme*, edited by Nielsen, Randsborg and Thrane, 1994, 78–88.

Haywood, John. *Dark Age Naval Power. A Reassessment of Frankish and Anglo-Saxon Seafaring Activity*. London and New York: Routledge, 1991.

Heather, Peter. 'The Anti-Scythian tirade of Synesius' *De Regno*', *Phoenix* 42 (1988), 152–72.

———. *Goths and Romans, 332–489*. Oxford: Clarendon Press, 1991.

———. 'Literacy and power in the migration period', in *Literacy and Power in the Ancient World*, edited by Alan K. Bowman and Greg Woolf. Cambridge: Cambridge University Press, 1994, 177–97.

———. 'The Huns and the end of the Roman Empire in Western Europe', *English Historical Review* 110 (1995), 4–41.

———. 'Theodoric King of the Goths', *Early Medieval Europe* 4 (1995), 145–73.

———. *The Goths*, The Peoples of Europe. Oxford: Blackwell, 1996.

———. 'Disappearing and reappearing tribes', in *Strategies of Distinction*, edited by Pohl and Reimitz, 1998, 95–112.

———. '*Foedera* and *foederati* of the fourth century', in *Kingdoms of the Empire*, edited by Walter Pohl, 1998, 57–74.

———. 'The barbarian in late antiquity: images, reality and transformations', in *Constructing Identities in Late Antiquity*, edited by Richard Miles. London: Routledge, 1999, 234–58.

———. 'The late Roman art of client management: imperial defence in the fourth century West', in *The Transformation of Frontiers*, edited by Pohl, Wood and Reimitz, 2001, 15–68.

———. '*Gens* and *regnum* among the Ostrogoths', in *Regna and Gentes*, edited by Goetz, Jarnut and Pohl, 2003, 85–133.

———. *The Fall of the Roman Empire: A New History*. London: Macmillan, 2005.

———. 'Merely an ideology? Gothic identity in Ostrogothic Italy', in *Ostrogoths*, edited by Barnish and Marazzi, 2007, 31–79.

——— and Matthews, John. *The Goths in the Fourth Century*, Translated Texts for Historians 11. Liverpool: Liverpool University Press, 1991.

———, ed. *The Visigoths from the Migration Period to the Seventh Century: An Ethnographic Perspective*, Studies in Historical Archaeoethnology 4. Woodbridge: Boydell, 1999.

Hedeager, Lotte. 'A quantitative analysis of Roman imports in Europe north of the *limes* and the question of Roman-Germanic exchange', in *New Directions in Scandinavian Archaeology*, edited by K. Kristiansen and C. Paludan-Müller. Copenhagen: National Museum, 1978, 191–216.

———. 'Empire, frontier and the barbarian hinterland: Rome and northern Europe from AD 1–400', in *Centre and Periphery in the Ancient World*, edited by Michael Rowlands, Mogens Larsen and Kristian Kristiansen. Cambridge: Cambridge University Press, 1987, 125–40.

———. *Iron Age Societies: From Tribe to State in Northern Europe 500 BC to AD 700*, translated by John Hines. Oxford: Blackwell, 1992.

———. 'Kingdoms, ethnicity and material culture: Denmark in a European perspective', in *The Age of Sutton Hoo*, edited by M. Carver. Woodbridge: Boydell, 1992, 279–300.

———. 'The creation of Germanic identity: a European origin-myth', in *Frontières d'Empire*, edited by Brun, Leeuw and Whittaker, 1993, 121–31.

———. 'Migration period Europe: the formation of a political mentality', in *Rituals of Power*, edited by Theuws and Nelson, 2000, 15–57.

———. '*Asgard* reconstructed: Gudme, a "central place" in the north', in *Topographies of Power*, edited by Jong and Theuws, 2001, 467–507.

Hen, Yitzhak. *Culture and Religion in Merovingian Gaul, AD 481–751*. Leiden: Brill, 1995.

———. *Roman Barbarians: The Royal Court and Culture in the Early Medieval West*. Basingstoke: Palgrave Macmillan, 2007.

Hendy, Michael F. 'From public to private: the western barbarian coinages as a mirror of the disintegration of late Roman state structures', *Viator* 19 (1988), 29–78.

Higham, Nick, ed. *Britons in Anglo-Saxon England*, Publications of the Manchester Centre for Anglo-Saxon Studies. Woodbridge: Boydell, 2007.

Hines, John. 'The becoming of the English: identity, material culture and language in early Anglo-Saxon England', *Anglo-Saxon Studies in Archaeology and History* 7 (1994), 49–59.

———. 'Culture groups and ethnic groups in northern Germany in and around the Migration Period', *Studien zur Sachsenforschung* 13 (1999), 219–32.

———, ed. *The Anglo-Saxons from the Migration Period to the Eighth Century. An Ethnographic Perspective*, Studies in Historical Archaeoethnology 2. Woodbridge: Boydell, 1997.

Hobsbawm, Eric and Ranger, Terence, eds. *The Invention of Tradition*. Cambridge: Cambridge University Press, 1983.

Hodges, Richard and Bowden, William, eds. *The Sixth Century: Production, Distribution, and Demand*, The Transformation of the Roman World 3. Leiden: Brill, 1998.

Hoffmann, D. *Das spätrömische Bewegungsheer und die Notitia Dignitatum*. 2 vols. Düsseldorf: Rheinland Verlag, 1969.

Horedt, K. and Protase, D. 'Das zweite Fürstengrab von Apahida', *Germania* 50 (1972), 174–220.

Howe, Nicholas. *Migration and Mythmaking in Anglo-Saxon England*. New Haven, CT: Yale University Press, 1989.

Hubert, Jean, Porcher, Jean and Volbach, W.F. *Europe in the Dark Ages*, The Arts of Mankind. London: Thames and Hudson, 1969.

Hunt, David. 'The outsider inside: Ammianus on the rebellion of Silvanus', in *The Late Roman World*, edited by Drijvers and Hunt, 1999, 51–63.

Isaac, Benjamin. *The Invention of Racism in Classical Antiquity*. Princeton, NJ: Princeton University Press, 2004.

Istvánovits, Eszter, and Kulcsár, Valéria, eds. *International Connections of the Barbarians of the Carpathian Basin in the 1st–5th Centuries A.D.* Nyíregyháza and Aszód, Hungary: Jósa András Museum and Osváth Gedeon Museum Foundation, 2001.

Jackson, K.H. *The Oldest Irish Tradition: A Window on the Iron Age*. Cambridge: Cambridge University Press, 1964.

James, Edward. *The Merovingian Archaeology of South-West Gaul*, 2 vols, British Archaeological Reportsementary Suppl Series. 25. Oxford: BAR, 1977.

———. 'Cemeteries and the problem of Frankish settlement in Gaul', in *Names, Words and Graves: Early Medieval Settlement*, edited by P.H. Sawyer. Leeds: School of History, University of Leeds, 1979, 55–89.

———. *The Origins of France: From Clovis to the Capetians, 500–100*. London and Basingstoke: Macmillan, 1982.

———. *The Franks*, The Peoples of Europe. Oxford: Blackwell, 1988.

———. 'The origins of barbarian kingdoms: the continental evidence', in *Origins*, edited by Bassett, 1989, 40–52.

———. 'The militarization of Roman society, AD 400–700', in *Military Aspects of Scandinavian Society in a European Perspective, AD 1–1300*, edited by A.M. Jørgensen and B.L. Clausen. Copenhagen: The National Museum, 1997, 19–24.

———. 'Gregory of Tours and the Franks', in *After Rome's Fall*, edited by Murray, 1998, 51–66.

———. *Britain in the First Millennium*. London: Edward Arnold, 2001.

———. 'The rise and function of the concept "late antiquity"', *Journal of Late Antiquity* 1 (2008), 20–30.

Jankuhn, Herbert. 'Siedlung, Wirtschaft und Gesellschaftsordnung der germanischen Stämme in der Zeit der römischen Angriffskriege', in *Aufstieg und Niedergang der Römischen Welt*, series II, vol. 5.1, edited by Hildegard Temporini. Berlin and New York: Walter De Gruyter, 1976, 65–126.

Jarnut, Jörg. 'Gregor von Tours, Frankengeschichte II, 12: Franci Egidium sibi regem adsciscunt. Faktum oder Sage?' in *Ethnogenese und Überlieferung*, edited by Brunner and Merta, 1994, 129–34.

———. '*Gens, rex* and *regnum* of the Lombards', in *Regna and Gentes*, edited by Goetz, Jarnut and Pohl, 2003, 409–27.

Jesch, Judith, ed. *The Scandinavians from the Vendel Period to the Tenth Century: An Ethnographic Perspective*, Studies in Historical Archaeoethnology 5. Woodbridge: Boydell, 2002.

Jolly, Karen Louise. *Popular Religion in Late Saxon England: Elf Charms in Context*. Chapel Hill: University of North Carolina Press, 1996.

Jones, A.H.M. 'Were ancient heresies national or social movements in disguise?' *Journal of Theological Studies* n.s. 10 (1959), 280–98.

——. *The Later Roman Empire, 284–602: A Social, Economic and Administrative Survey*. 3 vols. Oxford: Blackwell, 1964.

Jones, C.P. 'Stigma: tattooing and branding in Graeco-Roman Antiquity', *Journal of Roman Studies* 87 (1987), 139–55.

Jones, Michael E. *The End of Roman Britain*. Ithaca, NY: Cornell University Press, 1996.

Jones, Siân. *The Archaeology of Ethnicity: Constructing Identities in the Past and Present*. London and New York: Routledge, 1997.

Jones, W.R. 'The image of the barbarian in medieval Europe', *Comparative Studies in Society and History* 13 (1971), 376–407.

Jong, Mayke de and Theuws, Frans, eds. *Topographies of Power in the Early Middle Ages*, The Transformation of the Roman World 6. Leiden: Brill, 2001.

Jørgensen, Anne Nørgård and Clausen, Berthe L., eds. *Military Aspects of Scandinavian Society in a European Perspective, AD 1–1300*, Studies in Archaeology and History 2. Copenhagen: The National Museum, 1997.

Jørgensen, Lars, ed. *Chronological Studies of Anglo-Saxon England, Lombard Italy and Vendel Period Sweden*, Arkaeologiske Skrifter 5. Copenhagen: University of Copenhagen, 1992.

Jørgensen, Lisa Bender. *North European Textiles until AD 1000*. Aarhus: Aarhus University Press, 1992.

Kazanski, Michel. *Les Goths (Ier-VIIe siècle après J.-C.)*. Paris: Errance, 1991.

——. 'La royaume de Vintharius: le récit de Jordanes et les données archéologiques', in *Strategies of Distinction*, edited by Pohl and Reimitz. Leiden: Brill, 1998, 221–40.

——. *Les Slaves: Les origines (Ier–VIIe siècle après J.-C.)*. Paris: Errance, 1999.

——. 'Les épées 'orientales' à garde cloisonné du Ve-VIe siècles', in *International Contacts*, edited by Istvánovits and Kulcsár, 2001, 389–418.

—— and Mastykova, Anna. *Les Peuples du Caucase du Nord: le début de l'histoire (Ier–VIIe siècle après. J.-C.)*. Paris: Errance, 2003.

—— and Périn, Patrick. 'Le mobilier funéraire de la tombe de Childéric Ier; état de la question et perspectives', *Revue archéologique de Picardie* (1988), 13–38.

Kelly, Fergus. *A Guide to Early Irish Law*, Early Irish Law 3. Dublin: Dublin Institute for Advanced Studies, 1988.

——. *Early Irish Farming: A Study Based Mainly on the Law-Texts of the 7th and 8th Centuries AD*, Early Irish Law 4. Dublin: Dublin Institute for Advanced Studies, 1997.

Kelly, J.N.D. *Jerome: His Life, Writings and Controversies*. London: Duckworth, 1975.

King, P.D. *Law and Society in the Visigothic Kingdom*, Cambridge Studies in Medieval Life and Thought, 3rd series 5. Cambridge: Cambridge University Press, 1972.

Kirby, D.P. *The Earliest English Kings*. London: Unwin Hyman, 1991.

Klein, Barbro and Widbom, Mats, eds. *Swedish Folk Art: All Tradition is Change*. New York: Abrams, 1994.

Klingshirn, William E. 'Charity and power: Caesarius of Arles and the ransoming of captives in Sub-Roman Gaul', *Journal of Roman Studies* 75 (1985), 183–203.

———. *Caesarius of Arles: The Making of a Christian Community in Late Antique Gaul*. Cambridge: Cambridge University Press, 1994.

Kolendo, J. 'L'importation des esclaves barbares dans l'empire romain', in *Le monde romain et ses périphéries sous la république et sous l'empire*, edited by Tadeusz Kotula and Andrzej Ładomirski. Wrocław: 2001, 39–53.

Kolník, T. 'Q. Atilius Primus – interprex, centurio und negotiator. Eine bedeutende Grabinschrit aus dem 1. Jh. u. Z. im Quadischen Limes-Vorland', *Acta Archaeologica Academiae Scientiarum Hungaricae* 30 (1978), 61–75.

Krapp, Karin. *Die Alamannen: Krieger – Siedler – frühe Christen*. Stuttgart: Theiss, 2007.

Kulikowski, Michael. 'Barbarians in Gaul, usurpers in Britain', *Britannia* 31 (2000), 325–45.

———. 'Marcellinus "of Dalmatia" and the dissolution of the fifth-century Empire', *Byzantion* 72 (2002), 177–91.

———. *Late Roman Spain and its Cities*. Baltimore: Johns Hopkins University Press, 2004.

———. 'Ethnicity, rulership, and early medieval frontiers', in *Borders, Barriers, and Ethnogenesis*, edited by Curta, 2005, 247–54.

———. 'Constantine and the northern barbarians', in *The Cambridge Companion to the Age of Constantine*, edited by Noel Lenski. New York: Cambridge University Press, 2006, 347–76.

———. *Rome's Gothic Wars from the Third Century to Alaric*. New York: Cambridge University Press, 2007.

Ladner, Gerhart. 'On Roman attitudes towards barbarians in late antiquity', *Viator* 7 (1976), 1–26.

Lambert, David. 'The barbarians in Salvian's *De Gubernatione Dei*', in *Ethnicity and Culture*, edited by Mitchell and Greatrex. London: 2000, 103–16.

Lamm, J.P. and Nordström, H.-Å., eds. *Vendel Period Studies. Transactions of the Boat-Grave Symposium in Stockholm, February 2–3, 1981*. Stockholm: Statens Historiska Museum, 1983.

Larsson, Lars and Hårdh, Birgitte. *Centrality – Regionality: The Social Structure of Sweden During the Iron Age (Uppåkrastudier 7)*, Acta Archaeologica Lundensia, Series in Octavo, 40. Stockholm: Almqvist & Wiksell International, 2003.

Leader-Newby, Ruth E. *Silver and Society in Late Antiquity: Functions and Meanings of Silver Plate in the Fourth to Seventh Centuries*. Aldershot: Ashgate, 2004.

Leeds, E.T. 'Visigoth or Vandal?' *Archaeologia* 94 (1951), 195–212.

Lemerle, P. 'Invasions et migrations dans les Balkans depuis la fin de l'époque romaine jusqu'au VIIe siècle', *Revue historique* 211 (1954), 264–308.

———. *Les plus anciens recueils des Miracles de Saint Démétrius et la pénétration des Slaves dans les Balkans. 2. Le commentaire*. Paris: Centre Nationale des Recherches Scientifiques, 1981.

Lenski, Noel. '*Initium mali Romano imperio*: contemporary reactions to the battle of Adrianople', *Transactions of the American Philological Association* 127 (1997), 129–68.

——. *Failure of Empire: Valens and the Roman State in the Fourth Century AD*. Berkeley: University of California Press, 2002.

Levi, Annalina Caló. *Barbarians on Roman imperial coins and sculpture*, Numismatic Notes and Monographs 123. New York: American Numismatic Society, 1952.

Liebeschuetz, J.H.W.G. *Barbarians and Bishops: Army, Church, and State in the Age of Arcadius and Chrysostom*. Oxford: Clarendon Press, 1990.

——. 'The end of the Roman army in the western empire', in *War and Society in the Roman World*, edited by John Rich and Graham Shipley. London: 1993, 265–76.

——. 'Cities, taxes, and the accommodation of the barbarians', in *Kingdoms of the Empire*, edited by Pohl, 1997, 135–51.

——. 'Citizen status and law in the Roman Empire and the Visigothic kingdom', in *Strategies of Distinction*, edited by Pohl and Reimitz, 1998, 131–52.

——. *The Decline and Fall of the Roman City*. Oxford: Oxford University Press, 2001.

——. '*Gens* into *regnum*: the Vandals', in *Regna and Gentes*, edited by Goetz, Jarnut and Pohl, 2003, 55–83.

——. 'The refugees and evacuees in the Age of Migrations', in *The Construction of Communities*, edited by Corradini, Diesenberger and Reimitz, 2003, 65–79.

Little, Lester K., ed. *Plague and the End of Antiquity: The Pandemic of 541–750*. Cambridge: Cambridge University Press, 2007.

—— and Shanzer, Danuta, eds. *Society and Culture in Late Antique Gaul: Revisiting the Sources*. Aldershot: Ashgate, 2001.

MacGeorge, Penny. *Late Roman Warlords*. Oxford: Oxford University Press, 2002.

MacMullen, Ramsey. *Corruption and the Decline of Rome*. New Haven, CT: Yale University Press, 1988.

Magnus, Bente, ed. *Roman Gold and the Development of the Early Germanic Kingdoms. Symposium in Stockholm, 14–16 November 1997*, Konferenser 51. Stockholm: Kungl. Vitterhets Historie och Antikvitets Akademien, 2001.

Mann, J.C. *Legionary Recruitment and Veteran Settlement during the Principate*. London: Institute of Archaeology, University of London, 1983.

Martens, Jes. 'The Vandals: myths and facts about a Germanic tribe of the first half of the first millennium AD', in *Archaeological Approaches to Cultural Identity*, edited by Stephan Shennan. London: Routledge, 1989, 57–65.

Mathisen, Ralph W. 'Resistance and reconciliation: Majorian and the Gallic aristocracy after the fall of Avitus', *Francia* 7 (1979), 597–627.

——. 'Barbarian bishops and the churches "in barbaricis gentibus" in late Antiquity', *Speculum* 72 (1997), 664–97.

———. 'The letters of Ruricius of Limoges and the passage from Roman to Frankish Gaul', in *Society and Culture*, edited by Mathisen and Shanzer, 2001, 101–15.

———. '*Peregrini, barbari*, and *cives Romani*: concepts of citizenship and the legal identity of barbarians in the later Roman Empire', *American Historical Review* 111 (2006), 1011–40.

McCone, Kim. *Pagan Past and Christian Present in Early Irish Literature*, Maynooth Monographs 3. Maynooth: An Sagart, 1990.

McCormick, Michael. 'Clovis at Tours, Byzantine public ritual and the origins of medieval ruler symbolism', in *Das Reich und die Barbaren*, edited by Chrysos and Schwarcz, 1989, 155–80.

——— and Sivan, Hagith. 'Forging a new identity: the kingdom of Toulouse and the frontiers of Visigothic Aquitania (418–507)', in *The Visigoths*, edited by Ferreiro, 1999, 1–62.

——— and Sivan, Hagith S., eds. *Shifting Frontiers in Late Antiquity*. Aldershot: Variorum, 1996.

Matthews, John F. *Western Aristocracies and Imperial Court, AD 364–425*. Oxford: Clarendon Press 1975.

———. *The Roman Empire of Ammianus*. London: Duckworth, 1988.

———. 'Roman laws and barbarian identity in the late Roman west', in *Ethnicity and Culture*, edited by Mitchell and Greatrex, 2000, 31–44.

Mattingly, David J. 'From one colonialism to another: imperialism and the Maghreb', in *Roman Imperialism*, edited by Webster and Cooper, 1996, 49–69.

Meier, Dirk. 'The North Sea coastal area: settlement history from Roman to early medieval times', in *Continental Saxons*, edited by Green and Siegmund, 2003, 37–76.

Menghin, Wilfried. *Das Schwert im frühen Mittelalter: chronologisch-typologische Untersuchungen zu Langschwertern aus germanischen Gräbern des 5. bis 7. Jahrhunderts n. Chr.* Stuttgart: Theiss, 1983.

———. *Die Langobarden: Archäologie und Geschichte*. Stuttgart: Theiss, 1985.

———. *Frühgeschichte Bayerns: Römer und Germanen, Baiern und Schwaben, Franken und Slawen*. Stuttgart: Theiss, 1990.

———, Springer, Tobias and Wamers, Egon, eds. *Germanen, Hunnen und Awaren: Schätze der Völkerwanderungszeit. Die Archäologie des 5. und 6. Jahrhunderts an der mittleren Donau und der östlich-merowingische Reihengräberkreis*. Nürnberg: Verlag des Germanischen Nationalmueums, 1987.

Menis, Gian Carlo *et al.*, ed. *I Longobardi*. Milan: Electa, 1990.

Merrills, A.H. *History and Geography in Late Antiquity*. Cambridge: Cambridge University Press, 2005.

Mildenberger, G. 'Die Germanen in der archäologischen Forschung nach Kossinna', in *Germanenprobleme in heutigen Sicht*, edited by Beck, 1986, 310–20.

Miles, Richard, ed. *Constructing Identities in Late Antiquity*. London and New York: Routledge, 1999.

Millar, Fergus. 'P. Herennius Dexippus: the Greek world and the third-century invasions', *Journal of Roman Studies* 59 (1969), 13–29.

———. 'Emperors, frontiers, and foreign relations, 31 B.C. to A.D. 378', *Britannia* 13 (1982), 1–23.

———. *The Roman Empire and its Neighbours*. London: Weidenfeld and Nicolson, 1983.

———. 'Ethnic identity in the Roman Near East, AD 325–450: language, religion and culture', in *Identities in the Eastern Mediterranean*, edited by Clarke, 1998.

———. *A Greek Roman Empire: Power and Belief under Theodosius II (408–450)*. Berkeley: University of California Press, 2006.

Miller, D.H. 'Frontier societies and the transition between late Antiquity and the early Middle Ages', in *Shifting Frontiers*, edited by Mathisen and Sivan, 1996, 158–71.

Mitchell, Kathleen and Wood, Ian, eds. *The World of Gregory of Tours*. Leiden: Brill, 2002.

Mitchell, Stephen. 'Ethnicity, acculturation and empire in Roman and late Roman Asia Minor', in *Ethnicity and Culture*, edited by Mitchell and Greatrex, 2000, 117–50.

——— and Greatrex, Geoffrey, eds. *Ethnicity and Culture in Late Antiquity*. London: Duckworth and the Classical Press of Wales, 2000.

Moisl, Hermann. 'Anglo-Saxon royal genealogies and Germanic oral tradition', *Journal of Medieval History* 7 (1981), 215–48.

———. *Lordship and Tradition in Barbarian Europe*. Lewiston, NY: Edwin Mellon, 1999.

Momigliano, Arnaldo. 'The lonely historian Ammianus Marcellinus', in Arnaldo Momigliano, *Essays in Ancient and Modern Historiography*. Oxford: Blackwell, 1977, 127–40.

Moorhead, John. 'Boethius and Romans in Ostrogothic service', *Historia* 27 (1978), 604–12.

———. 'The last years of Theodoric', *Historia* 31 (1982), 106–20.

———. 'Italian loyalties during Justinian's Gothic war', *Byzantion* 53 (1983), 575–96.

———. 'Clovis's motives for becoming a Catholic Christian', *Journal of Religious History* 13 (1985), 329–39.

———. *Theodoric in Italy*. Oxford: Clarendon, 1992.

———. *The Roman Empire Divided, 400–700*. London: Longman, 2001.

Moreland, John. 'Ethnicity, power and the English', in *Social Identity in Early Medieval Britain*, edited by William O. Frazer and Andrew Tyrell. London and New York: Leicester University Press, 2000, 23–51.

Moss, J.R. 'The effects of the politics of Aetius on the history of Western Europe', *Historia* 22 (1973), 711–37.

Muhlberger, Steven. 'The Gallic Chronicle of 452 and its authority for British events', *Britannia* 14 (1983), 23–33.

———. *The Fifth-Century Chroniclers: Prosper, Hydatius and the Gallic Chronicler of 452*. Leeds, 1990.

──────. 'Looking back from mid-century: the Gallic Chronicler of 452 and the crisis of Honorius' reign', in *Fifth-Century Gaul*, edited by Drinkwater and Elton, 1992, 28–37.

──────. 'War. warlords, and Christian historians from the fifth to the seventh century', in *After Rome's Fall*, edited by Murray, 1998, 83–98.

Murphy, Trevor. *Pliny the Elder's Natural History: The Empire in the Encyclopedia*. Oxford: Oxford University Press, 2004.

Murray, Alexander Callander. *Germanic Kinship Structure: Studies on Law and Society in Antiquity and the Early Middle Ages*. Toronto: Pontifical Institute of Mediaeval Studies, 1983.

──────. 'Post vocantur Merohingii: Fredegar, Merovech and "Sacral Kingship"', in *After Rome's Fall*, edited by Murray, 1998, 121–52.

──────. *From Roman to Merovingian Gaul: A Reader*. Peterborough, Ontario: Broadview, 2000.

──────. 'Reinhard Wenskus on "Ethnogenesis", ethnicity and the origin of the Franks', in *On Barbarian Identity*, edited by Gillett, 2002, 39–68.

──────, ed. *After Rome's Fall: Narrators and Sources of Early Medieval History. Essays Presented to Walter Goffart*. Toronto and Buffalo: University of Toronto Press, 1998.

Musset, Lucien. *The Germanic Invasions: The Making of Europe AD 400–600*. Translated by Edward James and Columba James. London: Elek, 1975.

Myhre, Bjørn. 'Chieftain's graves and chiefdom territories in South Norway in the Migration Period', *Studien zur Sachsenforschung* 6 (1987), 169–87.

Myres, J.N.L. 'The Angles, the Saxons and the Jutes', *Proceedings of the British Academy* 56 (1970), 145–74.

────── and Green, B. *The Anglo-Saxon Cemeteries on Caistor-by-Norwich and Markshall, Norfolk*. London: Thamts and Hudson 1973.

Mytum, Harold. *The Origins of Early Christian Ireland*. London: Routledge, 1992.

Näsman, Ulf. 'The gates of Eketorp II: to the question of Roman prototypes of the Öland ringforts', in *The Birth of Europe: Archaeology and Social Development in the First Millennium AD*, edited by Klaus Randsborg. Rome: 'Erma di Bretschneider, 1989, 129–39.

──────. 'Strategies and tactics in Migration Period defence: on the art of defence on the basis of the settlement forts of Öland', in *Military Aspects of Scandinavian Society*, edited by Jørgensen and Clausen, 1997, 146–56.

──────. 'The Justinianic era of South Scandinavia: an archaeological view', in *The Sixth Century*, edited by Hodges and Bowden, 1998, 255–78.

Nicasie, Martijn. *Twilight of Empire. The Roman Army from the Reign of Diocletian until the Battle of Adrianople*. Amsterdam: Thesis Publishers, 1998.

Nielsen, P.O., Randsborg, K. and Thrane, H. *The Archaeology of Gudme and Lundeborg. Papers presented at a Conference at Svendborg, October 1991*, Arkæologiske Studier 10. Copenhagen: Akademisk Forlag, 1994.

Noble, Thomas F.X., ed. *From Roman Provinces to Medieval Kingdoms*, Rewriting Histories. London and New York: Routledge, 2006.

Norman, E.R. and St Joseph, J.K.S. *The Early Development of Irish Society: The Evidence of Aerial Photography.* Cambridge: Cambridge University Press, 1969.

Ó Cróinín, Dáibhí. *Early Medieval Ireland, 400–1200.* London: Longman, 1995.

———, ed. *A New History of Ireland. I. Prehistoric and Early Ireland.* Oxford: Oxford University Press, 2005.

O'Donnell, J.J. 'Liberius the Patrician', *Traditio* 37 (1981), 31–72.

———. 'The aims of Jordanes', *Historia* 31 (1982), 223–40.

Okamura, Lawrence. 'Roman withdrawals from three transfluvial frontiers', in *Shifting Frontiers,* edited by Mathisen and Sivan, 1996, 11–19.

Oppenheimer, Stephen. *The Origins of the British: A Genetic Detective Story.* London: Constable, 2006.

Ossel, Paul van. *Établissments ruraux de l'Antiquité tardive dans le nord de la Gaule,* Supplément à Gallia, 51. Paris: Centre Nationale des Recherches Scientifiques, 1992.

———. 'L'insécurité et militarisation en Gaul du nord au Bas-empire. L'exemple des campagnes', *Revue du Nord* 77 (1995), 27–36.

Pallas-Brown, Rachael. 'East Roman perceptions of the Avars in the mid- and late-sixth century', in *Ethnicity and Culture,* edited by Mitchell and Greatrex, 2000, 309–30.

Parczewski, M. 'Beginnings of the Slavs' culture', in *Origins of Central Europe,* edited by Urbańczyk, 1997, 79–90.

Parker Pearson, Michael. 'Beyond the pale: barbarian social dynamics in Western Europe', in *Barbarians and Romans,* edited by Barrett, Fitzpatrick and Macinnes, 1989, 198–226.

Périn, Patrick. *La Datation des tombes mérovingiennes: Historique – Méthodes – Applications.* Geneva: Droz, 1980.

———. 'Les tombes de "chefs" du début de l'époque mérovingienne. Datation et interprétation historique', in *La Noblesse romaine,* edited by Vallet and Kazanski, 1995, 247–307.

Phillips, B.B. 'Circus factions and barbarian dress in sixth-century Constantinople', in *Awarenforschungen,* edited by Daim, 1992, 25–32.

Piganiol, André. *L'Empire chrétien, 325–395.* Paris: Presses Universitaires de France, 1947.

Pitts, Lynn F. 'Relations between Rome and the German "kings" on the Middle Danube in the first to the fourth century AD', *Journal of Roman Studies* 79 (1989), 45–58.

Pohl, Walter. 'Die Gepiden und die Gentes an der mittleren Donau nach dem Zerfall des Attilareiches', in *Die Völker an der mittleren und unteren Donau,* edited by Wolfram and Daim, 1980, 240–72.

———. *Die Awaren: ein Steppenvolk im Mitteleuropa, 567–822 n. Chr,* Fruhe Völker. Munich: Beck, 1988.

———. 'Ethnicity in early medieval studies', *Archaeologia Polona* 29 (1991), 39–49.

———. 'The Empire and the Lombards: treaties and negotiations in the sixth century', in *Kingdoms of the Empire,* edited by Pohl, 1997, 75–133.

———. 'The role of the steppe peoples in eastern and central Europe in the first millennium AD', in *Origins of Central Europe*, edited by Urbańczyk, 1997, 65–78.

———. 'Telling the difference: signs of ethnic identity', in *Strategies of Distinction*, edited by Pohl, 1998, 17–69.

———. 'The *regia* and the *hring* – barbarian places of power', in *Topographies of Power*, edited by Jong and Theuws, 2001, 439–66.

———. *Die Völkerwanderung: Eroberung und Integration*. Stuttgart: Kohlhammer, 2002.

———. 'Ethnicity, theory, and tradition: a response', in *On Barbarian Identity*, edited by Gillett, 2002, 221–39.

———. 'A non-Roman empire in Central Europe: the Avars', in *Regna and Gentes*, edited by Goetz, Jarnut and Pohl, 2003, 571–95.

——— and Diesenberger, Max, eds. *Eugippius und Severin: Der Autor, der Text und der Heilige*, Forschungen zur Geschichte des Mittelalters 2. Vienna: Verlag der Österreichische Akademie der Wissenschaften, 2001.

——— and Erhart, Peter, eds. *Die Langobarden: Herrschaft und Identität*, Forschungen zur Geschichte des Mittelalters 9. Vienna: Verlag der Österreichischen Akademie der Wissenschaften, 2005.

——— and Reimitz, Helmut, eds. *Strategies of Distinction: The Construction of Ethnic Communities, 300–800*, The Transformation of the Roman World 2. Leiden: Brill, 1998.

———, ed. *Kingdoms of the Empire: The Integration of Barbarians in Late Antiquity*, The Transformation of the Roman World 1. Leiden: Brill, 1997.

———, Wood, Ian and Reimitz, Helmut, eds. *The Transformation of Frontiers from Late Antiquity to the Carolingians*, The Transformation of the Roman World 10. Leiden: Brill, 2001.

Poliakov, Léon. *The Aryan Myth: A History of Racist and Nationalist Ideas in Europe*. Translated by E. Howard. London: Chatto Heinemann, 1974.

Potter, David S. *The Roman Empire at Bay, AD 180–395*. London and New York: Routledge, 2004.

Powlesland, Dominic. *25 Years of Archaeological Research on the Sands and Gravels of Heslerton*. Yedingham, North Yorks: Landscape Research Centre, 2003.

Price, G., ed. *Encyclopedia of the Languages of Europe*. Oxford: Blackwell, 1998.

Raev, B.A. *Roman Imports in the Lower Don Basin*, British Archaeological Reports, International Series 278. Oxford: BAR, 1986.

Rankin, David. 'Arianism', in *The Early Christian World*, edited by Philip F. Esler. London and New York: Routledge, 2000, 975–1001.

Rawson, Claude. *God, Gulliver, and Genocide: Barbarism and the European Imagination, 1492–1945*. Oxford: Oxford University Press, 2001.

Reuter, Timothy. 'The recruitment of armies in the Early Middle Ages: what can we know?' in *Military Aspects of Scandinavian Society*, edited by Jørgensen and Claussen, 1997, 32–7.

Reynolds, Susan. 'Medieval *Origines Gentium* and the community of the realm', *History* 68 (1983), 375–90.

———. 'What do we mean by "Anglo-Saxon" and "Anglo-Saxons"?', *Journal of British Studies* 24 (1985), 395–414.

———. 'Our forefathers? Tribes, peoples, and nations in the historiography of migrations', in *After Rome's Fall*, edited by Murray, 1998, 17–36.

Riché, Pierre. *Les Invasions Barbares*. Que Sais-Je? Paris: Presses Universitaires de France, 1968.

Ridyard, Susan J. and Benson, Robert, eds. *Minorities and Barbarians in Medieval Life and Thought*. Sewanee, TN: University of the South Press, 1996.

Ripoll López, Gisela. 'The arrival of the Visigoths in Hispania: population problems and the process of acculturation', in *Strategies of Distinction*, edited by Pohl and Reimitz, 1998, 153–87.

Roberts, Michael. 'Barbarians in Gaul: the response of the poets', in *Fifth-Century Gaul*, edited by Drinkwater and Elton, 1992, 97–106.

Rousseau, Philip. 'Visigothic migration and settlement, 376–418: some excluded hypotheses', *Historia* 41 (1992), 34–61.

———. 'Inheriting the fifth century: who bequeathed what?' in *The Sixth Century*, edited by Allen and Jeffreys, 1996, 1–19.

Said, Edward W. *Oritntalism*. New York: Pantheon, 1978.

Salin, Bernhard. *Die altgermanische Thierornamentik: Typologische Studie über germanische Metallgegenstände aus dem IV. bis IX. Jahrhundrt, nebst einer Studie über irische Ornamentik*. 2nd ed. Stockholm: Wahlström & Widstrand, 1935.

Sawyer, P.H. and Wood, I.N., eds. *Early Medieval Kingship*. Leeds: School of History, University of Leeds, 1977.

Scheibelreiter, Georg. *Die barbarische Gesellschaft. Mentalitätsgeschichte der europäischen Achsenzeit 5.–8. Jahrhundert*. Darmstadt: Wissenchaftliche Buchgesellschaft, 1999.

Scheidel, Walter. 'Finances, figures and fiction', *Classical Quarterly* 46 (1996), 222–38.

Schlesinger, Roger. *In the Wake of Columbus. The Impact of the New World on Europe, 1492–1650*. 2nd ed. Wheeling, IL: Harlan Davidson, 2007.

Schluter, W. and Wiegels, R., eds. *Rom, Germanien und die Ausgrabungen in Kalkriese*. Osnabrück, 1999.

Schmauder, Michael. 'Imperial representation or barbaric imitation? The imperial brooches (Kaiserfibeln)', in *Strategies of Distinction*, edited by Pohl and Reimitz, 1998, 281–96.

———. 'The relationship between Frankish *gens* and *regnum*: a proposal based on the archaeological evidence', in *Regna and Gentes*, edited by Goetz, Jarnut and Pohl, 2003, 271–306.

Schwarcz, Andreas. 'Die Goten in Pannonia und auf dem Balkan nach dem Ende des Hunnenreiches bis zum Italienzug Theoderichs des Grossen', *Mitteilungen des Instituts für Österreichische Geschichtsforschung* 100 (1992), 50–83.

———. 'Severinus of Noricum between fact and fiction', in *Eugippius und Severin*, edited by Pohl and Diesenberger, 2001, 25–31.

————. 'The Visigothic settlement in Aquitania: chronology and archaeology', in *Society and Culture*, edited by Mathisen and Shanzer, 2001, 15–25.

Semple, Sarah. 'Defining the OE *hearg*: a preliminary archaeological and topographic examination of *hearg* place-names and their hinterlands', *Early Medieval Europe* 15 (2007), 364–85.

Shanzer, Danuta. 'Dating the baptism of Clovis: the bishop of Vienne vs the bishop of Tours', *Early Medieval Europe* 7 (1998), 29–57.

————. 'Two clocks and a wedding: Theodoric's diplomatic relations with the Burgundians', *Romanobarbarica* 14 (1998), 225–58.

Shaw, Brent D. ' "Eaters of flesh and drinkers of milk': the ancient Mediterranean ideology of the pastoral nomad', *Ancient Society* 13/14 (1982–3), 5–31.

————. 'Bandits in the Roman Empire', *Past and Present* 105 (1984), 3–52.

Shaw, Philip. 'The origins of the theophoric week in the Germanic languages', *Early Medieval Europe* 15 (2007), 386–401.

Shchukin, Mark. *Rome and the Barbarians in Central and Eastern Europe, 1st Century BC–1st Century AD*, British Archaeological Reports International Series 542. Oxford: BAR, 1989.

————. 'Forgotten Bastarnae', in *International Connections*, edited by Istvánovits and Kulcsár, 2001, 57–64.

————, Kazanski, Michel and Sharov, Oleg. *Dès les Goths aux Huns: le nord de la mer moire au Bas-empire et à l'époque des grandes invasions*, Archaeological Studies on Late Antiquity and Early Medieval Europe, 1; British Archaeological Reports International Series 1535. Oxford: BAR, 2006.

Sherwin-White, A.N. *The Roman Citizenship*. 2nd ed. Oxford: Clarendon Press, 1973.

Sivan, Hagith. 'Why not marry a barbarian? Marital frontiers in late antiquity (the example of CTh 3.14.1)', in *Shifting Frontiers*, edited by Mathisen and Sivan, 1996, 136–45.

————. 'The appropriation of Roman law in barbarian hands: "Roman-barbarian" marriage in Visigothic Gaul and Spain', in *Strategies of Distinction*, edited by Pohl and Reimitz, 1998, 189–203.

————. '*Alaricus Rex*: legitimising a Gothic king', in *The Construction of Communities*, edited by Corradini, Diesenberger and Reimitz, 2003, 109–21.

Smith, Anthony D. *Chosen Peoples*. Oxford: Oxford University Press, 2003.

Snowden, Frank M. *Before Color Prejudice: The Ancient View of Blacks*. Cambridge, MA: Harvard University Press, 1983.

Sogno, Cristiana. *Q. Aurelius Symmachus: A Political Biography*. Ann Arbor: University of Michigan Press, 2006.

Soraci, Rosario. *Ricerche sui conubia tra Romani e germani nei secoli IV-VI*. 2nd ed. Catania: Muglia 1974.

Southern, Pat. *The Roman Empire from Severus to Constantine*. London and New York: Routledge, 2001.

Stahl, Alan M. 'The nature of the Sutton Hoo coin parcel', in *Voyage to the Other World: The Legacy of Sutton Hoo*, edited by Calvin B. Kendall and Peter S. Wells. Minneapolis: University of Minnesota Press, 1992, 3–14.

Starkey, Kathryn. 'Imagining an early Odin: gold bracteates as visual evidence?' *Scandinavian Studies* 71 (1999), 373–92.

Stenton, F.M. 'The historical bearing of place-name studies: Anglo-Saxon heathenism', *Transactions of the Royal Historical Society* 4th series 23 (1941), 1–24.

Steuer, Heiko. 'Handwerk auf spätantiken Höhensiedlungen des 4./5. Jahrhunderts in Südwestdeutschland', in *The Archaeology of Gudme* edited by Nielsen, Randsborg and Thrane, 1994, 128–44.

Stevens, C.E. *Sidonius Apollinaris and His Age*. Oxford: Clarendon Press, 1933.

Stickler, Timo. 'The *Foederati*', in *A Companion to the Roman Army*, edited by Erdkamp, 2007, 495–514.

Sulimirski, Tadeusz. *The Sarmatians*, Ancient Peoples and Places. London: Thames and Hudson, 1960.

Swain, Simon and Edwards, Mark, eds. *Approaching Late Antiquity: The Transformation from Early to Late Empire*. Oxford: Oxford University Press, 2004.

Sykes, Bryan. *Blood of the Isles: Exploring the Genetic Roots of Our Tribal History*. London: Bantam, 2006.

Teall, J.L. 'The barbarians in Justinian's armies', *Speculum* 40 (1965), 294–322.

Teillet, Suzanne. *Dès Goths à la nation gothique: les origines de l'idée de nation en Occident du Ve au VIIe siècle*. Paris: Les Belles Lettres 1984.

Teitler, H.C. 'Un-Roman activities in late antique Gaul: the cases of Arvandus and Seronatus', in *Fifth-Century Gaul*, edited by Drinkwater and Elton, 1992, 309–17.

Teodor, Eugen S. 'The shadow of a frontier: the Wallachian Plain during the Justinianic Age', in *Borders, Barriers*, edited by Curta, 2005, 205–46.

Themos, Frans and Nelson, Janet L., eds. *Topographies of Power: From Late Antiquity to the Early Middle Ages*, The Transformation of the Roman World 8. Leiden: Brill, 2000.

Thomas, Mark G., Stumpf, Michael P.H. and Härke, Heinrich. 'Evidence for an apartheid-like social structure in early Anglo-Saxon England', *Proceedings of the Royal Society, B* (2006), doi: 10.1098/rspb.2006.3627.

Thompson, E.A. 'Peasant revolts in late Roman Gaul and Spain', *Past and Present* 2 (1952), 11–23.

———. 'Christianity and the northern barbarians', in *The Conflict between Paganism and Christianity in the Fourth Century*, edited by A.D. Momigliano. Oxford: Clarendon Press, 1963, 56–78.

———. *The Early Germans*. Oxford: Clarendon Press, 1965.

———. *The Visigoths in the Time of Ulfila*. Oxford: Clarendon Press, 1966.

———. *The Goths in Spain*. Oxford: Clarendon Press, 1969.

———. 'The conversion of the Spanish Suevi to Catholicism', in *Visigothic Spain: New Approaches*, edited by Edward James. Oxford: Clarendon, 1980, 77–92.

———. 'Barbarian invaders and Roman collaborators', *Florilegium* 2 (1980), 71–88.

———. *Romans and Barbarians: The Decline of the Western Empire*. Madison: University of Wisconsin Press, 1982.

————. *The Huns*, The Peoples of Europe. Oxford: Blackwell, 1996.

Todd, Malcolm. *Migrants and Invaders: The Movement of Peoples in the Ancient World*. Stroud: Tempus, 2001.

————. *The Early Germans*. 2nd ed. The Peoples of Europe. Oxford: Blackwell, 2004.

Urbańczyk, Przemysław, ed. *Origins of Central Europe*. Warsaw: Scientific Society of Polish Archaeologists, 1997.

Vallet, Françoise, and Kazanski, Michel, eds. *L'Armée romaine et les barbares du IIIe au VIIe siècle*, Mémoires Publiées par l'Association Française d'Archéologie Mérovingienne 5. Paris: AFAM and Musée des Antiquités Nationales, 1993.

————, eds. *La Noblesse romaine et les chefs barbares du IIIe au VIIe siècle*, Mémoires Publiées par l'Association Française d'Archéologie Mérovingienne 9. Paris: AFAM and Musée des Antiquités Nationales, 1995.

Vanderspoel, John. *Themistius and the Imperial Court: Oratory, Civic Duty, and Paideia from Constantius to Theodosius*. Ann Arbor: University of Michigan Press, 1995.

Veit, Ulrich. 'Gustaf Kossinna and his concept of a national archaeology', in *Archaeology, Ideology and Society*, edited by Härke, 2002, 41–61.

Velásquez, Isabel. '*Pro patriae gentisque Gothorum statu* (4th Council of Toledo, Canon 75, A.633)', in *Regna and Gentes*, edited by Goetz, Jarnut and Pohl, 2003, 161–217.

Wallace-Hadrill, J.M. 'Gothia and Romania', *Bulletin of the John Rylands Library* (1961), 213–37.

————. *The Long-Haired Kings: And Other Studies in Frankish History*. London: Methuen, 1962.

————. *Early Germanic Kingship in England and on the Continent*. Oxford: Clarendon Press, 1971.

————. *Early Medieval History*. Oxford: Blackwell, 1975.

————. *Bede's* Ecclesiastical History of the English People: *A Historical Commentary*. Oxford: Clarendon, 1988.

Ward-Perkins, Bryan. 'Why did the Anglo-Saxons not become more British?' *English Historical Review* 115 (2000), 513–33.

————. *The Fall of Rome and the End of Civilization*. Oxford: Oxford University Press, 2005.

Watson, Alaric. *Aurelian and the Third Century*. London and New York: Routledge, 1999.

Webster, Jane. 'Ethnographic barbarity: colonial discourse and "Celtic warrior societies"', in *Roman Imperialism*, edited by Webster and Cooper, 1996, 111–23.

Webster, Jane and Cooper, Nick, eds. *Roman Imperialism: Post-Colonial Perspectives*, Leicester Archaeology Monographs 3. Leicester: School of Archaeological Sciences, University of Leicester, 1996.

Webster, Leslie and Brown, Michelle P. *The Transformation of the Roman World, AD 400–900*. London: British Museum, 1997.

Weissensteiner, Johann. 'Cassiodors Gotengeschichte bei Gregor von Tours und Paulus Diaconus? Eine Spurensuche', in *Ethnogenese und Überlieferung*, edited by Brunner and Merta, 1994, 123–28.

Wells, Peter S. *The Barbarians Speak: How the Conquered Peoples Shaped Roman Europe*. Princeton, NJ: Princeton University Press, 1999.

Wenskus, Reinhard. *Stammesbildung und Verfassung: Das Werden der frühmittelalterlichen Gentes*. Cologne: Graz, 1961.

Werner, Joachim. 'Zur Entstehung der Reihengräberzvilisation', *Archaeologia Geographica* 1 (1950), 23–32.

———. 'Zu den alamannischen Burgen des 4. und 5. Jahrhunderts', in *Speculum Historiale: Festschrift für Johannes Spörl*, 1965, 439–53.

———. 'Childerichs Pferde', in *Germanische Religionsgeschichte*, edited by Heinrich Beck, 1992, 145–61.

Whitby, Michael. 'Army and society in the late Roman world: a context for decline?', in *A Companion to the Roman Army*, edited by Erdkamp, 2007, 515–31.

Whittaker, C.R. 'What happens when frontiers come to an end?' in *Frontières d'Empire*, edited by Brun Leeuw and Whittaker, 1993, 133–41.

———. *Frontiers of the Roman Empire: A Social and Economic Study*. Baltimore and London: Johns Hopkins University Press, 1994.

———. *Rome and its Frontiers: The Dynamics of Empire*. London: Routledge, 2004.

Wieczorek, Alfried and Périn, Patrick, eds. *Das Gold der Barbarenfürsten: Schätze aus Prunkgräbern des 5. Jahrhunderts n. Chr. zwischen Kaukasus und Gallien*. Stuttgart: Theiss, 2001.

———, Périn, Patrick, Von Welck, Karin and Menghin, Wilfried, eds. *Die Franken, Wegbereiter Europas*. 2nd ed. 2 vols. Mainz: Reiss-Museum Mannheim/ Philipp von Zabern, 1997.

Wiedemann, T.E.J. 'Between men and beasts: barbarians in Ammianus Marcellinus', in *Past Perspectives: Studies in Greek and Roman Historical Writing*, edited by I.S. Moxon, J.D. Smart and A.J. Woodman. Cambridge: Cambridge University Press, 1984.

Wielowiejski, P. 'Bernstein in der Przeworsk-Kultur', *Bericht der Römisch-Germanische Kommission* 77 (1996), 215–347.

Williams, Howard. 'Ancient landscapes and the dead: the reuse of prehistoric and Roman monuments as early Anglo-Saxon burial sites', *Medieval Archaeology* 41 (1997), 1–31.

———. 'Cemeteries as central places – place and identity in migration period eastern England', in *Central Places*, edited by Hårdh and Larsson, 2002, 341–62.

———. *Death and Memory in Early Medieval Britain*. Cambridge: Cambridge University Press, 2006.

Winkelmann, Friedhelm. 'Die Bewertung der Barbaren in den Werken der oströmischen Kirchenhistoriker', in *Das Reich und die Barbaren*, edited by Chrysos and Schwarcz, 1989, 221–35.

Wirth, Gerhard. 'Rome and its Germanic partners in the fourth century', in *Kingdoms of the Empire*, edited by Pohl, 1997, 13–55.

Wolfram, Herwig. *History of the Goths.* Revised from the 2nd German ed. Berkeley: University of California Press, 1988.

———. '*Origo et religio*: ethnic traditions and literature in early medieval texts', *Early Medieval Europe* 3 (1994), 19–38.

———. *Die Germanen.* Munich: C.H. Beck, 1995.

———. *The Roman Empire and its Germanic Peoples.* Berkeley: University of California Press, 1997.

———. *Die Goten und ihre Geschichte.* Munich: C.H. Beck, 2001.

———. '*Origo Gentis*: the literature of German origins', in *Early Germanic Literature and Culture*, edited by Brian Murdoch and Malcolm Read. Rochester, NY, 2004, 39–54.

——— and Daim, Falko, eds. *Die Völker an der mittleren und unteren Donau im fünften und sechsten Jahrhundert*, Denkschriften der Österreichischen Akademie der Wissenschaften, Phil.-Hist. Klasse 145. Vienna: 1980.

——— and Langthaler, Gerhart. *Treasures on the Danube: Barbarian Invaders and their Roman Inheritance.* Wien: Böhlau, 1985.

——— and Schwarcz, Andreas, eds. *Anerkennung und Integration: Zu den wirtschaftlichen Grundlagen der Völkerwanderungszeit, 400–600*, Denkschriften der österreichischen Akademie der Wissenschaften, Phil.-Hist. Klasse 193. Vienna: 1988.

Wood, Ian N. 'Kings, kingdoms and consent', in *Early Medieval Kingship*, edited by Sawyer and Wood, 1977, 6–29.

———. 'Ethnicity and the ethnogenesis of the Burgundians', in *Typen der Ethnogenese unter besonderer Berücksichtigung der Bayern*, edited by Herwig Wolfram and Walter Pohl. Vienna: Verlag der Österreichischen Akademie der Wissenschaften, 1990, 53–69.

———. 'The Code in Merovingian Gaul', in *The Theodosian Code: Studies in the Imperial Law of Late Antiquity*, edited by Jill Harries and Ian Wood. London: Duckworth, 1993, 161–77.

———. *The Merovingian Kingdoms, 450–751.* London: Longman, 1994.

———. 'Defining the Franks: Frankish origins in early medieval historiography', in *Concepts of National Identity in the Middle Ages*, edited by Simon Forde, Lesley Johnson and Alan V. Murray. Leeds: University of Leeds, 1995, 47–57.

———. 'The barbarian invasions and the first settlements', in *The Cambridge Ancient History*, edited by Cameron and Garnsey. Cambridge: Cambridge University Press, 1998, 187–98.

———. *The Missionary Life: Saints and the Evangelisation of Europe, 400–1050.* Harlow: Longman, 2001.

———. '*Gentes*, kings and kingdoms – the emergence of states: the kingdom of the Gibichungs', in *Regna and Gentes*, edited by Goetz, Jarnut and Pohl, 2003, 243–69.

———. 'Misremembering the Burgundians', in *Die Suche nach den Ursprüngen: von der Bedeutung des frühen Mittelalters*, edited by Walter Pohl. Vienna: Verlag der Österreichischen Akademie der Wissenschaften, 2004, 139–48.

Wood, Ian, ed., *Franks and Alamanni in the Merovingian Period: An Ethnographic Perspective*, Studies in Historical Archaeoethnology 3. Woodbridge: Boydell, 1998.

Woolf, Alex. 'The Britons: from Romans to barbarians', in *Regna and Gentes*, edited by Goetz, Jarnut and Pohl, 2003, 345–80.

Wormald, Patrick. 'The decline of the Western Empire and the survival of its aristocracy', *Journal of Roman Studies* 66 (1976), 217–26.

———. '*Lex scripta* and *verbum regis*: legislation and Germanic kingship from Euric to Cnut', in *Early Medieval Kingship*, edited by Sawyer and Wood, 1977, 105–38.

———; Bullough, Donald; and Collins, Roger, eds. *Ideal and Reality in Frankish and Anglo-Saxon Society: Studies Presented to J.M. Wallace-Hadrill*. Oxford: Blackwell, 1983.

———. 'Bede, the *Bretwaldas* and the origins of the *Gens Anglorum*', in *Ideal and Reality*, edited by Wormald, Bullough and Collins, 99–129.

———. 'Celtic and Anglo-Saxon kingship: some further thoughts', in *Sources of Anglo-Saxon Culture*, edited by Paul E. Szarmach. Kalamazoo: Medieval Institute Publications, 1986, 151–83.

———. 'The *Leges Barbarorum*: law and ethnicity in the post-Roman west', in *Regna and Gentes*, edited by Goetz, Jarnut and Pohl, 2003, 21–53.

Wynn, Philip. 'Frigeridus, the British tyrants, and the early fifth-century barbarian invasions of Gaul and Spain', *Athenaeum: Studi di letteratura e storia dell'Antichità* 85 (1997), 69–117.

Yorke, Barbara. 'The Jutes of Hampshire and Wight and the origins of Wessex', in *Origins*, edited by Bassett, 1989, 84–96.

———. 'Anglo-Saxon *gentes* and *regna*', in *Regna and Gentes*, edited by Goetz, Jarnut and Pohl, 2003, 381–407.

INDEX